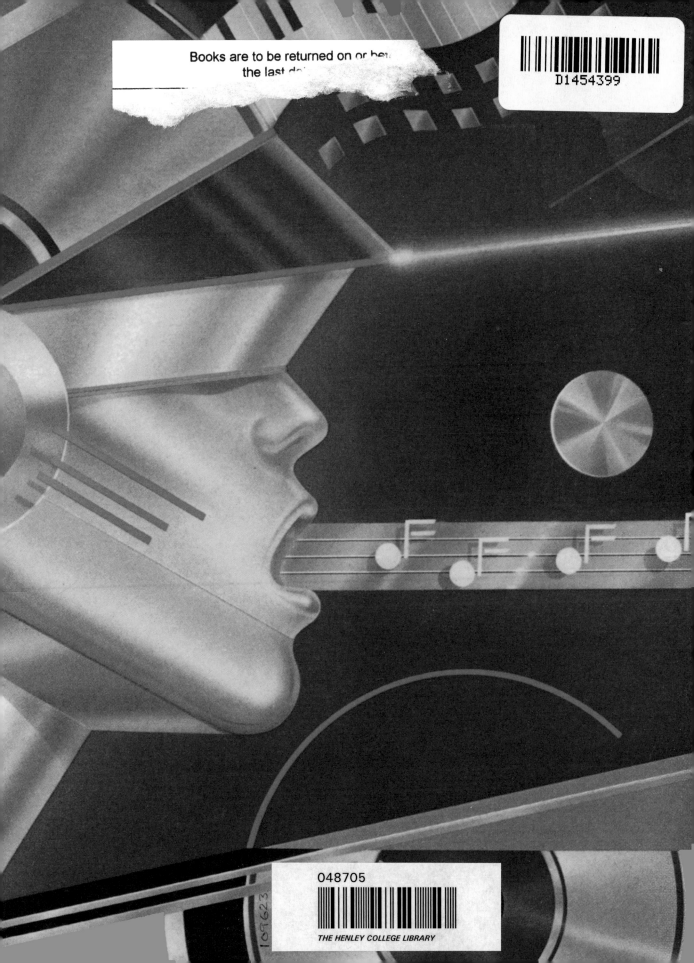

80^s

All-American Ads

LIGHTS: 9 mg. "tar", 0.6 mg. nicotine,
FILTERS: 16 mg. "tar", 1.0 mg. nicotine,
av. per cigarette by FTC method.

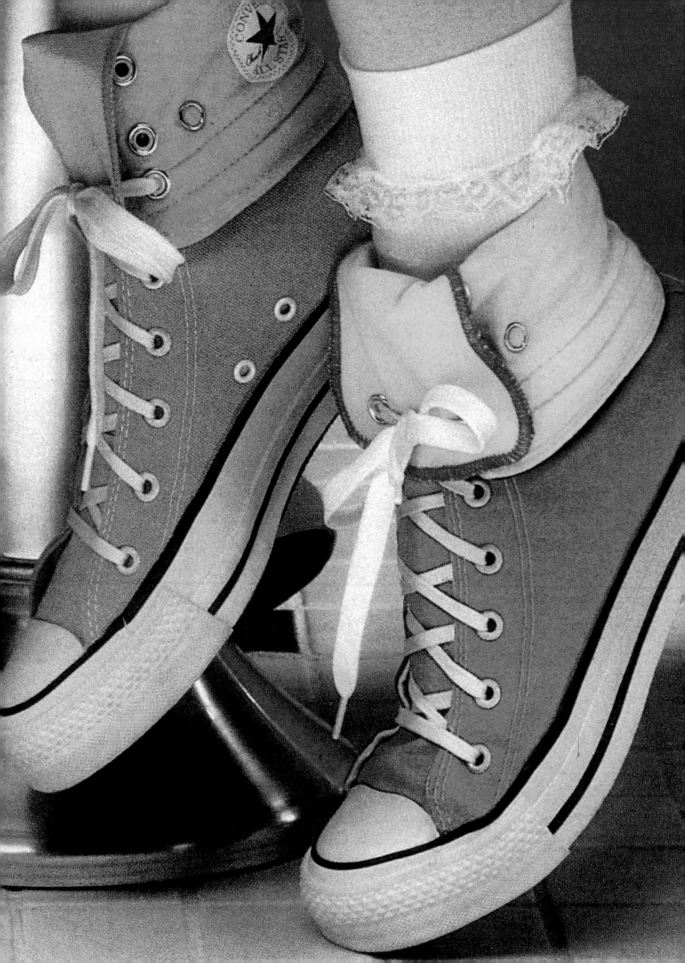

Acknowledgements

This volume of historical material would never have been completed without the help of numerous individuals. Among them are Cindy Vance of Modern Art & Design, who continues to labor on these massive volumes with her enthusiasm intact while infusing them with her design and image-editing expertise; Nina Wiener, who managed to keep this project and countless others at TASCHEN on track, in order and beautifully edited; Steven Heller for his impeccable and swift writing; and Sonja Altmeppen, Andy Disl, Stefan Klatte, Horst Neuzner, and the rest of the TASCHEN staff in Cologne for their help and guidance in consistently producing a quality product. Special thanks to our totally awesome interns, Kristie Wang and Morgan Weatherford, whose enthusiasm for the material fueled hours of fact-checking and image organization.

As always, a special thanks is due to all of those who provided the magazines and material that eventually wound up in this book, including Dan DePalma, Ralph Bowman, Gary Fredericks, Jeff and Pat Carr, Gerry Aboud, Cindy and Steve Vance, Sherry Sonnet, and all the other dealers of paper ephemera. I couldn't have done it without you.

Jim Heimann, Los Angeles

Cover: *Rio*, © Patrick Nagel, 1982. Courtesy of Jennifer Dumas
Endpapers: Marantz Sound Systems, 1983
Page 1: The Art Institute, 1985
Pages 2-3: Camel Cigarettes, 1988
Pages 4-5: Jensen Car Stereo, 1984
Pages 6-7: CompuServe, 1988
Pages 8-9: JCPenney, 1983
Pages 10-11: Teac Electronics, 1987
Pages 12-13: Rolling Stones, 1989
Pages 14-15: Converse All Star Athletic Shoes, 1987
Pages 16-17: Lipton Oriental Treasures Herbal Tea, 1988

Imprint

To stay informed about upcoming TASCHEN titles, please request our magazine at www.taschen.com or write to TASCHEN, Hohenzollernring 53, D–50672 Cologne, Germany, Fax: +49-221-254919. We will be happy to send you a free copy of our magazine which is filled with information about all of our books.

© 2005 TASCHEN GmbH
Hohenzollernring 53, D-50672 Köln
www.taschen.com

Art direction & design: Jim Heimann, L. A.
Digital composition & design:
Cindy Vance, Modern Art & Design, L. A.
Cover design: Sense/Net, Andy Disl, Cologne
Production: Stefan Klatte, Cologne
German translation: Anke Burger, Berlin
French translation: Lien, Amsterdam
Spanish translation: Gemma Deza Guil for LocTeam, S. L., Barcelona
Japanese translation: Hiromi Kakubari, Tokyo

Printed in Spain
ISBN: 3–8228–3833–0

Acknowledgements

This volume of historical material would never have been completed without the help of numerous individuals. Among them are Cindy Vance of Modern Art & Design, who continues to labor on these massive volumes with her enthusiasm intact while infusing them with her design and image-editing expertise; Nina Wiener, who managed to keep this project and countless others at TASCHEN on track, in order and beautifully edited; Steven Heller for his impeccable and swift writing; and Sonja Altmeppen, Andy Disl, Stefan Klatte, Horst Neuzner, and the rest of the TASCHEN staff in Cologne for their help and guidance in consistently producing a quality product. Special thanks to our totally awesome interns, Kristie Wang and Morgan Weatherford, whose enthusiasm for the material fueled hours of fact-checking and image organization.

As always, a special thanks is due to all of those who provided the magazines and material that eventually wound up in this book, including Dan DePalma, Ralph Bowman, Gary Fredericks, Jeff and Pat Carr, Gerry Aboud, Cindy and Steve Vance, Sherry Sonnet, and all the other dealers of paper ephemera. I couldn't have done it without you.

Jim Heimann, Los Angeles

Cover: *Rio*, © Patrick Nagel, 1982. Courtesy of Jennifer Dumas
Endpapers: Marantz Sound Systems, 1983
Page 1: The Art Institute, 1985
Pages 2-3: Camel Cigarettes, 1988
Pages 4-5: Jensen Car Stereo, 1984
Pages 6-7: CompuServe, 1988
Pages 8-9: JCPenney, 1983
Pages 10-11: Teac Electronics, 1987
Pages 12-13: Rolling Stones, 1989
Pages 14-15: Converse All Star Athletic Shoes, 1987
Pages 16-17: Lipton Oriental Treasures Herbal Tea, 1988

Imprint

To stay informed about upcoming TASCHEN titles, please request our magazine at www.taschen.com or write to TASCHEN, Hohenzollernring 53, D–50672 Cologne, Germany, Fax: +49-221-254919. We will be happy to send you a free copy of our magazine which is filled with information about all of our books.

© 2005 TASCHEN GmbH
Hohenzollernring 53, D-50672 Köln
www.taschen.com

Art direction & design: Jim Heimann, L. A.
Digital composition & design:
Cindy Vance, Modern Art & Design, L. A.
Cover design: Sense/Net, Andy Disl, Cologne
Production: Stefan Klatte, Cologne
German translation: Anke Burger, Berlin
French translation: Lien, Amsterdam
Spanish translation: Gemma Deza Guil for LocTeam, S. L., Barcelona
Japanese translation: Hiromi Kakubari, Tokyo

Printed in Spain
ISBN: 3–8228–3833–0

All-American Ads

Edited by Jim Heimann
with an introduction by Steven Heller

TASCHEN

KOLN LONDON LOS ANGELES MADRID PARIS TOKYO

Alcohol &
Tobacco
42

Automobiles
96

Business
& Industry
158

Consumer
Products
200

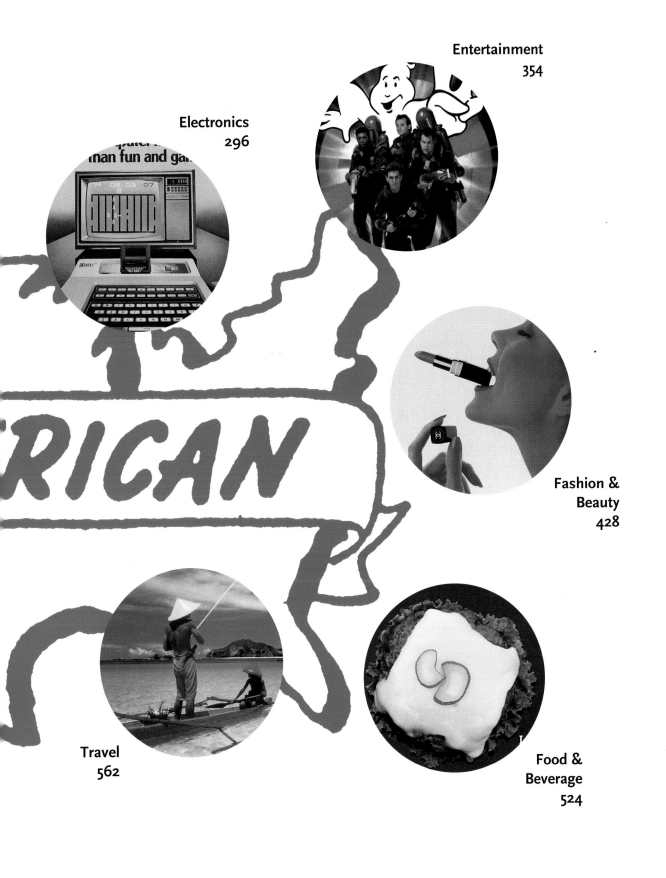

RICAN

The Eighties:
Advertising the Reagan Years

by Steven Heller

Crotch bulge: the new frontier

In 1980, Americans elected Ronald Reagan as President of the United States. The former host of TV's *General Electric Theater* (and ex-governor of California) was given a sizeable mandate to pitch the campaign of his life: a new American dominion. Globalization was on the horizon, a new social order was in the air, and Reagan was poised.

Reagan's eighties were indeed tumultuous. The Soviet Union made its final Iron Curtain call and the people of all Soviet bloc nations won freedom from oppression. Meanwhile, Calvin Klein® unveiled its first "Underwear for Men" advertisements and billboards and the American people earned the right freely to view crotch-bulge in public. As the surly Communist superpower succumbed to American, cold-war might, sensuous supermodels (Kathy Ireland, Christie Brinkley, and Cindy Crawford) conquered the American mass media, especially advertising.

The eighties saw Communism's defeat and gave rise to Reagan-era accomplishments, including trickle-down economics, Star Wars missile defense, and the Iran-Contragate. It also debuted Madison Avenue's major feats, including Joe Camel's Smooth Character, Coors'® Silver Bullet®,

and Spuds MacKenzie, the Bud Light® party dog. AIDS emerged as a deadly pandemic and the decade was besieged by various other crises, yet, true to character, the advertising industry ignored any disagreeable contradictions for the sake of its messages.

The wallpaper of capitalism

"Advertising as a whole is a fantastic fraud, presenting an image of America taken seriously by no one, least of all by the advertising men who create it," wrote sociologist David Riesman in his groundbreaking study *The Lonely Crowd: A Study of the Changing American Character* (Yale University Press, 1950). His statement is not entirely accurate, however; after all, consumers are complicit in fraud every time they submit to the idea that the pursuit of happiness can be advanced through the purchase of nationally advertised brands. For advertising to succeed there must be a symbiotic relationship between producer and consumer, in which each has something to gain. Therefore, when taken as the raw material of social and cultural history, the advertisements collected in this volume must be skeptically viewed as evidence of a mutually advantageous scam that, according to social critic Ernest van den

Haag, aims "to unify taste, to de-individualize it, and thus to make mass production possible." Indeed, anything that impedes Americans' consumption of mass-produced goods is wallpapered over with marketing propaganda—and consumption of mass-produced goods is wallpapered over with marketing propaganda—and advertising is the wallpaper of capitalism.

Print had been the primary creative medium until the sixties; by the seventies, television commercials had stolen the creative thunder; so, by the eighties, print had become the table scraps of the advertising industry and a paltry number of memorable print campaigns emerged. The few that did are noteworthy because they migrated into the general culture (sometimes together with TV commercials, but also on their own).

The exemplars represented in this book include Sony®'s "Full Color Sound" (page 313), illustrated by Milton Glaser, an elegantly eye-catching and smartly conceived metaphor that transformed sound into sight; Benetton®'s "United Colors of Benetton" (page 466), photographed by Oliviero Toscani, playfully iconic and with its long-running series of ads evolving into mild social commentary; Nike®'s "Just Do It." (page 480), accelerating an urban trend that trans-

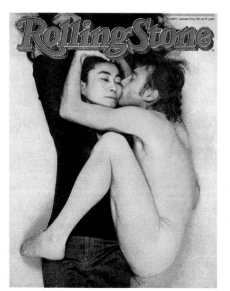

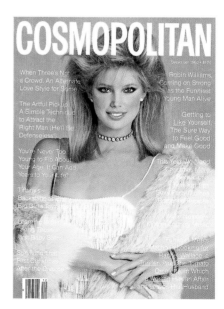

formed mere sneakers into prestigiously fashionable athletic *shoes*; Swatch®'s retro ads (page 202), conceived by Paula Scher, underscoring the stylishness of a new commercial commodity, the ephemeral wristwatch; and IBM®'s inspired mascotization of Charlie Chaplin (page 171), wedding a pioneer film comedian with the pioneer computer producer (nostalgia was also an effective way to ease PC customers gently into the computer age). Speaking of computers, the eighties saw the introduction of the Apple Macintosh® (and the less successful Lisa®) (page 173) with safely straightforward ad pitches serving as a gateway to an incredible new technology.

Perhaps the most resonant advertisement of the decade was Maxell®'s "No Other Audio Tape Delivers Higher Fidelity." (page 313), with its sleek black-and-white photograph of a leather-clad hipster white-knuckling the arms of a Le Corbusier chair—Maxell®'s audio cassette blasting sound, as though in a wind tunnel, directly into his face from a single, diminutive speaker. This was an exceptional fusing of concept, aesthetics, and message. This basic formula continued to promote the product's positive image in print and on TV for well over a decade. Nonetheless, these few superlative ads com-

prise a memorable molehill on a forgettable mountain.

Doomed to inconsequence

The campaigns cited above resonate because they either touched a collective nerve or implanted a subconscious alarm. Conversely, the vast majority of the ads in this book adhered to stylistic clichés that effectively lessened their impact over the long haul. Even when a single component (a slogan or an image) sparked momentary recognition, if all the elements did not perform in harmony, the particular ad was doomed to inconsequence. Take the dramatically lit, still-life photographs and demonstrative headlines for the Gillette® Atra razor (page 223), Close-Up® toothpaste (page 229), Dry Idea® (page 226), and Marriott Resorts® (page 580): they announced their respective wares, but failed as mnemonics to convey an identity beyond the initial viewing—and these were fairly well-designed ads. Clearly, good design does not succeed in a vacuum. Some ads strain when trying to connect with an audience, such as Life Savers'® "Hole Lotta Fresh!" (page 540) with its graphically startling, mammoth lifesaver, but moronic slogan.

A large number of print advertisements

produced during the eighties tried too hard to convey their pitches. Although scores of them were full-page bleed pictures, those laden with many words and complex images seemed to suggest that advertising agencies were admitting that the major budgets were spent on television, so print ads could not afford to be creative. Jazzercise® (page 239) is representative of the overkill methodology that lacked aesthetic savvy and conceptual nuance. In fact, nuance is exactly what separates the first-rate from the mediocre, as with "Speedo Suits Men." (page 456). Though arguably no less visually startling than "Calvin Klein Jeans" (page 458), it is awkwardly designed (the headline typography is as crass as if the buff model were wearing argyle socks) and the photograph is uninspired.

Aesthetics aside, advertisements tell stories, and if a narrative is compelling consumers are more apt to make a particular brand their own. But since these hucksters' tales perpetuate myths and fallacies it takes a whole lot of snake oil and patent medicine promises to bait the customer. Take Fudgsicle®'s "All Fudge. No Pudge." (page 538), which tells the story of Americans' competing compulsions to be svelte yet eat sweets. In one broad stroke, this clumsy-looking ad presents a physically beautiful ideal while ex-

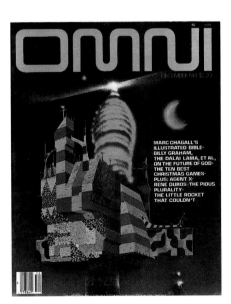

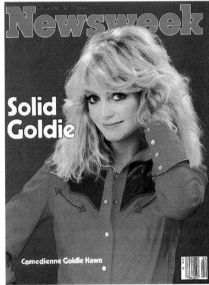

tolling the benefits of an essentially unexciting product. Who wouldn't be attracted by the promise of guiltless (and weightless) pleasure?

Unhealthy mythologies

The reality versus fantasy (truth versus lies) cliché is, however, really a red herring, because advertising does not pretend that it does *not* pretend. Everyone accepts that, either overtly or covertly, advertising is based on evasion. In some cases, however, advertising myths can be quite damaging to the body and mind. The most dishonest (and unhealthy) of modern advertising's mythologies, especially in the decades preceding the eighties, was the one that promoted cigarettes as somehow life enhancing. From the thirties through the fifties, advertisements claimed certain cigarettes reduced stress and were therefore good for mental health. During the seventies, a long-overdue ban on televised cigarette ads came into force, and by the mid-eighties the last hurrah for cigarette advertising (that was already required to display the Surgeon General's warning label prominently on every ad) was approaching. Conventional ads urged consumers to buck popular wisdom, succumb to their

habits, and smoke cigarettes regardless of all the proven ill effects. One insidious ad, the minimalist "If you smoke *please try Carlton.*" (page 88), made no claims yet did not dissuade the "existing" smoker from engaging in risky behavior. Most other tobacco advertisers removed any subtlety from their repertoires and created impressions that continued to perpetuate false social and cultural myths that cigarette smoking was hip, cool, elegant, and even radical. Some ads were so relentlessly devious it took a while to realize what they were up to.

When Camel® cigarettes grasped that its consumer base was fast eroding, owing to attrition both from catastrophic illness and breaking the habit, the company targeted its "Smooth Character" (pages 92) cartoon mascot at teenagers (and even younger kids). The phallic-shaped, anthropomorphized, leather-clad dromedary appeared in magazines that teens read (like *Rolling Stone*), clearly revealing its intended market.

When pitch-dogs reigned

Alcohol consumption among teens was also on the rise in the eighties and, not surprisingly, the beer and liquor companies, which were among the highest spenders for

print ad campaigns, sought to portray drinking as not just acceptable but expectable. Although not aimed at teens, but rather at the twenty-something consumer, the most brilliant of all the eighties' campaigns was (and remains) Absolut® Vodka (page 60), which launched in 1980 with the fusion of art and commerce into high-concept iconography. The intelligence in commissioning avant-garde artists including Keith Haring, Jean Michel Basquiat, and Andy Warhol to visually interpret (and ultimately lend their credibility to) the Absolut® bottle ensured this ad rose above the mundane and mediocre pap of the day.

Many brands tried to duplicate Absolut®'s success, but pretentious ads like Rumple Minze®'s "White Magic from the Black Forest" (page 69), featuring a fantasy super-babe mascot, and Grand Marnier®'s slavishly faux René Magritte Surrealist landscape (page 72) were never as creatively engaging. Mainstream liquors that were not looking for hip new customers continued to follow lackluster convention.

Unlike cigarettes and hard alcohol, ads for brewski have not been banned in print since the 1920s' prohibition (or ever on TV); and during the eighties a spate of them made a huge media impact. Venerable

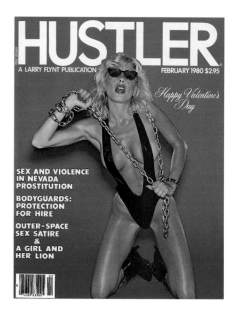

brands like Miller High Life® (page 52) and Moosehead® (page 46) focused in on their logos as selling points, but upstarts like the new generation of "lite" beers needed more provocative hooks to capture market share. One of the most popular was a quirky bull terrier named Spuds MacKenzie, Bud Light®'s "Original Party Animal" (page 55). Anheuser-Busch® had stumbled on a billion-dollar property in this pitch-dog that was so popular (and well known even among non-drinkers) they ran him for President. Given that Bud®'s advertising had such incredible power to influence public opinion—at times even erasing world concerns from the public's collective mind—if Spuds had seriously run against Ronald Reagan he just might have won.

By the end of the eighties, print advertising was slowly regaining strength as a creative medium because new niche magazines (some devoted entirely to customer service) appealed to audiences focused on the products presented therein. Moreover, ads for Absolut® and IBM® were being recognized as entertaining diversions in an editorial context. The industry was actively seeking both new and old venues apart from television. The cathode-ray tube was no longer the brightest advertising buy; billboards were on the upswing as were point-of-purchase display sites. New printing technologies were being added to the industry repertoire and art directors and designers were meeting the challenge. By the nineties, print advertising had really begun to experience a renaissance in its creative potential and, with the new American prosperity of the succeeding White House administration, even started to break new ground. Advertising marched once again to the fore to lead the pop-culture parade, a development that was as good for clients as it was dubious for society.

Steven Heller is the art director of *The New York Times Book Review* and co-chair of MFA Design at the School of Visual Arts. He has edited or authored over eighty books on design and popular culture, including *Merz to Emigre and Beyond: Avant-Garde Magazine Design of the 20th Century* and *Design Literacy Revised*.

Die Achtziger:
Werbung für die Reagan-Jahre

von Steven Heller

Auf zu neuen Ufern: Der prall gewölbte Männerslip

1980 wurde Ronald Reagan zum Präsidenten der Vereinigten Staaten von Amerika gewählt. Der ehemalige Showmaster der TV-Werbesendung *General Electric Theater* (und Ex-Gouverneur von Kalifornien) erhielt eine beachtliche Mehrheit für die Kampagne seines Lebens: die amerikanische Weltherrschaft. Die Globalisierung und eine neue Gesellschaftsordnung lagen in der Luft und Reagan war startklar.

Die Achtziger unter Reagan sollten sich als enorm ereignisreich erweisen. Die Sowjetunion machte den letzten Knicks vor dem Eisernen Vorhang und die Bevölkerungen der Ostblockländer befreiten sich aus kommunistischer Unterdrückung. Gleichzeitig präsentierte Calvin Klein® die ersten Anzeigen und Werbeplakate für „Unterwäsche für Männer", und das amerikanische Volk errang das Recht, sich frei und in aller Öffentlichkeit prall gewölbte Männerslips anzusehen. Während die kommunistische Supermacht im Wettrüsten Amerika unterlag, eroberten sinnliche Supermodels (Kathy Ireland, Christie Brinkley und Cindy Crawford) die amerikanischen Massenmedien, insbesondere die Werbung.

In den Achtzigern erlebten wir nicht nur das Ende des Kommunismus, sondern auch glorreiche Neuerungen der Reagan-Ära wie die „Trickle-Down-Theorie" zur Steuersenkung für Spitzenverdiener, das „Krieg der Sterne"-Raketenabwehrprogramm und den Iran-Contra-Skandal. Die größten Erfindungen der amerikanischen Werbebranche entstammen ebenfalls dieser Zeit: das Dromedar Joe Camel, Coors'® Silver Bullet® und Spuds MacKenzie, der Bud-Light®-Partyhund. Die tödliche Seuche AIDS breitete sich aus und das Jahrzehnt erlebte eine ganze Reihe anderer großer Krisen, doch in der Werbung wurde alles ausgeblendet, was in unerfreulichem Widerspruch zu ihrer Botschaft hätte stehen können.

Der Kleister des Kapitalismus

Die gesamte Werbung sei ein unglaublicher Betrug. Sie präsentiere ein Bild von Amerika, das von niemandem ernst genommen werde, am wenigsten von den Werbeleuten selbst, so der Soziologe David Riesman in seiner wegweisenden Studie *Die einsame Masse: Eine Untersuchung der Wandlungen des amerikanischen Charakters* (Rowohlt 1958). Seine Aussage ist allerdings nicht ganz zutreffend. Wenn die Verbraucher der Behauptung glauben, dass Glück durch den Erwerb von Markenprodukten käuflich sei, sind sie Komplizen bei diesem Betrug. Soll Werbung funktionieren, muss es ein symbiotisches Verhältnis zwischen Produzent und Konsument geben, von dem beide Seiten profitieren. Wenn man die in diesem Band gesammelten Anzeigen als Quellenmaterial für sozial- und kulturwissenschaftliche Studien benutzen will, muss man sie skeptisch als Beweisstücke eines beiderseitig vorteilhaften Betrugs betrachten, der in den Worten des Sozialkritikers Ernest van den Haag darauf abzielt, „Geschmack zu vereinheitlichen, zu deindividualisieren und so Massenproduktion zu ermöglichen". Und tatsächlich ist Werbung der Kleister des Kapitalismus.

Bis in die Sechziger hinein waren Druckerzeugnisse das wichtigste kreative Medium gewesen, doch in den Siebzigern wurde ihnen die kreative Durchschlagskraft von der Fernsehwerbung gestohlen. In den Achtzigern waren gedruckte Anzeigen nicht mehr als die mageren Brosamen der Werbebranche, unvergessliche Anzeigenkampagnen waren rar. Die paar, die es gab, waren insofern bemerkenswert, als sie Teil der Alltagskultur wurden (manchmal mithilfe von TV-Spots).

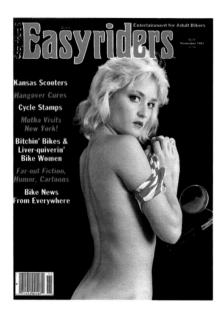

Zu ihnen zählen Sony® mit „Full Color Sound" (S. 313), illustriert von Milton Glaser, eine raffinierte Metapher, die Klang in etwas Sichtbares verwandelte; die von Oliviero Toscani fotografierten „United Colors of Benetton" (S. 466), eine Anzeigenserie, die zur Sozialkritik tendierte; Nike's® „Just Do It." (S. 480) beschleunigte den urbanen Trend, der aus einfachen Turnschuhen modische Prestigeobjekte machte; durch die Swatch®-Retroanzeigen (S. 202), entworfen von Paula Scher, wurden kurzlebige Armbanduhren schick, und Charlie Chaplin als IBM®-Maskottchen (S. 171) war die Liaison des Pioniers der Filmkomödie mit dem der Computerindustrie (Nostalgie erwies sich als effektive Strategie, um die frühen Computernutzer sanft auf das EDV-Zeitalter vorzubereiten). Apropos Computer: In den Achtzigern wurde auch der Apple Macintosh® (und der weniger erfolgreiche Lisa®) (S. 173) erfunden, dessen klare Werbeaussagen den Zugang zu einer unglaublichen neuen Technologie erleichterten.

Am stärksten in Erinnerung geblieben ist vielleicht die Anzeige für Maxell®-Audiokassetten (S. 313) mit dem schicken Schwarzweißfoto eines coolen Lederjackenträgers, der mit weißen Knöcheln die Lehnen eines Le-Corbusier-Sessels umklammert hält, während ihm die Maxell®-Kassette die Musik wie in einem Windtunnel aus einem Lautsprecher mit voller Kraft ins Gesicht bläst. In dieser Anzeige verschmolzen Konzept, Ästhetik und Botschaft, was dazu führte, dass sich das positive Image des Produkts mehr als zehn Jahre halten konnte. Doch diese wenigen Superlative stellten nicht viel mehr als den erinnerungswürdigen Maulwurfshügel auf einem unbedeutenden Berg dar.

Verdammt zur Bedeutungslosigkeit

Die oben genannten Kampagnen waren wirksam, weil sie entweder den kollektiven Nerv trafen oder unterbewusst verstörend wirkten. Die große Mehrheit der Anzeigen jedoch blieb stilistischen Klischees verhaftet, die ihre langfristige Wirkung minderten. Selbst wenn einer der Bestandteile (ein Slogan oder ein Bild) kurzzeitig einen Wiedererkennungseffekt besaß, war die Anzeige doch zur Bedeutungslosigkeit verdammt, wenn nicht alle Elemente harmonisch zusammenwirkten. Die dramatisch beleuchtete Still-Life-Fotografie und die demonstrativen Headlines für den Gillette®-Atra-Rasierer (S. 223), für Close-Up®-Zahnpasta (S. 229), Dry Idea® (S. 226) und Marriott Resorts®

(S. 580) zum Beispiel: Sie präsentierten zwar die jeweiligen Waren, versagten aber als einprägsame Sinnsprüche, die eine über den ersten Eindruck hinausgehende Identität hätten vermitteln können – und das waren noch die besseren Werbungen! Offensichtlich gedeiht gutes Design nicht in einem Vakuum. Manche Anzeigen wirken bemüht bei dem Versuch, die Käufer anzusprechen, so Life Savers® mit „Hole Lotta Fresh!" (S. 540), die zwar grafisch ins Auge springt, aber leider von einem idiotischen Slogan begleitet wird.

Sehr viele der in den achtziger Jahren produzierten Printanzeigen versuchten zu angestrengt, ihre Message herüberzubringen. Viele verwendeten zwar ganzseitige, randlose Bilder, die jedoch mit vielen Worten und komplexen Bildern überladen waren und einzugestehen schienen, dass die Werbeagenturen das große Geld mit TV-Werbung machten und sich deswegen keine kreativen Druckanzeigen leisten konnten. Jazzercise® (S. 239) beispielsweise fehlen ästhetisches Können und konzeptionelle Nuancen. Insbesondere Nuancenreichtum ist der Faktor, der Erstklassiges von Mittelmäßigem trennt, wie zum Beispiel in „Speedo Suits Men" (S. 456). Es ist zwar visuell kaum weniger auffallend als „Calvin Klein Jeans" (S. 458), aber unbeholfen gestaltet (die Typografie in der Schlag-

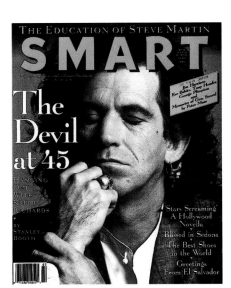

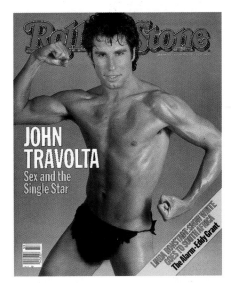

zeile passt so wenig zum sexy Model wie Karosocken), und die Fotografie ist fantasielos.

Wenn man den ästhetischen Aspekt außer Acht lässt, werden in der Werbung vor allem Geschichten erzählt. Sind sie spannend, neigen Verbraucher eher dazu, die Marke zu ihrer eigenen zu machen. Doch da die von Werbefuzzis ausgedachten Geschichten die immergleichen Märchen verbreiten, muss viel Brimborium drumherum gemacht werden, um die Kunden in den Bann zu ziehen. „All Fudge. No Pudge." (S. 538) von Fudgsicle® zum Beispiel erzählt von der Sünde ohne Reue. Mit einem derben Pinselstrich präsentiert diese plumpe Anzeige für ein im Grunde langweiliges Produkt zugleich das Ideal körperlicher Schönheit. Wer's glaubt, wird selig.

Ungesunde Mythen

Das Gegensatzpaar Realität und Fantasie (Wahrheit und Lüge) ist allerdings ein irreführendes Klischee, da die Werbung nie so tut, als würde sie Realität präsentieren. Bewusst oder unbewusst ist allgemein anerkannt, dass in der Werbung viele Fakten unter den Tisch fallen. In einigen Fällen können sich die von der Werbung propagierten My-

then jedoch als äußerst schädlich für Körper und Geist erweisen. Der verlogenste (und ungesundeste) Mythos der modernen Werbung, insbesondere in den Jahrzehnten vor den Achtzigern, war die Darstellung von Zigaretten als gesundheitsförderlich. Von den Dreißigern bis in die Fünfziger wurde in der Reklame behauptet, dass bestimmte Zigaretten Stress abbauen helfen und sich daher positiv auf die Gesundheit auswirken. In den siebziger Jahren trat das längst fällige Verbot von TV-Werbung für Zigaretten in Kraft und Mitte der Achtziger lag auch die Printwerbung in den letzten Zügen (sie war bereits gezwungen, den Warnhinweis des Gesundheitsministers groß in jeder Anzeige abzudrucken).

Herkömmliche Anzeigen drängten die Verbraucher dazu, nicht auf den gesunden Menschenverstand zu hören, ihrer Gewohnheit zu folgen und trotz aller bewiesenen negativen Wirkungen zu rauchen. Eine subtile Anzeige dieser Art, die minimalistische „Wenn Sie rauchen, *probieren Sie bitte Carlton*" (S. 88) machte keine Versprechungen, hielt den Raucher jedoch auch nicht von seinem riskanten Verhalten ab. Die meisten anderen Tabakkonzerne strichen jegliche Subtilität aus ihrem Repertoire und verfestigten mit ihren Bildern die falschen Sozial- und

Kulturmythen, dass Rauchen cool, lässig, elegant und sogar radikal sei. Manche Anzeigen waren so total unaufrichtig, dass es lange dauerte, bis man sie überhaupt durchschaute.

Als Camel® merkte, dass sein Kundenstamm schnell dahinzuschwinden drohte, stellte das Unternehmen sein gezeichnetes Maskottchen (S. 92) auf die Zielgruppe Jugendliche und Kinder ab. Das phallisch geformte, sich menschlich verhaltende, in Leder gekleidete Dromedar erschien in Teenager-Zeitschriften (wie *Rolling Stone*), was die Zielgruppe sehr deutlich macht.

Die Herrschaft des Bierhundes

Der Alkoholkonsum bei Jugendlichen stieg in den Achtzigern ebenfalls an, und die Bier- und Schnapsproduzenten, die das meiste Geld für Printkampagnen ausgaben, stellten Trinken nicht nur als akzeptabel, sondern als normal dar. Die genialste in den Achtzigern gestartete Kampagne war (und ist) die für Absolut® Wodka (S. 60). Sie war allerdings nicht auf Teenager, sondern auf Mittzwanziger abgestimmt und schuf 1980 mit der Fusion von Kunst und Kommerz eine einprägsame Ikonografie. Dass man so intelligent war, Avantgarde-Künstler wie Keith

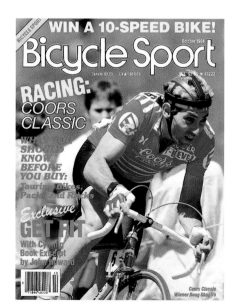

Haring, Jean Michel Basquiat und Andy Warhol zur visuellen Interpretation der Absolut®-Flasche (und dadurch zur Übertragung ihrer Glaubwürdigkeit auf diese) zu verpflichten, sorgte dafür, dass sich die Anzeigenserie über alles Mittelmäßige erhob.

Viele Marken versuchten, den Erfolg von Absolut® zu kopieren, aber prätentiöse Anzeigen wie die für Rumple Minze® mit seiner „Weißen Magie aus dem Schwarzwald" (S. 69) in Gestalt eines Fantasy-Superweibs oder die surrealistische Pseudo-René-Magritte-Landschaft von Grand Marnier® (S. 72) waren nie so kreativ oder interessant. Die Werbung für durchschnittliche Liköre und Schnäpse, die keine neuen, hippen Kundenkreise erschließen sollte, folgte einfach den fantasielosen Konventionen.

Im Gegensatz zur Zigaretten- und Spirituosenwerbung war Reklame für Bier seit der Prohibitonszeit in den zwanziger Jahren immer erlaubt. In den Achtzigern hatte sie einen enormen Medieneinfluss. Altehrwürdige Marken wie Miller High Life® (S. 52) und Moosehead® (S. 46) setzten auf ihre Logos, aber neue Produkte wie die Leicht-Biere brauchten aufsehenerregendere Köder, um sich einen Marktanteil zu sichern. Einer der beliebtesten war ein Bullterrier namens Spuds MacKenzie, das „Original Partytier"

von Bud Light® (S. 55). Anheuser-Busch® machte mit diesem Werbehund ein Milliardengeschäft. Die Figur war derart populär (selbst bei Antialkoholikern), dass sie bei der Präsidentschaftswahl aufgestellt wurde. Wenn man bedenkt, welche unglaubliche Macht über die öffentliche Meinung Bud® mit dieser Werbung hatte – die es mitunter schaffte, die weltpolitischen Sorgen aus dem Bewusstsein der Öffentlichkeit zu verbannen –, hätte Spuds vielleicht sogar gewonnen, wenn er wirklich gegen Ronald Reagan angetreten wäre.

Gegen Ende des Jahrzehnts gewann die Werbung in den Printmedien allmählich ihre Kreativität zurück, weil die neuen Nischen-Magazine (von denen manche ausschließlich Kundenservice boten) ganz zielgruppenspezifisch warben. Auch wurden Anzeigen für Absolut® und IBM® als unterhaltsame Unterbrechung des redaktionellen Teils gesehen. Die Branche suchte aktiv nach alten und neuen Kanälen jenseits des Fernsehens. Der Kathodenstrahl des Bildschirms leuchtete am Werbehimmel nicht mehr am hellsten. Plakatwände und Displays am Point-of-Purchase waren im Kommen. Neue Druckverfahren wurden eingeführt, die von Artdirektoren und Designern dankbar genutzt wurden. Mit dem Beginn der Neunziger fand

eine wahre Renaissance der Printwerbung statt, die mit dem Wirtschaftsaufschwung unter der neuen Regierung im Weißen Haus sogar bahnbrechend Neues hervorbrachte. Die Werbung marschierte wieder an der Spitze der Popkultur-Parade, eine Entwicklung, die so gut für die Firmen wie zweifelhaft für die Gesellschaft war.

Steven Heller ist Artdirector der *New York Times Book Review* und Vorsitzender der Fakultät Gestaltung (MFA/Design) an der School of Visual Arts in New York. Er ist außerdem Autor und Herausgeber von mehr als 80 Büchern über Grafikdesign und Populärkultur, u. a. *Merz to Emigre and Beyond: Avant-Garde Magazine Design of the 20th Century* und *Design Literacy Revised*.

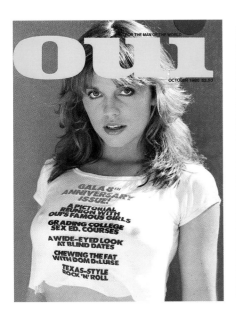

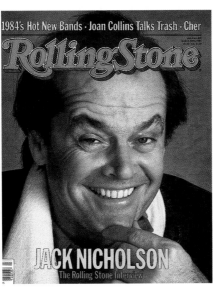

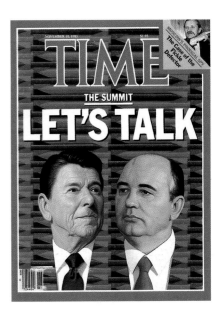

Les Années 80 :

La publicité des années Reagan

par Steven Heller

La bosse du slip : la nouvelle conquête

En 1980 les Américains élisaient Ronald Reagan à la présidence des Etats-Unis. Celui qui avait été l'animateur de *General Electric Theater* à la télévision (et gouverneur de la Californie) fut investi des pleins pouvoirs pour lancer la campagne de sa vie : la nouvelle puissance américaine. La mondialisation pointait à l'horizon, un nouvel ordre social était dans l'air et Reagan était en place.

En effet, les années Reagan se révélèrent mouvementées. L'Union Soviétique faisait ses adieux à la scène internationale et libérait de l'oppression les populations du bloc soviétique. A la même époque, Calvin Klein® dévoilait ses premières publicités et affiches « Underwear for Men » permettant ainsi au public américain de découvrir la bosse du slip. Le morne pouvoir communiste ayant perdu la guerre froide face à la puissance américaine, on vit de sensuels supermodèles (Kathy Ireland, Christie Brinkley, et Cindy Crawford) envahir les médias américains, et la publicité en particulier.

Les années 80 furent témoins de la chute du communisme et suscitèrent les grandes réalisations de l'ère Reagan, y compris les difficultés économiques, les missiles Star Wars et le scandale de « l'Irangate ». Ce fut aussi le début des grandes créations de Madison Avenue, comme le « Smooth Character » de Joe Camel, la Coors® Silver Bullet® et Spuds MacKenzie, le chien de Bud Light®. Le SIDA se révéla être une épidémie mortelle et la décennie fut affectée par d'autres crises diverses, bien que fidèle à sa tradition et par commodité, le monde de la publicité ignora les signaux contradictoires dans ses messages.

La façade du capitalisme

« La publicité n'est qu'une gigantesque escroquerie, qui nous montre une image de l'Amérique à laquelle personne ne croit et surtout pas ceux qui la fabriquent » écrit le sociologue David Riesman dans son analyse révolutionnaire *La foule solitaire : Anatomie de la société moderne* (Arthaud, 1968). Pourtant, son allégation n'est pas tout à fait exacte ; après tout, les consommateurs se font les complices de la tromperie à chaque fois qu'ils croient que leur bonheur dépend de l'achat de produits de grandes marques. Pour que la publicité marche, il faut qu'il y ait une symbiose entre le producteur et le consommateur, pour le plus grand bénéfice des deux. Voilà pourquoi les publicités rassemblées dans ce volume, en tant que matériau brut de l'histoire sociale et culturelle, doivent être considérées avec scepticisme comme l'évidence d'une arnaque profitable qui, d'après le critique social Ernest van den Haag, vise « à uniformiser le goût, à le désindividualiser et permet la production en série ». En effet, tout ce qui pourrait ralentir la consommation effrénée est occulté par la propagande publicitaire – et la publicité, c'est la façade du capitalisme.

La presse écrite avait été le principal support de créativité jusque dans les années 60 ; dans les années 70, la télévision lui avait volé la vedette ; de ce fait, dans les années 80, la publicité de presse était en miettes et très peu de campagnes publicitaires de l'époque sont restées dans les mémoires. Celles dont on se souvient sont remarquables parce qu'elles sont passées dans l'héritage culturel (quelquefois avec des publicités télévisées mais aussi indépendamment).

Parmi les publicités présentées dans ce livre on trouve « Full Color Sound » de Sony® (p. 313), illustrée par Milton Glaser, une métaphore qui accroche l'œil, élégante et pleine d'esprit sur la visualisation du son ; « United Colors of Benetton » de Benetton®

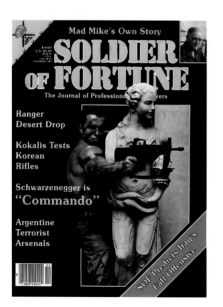
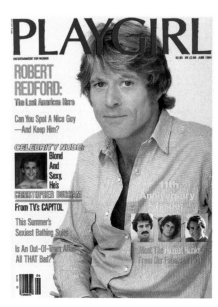
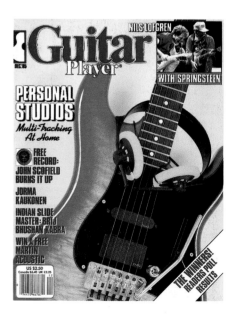

(p. 466), photographiée par d'Oliviero Toscani, une image espiègle avec une série d'affiches évoluant en une indulgente critique sociale; «Just Do It.» de Nike® (p. 480), qui lança une nouvelle mode dans la rue en transformant un simple sneaker en une prestigieuse chaussure de sports; la pub rétro de Swatch® (p. 202), conçue par Paula Scher, soulignant le style d'un nouveau produit, la montre éphémère; et l'inspiration d'IBM®, choisissant Charlie Chaplin comme mascotte (p. 171) et associant ainsi le pionnier des acteurs comiques au pionnier du fabricant d'ordinateurs (la nostalgie était aussi une manière effective de faciliter le passage des utilisateurs de PC à l'ère de l'informatique). En parlant d'ordinateurs, les années 80 ont vu le lancement de l'Apple Macintosh® (et dans une moindre mesure de LISA®) (p. 173), avec un argument publicitaire d'une sobriété calculée ouvrant la voie vers une incroyable nouvelle technologie.

La publicité la plus connue de la décennie est peut-être celle de Maxell® avec «No Other Audio Tape Delivers Higher Fidelity» (p. 313), une photographie sophistiquée en noir et blanc d'un yuppie vêtu de cuir, agrippé de toutes ses forces au bras d'un fauteuil Le Corbusier – la cassette Maxell® soufflant le son comme dans un tunnel aérodyna-mique à partir d'un petit haut-parleur situé en face de lui. C'était un remarquable amalgame d'idées, d'esthétique et de messages. Cette simple formule contribua à l'image positive du produit dans la presse et à la télévision pendant plus de dix ans. Cependant, ces quelques publicités ne sont qu'une taupinière par rapport à la montagne de celles que l'on a oubliées.

Condamnées à l'oubli

Les campagnes citées ci-dessus nous interpellent parce qu'elles avaient soit touché un nerf sensible collectif soit implanté une peur inconsciente. Par opposition, la grande majorité des publicités de ce livre utilisaient des clichés de style, ce qui effectivement diminuait leur impact avec les années. Même si l'on retenait l'un des éléments (un slogan ou une image), si l'ensemble ne formait pas un tout harmonieux, l'annonce en question était condamnée à tomber dans l'oubli. Voyez le côté dramatique, les photos figées et les gros titres péremptoires du rasoir Gillette® Atra (p. 223), du dentifrice Close-Up® (p. 229), de Dry Idea® (p. 226), et de Marriott Resorts® (p. 580): ils vantaient leurs produits respectifs, mais ont échoué dans leur tentative à graver le nom de la marque dans la mémoire du consommateur au-delà de la première exposition – et c'était des publicités plutôt bien faites. C'est clair, il ne suffit pas d'avoir une bonne idée. Certaines publicités s'efforçaient d'attirer l'attention du public, comme «Hole Lotta Fresh!» de Life Savers® (p. 540) avec une image impressionnante d'une bouée géante mais un slogan idiot.

Un grand nombre des publicités de presse produites dans les années 80 se donnait beaucoup de mal pour convaincre le public. Bien que beaucoup d'entre elles étaient en pleine page sans bordure, celles qui étaient surchargées de texte et d'images semblaient suggérer que les agences de publicité admettaient que les gros budgets étaient réservés pour la télévision, et que la publicité de presse n'avait pas les moyens d'être créative. Jazzercise® (p. 239) est un exemple de cet effet d'exagération qui manque totalement de talent artistique et de nuance. En fait, la nuance est exactement ce qui sépare l'excellence du médiocre, comme on peut le constater dans «Speedo Suits Men.» (p. 456). Bien qu'elle soit sans doute visuellement aussi attrayante que celle de «Calvin Klein Jeans» (p. 458), la composition manque de finesse (la typographie du titre est grossière, comme si le bel athlète portait des Burlingtons).

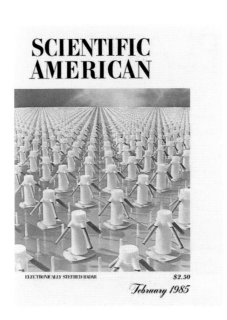

Esthétique mise à part, les publicités racontent des histoires et plus l'histoire est intéressante, plus le consommateur sera enclin à adopter cette marque en particulier. Mais puisque ces boniments entretiennent les mythes et les illusions, ils doivent faire de plus en plus de promesses, vraies ou fausses, pour tenter le client. Prenez « All Fudge. No Pudge. » de Fudgsicle® (p. 538), qui évoque les désirs contradictoires des Américains de rester minces tout en mangeant des bonbons. D'un grand trait, cette publicité maladroite nous montre l'idéal de la beauté physique tout en vantant les avantages d'un produit essentiellement banal. Qui ne serait pas attiré par la promesse d'un plaisir innocent (et léger) ?

Des mythologies nuisibles

Cependant, le cliché réalité/fantaisie (vérité/mensonges) est en réalité un faux problème, puisque la publicité ne prétend pas ne pas prétendre. Chacun reconnaît, ouvertement ou secrètement, que la publicité est basée sur l'évasion. Quoique dans certains cas, les mythes publicitaires soient nuisibles au physique comme au moral. Le mensonge le plus immoral (et nuisible) de la publicité moderne, surtout dans les décen-

nies précédant les années 80, c'est celui qui présentait la cigarette comme un produit pour agrémenter la vie. Des années 30 aux années 50, les annonces proclamaient que la cigarette diminuait le stress et de ce fait était bénéfique pour la santé mentale. Dans les années 70, l'interdiction de la publicité pour le tabac à la télévision, une décision longtemps attendue, entra en vigueur et au milieu des années 80, la publicité pour le tabac touchait à sa fin (on pouvait déjà voir l'avertissement du Directeur du service de santé publique bien en vue sur toutes les annonces).

Les publicités habituelles poussaient les consommateurs à faire fi des mises en garde, à céder à leurs habitudes et à fumer sans se soucier des effets néfastes démontrés. Une publicité insidieuse, le minimaliste « If you smoke *please try Carlton* » (p. 88), ne prétendait rien mais ne faisait rien non plus pour dissuader le fumeur « exercé » de prendre des risques. Les autres fabricants de tabac supprimèrent la subtilité de leurs répertoires et continuèrent à entretenir les fausses conceptions sociales et culturelles que fumer était branché, cool, élégant et même révolutionnaire. Certaines publicités étaient si bien faites qu'il fallait un moment pour comprendre de quoi il s'agissait.

Quand Camel® comprit que le nombre de ses clients déclinait rapidement, ce qui était provoqué par la peur d'une terrible maladie et par ceux qui arrêtaient de fumer, la compagnie chercha à intéresser les adolescents (et même les plus jeunes) avec sa mascotte « Smooth Character » (p. 92), un personnage de bande dessinée. Le chameau de forme phallique, anthropomorphe, habillé de cuir, apparut dans des magazines pour les jeunes (comme *Rolling Stone*), ce qui révéla clairement la population visée ...

Quand les chiens faisaient de la réclame

Dans les années 80, la consommation d'alcool était aussi en augmentation chez les jeunes et évidemment les fabricants de bière et de spiritueux, qui finançaient les plus grosses campagnes de presse, ont cherché à en donner l'image d'un comportement social non seulement accepté mais aussi souhaité. Bien que visant les jeunes de vingt à trente ans plutôt que les adolescents, la plus remarquable de toutes fût (et reste) Absolut® Vodka (p. 60) lancée en 1980, une fusion de l'art et du commerce dans une iconographie de haut niveau. L'intelligence d'avoir demandé à des artistes d'avant-garde comme Keith

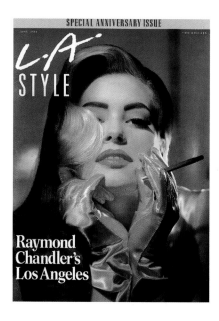

Haring, Jean Michel Basquiat et Andy Warhol de concevoir (et finalement de cautionner) la bouteille d'Absolut® lui permit de s'élever au-dessus de la masse banale et médiocre des publicités de l'époque.

Plusieurs marques essayèrent d'égaler le succès d'Absolut®, mais la prétentieuse publicité de Rumple Minze®, «White Magic from the Black Forest» (p. 69), symbolisée par un fantasme de super-nana et celle de Grand Marnier®, imitant servilement un tableau de René Magritte (p. 72), n'affichaient pas la même créativité. Les grandes marques de boissons alcoolisées qui ne cherchaient pas à conquérir un nouveau public ne changèrent rien à leur routine.

A la différence du tabac et des spiritueux, la publicité pour la bière n'a jamais plus été interdite dans la presse depuis la prohibition des années 20 (et jamais à la télévision); dans les années 80, un très grand nombre de ces publicités eurent un énorme retentissement dans les médias. Les marques classiques comme Miller High Life® (p. 52) et Moosehead® (p. 46) se concentrèrent sur leur logo comme argument de vente, mais les nouvelles marques, la génération des bières «light», nécessitaient des arguments plus percutants pour conquérir leur part de marché. L'un des plus connu fut un bizarre

bull-terrier dénommé Spuds MacKenzie, le «Original Party Animal» de Bud Light® (p. 55). Anheuser-Busch® est tombé sur une affaire en or avec ce chien, qui était si populaire (aussi parmi les non-buveurs) qu'il fut proposé comme candidat à la Présidence. Etant donné que Bud® avait énormément d'influence sur l'opinion publique grâce à ses publicités – parfois même à lui en faire oublier le reste du monde – si Spuds avait vraiment fait campagne contre Ronald Reagan, il aurait peut-être gagné.

A la fin des années 80, la publicité de presse regagna lentement du terrain en tant que support de créativité parce que les magazines des nouveaux secteurs du marché (certains entièrement consacrés au service de la clientèle) visaient le public intéressé par les produits qu'ils présentaient. De plus, les annonces pour Absolut® et IBM® étaient considérées comme une diversion amusante du contenu rédactionnel. Les annonceurs étaient activement à la recherche d'anciens et de nouveaux débouchés, indépendamment de la télévision. Le tube cathodique avait perdu son prestige; on lui préférait les panneaux publicitaires et les étalages des points de vente. De nouvelles techniques d'impression venaient s'ajouter à l'arsenal de l'industrie et les directeurs artistiques

ainsi que les créateurs étaient prêts à relever le défi. Dans les années 90, la publicité de presse vit la renaissance de son potentiel de créativité et, grâce à la nouvelle prospérité américaine due au succès de l'administration de la Maison blanche, commençait même à percer. La publicité était à nouveau en tête, donnant le ton à la culture populaire, un développement aussi bénéfique pour la clientèle que suspect pour la société.

Steven Heller est le directeur artistique de *The New York Times Book Review* et co-doyen de la section de MFA Design à la School of Visual Arts. Il a révisé ou écrit plus de quatre-vingts livres sur le dessin et la culture populaire, dont *Merz to Emigre and Beyond: Avant Garde Magazine Design of the 20th Century* et *Design Literacy Revised*.

His art caught the spirit of the Twenties (p. 94): here, Joe College leaves his hometown girl behind

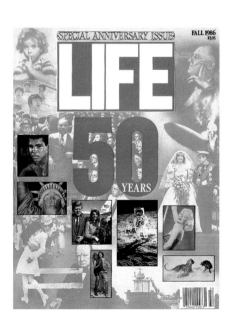

Los años ochenta:
La publicidad en la era Reagan

por Steven Heller

El bulto en la entrepierna: la nueva frontera

En 1980, los estadounidenses eligieron a Ronald Reagan presidente. Confiaron a aquel ex presentador del programa de televisión *General Electric Theater* (y ex gobernador de California) un mandato considerable para llevar a cabo la campaña de su vida: un nuevo dominio de Estados Unidos. La globalización y un nuevo orden social empezaban a perfilarse en el horizonte, y Reagan se hallaba en posición de asalto.

Los años ochenta de Reagan fueron tumultuosos cuando menos. El telón de acero se rasgó y los habitantes de las naciones del bloque soviético lograron zafarse de la opresión. Entre tanto, Calvin Klein® presentó sus primeros anuncios y vallas publicitarias de ropa interior para hombre y los norteamericanos obtuvieron el derecho a contemplar en público el bulto de la entrepierna. Mientras la hosca superpotencia comunista sucumbía al poderío de Estados Unidos en los últimos coletazos de la guerra fría, *top models* sensuales (Kathy Ireland, Christie Brinkley y Cindy Crawford) conquistaban los medios de comunicación, en especial, la publicidad.

La década de 1980 fue testigo de la derrota del comunismo y dio paso a los logros de la era Reagan, incluida la implantación de la economía de goteo descendente, la defensa contra misiles balísticos conocida como la «Guerra de las Galaxias» y el Iran-Contragate (el escándalo suscitado por la financiación de los contrarrevolucionarios nicaragüenses con los beneficios de la venta de armas a Irán). Pero también fue la década en la que debutaron algunos hitos de Madison Avenue, como Joe Camel, la mascota de los cigarrillos Camel; la Silver Bullet®, la cerveza «sin» de Coors®; y Spuds MacKenzie, el animal fiestero de Bud Light®. El sida se convirtió en una pandemia mortal y la década estuvo asediada por otras muchas crisis, si bien la industria de la publicidad, dando fe de su condición, hizo oídos sordos a cualquier contratiempo por el bien de sus mensajes.

El papel pintado del capitalismo

«La publicidad en su conjunto es un fraude fantástico que presenta una imagen de Estados Unidos que ningún ser humano se toma en serio, y menos que nadie los publicitarios que la crean», escribió en 1950 el sociólogo David Riesman en su rompedor estudio *The Lonely Crowd: A Study of the Changing American Character* (Yale University Press, 1950). Sin embargo, su aseveración

no es del todo precisa; al fin y al cabo, los consumidores son cómplices de fraude cada vez que se rinden a la idea de que la felicidad puede alcanzarse adquiriendo las marcas anunciadas. Para que la publicidad tenga éxito debe existir una relación simbiótica entre el productor y el consumidor en la cual ambas partes tengan algo que ganar. Por lo tanto, si se conciben como materia prima de la historia sociocultural, los anuncios recopilados en este volumen pueden contemplarse con escepticismo como prueba de un chanchullo mutuamente ventajoso que, de acuerdo con el crítico social Ernest van den Haag, tiene como fin «unificar el gusto, desindividualizarlo y, con ello, posibilitar la producción en serie». A decir verdad, cualquier cosa que obstaculice el consumo de artículos producidos en serie por parte de los estadounidenses se empapela con *marketing*... y la publicidad es el papel pintado del capitalismo.

La publicidad impresa había sido el medio creativo por excelencia hasta los años sesenta; en los setenta, los anuncios televisivos le habían arrebatado el protagonismo y, llegados a los ochenta, se había convertido en los despojos del sector, si bien fue el medio de campañas memorables que merece la pena destacar porque se abrieron camino en la cultura general (en ocasiones, junto con sus

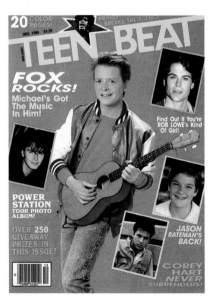

homólogas televisivas, pero también algunas por sí solas).

Los ejemplos representados en este libro incluyen «Sonido a todo color» de Sony® (pág. 313), una sinestesia inteligente y llamativa ilustrada por Milton Glaser que transformó el sonido en visión; «United Colors of Benetton» de Benetton® (pág. 466), una campaña icónica con fotografías de Oliviero Toscani, cuya serie de anuncios permaneció largo tiempo en cartelera y acabó por devenir una crítica social moderada; «Just Do It» de Nike® (pág. 480), que convirtió en tendencia urbana de moda el uso de las zapatillas deportivas; los anuncios retro de Swatch® (pág. 202), concebidos por Paula Scher, que subrayaban el estilo de un nuevo artículo comercial: el reloj de pulsera efímero, y la inspirada iconización que IBM® hizo de Charlie Chaplin (pág. 171), donde casó a un cómico cinematográfico pionero con un productor informático también pionero (la nostalgia demostró ser un método eficaz para facilitar la entrada de los usuarios de PC en la era informática). Y hablando de ordenadores, los ochenta fueron testigo del nacimiento de Apple Macintosh® (y de los menos exitosos Lisa®) (pág. 173) con anuncios que sirvieron como pasaporte a una nueva tecnología impresionante.

Sin embargo, tal vez el anuncio con más resonancia de la década fuera el de Maxell®: «Ninguna otra cinta ofrece mejor fidelidad» (pág. 313), con su elegante fotografía en blanco y negro de un joven enfundado en cuero agarrado a los brazos de un sillón de Le Corbusier soportando el embate del sonido del casete Maxell® como si se hallara en un túnel de viento, con las ondas sonoras que emanan de un único y diminuto altavoz azotándole el rostro. Este anuncio supuso una fusión excepcional de concepto, estética y mensaje. Y aquella fórmula básica continuó promocionando la imagen del producto tanto en prensa impresa como en televisión durante más de una década. No obstante, estos ejemplos superlativos componen una topera memorable en una montaña insulsa.

Sentenciados a la intrascendencia

Las campañas citadas anteriormente siguen sonándonos, bien porque tocaron el nervio de la memoria colectiva, bien porque implantaron una alarma inconsciente en nuestro cerebro. Por el contrario, la inmensa mayoría de los anuncios de este libro se sumaron a los clichés estilísticos cuyo impacto mermó considerablemente a largo plazo. Incluso aunque un componente

(un eslogan o una imagen) deslumbrara momentáneamente, si el resto de los elementos no estaba en sintonía con él, el anuncio estaba sentenciado a la intrascendencia. Pongamos por ejemplo las fotografías de naturalezas muertas con iluminación teatral y eslóganes concluyentes que presentaban las cuchillas Gillette® Atra (pág. 223), los dentríficos Close-Up® (pág. 229), Dry Idea® (pág. 226) y Marriott Resorts® (pág. 580): anunciaban el producto, pero fallaban en tanto que ayuda mnemotécnica para transmitir una identidad más allá de la imagen inicial; y eso que se trataba de anuncios bastante bien diseñados. Lógicamente, el diseño de calidad no funciona por sí solo. Algunos anuncios usaban recursos efectistas para conectar con el público –como el de Life Savers® (pág. 540), con su gigantesco salvavidas de composición gráfica impecable–, pero incorporaban un eslogan estúpido.

Bastantes anuncios impresos producidos durante los años ochenta procuraban con excesivo ahínco incrustar sus eslóganes en la mente del consumidor. Aunque muchos de ellos eran imágenes a sangre y a toda página, los anuncios recargados de texto e imágenes complejas parecían indicar que las agencias de publicidad admitían por fin que los presupuestos importantes se destinaban a

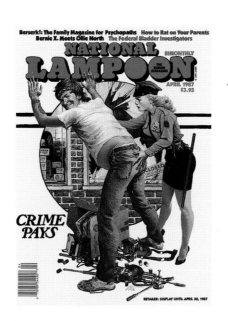

la publicidad en televisión, por lo que los anuncios en papel no podían permitirse ser creativos. Jazzercise® (pág. 239) es una muestra representativa de la metodología de la exageración carente de toda noción estética y matiz conceptual. A decir verdad, los matices son precisamente lo que diferencia los anuncios de primera de los mediocres, como en el caso de Speedo (pág. 456). Aunque podría decirse que visualmente no es menos llamativo que «Calvin Klein Jeans» (pág. 458), su diseño es torpe (la tipografía del eslogan es tan burda como si el modelo aficionado llevara calcetines con rombos) y en la fotografía la inspiración brilla por su ausencia.

Dejando de lado la estética, los anuncios cuentan historias y, si una narración tiene gancho, es más probable que los consumidores se identifiquen con la marca que la anuncia. Sin embargo, dado que estos cuentos publicitarios perpetúan mitos y falacias, hace falta desplegar todo un abanico de promesas de medicamentos con patente y aceite de serpiente para que el consumidor se trague el anzuelo. Por ejemplo, el anuncio de Fudgsicle® (pág. 538) da fe de la compulsión competitiva de los estadounidenses por mantener la línea aun comiendo dulces. De una pincelada, este anuncio falto de gracia presenta un ideal de belleza al tiempo que

ensalza los beneficios de un producto que en esencia carece de todo interés. ¿Quién no se sentiría atraído por la promesa de concederse un pequeño capricho sin sentirse culpable (y sin engordar ni un gramo)?

Mitos insanos

Con todo, el cliché de la realidad frente a la fantasía (o de la verdad frente a la mentira) sirve solo para desviar la atención, porque la publicidad no finge no fingir. Todo el mundo sabe, ya sea manifiesta o encubiertamente, que la publicidad se basa en evasivas. Pese a todo, en algunos casos, los mitos publicitarios pueden resultar perjudiciales para el cuerpo y para la mente. El mito más falaz (e insano) de la publicidad moderna, sobre todo de las décadas precedentes a los años ochenta, era el que presentaba el tabaco como un producto que mejoraba la calidad de vida. Desde los años treinta hasta bien entrados los cincuenta, los anuncios afirmaban que fumar reducía el estrés y, por lo tanto, era una práctica excelente para disfrutar de una buena salud mental. Durante los años setenta, entró en vigor la tan necesaria prohibición de anunciar tabaco en televisión y a mediados de los años ochenta empezó a sonar el canto de cisne de la publicidad

de cigarrillos, con la inclusión obligatoria en todos los anuncios y de manera visible de la etiqueta de advertencia de las autoridades.

Los anuncios convencionales alentaron a los consumidores a ir en contra de la sabiduría popular, sucumbir a sus hábitos y seguir fumando pese a los efectos nocivos probados. El anuncio insidioso «Si fuma, pruebe Carlton» (pág. 88) no buscaba nuevos adeptos, pero tampoco pretendía disuadir al fumador de abandonar su comportamiento de riesgo. Casi todas las demás tabacaleras eliminaron toda sutileza de su repertorio y perpetuaron el mito sociocultural falso de que fumar era moderno, elegante e incluso radical. Algunos anuncios utilizaban artimañas tan enrevesadas que había que observarlos con lupa para desvelar su cometido.

Cuando Camel® apreció que su base de consumidores se erosionaba a marchas forzadas debido tanto a las enfermedades catastróficas relacionadas con el tabaco como a la idea de que hay que dejar de fumar, la empresa creó un dibujo animado a modo de mascota, Joe Camel (pág. 92), para atraer a adolescentes (y niños). El dromedario con chupa de cuero, con forma fálica y antropomorfizado aparecía en revistas juveniles (como *Rolling Stone*), revelando con toda claridad cuál era su público objetivo...

El reinado canino

El consumo de alcohol entre adolescentes también estuvo en auge en los años ochenta y, como no es de extrañar, las empresas de cerveza y licores, que se contaban entre las mayores inversoras en campañas publicitarias impresas, retrataban la bebida no solo como algo aceptable sino deseable. La campaña más brillante de los años ochenta, destinada a un público objetivo de unos veintitantos, fue (y sigue siendo) la de Absolut® Vodka (pág. 60), lanzada en 1980, que combinaba el arte y el negocio en una iconografía sublime. La perspicacia para encargar a artistas de vanguardia como Keith Haring, Jean Michel Basquiat y Andy Warhol que interpretaran visualmente (y, en última instancia, que cedieran su credibilidad a) la botella de Absolut® garantizó que este anuncio destacara entre tanta mediocridad.

Muchas marcas intentaron repetir el éxito de Absolut®, pero anuncios pretenciosos como «Magia blanca desde la Selva Negra» de Rumple Minze® (pág. 69), protagonizado por una exhuberante heroína fantástica, y el paisaje surrealista falso a lo René Magritte de Grand Marnier® (pág. 72) carecían de todo atractivo creativo. Las bebidas corrientes no buscaban atraer al público «moderno»

y perpetuaron las convenciones mediocres.

A diferencia del tabaco y los licores fuertes, los anuncios de cerveza no se han prohibido en prensa impresa desde los años veinte (ni tampoco en televisión), y durante los ochenta inundaron los medios. Marcas venerables como Miller High Life® (pág. 52) y Moosehead® (pág. 46) se concentraron en sus logotipos como puntos de venta, mientras que las marcas advenedizas, como la nueva generación de cervezas «sin», recurrían a ganchos más provocativos para captar su nicho de mercado. Uno de los más populares fue el estrafalario bulterrier Spuds MacKenzie, el «animal fiestero» de Bud Light® (pág. 55). Anheuser-Busch®, proveedor de la cerveza, consciente de la popularidad (incluso entre los no bebedores) de aquel perro que reportó tantos miles de millones, lo presentó para Presidente. Dado que el anuncio de Bud® tenía un poder impresionante para influir en la opinión pública, e incluso para despertar conciencias mundiales, si Spuds hubiera rivalizado en serio con Ronald Reagan, quizá hubiera ganado.

Hacia finales de los ochenta, la publicidad impresa volvía a ganar poco a poco fuerza como medio creativo gracias a las nuevas revistas (algunas dedicadas en exclusiva a ofrecer servicios al consumidor), que atraían

a un público interesado en los productos presentados en su interior. Es más, los anuncios de Absolut® e IBM® se consideraban entretenimientos dentro de un contexto editorial. El sector buscaba otros campos aparte de la televisión. El tubo de rayos catódicos había dejado de ser la panacea de la publicidad; las vallas y los expositores estaban en alza. Al repertorio de la industria se añadían las nuevas tecnologías de impresión, mientras los directores de arte y diseñadores hacían frente a nuevos desafíos. Antes de entrar en los años noventa, la publicidad impresa empezó a experimentar un verdadero renacimiento de su potencial creativo y, con la nueva prosperidad estadounidense de la subsiguiente Administración de la Casa Blanca, incluso rompió moldes. La publicidad marchaba una vez más al frente del desfile de la cultura pop, un avance tan bueno para sus clientes como discutible para la sociedad.

Steven Heller es director de arte del *New York Times Book Review* y codirector del Máster de Diseño en la School of Visual Arts. Ha editado y escrito más de ochenta libros sobre diseño y cultura popular, entre los que se cuentan *Merz to Emigre and Beyond: Avant Garde Magazine Design of the 20th Century* y *Design Literacy Revised*.

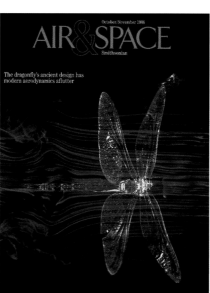

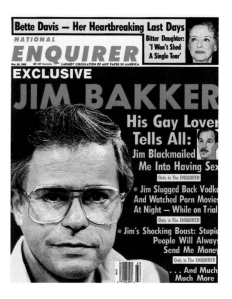

80年代－レーガン時代の広告

スティーヴン・ヘラー

股間の膨らみ：新しい領域

1980年、アメリカはロナルド・レーガンを合衆国大統領として選出した。ジェネラル・エレクトリック・シアター（TV番組）の前司会者、そしてカリフォルニア州元知事は、彼の新しい人生－アメリカの支配－のキャンペーンを打つ大きな権限を委託された。

全世界化の兆候が見えており、新しい社会体制が広まり、そしてレーガンは台頭したのである。

レーガンの80年代は実際騒がしいものだった。ソビエト連邦の鉄のカーテンは最後の"カーテンコール"となり、ソビエト圏の国の人々は圧制からの自由を獲得することとなった。その一方で、Calvin Klein が"男性用下着"の最初の広告を披露し、アメリカの人々は公共の場で股間の膨らみを自由に見る権利を得た。不機嫌な共産主義の超大国が冷戦の終了と共にアメリカに屈服し、そして審美的なスーパーモデル達（キャシー・アイルランド、クリスティー・ブリンクリー、シンディー・クロフォード）がアメリカのマスメディア、特に広告を征服していった。

80年代は共産主義の敗北とレーガン時代の完成、そしてわずかながらの経済の下降、スターウォーズばりのミサイル防御、イラン・コントラゲート事件を見ることとなった。そしてマディソン・アベニューの巨人達の偉業、Joe Camel の「Smooth Character」、Coors の「Silver Bullet」、そして Bud Light のパーティードッグ「Spuds MacKenzie」の登場である。エイズが致命的な世界的伝染病として現れ、この10年期は様々な危機に攻囲されてはいたが、広告産業はその特性に忠実に、メッセージを伝えるためにはどんな不愉快な反発をも無視するのである。

資本主義の壁紙

「広告とは総括してファンタスティックな欺瞞である。誰からも、とりわけ広告を作った本人である広告マンからもシリアスに受け取られないアメリカ人を表わしているのだ」と社会学者デイヴィッド・リースマンは彼の衝撃的な論文「孤独な群集：アメリカ人のキャラクターの変化（エール大学出版、1950）」の中で書いている。彼の著述は必ずしも完全に正確とは言いがたいが、結局、全国的に広告されたブランドを購入することで幸福の追求を進めることができるという考え方を常に甘受することによって、消費者達は欺瞞に共謀しているのである。広告が成功するためには生産者と消費者との双方にとって得る物があるという共生関係が必須である。結果、社会的・文化的歴史の材料として考える時、この本に集められた広告は社会評論家アーネスト・ヴァン・デン・ハーグによればすなわち「好みを単一化し、反個別化し、かように大量生産を可能にする」ことを目的とした相互利益のペテンの証拠として懐疑的に見られなければならない。実際、アメリカの大量生産製品の消費を妨げるものは何であれマーケティングのプロパガンダで覆い隠され、そして広告はそのための資本主義の壁紙となった。

印刷は60年代までは主たる創造媒体であった；70年代にはテレビCMがそのお株を奪った。そして80年代までには、印刷物は広告産業のスクラップと化し、数少ない忘れがたい印刷広告のキャンペーンが現れた。そのわずかな広告キャンペーンは時にはテレビCMと共に、しかしまた印刷媒体のみでやがて一般文化へと移行した点で注目すべきものである。

この本に収められた見本には、ミルトン・グレイザーにより描かれた音を視覚に変換するという洗練された隠喩、優雅な人目を惹く Sony の「Full Color Sound」（p.313）、オリヴィエロ・トスカーニ撮影の遊び心溢れる肖像写真からソフトな社会批評へと進化を遂げたロングランシリーズである Benet-

tonの「United Colors of Benetton」(p.466)、都会のトレンドを促進することによって単なるスニーカーを権威あるファッショナブルな "運動靴" へと変換したNikeの「Just Do It.」(p.480)、新しい日用品・短期使用目的の腕時計の粋を強調したポーラ・シェアー制作のSwatchのレトロな広告(p.202)、そして映画コメディアンの先駆者とコンピュータメーカーの先駆者との結合(ノスタルジアはまたパソコンユーザーを安心させコンピュータ時代へと優しく誘う効果的な手段でもある)によるIBMのチャーリー・チャップリンの創造的起用(p.171)、コンピュータと言えば、80年代はまた、驚くべき新テクノロジーの成功へと至る道として提供されたその明確な広告と共にApple Macintosh(そしてそれほど成功とは言えなかったLisa)の創始を目撃することとなった。

おそらくこの10年期に最も反響のあった広告はMaxellの「No Other Audio Tape Delivers Higher Fidelity.」(p.313)であろう。革張りの最新流行のル・コルビュジェの椅子の肘掛を握り、小型のシングルスピーカーから風のトンネルのように直接に顔へとMaxellのオーディオカセットの音を響かせている光沢のある白黒写真−それはコンセプト

と美とメッセージとの稀なる融合であった。この基本的な手法は製品の明確なイメージを上手にプロモートする方法としてこの10年期にTVでも印刷上でも多々行われていった。それでもなお、これらの最上無比の広告は山と埋もれた広告の中で忘れられない記念碑となっている。

宿命づけられた矛盾

上記に挙げたキャンペーンは集団的神経あるいは意識下に植え付けられた警報に触れたことで反響があったものである。逆に言えば、この本の大多数の広告が実質的にはインパクトを長期的に少なくしてしまっている様式的な決り文句に固執していると言えよう。たとえひとつの構成要素(スローガンやイメージ)が瞬間的に輝き認められたとしても、もし全ての要素が調和して構成されていなければ、その広告は取るに足りないものと宣告されるのである。Gilletteの「Atra razor」(p.223)、「Close-Up」の歯磨き粉(p.229)、「Dry Idea」(p.226)、そして「Marriott Resorts」(p.580)のドラマティックな光線、静物写真、明示された見出しを採ってみても、彼等はそれぞれの製品を発表し、しかし当初の意図を越えて独自性を伝達する記憶術に終わってい

る−そしてそれらは充分うまくデザインされた広告なのでる。明かに、良いデザインは吸引力としては成功しない。いくつかの広告は読者を繋ぎ止めようとするあまりやりすぎてしまっている−Life Saversの「Hole Lotta Fresh!」(p.540)の驚くべき巨大なライフセイバーの写真と、低能なスローガンのように。

80年代に制作された多数の印刷広告は売り込み口上を伝達しようとしすぎて失敗している。たとえその大多数がフルページの裁ち込み写真であっても、そのたくさんの言葉とごちゃごちゃと入り組んだ画像は、広告業者が、主な予算はテレビ用に使われてしまい印刷広告は創造的に制作できないと認めていたことを示唆しているようだ。

「Jazzercise」(p.239)は、その美的知性と概念的ニュアンスの欠如からやりすぎの方法論の典型である。事実、「Speedo Suits Men.」(p.456)のように、ニュアンスこそが一流と並とを明確に分けるものである。「Calvin Klein Jeans」(p.458)よりも刺激的でなくはないと論証できたとしても、ぎこちないデザインであり(見出し印刷は素裸のモデルがアーガイルの靴下を履いているかの様に愚鈍である)、写真は創造性に欠けている。

美の他にも、広告はストーリーを語り、そしてそ

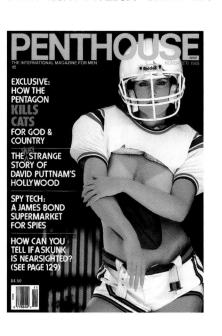

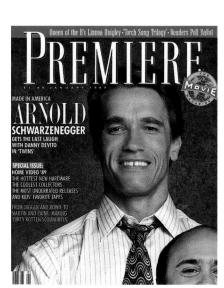

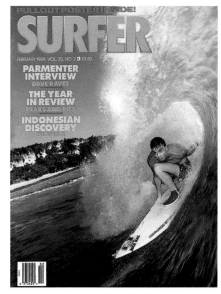

の物語が引き込まれるものであれば消費者達はそのブランドを自分達の物としがちである。が、しかし広告屋達の話には不朽の神話も当てにならない話もあり、きちんとした特許薬の他にたくさんのインチキ薬や何でもかんでもが顧客を餌にかける恐れがある。Fudgsicleの「All Fudge. No Pudge.」（p.538）を採ってみても、甘い物を食べてもなお痩せようとするアメリカ人の競合する脅迫観念を物語っている。下品な一言で、この不体裁な広告は本質的に退屈な製品の利点をほめつつも身体的な美の理想を述べている。罪悪感の無い（そして体重増加も無い）快楽の保証に誰が魅力を感じずにいられるだろうか？

不健康な神話

　現実対空想の（そして真実対嘘の）決り文句は、しかしながら本当にまやかし物であり、なぜならば広告は偽って「いない」という振りはしていないからである。公然とあるいは密やかに、広告は逃げ口上の上に成り立っているということは万人が受け入れている。しかしながら、いくつかのケースでは、広告の作り話は体も心もかなり傷つけ得る。現代の広告の作り話の中で最も不正直な（そして不健康な）物

は、特に80年代より前の時代においては、タバコをともかくも生活を高めるものとしてプロモートした物だろう。30年代から50年代にかけて、ある一部のタバコはストレスを軽減させそれ故に精神的健康に良いと広告で主張した。70年代の間、以前からの懸案とされていたテレビでのタバコの広告の禁止が実施され、80年代半ばにはタバコ広告への最後の応援（既に公衆衛生局長官による警告ラベルを全ての広告に目立つように掲示するよう要求付けられていた）が取り掛かられた。

　紋切り型の広告が消費者達に世間一般に普及している分別に抵抗し、習慣に屈服し、そして実証された全ての不健全な影響にも関わらずタバコを吸うよう強要した。一つの狡猾なミニマルな広告「If you smoke please try Carlton.」（p.88）は、何も要求してはいないが「既に存在する」スモーカーに対しても危険なふるまいに対する束縛を思い留まらせようともしていない。その他の殆どのタバコ広告業者はそのレパートリーから狡猾さを取り除き、喫煙は最新流行で、かっこ良く、エレガントで更には進んでいるという社会的・文化的に偽りの作り話を永続させ続ける印象を創造した。いくつかの広告はあまりに容赦無く、また遠回りであったため

一体何を言いたいのか認識するまでしばらくかかる程である。

　破滅的な病気と習慣からの脱出の双方により消費者が急速に減っていることをCamelが理解した時、会社は「Smooth Character」（p.92）の漫画キャラの対象をティーンエイジャー（そしてより小さな子供）へと向けた。男根のような形状の、擬人化した、革のジャケットを着たひとこぶラクダが10代の読む雑誌（Rolling Stone誌のような）に登場した……販路を目論んでいることは明白である。

宣伝犬の君臨

　10代におけるアルコール消費問題もまた80年代に発生し、驚くべきことでもないが、印刷広告の最大使用者であるビール・酒会社は飲酒は単に受け入れられる物ではなく当然のことであると描き出そうとした。

　10代を対象にしてではないが、20代の消費者に対する80年代最高のキャンペーン（今も行っているが）は、芸術と商業をハイコンセプトな図法で融合させた1980年立ち上げの「Absolut Vodka」（p.60）である。キース・ヘリング、ジャン・ミシェル・バスキアやアンディ・ウォーホルらアヴァンギャ

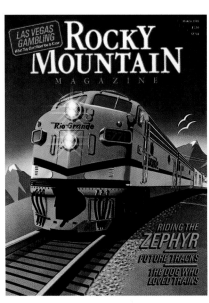

ルドな芸術家達に制作を依頼することによって Absolutのボトルを視覚的に演出し（更に究極的には彼等の信頼性を借用し）、この広告が世俗的な並の子供だましの域から脱することを確実にした。

多くのブランドがAbsolutのコピーをしようとした。が、空想のsuper-babeマスコットをフィーチャーしたRumple Minzeの「White Magic from the Black Forest」(p.69)のような偽物の広告や、Grand Marnierの独創性の無い失敗作、ルネ・マグリットの超現実的風景画（p.72）は決して創造的であるとは請合えない。最新流行の新しい消費者が活気の無い因襲についてくるとは大勢の酒業界は期待していなかった。

タバコやハードアルコールとは異なり、1920年の禁酒法以来ビールに対する広告は禁止されていなかった。そして80年代には巨大なメディアへの影響としてほとばしるのである。Miller High Life (p. 52)やMoosehead (p.46)のような崇拝すべきブランドはその名前やセールスポイントに焦点を置き、しかし新たに現れた"ライト"ビールのような新世代はマーケットシェアを獲得するためにもっと挑発的な餌を必要としていた。最も人気があったのはBud Lightの「Original Party Animal」(p. 55)

であるSpuds MacKenzieという名の気まぐれなブルテリアであった。Anheuser-Buschが10億ドルの資産に出くわすこととなったこの宣伝犬は、あまりに人気があったため（そしてアルコールを飲まない人々にも有名であった）、彼を大統領に立候補させた。Budの広告がこれほど公衆の意見に影響を与える信じがたいパワーを得ており−時々公衆の集合的意見から世界的関心事を消去さえした−もしSpudsが真剣にロナルド・レーガンに対抗したならば彼は勝ったかもしれない。

80年代の終わりまでに、新しいニッチな雑誌がその中で紹介した製品にフォーカスすることにより読者層にアピールしたため（いくつかの雑誌はひたすら顧客サービスに用いられた）、印刷広告はゆっくりと創造メディアとしての強みを取り戻した。さらに、編集的見地から、AbsolutとIBMの広告が楽しめる娯楽として認知されてきていた。業界はテレビから離れて積極的に新旧両方の場を探していた。ブラウン管はもはや広告の輝かしい掘り出し物ではなく、掲示板はPOP広告のディスプレイの場としても躍進していた。新しい印刷技術が業界にレパートリーを与え、ディレクターやデザイナー達は難問に取り組んだ。90年代までに、印刷広告はその創造

的可能性のルネッサンスを真に経験し始め、ホワイトハウス経営の成功による新しいアメリカの繁栄と共に新天地を拓きつつさえある。広告はポップカルチャーのパレードを日が当たる場所へ今一度導くために進展し、その発展はクライアントに有益であると同時に社会にとっても未知数であった。

スティーブン・ヘラーは、ニューヨークタイムズ・ブックレビューのアートディレクターで、ビジュアルアーツスクールMFAデザイン学科の共同主任である。彼はこれまで、デザインやポップカルチャーに関する80冊以上の本を編集、執筆している。代表作に『Merz to Émigré and Beyond: 20世紀におけるアバンギャルドマガジン』等がある。

FOR EVERYONE WHO CUTS THE BIG JOBS DOWN TO SIZE...

KING OF BEERS® • ANHEUSER-BUSCH, INC. • ST. LOUIS

THIS BUD'S FOR YOU.

San Miguel Beer, 1981

Moosehead Beer, 1984

Foster's Lager, 1982

Budweiser Beer, 1984

▶ *Budweiser Beer, 1983*

This is the famous Budweiser beer. We know of no brand produced by any other brewer which costs so much to brew and age. Our exclusive Beechwood Aging produces a taste, a smoothness and a drinkability you will find in no other beer at any price.

Budweiser.
KING OF BEERS®

GENUINE

GENUINE

Budweiser Beer, 1984 ◀ *Budweiser Beer, 1988*

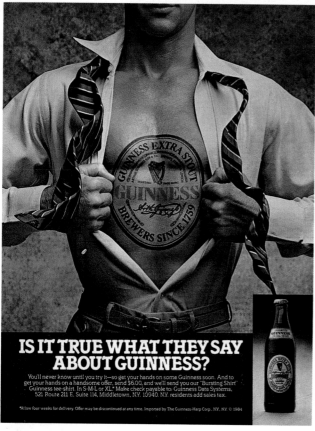

Guiness Extra Stout, 1984

Coors Light Beer, 1984

Miller Beer, 1984

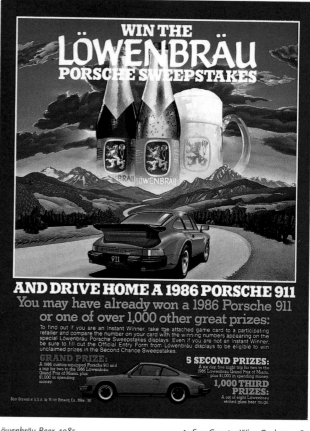

Löwenbräu Beer, 1985

▶ *Sun Country Wine Coolers, 1985*

TROPICAL FEVER

SUN COUNTRY
TROPICAL
COOLER
1 LITER
white wine & tropical fruit juice cooler

987 SUN COUNTRY CELLARS, CANANDAIGUA, N.Y.

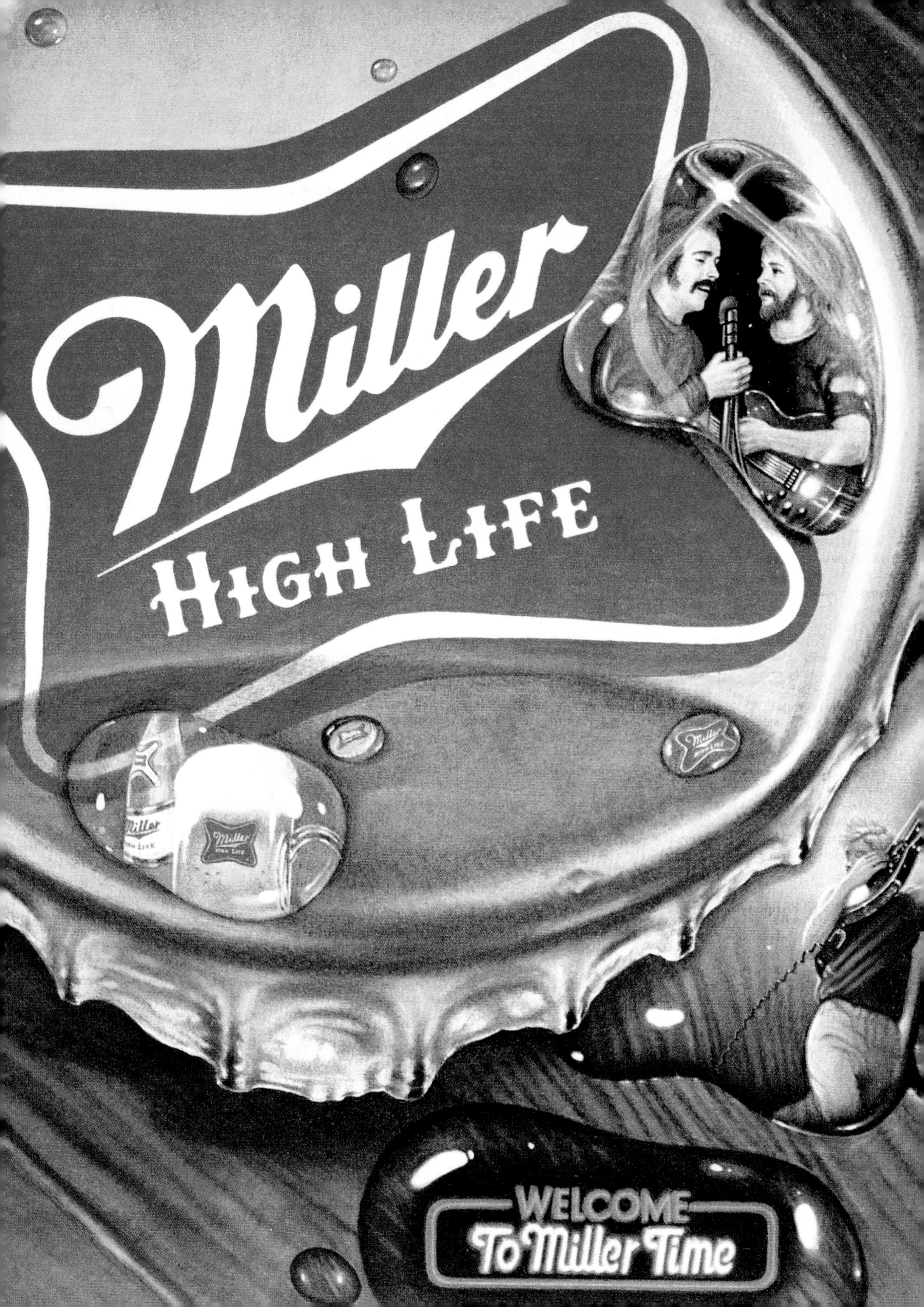
Miller
High Life
WELCOME
To Miller Time

Michelob Beer, 1988

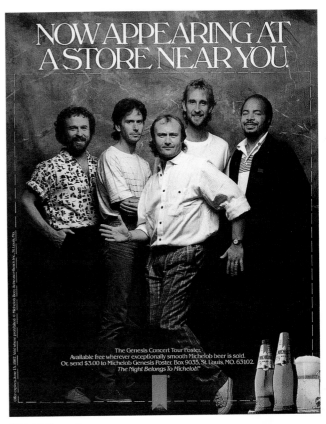

Michelob Beer, 1987

Miller Beer, 1983 ◄ Anheuser-Busch Beers, 1985

Erlanger Beer, 1980

Miller Lite Beer, 1989

Miller Beer, 1989

Coors Beer, 1989

Budweiser Beer, 1989

Bud Light Beer, 1988

UNCORK THE ULTIMATE.

La Différence
c'est Piper.

Champagne
of the
Connoisseur
since
1785.

Reims, France

Perrier-Jouët Champagne, 1981 ◄　*Piper-Heidsieck Champagne, 1988*

CUERVO ESPECIAL ® TEQUILA. 80 PROOF. IMPORTED AND BOTTLED BY © 1986 HEUBLEIN, INC., HARTFORD, CONN

Introducing Joan's Cuervo Solid Gold Collins.

A casual evening with Joan Collins means bringing out the caviar and Cuervo; clearly, a Collins Collins **must** be made with nothing less than Cuervo Gold. Mix 1½-oz. Cuervo with one tbsp. frozen lemonade concentrate. Add ice cubes and fill the glass with Collins mix. Recline casually. And of course never use anything other than Cuervo Gold, for the uniquely smooth taste of the premium tequila.

Rethink your drink

Cuervo®

Mix with Cuervo tequila

"Experts say Paul Masson Cabernet Sauvignon is a mature, complex wine, with nice wood. What they're trying to say is...it tastes good."

Paul Masson will sell no wine before its time.

Paul Masson Vineyards, Saratoga, California © 1980

Cuervo Tequila, 1986 ◄ *Paul Masson Wine, 1980*

ABSOLUT HARING.

Absolut Vodka, 1986

ABSOLUT SCHARF.

Absolut Vodka, 1987

M A L I B U

MORE FUN THAN RUM...

Anything rum can do, Malibu can do better.

If you like rum and cola, wait until you taste Malibu and cola. The same goes for tonic, fruit juice and anything else you mix with rum.

Plus, Malibu is refreshing straight or on the rocks. Some say the hint of tropical coconut is what makes it so smooth.

One thing is certain. Malibu is more fun than rum.

For a free recipe booklet, write to: P.O. Box 3391, Maple Plain, MN 55393.

It's not what it seems to be. TAKARA.

It's not vodka. It's not gin. It's unexpected.
It's clear, crisp and completely new.

Malibu Rum, 1983 ◄ *Takara Sochu, 1989*

Rose's. A 19th-century lime
juice—utterly steeped in
tradition—that has always
found its way into the drinks
and cupboards of those
who, if anything, prefer to
part with tradition.

ROSE'S LIME JUICE.

**THE UNCOMMON
DENOMINATOR.**

Rose's Lime Juice, 1985

SCHNAPPS

What a game. On the ground and in the air your team did the job.

Now taste the flavors you've always loved. Enjoy our new tangy Ginger, spicy

Arrow Schnapps

Cinnamon or minty Spearmint Schnapps over ice, with your favorite mixers, or along with a beer.

The two of you and Arrow Schnapps. What a play.

ARROW. THE FLAVOR OF AMERICA.

ARROW® SCHNAPPS. 60 PROOF, ARROW LIQUORS CO., ALLEN PARK, MICHIGAN.

Arrow Schnapps, 1980

Imported Bombay from England. Slowly, gently distilled from 100% grain neutral spirits. Your serve.

Play to win.

© Carillon Importers, Ltd., N.Y. 86 Proof. 100% grain neutral spirits.

Bombay Gin, 1985

▸ *Tanqueray Gin, 1988*

Imitation is the sincerest form of flattery.

Tanqueray. A singular experience.

HERE'S TO GUT FEELINGS AND THOSE WHO STILL FOLLOW THEM

Ted Turner does lots of things people advise him not to do. And he succeeds at them. He turned Atlanta's WTBS-TV into a "Superstation" using a communications satellite and recently founded Cable News Network, the world's first 24-hour TV news network. He bought the Atlanta Braves and moved them out of last place; won the 1977 America's Cup after being fired in the '74 races; and was named "Yachtsman of the Year" four times.

Ted Turner puts his feelings where his mouth is. He also puts a great scotch there: Cutty Sark. And while he's been called Captain Outrageous by some, one thing's sure: Ted Turner's enjoying himself.

Ted "Captain Outrageous" Turner

the Scotch with a following of leaders

CUTTY SARK

WHITE MAGIC
FROM THE BLACK FOREST.

RUMPLE MINZE. 100 PROOF PEPPERMINT SCHNAPPS. IMPORTED FROM GERMANY. ENJOY IN MODERATION.

FOR AN 18" X 22" POSTER OF THIS AD, PLEASE SEND $3 TO RUMPLE MINZE, DEPT A, PO BOX 2456, NEW BRITAIN CT 06050
Imported by The Paddington Corp., Fort Lee, NJ, USA

Cutty Sark Scotch, 1982 ◄ *Rumple Minze Schnapps, 1988*

Smooth as Velvet

IMPORTED BLACK VELVET. BLENDED CANADIAN WHISKY EIGHTY PROOF

"After you feel Velvet, you won't want to touch another Canadian."

Premium and Imported.

Black Velvet Whisky, 1981 ◄ *Black Velvet Whisky, 1981*

Having a Grand Time...

Grand Marnier Liqueur, 1985

Grand Marnier Liqueur, 1981

Grand Marnier Liqueur, 1986 ◄ *Drambuie Liqueur, 1985*

Drambuie Liqueur, 1989

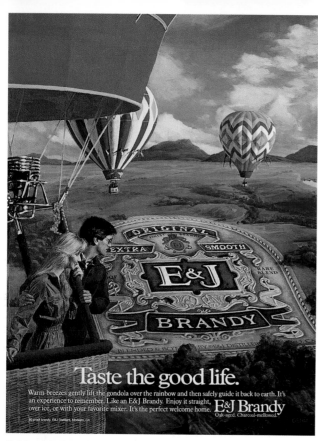

E&J Brandy, 1983

Chivas Regal Whiskey, 1983

Hennessy Cognac, 1984

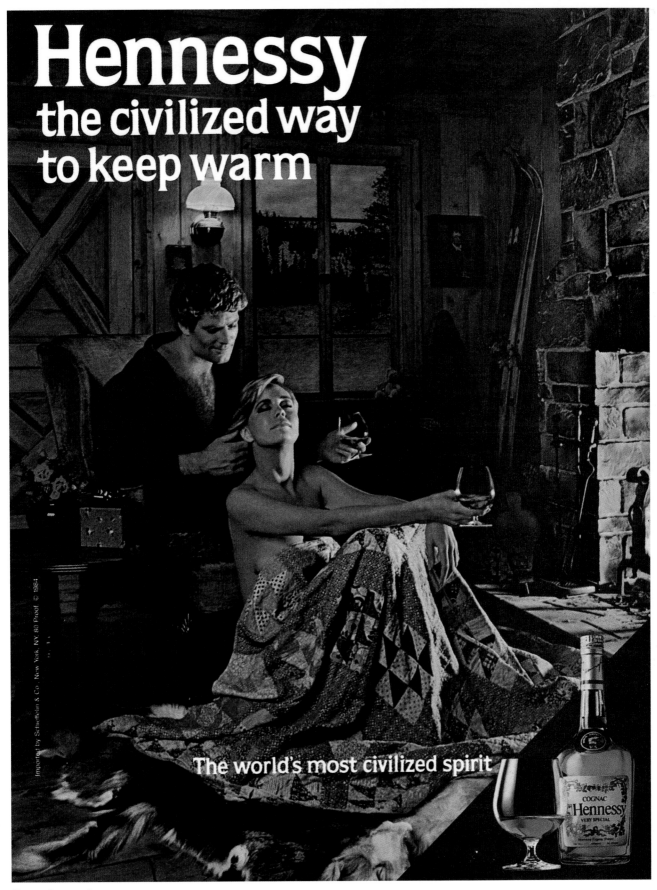

Hennessy Cognac, 1985

C.B. in orange.

WITH A LITTLE CB BRANDY AND ORANGE JUICE, JOHNNY B. VERY GOOD INDEED.

CIRCLE 7 ON READER SERVICE CARD

Christian Brothers Brandy, 1987

▶ *Monte Téca Liqueur, 1989*

**No longer the only thing from Mexico
that's fun to open at parties.**

Show your party animal instincts.
Open a bottle of Monte Téca, and surprise the crowd.
This unique tequila based liqueur adds just the right punch to
party punch.
Mix it with orange juice, cranberry juice—and that cute guy or
gal standing by the guacamole dip in the corner.
Buy a few bottles! Buy a case! After all, our case es su casa—
or something like that.

© 1989 Imported by Chatham Imports, Inc., N.Y., N.Y.   Liqueur 30% Alc. by Vol. (60 proof)
Made & Bottled in Mexico

MONTE TÉCA LIQUEUR
AN ORDER FROM THE BORDER

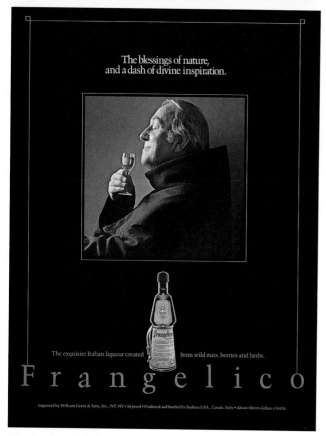

Frangelico Liqueur, 1983

DeKuyper Schnapps, 1986

Gordon's Gin, 1983

Baileys Irish Cream Liqueur, 1983

Courvoisier Cognac, 1981

Rémy Martin Cognac, 1981

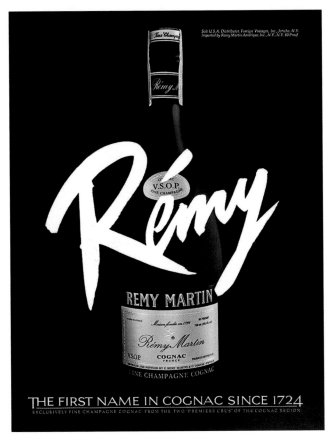

Rémy Martin Cognac, 1981

Kahlúa Liqueur, 1982

The pleasure is back.
BARCLAY

BARCLAY BARCLAY

99% tar free.™

1 MG TAR   1 MG TAR·MENTHOL

Regular, 1 mg. "tar", 0.2 mg. nicotine av. per cigarette, FTC Report Dec. '81;
Menthol, 1 mg. "tar", 0.2 mg. nicotine av. per cigarette by FTC method.

Warning: The Surgeon General Has Determined
That Cigarette Smoking Is Dangerous to Your Health.

© 1982 B&W T Co.

Barclay Cigarettes, 1982

▶ *Vantage Cigarettes, 1980*

The Vantage Point
Where great taste and low tar meet

VANTAGE

VANTAGE 100's

VANTAGE Menthol

FILTER: 9 mg. "tar", 0.8 mg. nicotine
av. per cigarette by FTC method;
MENTHOL: 11 mg. "tar", 0.8 mg. nicotine,
FILTER 100's: 12 mg. "tar", 0.9 mg. nicotine,
av. per cigarette, FTC Report DEC. '79.

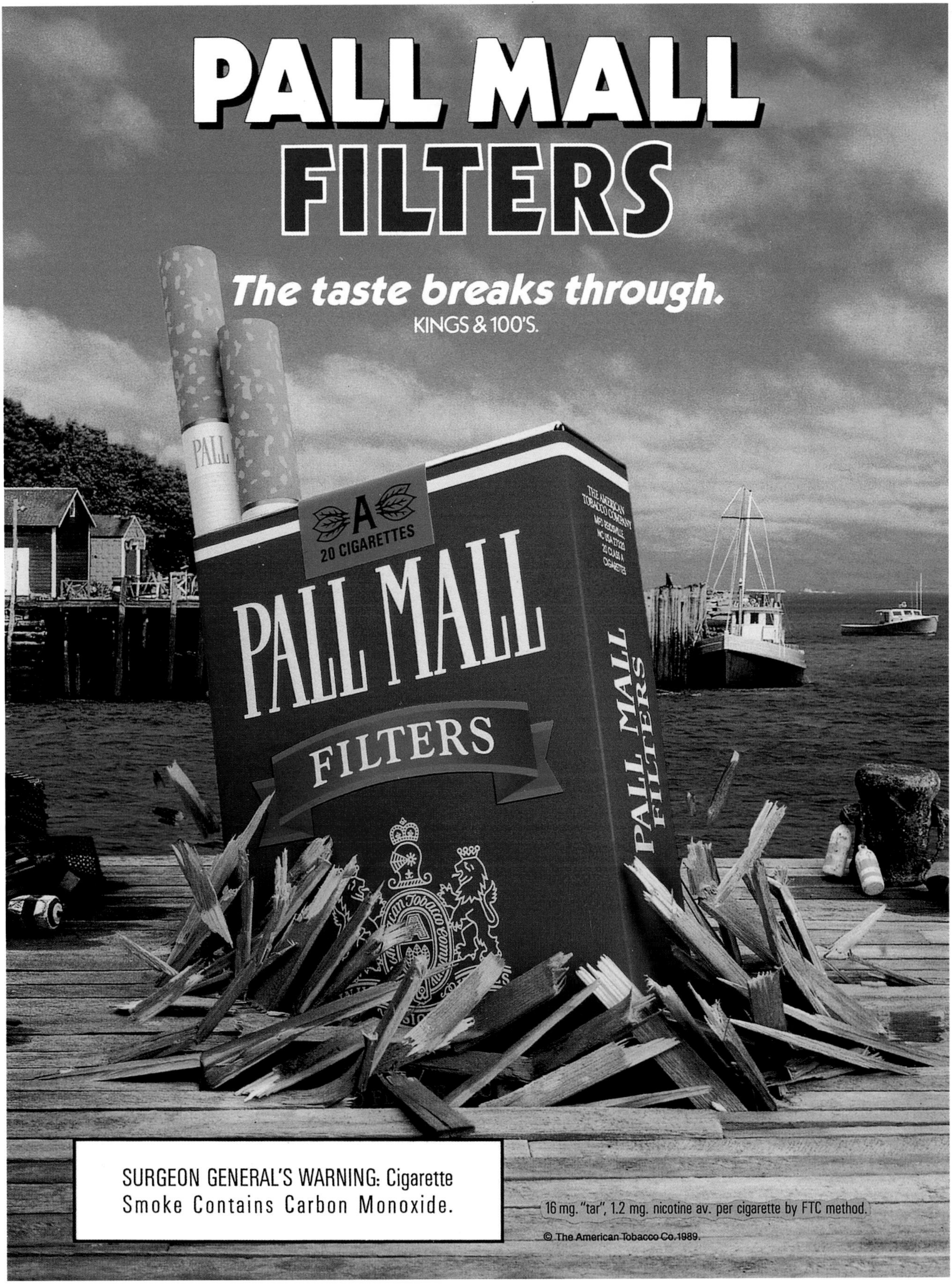

PALL MALL
FILTERS

The taste breaks through.
KINGS & 100'S.

A
20 CIGARETTES

PALL MALL
FILTERS

THE AMERICAN
TOBACCO COMPANY
MFD PRODUCT,
MO USA 27120
20 CLASS A
CIGARETTES

PALL MALL
FILTERS

SURGEON GENERAL'S WARNING: Cigarette
Smoke Contains Carbon Monoxide.

16 mg. "tar", 1.2 mg. nicotine av. per cigarette by FTC method.

© The American Tobacco Co. 1989.

Winston Cigarettes, 1989 ◄ *Pall Mall Cigarettes, 1989*

Marlboro Cigarettes, 1983

Marlboro

© 1989

Marl

Warning: The Surgeon General Has Determined That Cigarette Smoking Is Dangerous to Your Health.

17 mg "tar," 1.1 mg nicotine av. per cigarette, FTC Report Mar.'83

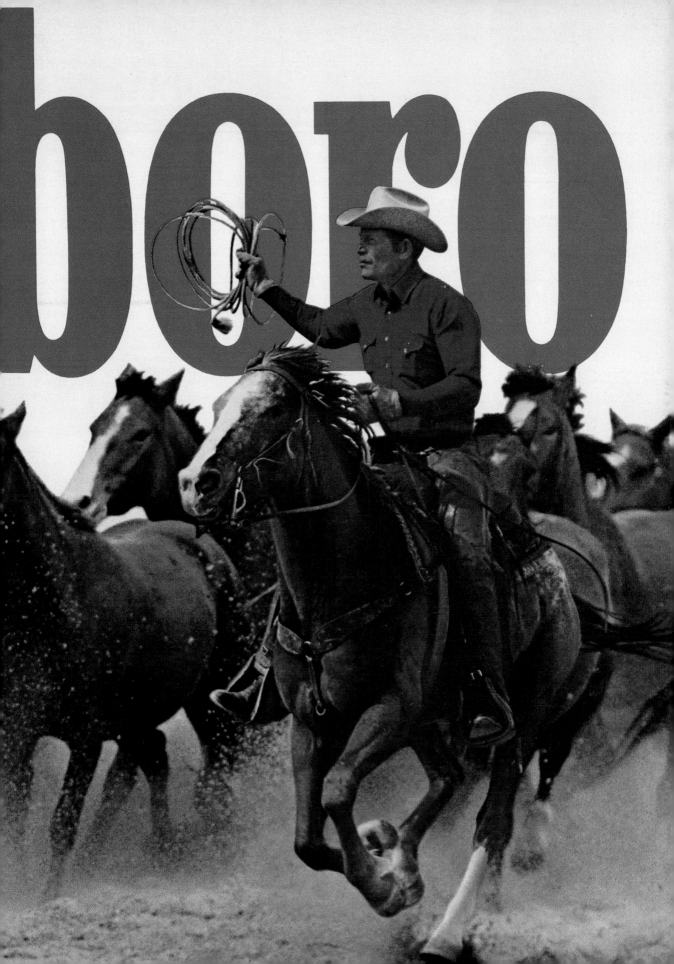

If you smoke
please try Carlton.

Carlton Cigarettes, 1984

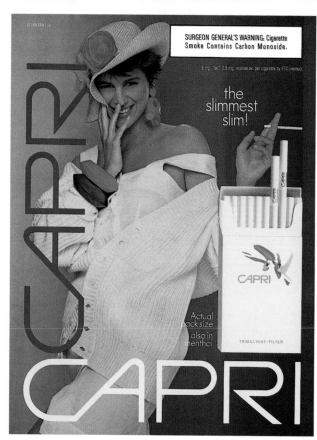

Capri Cigarettes, 1988

Virginia Slims Cigarettes, 1989

Kool Cigarettes, 1988

Merit Cigarettes, 1984

Benson & Hedges Cigarettes, 1988

THE REFRESHEST

© 1988 R.J. REYNOLDS TOBACCO CO.

17 mg. "tar", 1.3 mg. nicotine, av. per cigarette by FTC method.

CAMEL LIGHTS
It's a whole new world.

Today's
Camel Lights,
unexpectedly
mild.

LOW TAR
CAMEL TASTE

Warning: The Surgeon General Has Determined That Cigarette Smoking Is Dangerous to Your Health.

9 mg. "tar", 0.8 mg. nicotine av. per cigarette by FTC method.   © 1985 R.J. REYNOLDS TOBACCO CO.

Salem Cigarettes, 1988 ◄ *Camel Lights Cigarettes, 1985*

Smooth character.

World Championship

10 mg. "tar", 0.6 mg. nicotine av. per cigarette by FTC method.

SURGEON GENERAL'S WARNING: Smoking Causes Lung Cancer, Heart Disease, Emphysema, And May Complicate Pregnancy.

CAMEL LIGHTS

LOW TAR CAMEL TASTE

Camel Cigarettes, 1989

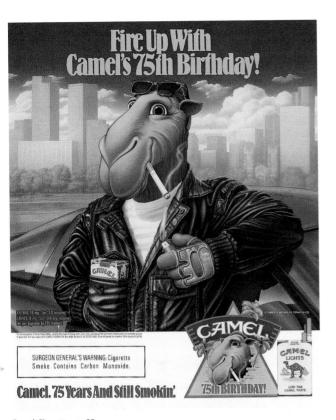

Camel Cigarettes, 1988

Camel Cigarettes, 1989

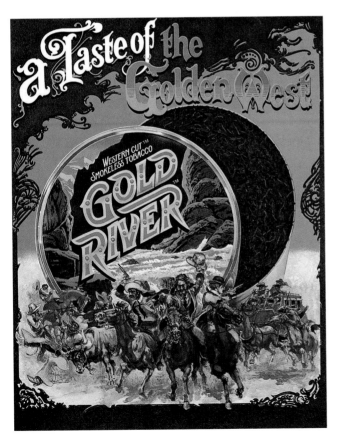

Gold River Tobacco, 1982

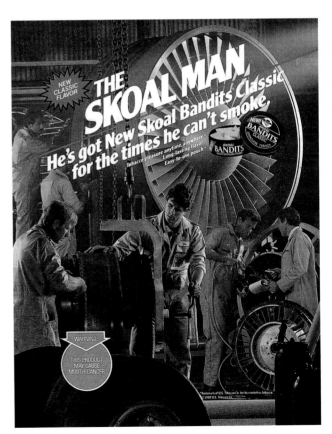

Skoal Bandits Chewing Tobacco, 1989

And the winner is...

And Nothing Else, Mickey?

Somewhere in the back room of the advertising agency that created this tasteful tribute to the women's movement, a couple of cases of Mickey's Big Mouth® must have been consumed. Slaps on the back and high fives would have greeted the completion of this frat-boy testament to bad taste. Anticipating the return of the "tits and ass" men's magazines that would appear a full decade later, the good ol' boy ethic was slowly creeping back into the eighties' zeitgeist ... much to the dismay of *Ms.* magazine subscribers.

Sonst ist dir nichts aufgefallen, Mickey?

Im Hinterzimmer der Werbeagentur, in dem dieses geschmackvolle Tribut an die Frauenbewegung kreiert wurde, müssen ein paar Kästen Mickeys Big Mouth® geleert worden sein. Der Schuljungenstreich wurde sicherlich mit Gejohle und Schulterklopfen gefeiert – hoch lebe der schlechte Geschmack! Der gute alte Machismo nahm langsam, aber sicher den Zeitgeist der Achtziger für sich ein und die Rückkehr der „Tittenmagazine" in den Neunzigern vorweg – sehr zum Missfallen der Abonnentinnen der Zeitschrift *Ms.*

Et rien d'autre, Mickey ?

Quelque part dans les bureaux de cette agence de publicité, on a sûrement vidé deux ou trois caisses de Mickey's Big Mouth® avant de rendre cet hommage plein de délicatesse à la cause féminine. Le couronnement de ce monument au mauvais goût a dû être fêté dans la grande tradition potache, à grands coups de claques dans le dos et de claquements de mains. Anticipant le retour des magazines pour hommes à la gloire des « nichons et des fesses » qui referont leur apparition une bonne dizaine d'années plus tard, les années 80 virent les «traditionnelles» valeurs masculines refaire peu à peu surface... à la grande consternation des abonnées de *Ms.*

¿Lo dices en serio, Mickey?

En algún lugar recóndito de la agencia de publicidad que creó este delicado tributo al movimiento femenino se debieron de consumir un par de cajas de Big Mouth®, de la marca Mickey. Seguramente la conclusión de este homenaje de machito al mal gusto se celebró con palmaditas en la espalda y apretones de manos. Anticipándose al retorno de las revistas masculinas de «tetas y culos» que reaparecerían una década después, la ética de los clubes masculinos trepaba sigilosamente por la columna vertebral de los años ochenta, para consternación de las suscriptoras a la revista *Ms...*

もっと他には無いの、ミッキー？

女性の動きに対するこの上品な賛辞を創造した広告代理店のどこか奥の方で、数ケースの Mickey's Big Mouth が消費されたに違いない。この悪趣味への男子学生の部活的な誓約の完成は、背中への平手打ちやハイファイブによって迎えられた事だろう。10年後に現れる「おっぱいとお尻」男性誌の来襲を予測しつつも、古き良き時代的な倫理観は80年代の時代精神へとゆっくりと戻っていた … 女性の雑誌定期購読者の狼狽は言うまでもない。

The first thing
I noticed
was her
Big Mouth.

MICKEYS FINE MALT LIQUOR

For a 14" x 25" poster of this ad, send $1.00
in check or money order (no cash), payable to:
Mickey's Poster I /P.O. Box 5188/New Milford,
CT. 06774
© 1988 G. Heileman Brewing Company, Inc., LaCrosse, WI

Mickey's Big Mouth Malt Liquor, 1988

America's most popular sports car.

Sleek. Surefooted. Aerodynamic. That's Mustang. A thoroughbred with the high gas mileage you might not expect from a high-spirited car.

23 EPA EST MPG* **34** EPA EST HWY* Choose from a wide range of standard features like rack and pinion steering and modified MacPherson front suspension to an impressive list of options—Michelin TRX radial tires, forged aluminum wheels...even a T-Roof to the sky.

Ford Mustang. Experience why it's America's most popular sports car.

*Estimates for comparison. Your mileage may differ depending on speed, distance and weather. Highway mileage and Calif. estimates lower.

MMMMUSTANG

FORD MUSTANG

FORD DIVISION. Ford

Excalibur West, 1981 ◄ Ford Mustang, 1981

► Renault Le Car, 1980

Le gas goes slowly. The car doesn't.

Renault Le Car gets you from point A to point B economically. Without taking all day to do it.

It has the economy to give you ③ estimated mpg/40 ghway estimate.* But it also has the performance to let u pass more than just gas stations.

Of course, Le Car gets you around curves as nimbly as own straightaways. With front wheel drive, road-hugging ichelin radials, and rack and pinion steering *Motor end* describes as "oh, so light and easy."

For potholes that can't be maneuvered around, four-heel independent suspension and a long wheelbase give u what *Motor Trend* calls bump-smoothing ride like no her car in its class."

And when you leave the highway and head for the city, *Motor Trend* says, "the combined capabilities of the steering, brakes, and suspension make inner-city motoring with Le Car an effortless experience."

Visit one of the more than 1100 Renault and American Motors dealers from coast to coast. For a car that makes your gas go slowly. Without doing the same to you.

40 HWY. EST. **30** EST. MPG*

*Remember: Compare these 1980 EPA estimates to estimated mpg for other cars. Your mileage may vary, depending on speed, trip length, and weather. Your actual highway mileage will probably be lower. California excluded. 1981 data not available at time of publication.

Renault Le Car
More than just economy
at American Motors

Ford Fiesta, 1980

Mazda RX-7, 1980

Volkswagen Vanagon, 1980

"WE CHALLENGE ANY SKI TEAM IN THE WORLD TO AN UPHILL."

UNITED STATES SKI TEAM

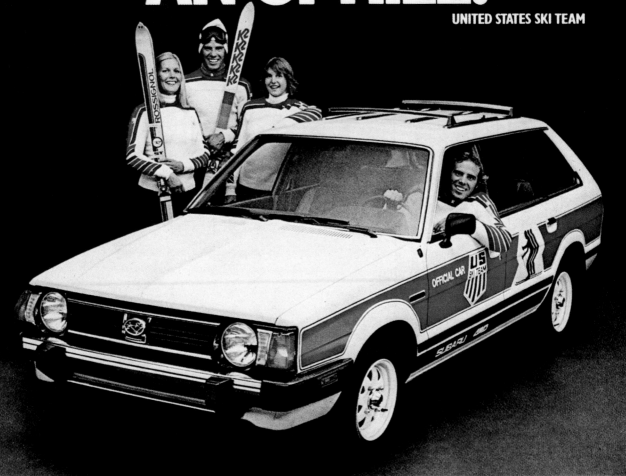

The inexpensive Subaru 4 wheel drive wagon shifts from front wheel to four wheel drive at the flick of a lever. Which makes driving up a snowy hill almost as much fun as skiing down one.

SUBARU.
OFFICIAL CAR OF THE UNITED STATES SKI TEAM.

Subaru, 1980

DATSUN OFFERS BLACK GOLD
10TH ANNIVERSARY 280-ZX

Here is precious metal many will desire, but few will possess. It's the limited-edition Datsun 280-ZX – created to celebrate the first decade of the legendary Datsun Z-car.

Come. Stroke its rich leathers on the thick, cushioned bucket seats. Ignite its restless soul with a fuel-injected six-cylinder power source. Control its seething passion with all around disc brakes, independent four-wheel suspension and road-feeling power steering.

Whisk over a twist of scenic route with the T-bar roof open to the sky.

So rare each is numbered on an engraved plaque. So rich all are lavished with optimum luxury – from pre-flight computer read-out to 40-watt power-boosted, four-speaker stereo.

It's Black. It's Gold. And it is <u>awesome</u>. Appraise one now at your Datsun dealer.

Toyota Celica Supra, 1980

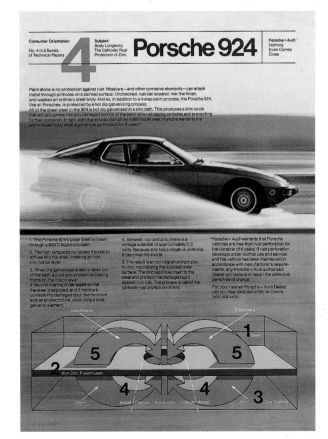

Porsche 924, 1980

Datsun 280-ZX, 1980 ◄   Honda Prelude, 1980

Ford Fairmont, 1980

Rover 3500, 1980

Oldsmobile Toronado, 1981

Cadillac Seville, 1981

DISAPPOINTING NEWS FOR AMERICA'S 520,000 MILLIONAIRES. ONLY 1,500 BERTONE COUPES WILL BE OFFERED THIS YEAR.

In an age when anyone with money can purchase a Mercedes, BMW or Cadillac Seville, it takes a good deal more to own a Bertone Coupe.

It takes luck.

The Bertone Coupe is a limited production luxury class touring car that combines Volvo engineering with the classic Italian craftsmanship of one of Europe's most distinguished coach builders: Bertone of Turin.

To fully appreciate the results of this collaboration—the handcrafted details, the supple leather upholstery, the rich wood veneers, the superb engineering—you have to see and drive this car for yourself.

Due to the extremely limited supply of these extraordinary automobiles, we urge you to use extreme haste in visiting a Volvo dealer.

If you should have money enough and luck enough to purchase a Bertone Coupe, you'll not only have the satisfaction of owning a car that shows you've arrived.

You won't see yourself coming and going.

VOLVO

Volvo Bertone Coupe, 1980

A *Lotus* is a rare sight.

Look at the *Lotus Esprit.*
The exotic car that holds the road like nothing else.

The roadholding secrets of the Esprit reach from Formula One to US 1.
The powerful four-cylinder 907 aluminum engine is placed amidships.
The gasoline supply is balanced ingeniously by connecting port and starboard tanks.
The low aerodynamic drag is enhanced by a wraparound spoiler.
The wide-track alloy wheels are widened further by hub-cap offsets.
The remarkable glass-fibre body is made even stronger by a steel-backbone chassis.
The gear box puts a fifth dimension at your fingertips.
And to dazzle the eye, the cockpit is finished by hand.
British inventor Colin Chapman and Italian designer Georgetto Giugiaro
would have it no other way.
Just so you can escape in an exotic car today that no one can touch tomorrow.

For the name of the Lotus Authorized Dealership nearest you,
call 800-325-6000 and use ID number 1000.
The two-passenger mid-engine Esprit S2. The Éclat 2 + 2. The four-passenger Elite 503.
One look will tell you: there is nothing else in sight.

Lotus
The rarest exotic cars.

Evolution moves selectively toward perfection

*Introducing
the Mondial 8 ... an evolutionary sportscoupe –
perfect for your two plus two lifestyle.*

For the name of the authorized Ferrari dealer nearest you, call toll-free:
(800)447-4700, in Illinois, (800)322-4400, in Alaska and Hawaii, (800)447-0890.

Ferrari

Lotus Esprit, 1980 ◄ *Ferrari Mondial 8, 1981*

GM

Obviously, a lot of people like our Skylark Limited because of its luxury.

24 EPA EST. MPG 36 EST. HWY.

Skylark gets a lot of votes for its stand on economy, thanks to its 2.5 liter four (with available automatic transmission, without air conditioning).*

In all kinds of climates, on all kinds of roads, drivers are very impressed with Skylark's front-wheel-drive traction.

Others like the fact that Skylark offers roomy accommodations for five—plus an accommodating trunk.

Lots of folks are taken with Skylark's good looks. And we modestly submit, who can blame them?

We couldn't get all the reasons people like Skylark on this page. But we sure got them into the car.

BUICK

*Use "estimated mpg" for comparison. Your mileage may differ depending on speed, distance, weather. Actual highway mileage lower. Estimates lower in California. Buicks are equipped with GM-built engines supplied by various divisions. See your dealer for details.

Buick Skylark, 1981

Dodge Charger 2.2
A lot of go without the guzzle.
0 to 50 in 6.6 seconds. 41 26 mpg.*
EST. HWY   EPA EST. MPG

The Charger legend lives again in the new Charger 2.2. A sports car that we call a Driving Machine.

A Driving Machine that's a performance machine.

We took Chrysler's gutsy 2.2 liter OHC powerplant that cranks out 111 foot pounds of torque at 2800 RPM. Hooked it on a 3.13:1 final drive ratio and put it together with a slippery aerodynamic exterior that weighs-in under 2400 pounds. On the street, according to NHRA acceleration tests, that translates into 0 to 50 in only 6.6 seconds!

We've got a lot more than just muscle up our sleeve.

41 EST. HWY. 26 EPA EST. MPG.*

Only a handful of other machines can even compete with Charger 2.2. Those that do, for the most part, are conventional rear-wheel-drive. Years behind the technology that makes Charger 2.2 a driving machine.

A USAC certified sports car.

There's a good reason why USAC certified Charger 2.2 as a sports car. It gives you the handling you can expect from front-wheel-drive and rack-and-pinion steering. It sits firmly on the road with its Sports Suspension System and performance raised white letter tires. Notice that Charger 2.2 comes with a Rallye Instrument cluster that includes a tachometer and quartz clock. Notice the reclining bucket seats with lateral support, remote control dual sport mirrors and performance exhaust system. All standard equipment. And if you're into off-road racing, there's a Direct Connection dealer waiting to help you tool up your Charger 2.2.

With all that torque Charger 2.2 zips past the pump at an incredible

A Driving Machine for less than the cost of a lot of cars.*7,242.*

Dodge Charger 2.2. The new standard by which all thoroughbred driving machines will be judged. Buy or lease one at your Dodge dealer. You'll have a hard time beating her on the road. At $7,242** you'll have an even harder time beating the price. The Charger legend lives again. Unchallenged.

Dodge

America's Driving Machines

MODEL	EPA* EST	HWY* EST	ENGINE	DSPL/ WT†	0-50††
'82 Charger 2.2	26	41	2.2-Liter 135 CID	.060	6.62
'81 Datsun 280ZX 2+2	21	32	2.8-Liter 168 CID	.056	7.30
'81 Mustang Cobra	23	34	2.3-Liter 140 CID	.053	9.04
'81 Porsche 924	20	35	2.0-Liter 121 CID	.046	7.77
'81 Pontiac Trans Am	16	22	4.9-Liter 301 CID	.087	7.32

*Use EPA EST MPG numbers for comparison. Actual mileage may vary depending on speed, trip length, and weather. Actual HWY mileage probably lower. CA mileage lower.
**Sticker price excluding taxes and destination charges. †Calculated by dividing cubic inch displacement by curb weight. ††Based on National Hot Rod Association acceleration tests.

Dodge Charger, 1981

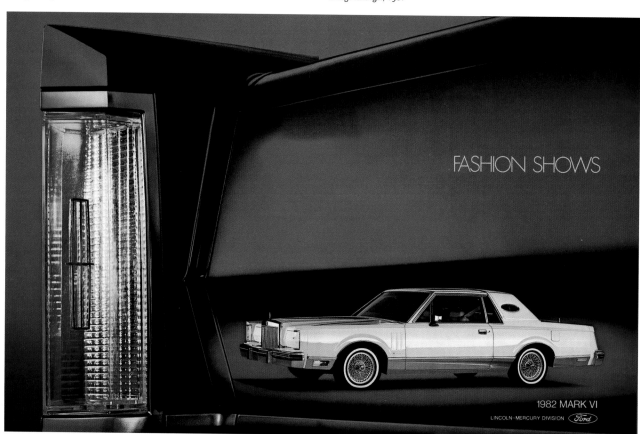

FASHION SHOWS

1982 MARK VI

LINCOLN-MERCURY DIVISION Ford

Ford Mark VI, 1981

American Motors Concord, 1981

Nissan Stanza, 1981

Toyota Corolla Tercel, 1981

Toyota Corolla, 1981

The Renault 18i is available at more than 1300 Renault and American Motors Dealers in Sedan and Sportswagon models with standard four-speed transmission. Five-speed manual and three-speed fully automatic transmissions are optional.

Renault 18i, 1981

► *Buick Regal, 1981*

It flies through the air with the greatest of ease.

The aerodynamic Buick Regal.

When an object is shaped to reduce aerodynamic drag, it often becomes more handsome in the process. We think that fact is happily attested to by the two sleek profiles above, the one in the foreground being our Buick Regal.

With its low-sloping front end and high-sailing rear deck, Regal moves through the air easily, so it moves over the road efficiently. A factor which contributes to these rather gratifying Buick projections of mileage estimates.

30 EST. HWY.	**21** EPA EST. MPG

Buick projections of 1982 EPA estimates. See your dealer for actual EPA estimates.

And that, mind you, is for a Regal Limited Coupe, powered by a responsive 3.8 liter V-6. Fitted out with all our customary interior niceties and refinements.

Which shows you don't have to strip a car of comforts to achieve economy when you can outstrip the wind.

The aerodynamic Buick Regal. It flies through the air with the greatest of ease without even leaving the ground.

Use estimated MPG for comparison. Your mileage may differ depending on speed, distance, weather. Actual highway mileage lower. Estimates lower in California. Some Buicks are

equipped with engines produced by other GM Divisions, subsidiaries, or affiliated companies worldwide. See your Buick dealer for details.

BUICK

Wouldn't you really rather have a Buick?

Only those who dare... truly live

Ferrari

Ferrari, 1981

TAKE YOUR SEAT. THE PERFORMANCE IS ABOUT TO BEGIN.

DATSUN 280-ZX.
Slip into something comfortable: a multi-adjustable bucket seat you fine-tune to the perfect driving position.

A quick systems checkout assures you all is in readiness: computer sensors report on lights and vital fluids; a vocalized system alerts you if doors are open, fuel level low, parking brake on.

Remote-control mirrors? Check. Four-speaker stereo/cassette? Check. Power windows? Check.

Now, unleash the fuel-injected, computer-controlled powerplant. As energy surges effortlessly, a tingle travels down your spine. No wonder Z-cars have won national racing championships 11 of the past 12 years.

The 1982 Datsun 280-ZX and Turbo-ZX. Now both models are available in 2-seater and 2+2.

Come and see the four newest faces of "awesome."

DATSUN WE ARE DRIVEN

Product of **NISSAN**

Datsun 280-ZX, 1982

© 1981 Toyota Motor Sales, U.S.A., Inc.

Presenting the newest addition to the best-selling line of cars in the world. The 1981½ Toyota Corolla Sports Hardtop. A totally new kind of Corolla from the roof down.

Fresh, crisp, contemporary lines. Distinctively subtle, yet the very latest in sporty good looks. The hardtop design gives you a wide-open airy feeling...even with the windows up. The spacious trunk allows you to lock valuables out of sight. And the roomy interior is loaded with the kinds of standard equipment you'd expect to pay extra for on most other cars. Full instrumentation. 5-speed overdrive transmission. A swivel AM/FM/MPX stereo radio. Tinted glass. Steel-belted radials. And more.

But best of all, beneath that beautiful, sporty exterior, the Sports Hardtop is all Corolla. And it acts like one. It's incredibly dependable. Totally economical. And extremely thrifty at the pumps.

With Corolla's 1.8 liter 4-cylinder engine and 5-speed overdrive transmission, the Sports Hardtop is rated at 39 EPA EST. HWY. MPG, 28 EPA EST. MPG. Remember: Compare this estimate to the EPA "Estimated MPG" of other cars with manual transmission. You may get different mileage, depending on how fast you drive, weather conditions and trip length. Actual highway mileage will probably be less than the EPA "Highway Estimate."

The 1981½ Toyota Corolla Sports Hardtop. It's a whole new sport that's hard to top.

OH WHAT A FEELING

TOYOTA

A WHOLE NEW SPORT.
INTRODUCING THE COROLLA SPORTS HARDTOP.

Toyota Corolla, 1981

The evolution of the new Mercedes-Benz Coupe.

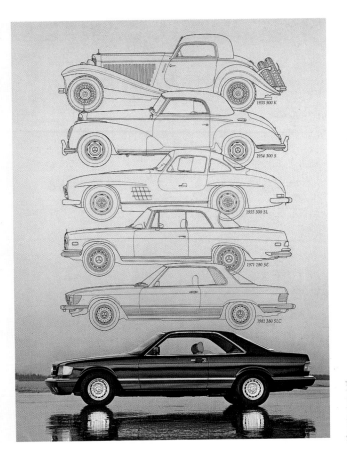

The new 380 SEC is the coupe that Mercedes-Benz has been readying itself to create for 83 years. There is no automobile like it, at $52,000* or any price.

A motorized carriage built by the co-founder of Mercedes-Benz in 1899 was the first automobile ever to be called a coupe.

This Benz "My Lord" founded a coupe lineage that must by now be the most aristocratic and most envied anywhere: evolving after 1927 from thinly disguised racing machines into roadsters and cabriolets as sumptuous as they were powerful; gaining fixed steel roofs; ever more civilized as driving itself became more civilized.

Until today when, whatever its character or type or age—if it is a Mercedes-Benz coupe, it is probably a collector's item.

There is now a new coupe, the 380 SEC. It is Mercedes-Benz at its technological zenith. List all those things a car of this kind should do well and point for point it is meant to score more highly, more often, than any other—even any other Mercedes-Benz coupe.

Its 0.35 drag coefficient makes this one of the most aerodynamically advanced designs in production today.

Inside, four persons are accommodated in four individual seats that feel sculpted in leather. They are served by virtually every electric assist and other amenity in the Mercedes-Benz repertoire.

Mechanical butler

Burled walnut veneer lends this cabin a warm and clubby atmosphere. So pampered is the driver that, as he turns on the ignition, he is served up his seat belt by a mechanical butler. "If you dare to ignore it," reports *Autocar*, "it continues to hold out the belt for half a minute, then—you *feel* the disapproval—it sadly retires again into its hole."

The 380 SEC, meanwhile handles and corners with the best sports cars. Its suspension is so supple, lending the tires such bite, that you can make good time even on atrocious roads.

Yet the car is so soothingly quiet that there is barely any wind noise at highway speeds.

The 380 SEC is engined with the most efficient V-8 in Mercedes-Benz history, a light alloy 3.8 liter whisperer. Your gearshifts are made for you hydraulically, by a highly auto-

mated four-speed automatic gearbox.

There is something notable about almost every aspect of the 380 SEC. This coupe provides a sedan-sized trunk of more than 14 cu. ft. capacity. The outside door handles wear aerodynamically shaped gauntlets. Every car has windshield washers, but the 380 SEC's washer nozzles are *heated*, as a deicing measure.

Quantities limited, significance universal

The 380 SEC will be minted in restricted numbers for a few fortunate customers per year. For the rest of the world it will stand as a landmark of automotive design—probably through this decade and beyond.

*Approximate suggested advertised delivered price at port of entry.

© 1982 Mercedes-Benz N.A., Inc., Montvale, N.J.

Engineered like no other car in the world

Mercedes-Benz 380 SEC, 1982

The new Renault Fuego. Racy. Exciting. A heritage born of Grand Prix. Windsmooth styling that simmers with the performance of a fuel injected 1.6 litre engine. EPA's that give you 24 est. MPG, 36 est. hwy.*

Renault Fuego. Five forward speeds or optional 3-speed automatic. Front disc and rear drum brakes that have power-assisted hydraulics for extra safety.

Renault Fuego. Front wheel drive efficiency with independent front suspension and standard Michelin steel-belted radials. All give Fuego the handling you'd expect from the leader in front-wheel drive. Renault Fuego. Over a hundred

designers produced exterior lines more slippery than even the $39,000 Porsche 928. Inside, body contoured seating, full instrumentation, and a leather-wrapped sport steering wheel for an overall concept of driver comfort and control. There's even an optional sunroof

that reaches all the way to the back seat. Renault Fuego. Covered by American Motors' exclusive Buyer Protection Plan, with the only full warranty that gives you 12-months/12,000 miles coverage of everything except tires. Every part covered, even if it just wears out.

Renault Fuego. For an extra boost of excitement, optional Turbo package available. Fuego Turbo, performance that's responsive yet offers EPA's of 26 est. MPG, 39 est. hwy.*

The new Renault Fuego. Racy and less than $8500.**

*Compare 1982 EPA Estimates with estimated MPG for other cars. Your actual mileage depends on speed, trip length, and weather. Actual highway mileage will probably be lower.

**Manufacturer's suggested retail price. Price does not include tax, license, destination charges, aluminum sport wheels, touring interior, and other optional or regionally required equipment.

Fuego

New. Racy. Fuego.

RENAULT
American Motors

Renault Fuego, 1982

The Dayton Thorobreds are with you...

mile after mile.

With a full stable of famous Thorobred radials... including the steel-belted Blue Ribbon, the all-season Quadra and the wide track Daytona. Great radials for virtually every car and light truck on the road.

From coast to coast, our national dealer network is over 3,000 strong, to provide you full service and support. Check the Yellow Pages for the dealer nearest you and ask him about our written mileage warranties that help protect you and your investment.

Down the road, Dayton's Thorobreds give you the long mileage, handling and traction you need, mile, after mile...

Dayton.
△ TIRES

P.O. Box 1075 AMF
Cleveland, Ohio 44181

Dayton Tires, 1983

GET YOUR HANDS ON A CHEVROLET THE COMPETITION CAN'T TOUCH.

That Chevrolet is Camaro, and it's flat outselling every other 2+2 sport coupe on the road today.*

Camaro. Designed and engineered with some of the newest performance technology you'll find on any road, anywhere. Including Ground Effects technology. A cockpit designed to link driver and machine together.

And now, Camaro is led by a new standard 5-speed, 5-liter** Z28 with the lowest aerodynamic drag coefficient of any production Chevrolet ever tested.

Get your hands on a hot-selling Camaro today. And experience what it's like to take hold of a Chevrolet that was chosen in February as Motor Trend's "Car of the Year."

*Source: Ward's Automotive Reports; Specialty Subcompact Segment. **Some Chevrolets are equipped with engines produced by other GM divisions, subsidiaries, or affiliated companies worldwide. See your dealer for details.

GM Let's get it together. buckle up.   CHEVROLET CAMARO Z28

USA-1 IS TAKING CHARGE   Chevrolet

CAMARO • CELEBRITY • CAVALIER • CHEVETTE • CITATION • MALIBU • MONTE CARLO • CAPRICE • CORVETTE

Chevrolet Camaro, 1982

IT'S HOT, IT'S HERE, IT'S FIERO!

Throw away those old maps. Pontiac just paved a new road to driving excitement.

Fiero is an all-new kind of car. Designed and built to be exhilarating to drive, yet easy to own. Its mid-engine design and balanced weight distribution give Fiero an amazing command of the road. And its innovative high-strength space frame chassis is wrapped with a beautifully aerodynamic Enduraflex™ body that resists minor dents and will never rust.

Fiero's standard equipment makes serious roadwork a distinct pleasure: A fully independent suspension that keeps it glued to the road. 4-wheel disc brakes that pull it down from speed quickly. Rack and pinion steering that delivers precise road feel and directional control. A quick-shifting manual transmission. Bolstered, body-contoured bucket seats. Full instrumentation. And an electronically fuel injected 2.5 liter engine that gives instant throttle response and outstanding mileage.*

The totally new Fiero, America's first and only mid-engine production car.

Only at your Pontiac dealer.

PONTIAC ▼ WE BUILD EXCITEMENT

EXCITEMENT AHEAD

Fiero

GM *Pontiac Fiero Sport Coupe with available automatic transmission offers an EPA EST MPG of 27 and a highway estimate of 40. Use estimated MPG for comparisons. Your mileage may differ depending on speed, distance, weather. Actual highway mileage lower. Some Pontiacs are equipped with engines produced by other GM divisions, subsidiaries or affiliated companies worldwide. See your Pontiac dealer for details.

Mercedes-Benz 300 SD, 1983 ◄   Pontiac Fiero, 1983

THE REMARKABLE 1981 JAGUAR
BRED TO BE THE BEST JAGUAR IN HISTORY.

For more than fifty years, the superb thoroughbred motorcars of Jaguar have made history on the world's racetracks and in the annals of classic automotive design.

This newest Jaguar, the Series III, also makes history, simply by being the best Jaguar sedan ever built.

The Series III is powered by the most advanced version of Jaguar's legendary 4.2 liter double overhead-cam Six. Electronically fuel injected, with a Bosch/Lucas system, this vividly responsive power plant also has a thoroughly dependable electronic ignition and a separate, electronic cold start enrichment system, making this latest Jaguar the most reliable ever.

Like all Jaguars, the Series III moves, handles and responds with a special grace. Four wheel independent suspension gives the car a remarkable feel for the road, regardless of the quality of the road surface. A very precise rack and pinion power steering system assures positive directional response. Power disc brakes on all four wheels stop the Jaguar decisively.

Bred in a tradition of rich but understated luxury, the Jaguar Series III provides both an elegant ambience and the latest in electronic technology. The classic Jaguar luxury is reflected in such things as the dashboard veneered in rare walnut burl, the seat facings covered in supple topgrain leather and impressive silence in motion. The latest technology is apparent in the self adjusting heating and air conditioning, power driver's seat, power sideview mirrors, stereo AM/FM radio with station-seeking tuner and cassette, an antenna that disappears when the engine is turned off, cruise control, electric sunroof, and alloy wheels: all standard.

THE BEST JAGUAR WARRANTY IN HISTORY.
So great is Jaguar's confidence in the Series III that for 1981 models the basic 12-month limited warranty is extended to cover the power train for a full two years or 50,000 miles, whichever comes first. For full details of this remarkable warranty, see your Jaguar dealer. For your nearest dealer call toll-free: (800) 447-4700 or, in Illinois, (800) 322-4400.

JAGUAR
A BLENDING OF ART AND MACHINE

© Jaguar Rover Triumph Inc. Leonia, N.J. 07605.

Jaguar Series III, 1981

IT'S A NEW KIND OF CADILLAC...

...for a new kind of Cadillac owner. Compare Cimarron to the likes of the BMW 320i, Audi 5000 and Saab 900s. Spec for spec, feature for feature. Only Cimarron has front-wheel drive, air conditioning and genuine leather seating areas with lumbar support, all standard. Plus Cadillac's exclusively tuned touring suspension. Take a Cimarron test drive today, at the Cadillac dealership nearest you.

CIMARRON
BEST OF ALL...IT'S BY CADILLAC.

Cadillac Cimarron, 1982

YOUR TIME HAS COME

1982 TRANS AM
The excitement began 15 years ago when those electrifying "Birds" came down like rolling thunder to capture the hearts of enthusiasts everywhere. And a legend was born.

Now comes the road machine that will fire-up a new generation! From saber-like nose to rakish tail, Trans Am is a brilliant orchestration of aerodynamic function. Its .31 drag coefficient is the best of any production car GM has ever tested.

But the new Trans Am is much more than a beautiful piece of automotive sculpture. It's a

driver's car that's totally engineered for serious roadwork.

Trans Am with options shown, $10,076. Trans Am's base price? Only $9,659! This is a manufacturer's suggested retail price including dealer prep. Taxes, license, destination charges and optional equipment additional.

One "hands-on" impression will convince you that Trans Am is a driving sensation!

The legend makers at Pontiac have done it again!

THE DRIVER'S CAR
The makings of a legend:
• 5.0 liter 4-bbl. V-8 with dual free-flow resonator exhausts
• 4-speed manual transmission
• Quick-ratio power steering
• MacPherson front struts
• Front and rear stabilizer bars
• Torque arm rear suspension
• Turbo cast aluminum wheels
• P205/70R14 steel radials
• 14½" Formula steering wheel
• Reclining front bucket seats

Some Pontiacs are equipped with engines produced by other GM divisions, subsidiaries, or affiliated companies worldwide. See your Pontiac dealer for details.

PONTIAC ▼ NOW THE EXCITEMENT REALLY BEGINS

Pontiac Trans Am, 1982

CAMARO
PRICED TO HAVE THE COMPETITION CHASING SHADOWS.

$7,731

Of all the innovations that went into the new Camaro Sport Coupe, the best one of all just might be the price.

At $7,731 with options shown, it makes a lot of those high-priced imported sports cars seem a bit outrageous. Especially when you consider all of Camaro's advanced engineering and technology.

Like a new computer-controlled fuel injection system that's standard on the four-cylinder engine. Ultrasleek aerodynamics. And a beautifully designed cockpit where driver and machine come together as one.

The new Camaro Sport Coupe. Styled so new and priced so low, it'll have the competition chasing shadows.

*Manufacturer's Suggested Retail Price, including full wheel covers, sport mirrors and dealer prep. Tax, license, destination charges and other available equipment are additional. Some Chevrolets are equipped with engines produced by other GM divisions, subsidiaries, or affiliated companies worldwide. See your dealer for details.

Chevrolet

Chevrolet Camaro, 1982

▶ *Saab, 1982*

Thunderbird for '83.
Before we made it beautiful, we made it right.

1983 Thunderbird

From the slope of its hood, to the flip of its tail, Thunderbird is obviously aerodynamic. It uses the air to reduce lift in the front and rear of the car. This improves handling and road stability.

Thunderbird responds to commands as if it were an extension of the driver's body. From its 3.8 liter V-6 engine, to its gas-filled shocks to its variable ratio steering, Thunderbird is your sixth sense on the road.

Thunderbird can be equipped to fit you in the most personal sense.

Contoured seats adjust six ways. Side view mirrors adjust electrically from a command pod placed between the seats. Other choices include an electronically fuel-injected 5.0 liter V-8, automatic overdrive transmission and Tripminder® computer.

Outside, inside and underneath, the new Thunderbird has been designed to give you every tool for road command. In a phrase, it's a pleasure to drive. In a word, it's Thunderbird.

Get it together—
Buckle up.

HAVE YOU DRIVEN A FORD... LATELY?

Ford Thunderbird, 1983

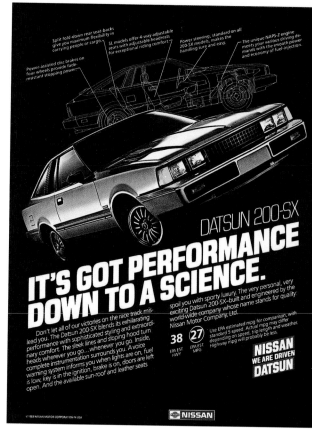

Split fold-down rear seat-backs give you maximum flexibility in carrying people or cargo.

SL models offer 4-way adjustable seats with adjustable headrests for exceptional riding comfort.

Power steering, standard on all 200-SX models, makes the handling sure and easy.

The unique NAPS-Z engine meets your various driving demands with the smooth power and economy of fuel-injection.

Power-assisted disc brakes on four wheels provide fade-resistant stopping power.

DATSUN 200-SX
IT'S GOT PERFORMANCE DOWN TO A SCIENCE.

Don't let all of our victories on the race track mislead you. The Datsun 200-SX blends its exhilarating performance with sophisticated styling and extraordinary comfort. The sleek lines and sloping hood turn heads wherever you go...whenever you go. Inside, complete instrumentation surrounds you. A voice warning system informs you when lights are on, fuel is low, key is in the ignition, brake is on, doors are left open. And the available sun-roof and leather seats spoil you with sporty luxury. The very personal, very exciting Datsun 200-SX–built and engineered by the world-wide company whose name stands for quality: Nissan Motor Company, Ltd.

38 EPA EST HWY **27** EPA EST MPG

Use EPA estimated mpg for comparison, with standard 5-speed. Actual mpg may differ depending on speed, trip length and weather. Highway mpg will probably be less.

NISSAN
WE ARE DRIVEN
DATSUN

Datsun 200-SX, 1983

STOP WISHING

THE TOTALLY NEW FIERO IS HERE!
Your most fervent automotive hope just came true.

Fiero is totally new from the ground up, from the inside out, from front to rear. Even the way it's built, to provide consistent, high-quality fit and finish, is unique.

Fiero is America's first and only mid-engine production car. The balanced weight distribution of this mid-engine design, along with its rigid space frame, fully independent suspension, power four-wheel disc brakes, and rack and pinion steering, give an amazing command of the road.

Fiero is strong. It hugs the road. And its electronically fuel-injected 2.5 liter engine features "swirl-port" technology for a smooth, fast burning combustion process. The result? Snappy acceleration and impressive performance.

Fiero also has a unique Enduraflex™ body that resists minor dents and will never rust.

Fiero Coupe prices start at just $7,999† (the Sport Coupe shown is $8,499).†

Fiero truly is an astounding car. Especially when you walk around it, look at it from different angles, sit in it, and take it for a spin. And there's only one place to do that. At your Pontiac dealer.

PONTIAC ▼ WE BUILD EXCITEMENT

Pontiac Fiero, 1983

Dodge Vista, 1983

ONLY NISSAN MAKES 35 MPG THIS ROOMY.

Go ahead, give the new Nissan Sentra Wagon your precious cargo. This wagon can handle it.

Its cavernous cargo area measures 60 cubic feet with rear seats folded, and 23.5 cubic feet when carrying 5 passengers. That's major space.

Of course, Nissan technology doesn't stop at space. The gas mileage is big too: the biggest of any wagon. 35 estimated MPG, 49 highway.* In fact, the only thing that isn't big is the price.

What's more, this wagon's a dream to drive. With rack-and-pinion steering and fully independent suspension for safe, solid handling. And front-wheel drive for sure-footed traction.

So look into our new Sentra Wagon. And see how Nissan technology takes it far beyond other wagons.

All the way to Major Motion.

*Use EPA estimated MPG for comparison, with standard 5-speed. Actual mileage may differ depending on speed, trip length and weather. Highway mileage will probably be less.

AT YOUR DATSUN DEALER.

COME ALIVE, COME AND DRIVE **SENTRA**

MAJOR MOTION FROM NISSAN

NISSAN

Nissan Sentra, 1984

Jeep Wagoneer, 1982

Cougar Wagon, 1982

► *Volkswagen Scirocco, 1983*

Driving takes on a new

The Scirocco was not built for this country. It was made to be driven in Germany.

And it is for this precise reason that you should be interested in it.

Consider the following: There is no speed limit on Germany's autobahns.

Think about that for a moment.

Think about the level of engineering required to make a sports car that can respond precisely under such driving conditions.

Now consider the fact that most other sports cars on the market today are created to perform in, shall we say, a less demanding world?

It is this difference of standards makes the Scirocco superior.

Any test drive will prove it.

When you get into a Scirocco, the thing you notice is getting in. The se set low to the ground.

Now, as you drive along, you'll n the Scirocco's linear response.

perspective in a Scirocco.

What that means is that the suspension, braking, and steering systems communicate with you directly. And they react predictably to your commands. As you accelerate down straightaways and track through turns, you feel that you are an integral part of the car.

It's an exhilarating feeling.

To enhance this performance, VW engineers recently broke new ground with techniques as simple as cutting grooves down the roof. Better aerodynamics lessen drag and enable the car to move faster.

What's more, the Scirocco has maximal glass space, making it easier to see everything around you.

But that shouldn't come as a surprise. Like we said at the beginning, the Scirocco gives you a new viewpoint on driving. Seatbelts save lives.

Nothing else is a Volkswagen

Porsche 928S, 1983

Porsche 911SC, 1983

▶ Isuzu Impulse, 1983

The fuel injected, I-TEC controlled engine comes instantly alive. The satellite control modules are moved into driving position. And suddenly, the world is set in motion. On board, three computers begin to monitor and record on-going functions; as the wedge-shaped vehicle plunges into the night. Third gear. Fourth gear. The Impulse clings to a curve as you shift into fifth, the wind slipping over the flush aerodynamic skin. This is the Isuzu Impulse. Once the private fantasy of world renowned designer, Giorgio Giugiaro. Now the embodiment of an Isuzu dream: to build one of the most advanced, most practical, four passenger production cars the world has ever known. The all new Isuzu Impulse. Soon at your Isuzu automobile dealer.

ISUZU

ISUZU IMPULSE

FOLLOW YOUR IMPULSE

A "Touch of Class"

The Kamei **x1**™ System.

Kamei, the world leader in automotive aero-dynamic products, introduces the X1 system for Sciroccos. Other applications soon to follow.

The X1 system includes aerodynamic spoilers, side skirts, rear skirt, grille and decor set.

Kamei X1 spoilers and skirts have been wind tunnel designed and tested to provide improved handling, fuel economy and style.

Send $2.00 for X1 ordering information and a full-color catalog to: Kamei Auto Extras, 300 Montowese Ave., Dept. PB, North Haven, CT 06473.

⧸☰KAMEi ®

Kamei, 1983

▶ *Ford Mustang, 1983*

1983 FORD MUSTANG

IT'S MORE THAN A CONVERTIBLE. IT'S A MUSTANG.

Mustang Convertible. It comes complete with an electric convertible top, a real glass rear window, and room for four. And, that makes it a complete convertible.

But, it also comes complete with the wind in your hair and a pounding in your heart. And that makes it a Mustang.

Limited availability. Whether you buy or lease, see your Ford Dealer and place your order now. And remember, get it together — buckle up.

HAVE YOU DRIVEN A FORD...LATELY?

FORD DIVISION

FIRST CLASS.

For you, first class is a way of life. In everything you
do...including the car you drive. Seville. Cadillac's
finest. Elegant. Distinctive. Superbly crafted.
A car for those who choose to go
first class...all the way. Seville for 1984.

BEST OF ALL...IT'S A CADILLAC.

Let's Get It Together...Buckle Up.

Cadillac Seville, 1984

▶ *Oldsmobile Cutlass Ciera, 1984*

Olds Cutlass Ciera.
Technology that's state of the art.
And style that's all Cutlass.

Cutlass Ciera's technology is most impressive. The engine is constantly tuned by a computer. There's front-wheel drive, and options like an electronic instrument panel and 3.8L V6 engine with multi-port fuel injection.

But above all Ciera is a Cutlass. So along with great engineering, this mid-size carries with it a great heritage. And it shows. It shows in the stylish, contemporary design. In the clean lines, and attractive new front end.

Inside, you enjoy a most handsome interior, with ample room for six. The Brougham even offers available rich, supple leather in the seating areas.

Olds Cutlass Ciera. It never forgets it's a Cutlass. And neither will you.

Oldsmobiles are equipped with engines produced at facilities operated by GM car groups, subsidiaries or affiliated companies worldwide.

There is a special feel in an *Oldsmobile*

Still, The Standard.

Today, the Honda Accord 4-Door Sedan is bigger than when it was first introduced. Both inside and out. It is more aerodynamic. More powerful. More luxurious. And it has become the number one selling small car in America.*

Only one thing has not changed. It is still the standard by which every car in its class is judged.

H O N D A

Accord 4-Door Sedan

© 1984 American Honda Motor Co., Inc. *Based on 1983 calendar year Ward's Automotive Reports and EPA Interior Volume Index for subcompacts.

Honda Accord, 1984

COME ALIVE, COME AND DRIVE **NISSAN**
MAJOR MOTION

NEW NISSAN MAXIMA GL. A WORLD CLASS SEDAN THAT DOESN'T COST THE WORLD.

Thinking about a luxury sedan? We invite you to compare the performance, features and styling of Nissan's Maxima GL to any import or domestic available. Best of all...compare the price!

FUNCTIONAL TECHNOLOGY
A keyless entry system is just the beginning. Choose the electronics package, and see fuel capacity and engine torque monitored in digital. Choose leather seats that adjust eight ways. Standard power windows, air conditioning, cruise control, 6-speaker stereo with cassette, all add up to one of the world's most sophisticated sedans, at any price.

NEW FUEL-INJECTED, 3-LITER V-6
Nissan doesn't believe in lethargic

luxury. The new Maxima power plant generates more horsepower than BMW 325e, Audi 5000,...even more than a Porsche 944.

QUALITY IN MOTION
Nissan's commitment to quality is legend. Their skilled craftsmen have made this Maxima the best ever. Drive the 4-door sedan or wagon at your Datsun dealer. Both are luxury in motion.

THE BEST EXTENDED-SERVICE PLAN AVAILABLE:
Up to 5 years/100,000 miles. Ask about Nissan's Security Plus at participating Datsun dealers.

NISSAN

Nissan Maxima, 1984

It's amazing what $6990 can handle.

The engineers at Volkswagen who designed the new Golf achieved a goal that has eluded engineers elsewhere: They created a new generation of hatchbacks that is so advanced—it establishes the new definition by which all other hatchbacks will be judged.

The new Golf can handle any situation with ease.

Handling People. Once hatchbacks were small and cramped. But the Golf comfortably seats a family of five.

For details call 1-800-85-VOWS. *MN's suggest retail pricing, excluding tax, title, dealer prep, and transportation. $6,990 for 2-door fuel-injected gasoline model as shown. (rear wiper, full-wheel covers, metallic paint optional at extra cost).

Handling Things. The Golf holds 17.8 cubic feet of cargo. Up to 40 cubic feet with its back seat down.

Handling the Road. The Golf has to be driven to be experienced. Its German-engineered steering, suspension, and brakes provide precise, responsive handling.

Handling the Future. The Golf is built to last. We torture tested it in over 3,750,000 miles of driving. And we back it with our new 2-year Unlimited-mileage Protection Plan** that's as simple and straightforward as a VW itself.

Handling the Budget. Prices start at $6,790* for a Golf with a durable VW diesel engine. We also offer a Golf with a responsive fuel-injected gas engine for $6,990.*

How can we offer so much for so little?

The answer is simple: At Volkswagen, the engineers outnumber the accountants.

The new Golf. **It's not a car. It's a Volkswagen.**

$6,790 for 2-door diesel model. **Protection Plan: 2-year unlimited mileage, limited warranty on drive train, except brake, 3-year unlimited mileage limited warranty on corrosion perforation. See U.S. dealer for details.

Volkswagen Golf, 1984

How to live generously
without spending
lavishly.

The Buick LeSabre
has always been big on
value, and big on tradi-
tional values.
That's because the
LeSabre is large, and
roomy, and comfortable,
and solid.
Now these truths
become even more self-
evident. For now you can
order the LeSabre Collec-
tors Edition. Its interior
treatment goes far
beyond mere comfort
and convenience — it is
truly sumptuous.
Yet, the LeSabre is
still priced at very little
more than an ordinary car.
Buckle up and visit
your Buick dealer.
To ask any questions,
request a brochure or
test drive, call the Buick
Product Information
Center, 8 a.m. to 8 p.m.
Eastern time, weekdays.
1-800-65-BUICK
(1-800-852-8425).

Wouldn't you
really rather have a Buick?

Buick LeSabre Collectors Edition.

Buick LeSabre, 1984

After all, who knows more about
German cars than the Germans?

Audi 4000S Sports Sedan

$12,950. Mfrs. sugg. retail price 4-door sedan. Title, taxes, transp., registration, dealer delivery charges add'l. Sunroof optional.

The fact that our Audi 4000S
tells you a great deal about the kind of
automobile it is.
Ask the person who makes one. It
enjoys a reputation for advanced engineering in a country where the level of
automotive engineering is already the
most advanced in the world, and where
they expect to be able to drive a sports
sedan like this on the Autobahn at sus-
tained speeds of over 100 miles an hour.

It has a new 1.8-liter Audi-designed
engine with an advanced fuel injection
system and a five-speed manual transmission that, together, take you smoothly
from 0 to 50 in 7.9 seconds. Fuel efficiency
is [26] mpg city, 40 mpg on the highway.*
Legendary Audi handling. Front-
wheel drive, built with a mastery that
goes back over fifty years. And an afford-
ability that comes as a pleasant surprise,
especially when you
consider how well

equipped it is.
But if you want to know why they love
the Audi 4000S, you really have to drive it.
For your nearest dealer location, call toll-
free (800) 447-4700.
*Use estimated mpg for comparison.
Mileage varies with speed, trip length,
weather. Actual highway mileage will
probably be less.
PORSCHE+AUDI ©1984 Porsche Audi

Audi: the art of engineering.

Audi 4000S, 1984

THE LUXURY CAR FOR THOSE WHO REFUSE
TO RELAX THEIR STANDARDS.

Anyone who pays $40,000 for
a luxury sedan should not be asked
to do so in a spirit of forgiveness for
its deficiencies.
The BMW 733i makes no such
requests. And one of the world's
most unforgiving production processes makes certain that none is
ever needed.
That process mandates over
3 million operations for the assembly
of the body alone. It controls chassis alignments to within 4/1,000ths
of an inch. And it assesses the cor-
rosion-resistance of structural metals
by submerging them in salt water
for at least ten days.
It also endows the BMW 733i
with such technological innovations as an optional four-speed auto-

matic transmission that doesn't
force you to sacrifice the precision
of a manual gearbox, but rather
"gives the best of both worlds" (Auto-
sport magazine).
But the 733i is freer of compromise than even that implies. Of its
more than 4,000 parts, none ever
suffers from inattention because it's
judged "minor."
The electrically-powered leather
bucket seats are orthopedically
molded to the contours of the spine.
And because they're infinitely adjustable, being uncomfortable is all
but an anatomical impossibility.
Human anatomy even dictates
the design of the buttons that operate the power windows and the
two-position electric sunroof.

They are precisely shaped to fit the
natural curvature of the fingertip.
The 733i, in short, is an automobile in which nothing has been
left to chance, in which luxury is the
result of—rather than a substitute
for—genuinely superior design and
craftsmanship.
Providing something life commonly denies the perfectionist: Vin-
dication, instead of disappointment.

THE ULTIMATE DRIVING MACHINE.

© 1984 BMW of North America, Inc. The BMW trademark and logo are registered. European Delivery can be arranged through your authorized U.S. BMW dealer.

BMW 733i, 1984

129

A logical extension of the Buick philosophy.

Introducing the Buick Century Estate Wagon. What makes it exceptional is that, in addition to the spaciousness and convenience of a traditional station wagon, it also offers you all the advantages of a very advanced Buick.

It has the tight, firm control of front-wheel drive. The confident, dependable performance of a computer-controlled V-6 engine. And the smooth, quiet ride provided by its computer-tuned suspension system.

Beyond these highly advanced characteristics, you will also appreciate the careful attention to workmanship that goes into the new Century Wagon—and into all new Buicks.

Of course, you will also discover the plush, comfortable, convenient interior that discriminating car owners have come to expect in Buicks.

If you're looking for a wagon that offers more than just extra space, visit your Buick dealer and buckle yourself into the Century Estate Wagon.

Not only is it logical. It's also very, very comforting.

Wouldn't you really rather have a Buick?

Some Buicks are equipped with engines produced by other GM divisions, subsidiaries or affiliated companies worldwide. See your Buick dealer for details.

Buick Century Estate Wagon, 1984

The new Continental. Its luxury is simply a reflection of its high technology.

We're speaking now about a world of luxury that lies beyond Continental's fine fabrics and real wood trim.

The luxury of high technology.

Consider the luxury of Continental's ride, for instance. This car rides smoothly and serenely. On air. Its electronically controlled air suspension gives you an unusual combination of riding comfort and control. A technological advance offered by no other car maker, it automatically levels the car to compensate for changes in passenger or luggage load.

That's one example of the way high technology contributes to Continental's luxury. And there are others.

Such as the responsive power of its electronically fuel-injected V8 or European-designed turbocharged diesel. Even the electronic climate control system that automatically keeps the interior at any temperature you select.

High technology and luxury. One exists because of the other in the new Continental. From Lincoln—maker of the highest quality luxury cars built in America.*

*Based on a survey of owner-reported problems during the first three months of ownership of 1983 luxury cars.

LINCOLN-MERCURY DIVISION

Get it together—buckle up.

Lincoln Continental, 1984

Dodge Caravan. A truly revolutionary vehicle. It can handle two adults plus 125 cubic feet of cargo. Or five adults. Even seven with the available rear seat. Yet it's shorter than a full-size station wagon, so it's easier to maneuver and park. And since Caravan stands a mere 5'5", it's easy for you to get in and out of. And it's easy to get Caravan in and out of your garage.

Caravan's 2.2-liter engine rates an est. hwy. of 37 and EPA est. mpg of 24*— impressive mileage for a vehicle of this sort. Caravan also has front-wheel drive to handle slippery surfaces outside and give you more room inside. Yet for all of this, Caravan is remarkably low-priced and even backed by Dodge's 5 year/50,000 mile Protection Plan on engine, powertrain and outer body rust-through.*

The totally new Dodge Caravan. You've got to see it, sit in it, and drive it to believe it. All of which can happen at your Dodge dealer —where you can buy or lease** your very own transportation revolution. Order one now.

The New Chrysler Technology. Quality backed by 5/50 Protection.

INTRODUCING DODGE CARAVAN. A TRANSPORTATION REVOLUTION.

NOT AS LONG AS A FULL-SIZE STATION WAGON, YET IT HOLDS 40% MORE CARGO. AND IT'S ABOUT THE SAME HEIGHT AS THE AVERAGE AMERICAN WOMAN. IT HAS FRONT-WHEEL DRIVE, GETS INCREDIBLE MILEAGE, AND IS BACKED BY 5/50 PROTECTION.

FULL-SIZE VAN   DODGE CARAVAN

WE ARE DODGE. **Dodge** AN AMERICAN REVOLUTION.

BUCKLE UP FOR SAFETY.

*Use EPA est. mpg for comparison. Your mileage may vary depending on speed, distance and weather. Actual hwy. mpg and CA ests. lower.   **5 years or 50,000 miles, whichever comes first.   Limited warranty. A deductible applies. Excludes leases. SEE DEALER FOR DETAILS.

Dodge Caravan, 1984

1984 Mercury Cougar

1984 Thunderbird

Get it together—Buckle up.

Vision Becomes Reality.

The Vision

The visionary cars of the future are always sleek and elegant and technologically

Probe III

sophisticated. Unfortunately, they usually possess one terrible flaw. They're never real, always remaining the stuff of dreams and imagination, always on the drawing board, but never on the road.

In the late seventies, Ford Motor Company began development of the Probe Series, producing some of the most aerodynamically-efficient cars of the time. Aerodynamically-efficient design can achieve better handling and stability, better fuel economy and a quiet ride.

The Reality

You saw the reality born of that vision in February of last year, with the introduction of the Thunderbird and Cougar.

You saw it again in May, with the debut of our Ford Tempo and Mercury Topaz. And in November, when we introduced the new Mark VII.

Making our vision a reality required inventiveness and creativity, a renewed commitment to quality and

workmanship, and a new spirit of cooperation between labor and management.

But most of all, it required a desire to be the best.

1983 was the beginning of the greatest outpouring of new products in our history: Automobiles of elegance and power, sleekness and beauty, quality and precision. Automobiles that in the words of Car and Driver "simply change the rules in the domestic car business."

You can see all the 1984 models at Ford and Lincoln-Mercury dealers everywhere.

Quality is Job 1.

FORD · LINCOLN · MERCURY · FORD TRUCKS · FORD TRACTORS

Ford, 1984

PERSONAL LUXURY WITH PONTIAC FLAIR

GRAND PRIX

This is one luxury car that doesn't compromise on performance. Sure, Grand Prix's full coil suspension has been calibrated for smooth, comfortable ride. The body-contoured seats are covered with a rich textured cloth that's gentle to the touch. And virtually every feature you'd ever want in a luxury car is available. Yet, Grand Prix is still a Pontiac. And that means driving excitement. With quick-ratio power steering. Fade-resistant power brakes. A front stabilizer bar that helps keep it square to the road in tight turns. And a responsive 3.8 liter V-6 engine. (For an even greater "kick" order the 5.0 liter, 4-barrel V-8 engine and Y99 Rally Suspension.)

Pontiac Grand Prix. It doesn't compromise on luxury or performance. So why should you?

Some Pontiacs are equipped with engines produced by other GM divisions, subsidiaries or affiliated companies worldwide. See your Pontiac dealer for details.

PONTIAC ▼ WE BUILD EXCITEMENT

Pontiac Grand Prix, 1984

How to find the best wagon without spinning your 車輪.

There seems to be a mini-boom.

Nearly every car maker now has a small wagon. And while they're all designed to be more roomy, one is also designed to be more you: the 7-passenger 1988 Colt Vista.

To begin with, it's the most versatile wagon in its class. With seats that fold into more different configurations than anybody else's. To hold just about any combination of family, friends and freight in grand style.

Its trim size means it's easy to maneuver and park.

And it's full of thoughtful features like a center console, map pockets and underseat storage to keep everything in its place.

Vista even offers you an optional push-button **4WD** 4-wheel drive to help make sure snow and steep hills never stand in your way.

And Vista's sticker price is hundreds less than Nissan's 4WD Stanza wagon.* Even though Vista has more standard seating and offers options you can't even get on their wagon.

For excellent reliability, Vista is built by Mitsubishi in Japan.

You can test drive the new Colt Vista at your Chrysler-Plymouth or Dodge Dealer.

Which is nice.

Because owning a wagon that caters to your every 希望する事 is even better when it's sold by a dealer who does the same.

優秀 Colt
It's all the Japanese you need to know.

Colts are built by Mitsubishi Motors Corp. and sold exclusively at Chrysler-Plymouth and Dodge Dealers.
*Sticker price comparison of base models. Standard equipment levels vary.

Buckle up for safety.

Dodge Colt, 1988

Sometimes your toughest competition is yourself.

Motor Trend magazine recently named its 1984 Import Car of the Year. And for the first time ever, one manufacturer swept the top three places. Thank you, thank you, thank you.

Motor Trend
Import Car of the Year
HONDA

MOTOR TREND MAGAZINE
IMPORT CAR OF THE YEAR

Civic CRX,
Import Car of the Year.

Prelude,
First Runner-Up.

Civic S Hatchback,
Second Runner-Up.

© 1984 American Honda Motor Co., Inc.

Honda, 1984

THE NEW NISSAN 300 ZX PACE CAR FOR THE PERFORMANCE GENERATION.

Very few automobiles in the world have generated the excitement and emotional involvement associated with the Z-car. Keeping this in mind, it's not surprising to read that Motor Trend Magazine called the 300 ZX, "the best all-around Z-car ever built."

For 1986, Nissan has taken one more step in the thoughtful evolution of a classic.

At the heart of this Z is a 3-liter V-6 that is actually eight inches shorter and 15 percent lighter than the 280 ZX. Yet the turbo model puts out 11% more power; a rousing 200 horsepower. That power gets to the road by way of an electronic control system that gives you the most efficient transmission of power at any speed. Combined with shocks you adjust electronically from the cockpit, the result is startling.

In addition, an electronic monitoring system keeps track of spark plugs that fire 42 times a second at 5000 RPM and a micro computer controls the fuel injection system making the Z a marvel of functional electronic wizardry.

Outside, fender flares, housing wider tires, were integrated into the body. The air dam was extended and rocker panel extensions were added to reduce air turbulence under the car. All this, plus a wider track results in better handling than ever.

Inside, a choice of electronic or analog instrumentation is offered, along with every conceivable luxury, including a resounding 80-watt, 6-speaker stereo system.

The 300 ZX, turbo or fuel injected. Once you get inside a Z, a Z will get inside of you.

THE NAME IS NISSAN

NISSAN · BELT YOURSELF

Nissan 300 ZX, 1985

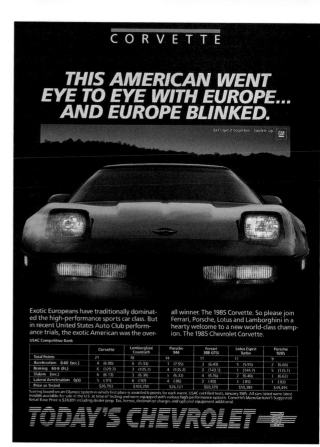

CORVETTE

THIS AMERICAN WENT EYE TO EYE WITH EUROPE... AND EUROPE BLINKED.

Let's get it together...buckle up. GM

Exotic Europeans have traditionally dominated the high-performance sports car class. But in recent United States Auto Club performance trials, the exotic American was the over-

all winner. The 1985 Corvette. So please join Ferrari, Porsche, Lotus and Lamborghini in a hearty welcome to a new world-class champion. The 1985 Chevrolet Corvette.

USAC Competitive Rank

	Corvette	Lamborghini Countach	Porsche 944	Ferrari 308 GTSi	Lotus Esprit Turbo	Porsche 928S
Total Points	21	16	14	11	11	9
Acceleration 0-60 (sec.)	4 (6.00)	6 (5.33)	1 (7.95)	3 (6.43)	5 (5.95)	2 (6.66)
Braking 60-0 (ft.)	6 (129.2)	3 (135.7)	4 (135.2)	4 (143.1)	1 (144.7)	5 (135.1)
Slalom (sec.)	6 (6.13)	3 (6.18)	5 (6.33)	4 (6.36)	2 (6.40)	1 (6.62)
Lateral Acceleration (g's)	5 (.91)	6 (.92)	4 (.86)	2 (.83)	3 (.85)	1 (.82)
Price as Tested	$26,703	$103,700	$26,121	$60,370	$50,384	$49,495

Scoring based on an Olympic system in which first place is awarded 6 points for each event. USAC certified tests, January 1985. All cars listed were latest models available for sale in the U.S. at time of testing and were equipped with various high-performance options. Corvette's Manufacturer's Suggested Retail Base Price is $24,891 including dealer prep. Tax, license, destination charges and optional equipment additional.

TODAY'S CHEVROLET

Chevrolet Corvette, 1985

Buckle up – together we can save lives.

1986 Mercury Cougar. It moves the way it moves because it looks the way it looks.

MERCURY. The shape you want to be in.

For more information, call 1-800 MERCFAX

LINCOLN-MERCURY DIVISION Ford

Mercury Cougar, 1985

Safari is ideal for all sorts of demanding expeditions.

Any van is useful for the mundane, dreary, go-to-the-market episodes of life.

Certain kinds of more vibrant lifestyles, however, demand a certain kind of vehicular style. It's found at last in Safari, a van one can take anywhere.

With available seating, Safari has room for eight friends and/or family members. And the creature comforts they're accustomed to expecting from fine automobiles.

You demand the best from life. So don't just get a van. Demand a Safari. By GMC. From your nearest GMC Truck dealer. You'll find a listing in the Yellow Pages.

GMC TRUCK

A truck you can live with

Let's get it together. . buckle up.

GMC Safari, 1985

135

One good turn deserves another.

Look what the Honda Prelude can do for you.

For openers, there's a power Moonroof. For your listening pleasure there's an AM/FM stereo with cassette. The steering column is adjustable and the front buckets recline. These amenities, and more, are guaranteed to make you feel comfortable by surrounding you in luxury. Of course, nobody needs to know how affordable this luxury really is.

You also will feel power. Hidden neatly under the sloping hood is a 12-valve, 1.8 liter, dual-carbureted engine ready to respond. On command. Or ask the Prelude to stop. Four-wheel disc brakes will have you back to zero in practically no time.

And thanks to an ingeniously engineered double wishbone front suspension combined with front and rear stabilizer bars and Mac-Pherson struts in the rear, you'll know what it feels like to drive a performance car.

Now, when a car is willing to do so much for you, don't you think it deserves at least one good turn? Then go find one. In a Honda Prelude. Naturally.

HONDA The Prelude

Honda Prelude, 1987

Colt joins the crème de la 最高.

The totally re-designed Colt GT Turbo. Recently named one of *Car and Driver* magazine's 10 best cars of the year.

"One of the 10 best cars of the year."

Car and Driver magazine

And it earned that distinction by delivering something Colts aren't known for. *A rush.*

With performance enhancements that include a turbocharged 16-valve, DOHC 1.6 liter powerplant, power rack and pinion steering, power 4-wheel disc brakes, taut sports suspension, performance radials, a super slippery new profile and more spunk than a lot of high-ticket turbo coupes.

Its refinements didn't stop under the hood, either.

Inside you'll find the Colt GT has ample elbow room, comfortable sport buckets, a telescoping tilt steering wheel, an ergonomically advanced interior and impressive dash graphics and instrumentation.

They're available in limited numbers at Plymouth and Dodge dealers who can promise you one thing:

A test drive that's a real kick in the 後背部.

優秀 Colt

It's all the Japanese you need to know.

3/36 Bumper To Bumper Warranty
See limited warranty at dealer, restrictions apply. Excludes normal maintenance, adjustments and wear items.

Buckle up for safety.

Dodge Plymouth IMPORTS

Dodge Colt, 1989

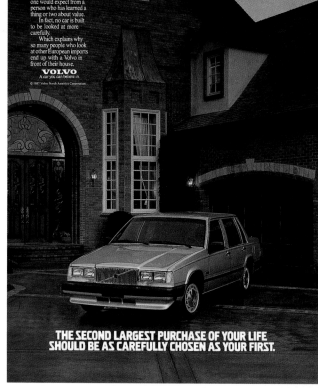

The Volvo 740 is built and engineered to withstand the kind of scrutiny one would expect from a person who has learned a thing or two about value.

In fact, no car is built to be looked at more carefully.

Which explains why so many people who look at other European imports end up with a Volvo in front of their house.

VOLVO
A car you can believe in.
© 1987 Volvo North America Corporation

THE SECOND LARGEST PURCHASE OF YOUR LIFE SHOULD BE AS CAREFULLY CHOSEN AS YOUR FIRST.

Volvo 740, 1987   ▶ *Chevrolet Spectrum, 1988*   ▶▶ *Honda CRX Si, 1989*

THE RED
SPECTRUM

Red hot.
Turbo charged.
Designed in Italy.
Made in Japan.
Warranteed by GM.*
**$9,305.00
To make them see red.

CHEVROLET

Shrouded in secrecy for years, the Stealth Bomber was finally introduce

public. For the record, we introduced ours first. The CRX Si. H O N D A

Datsun Trucks, 1980

Ford 4 x 4, 1980

Toyota Trucks, 1988

Toyota SR-5 Sport Truck, 1980

▶ *Volkswagen Pickup Truck, 1980*

Volkswagen's new Pickup: It's built like a truck, but drives like something else.

Where is it written that a truck has to drive like a truck? Certainly not on that brand new Volkswagen Pickup Truck. When it comes to going, a VW Pickup can pick 'em up and lay 'em down with the best of 'em. Under its aerodynamic hood is a very dynamic engine. A fuel-injected, overhead cam powerhouse that can outaccelerate even an MGB.

And should you ever catch up to a VW Pickup, you'll never catch it wallowing through corners like other trucks. Its front-wheel drive and front-mounted transverse engine help keep it moving nimbly. Even when the road throws it a curve. The steering is precise and quick because it's Volkswagen's rack-and-pinion system. What's equally impressive is how good a pickup a VW Pickup is. It's the only truck in its class with a fully unitized body and double-wall bed construction for extra strength. And its heavy-duty suspension takes the tension out of hauling over 1100 pounds of stuff. So a truck is a truck is a truck, eh? Well, not if it's a Volkswagen Pickup Truck. Then it's something else.

VOLKSWAGEN DOES IT AGAIN

Beauty in the rough.

Ford Bronco II, 1984

Ford Bronco II, 1984

Toyota 4Runner, 1987

▶ *Nissan Sport Truck, 1984*

NISSAN S/T: RULE THE TURF.

Dare the dunes. Challenge the concrete. You're in the new Nissan Sport Truck, a hunk of truck that's tough enough for almost anybody's turf.

From its high profile wheels and tires to its performance cockpit, this brute makes tracks with a combination of muscle, styling and control you won't find anywhere else.

- Biggest standard engine in the class, geared to go.
- Wide-Clearance independent front suspension steps over rough stuff instead of bouncing like solid axles.
- Four-by-four has auto-locking hubs.
- Tightest turning circle. • Double-wall cargo bed.
- 4x2: alloy wheels, P205/75R14 radials. 4x4: P215/75R15.

- 5-speed overdrive, ventilated power front disc brakes.

Tough on the competition, easy on you—with all these standards:
- Cloth-covered bucket seats.
- Sliding rear window; intermittent wipers.
- Power steering with tilt column.
- AM/FM multiplex stereo and full instrumentation.
- Leather-wrapped sports steering wheel.
- Dual outside mirrors; day/night rear-view mirror–plus. Grab your share of the excitement with a truck that runs beyond sport to... Major Motion.

AT YOUR DATSUN DEALER.

COME ALIVE, COME AND DRIVE S/T

MAJOR MOTION FROM NISSAN

ISUZU

Buckle up — for life!

THERE ARE PLACES ON EARTH WHERE NO LIFE EXISTS EXCEPT SMALL COLONIES OF ISUZUS.

In some of the farthest corners of the earth, you'll find the only form of transportation is an Isuzu. Or a donkey.

Take the small colony of Isuzus you see here. Clockwise, you'll see our new Space Cab,* standard bed pick-up, Trooper II, longbed pick-up and another Trooper II. Five versions of high adventure powered this year by an all new 2.3 liter gas engine. (An optional turbo-diesel engine is available for the pick-ups and the Trooper II.**)

The Trooper II is a go anywhere, do anything, four-wheel drive that thinks it's a utility truck. With its huge 21.9 gallon fuel tank, you can leave civilization and go up to 613 miles without refueling.*** The

versatile Trooper II was voted "4x4 of the Year" by *4 Wheel & Off-Road* magazine. And still, it's the least expensive 4x4 in its class!

Then there's our Space Cab. In its cab, there's room for up to four people, with the optional jumpseats. Plus, there's extra storage space for your equipment, with a built-in tonneau cover for security. There's even a sunroof standard on the LS model.

And now our most popular Isuzu. Our longbed and standard bed. No other truck in its class has a larger bed than our longbed; it also has the largest standard fuel tank in the field. And our standard bed just won the stock mini pick-up class in the toughest off-road race in the world — the Baja 1000.

Isuzu trucks. You'll find a small colony right at your Isuzu dealer. Ready to go. Anyplace.

ISUZU
THE FIRST CAR BUILDERS OF JAPAN.

*Space Cab available summer of 1985. **Turbo-diesel not available in California. Turbo-diesel trucks available summer of 1985. ***Turbo-diesel Trooper II, 28 estimated MPG. Use estimated MPG for comparison. Actual mileage may vary.

Isuzu, 1985

Slip into something comfortable.
The 1987 Ford Bronco II is here.

<u>Now Bronco II is even more versatile!</u> For top performance, a 140 hp* V-6 is standard. So are new rear antilock brakes. And there's a choice of a new 2-wheel drive model as well as traditional 4-wheel drive.

5:38 p.m.
The work day's <u>finally</u> over!

As you walk across the company parking lot, you spot your Eddie Bauer

Eddie Bauer

Bronco II waiting for you. Pop open the door and ahh…slide into your Captain's Chair, with its commanding view of the road. Adjust the tilt wheel just right and feel the comfort and luxury of your Bronco II's high-style interior. Now you've *really* slipped into something comfortable.

Start your engine.
Turn the key. You just brought the Bronco II's 2.9L electronically fuel-injected multi-port V-6 engine alive. This powerplant is unbeaten by any standard engine in its class.

That's the brakes.
First stop is the florist. Pull out smartly into traffic. Wait…*hit the brakes!* Where did that puppy come from? Extra glad the Bronco II has rear antilock brakes. They help you make straight stops when operating in 2-wheel drive.

4-wheel drive detour.
Freeway traffic looks pretty bad. You should try this side road. Uh-oh—

mud! Oh well, the Bronco II can handle it. Just press the optional electric "Touch-Drive" button and your Bronco II transforms to a 4-wheel drive machine—ready to give you the traction to ease through mud and snow. No stopping. No shifting. (Ford also offers a Bronco II 2-wheel drive model.)

It fits right in.
Everyone in town must be shopping at once. Good thing the Bronco II is small and compact. Yet, it's still large enough to carry all our camping equipment for the weekend. And the Eddie Bauer Bronco II comes with the "Ford Care" extended service plan**—24 months or 24,000 miles, whichever

comes first. With 2 Captain's Chairs, there's only one problem you may have with Bronco II —deciding *who* gets to be captain and who's co-pilot!

Free air conditioning.
Free air conditioning is available when you buy any Bronco II Special Value Option Package. The option content varies with your choice of package. The savings are based on the manufacturer's suggested retail price for the Special Value Package compared to traditional suggested pricing for the options purchased separately.

Best-Built American Trucks six years running.
"Quality is Job 1." In fact, for the past six consecutive years, Ford quality has led all other American automobile companies. This is based on an average of owner-reported problems in the first three months of service on '86 models and in a six-month period on '81-'85 models designed and built in North America.

Buckle up—together we can save lives.
*Based on SAE standard J1349. **Limited warranty. Ask to see a copy at your dealer.

Bronco II
BUILT FUN TOUGH

Ford Bronco II, 1987

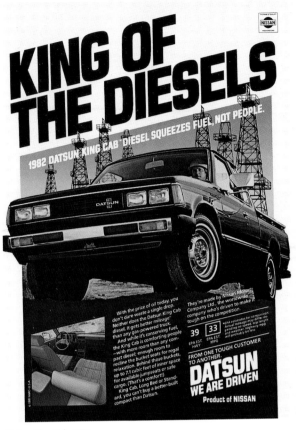

Datsun King Cab, 1982

Ford Bronco, 1981

Nissan Hardbody, 1988

"If it's tough enough for the Guinness Book of World Records...

It was a truly incredible journey. From Tierra del Fuego to the Arctic Circle — from the southern tip of South America to the northern tip of North America.

Garry Sowerby made this adventurous, record-setting trip in just 23 days, 22 hours and 40 minutes. And oh, the stories he could tell.

Naturally, to set a world record, Garry Sowerby didn't take chances — he took a Sierra, GMC Truck's ultimate full-size pickup. The comfortable, reliable Sierra Insta-Trac 4 X 4, with standard anti-lock rear brake system (operates only in two-wheel-drive mode on 4 X 4s), not only survived, it thrived. For 15,000 grueling miles — from mud to snow, through jungles and over mountains.

If the Sierra is tough enough to handle a trek like Sowerby's, imagine how well it can handle your everyday needs.

...it's tough enough for you."
— Garry Sowerby

You don't have to go for a world record to appreciate all the qualities the Sierra has to offer. The Sierra is much more than a full-size pickup — it's a GMC Truck full-size pickup.

Its toughness and reliability are evidenced by Garry Sowerby's record-setting journey. Its aerodynamic good looks speak for themselves. Its 4' X 8' bed and standard GVWR of 5,200 pounds (including passengers, cargo and vehicle) show its capacity to take care of business.

Its choice of five engines — from the standard 4.3-liter V-6 to the 454 V-8 (all with electronic throttle body fuel injection) to the 6.2-liter diesel — proves its versatility. And its roomy, civilized interior will almost make you forget you're driving a truck.

If you depend on a pickup, buckle up and see your GMC Truck dealer. Don't take chances — take a Sierra.

For a catalog and the name of your nearest dealer, call: 1-800-VALUE88 (1-800-825-8388).

GMC TRUCK
IT'S NOT JUST A TRUCK ANYMORE.

GMC Trucks, 1988

You can drive it as if it were your brother-in-law's.

Don't be misled by a Range Rover. Taken in by its elegant design. Seduced by its comfort. Thrown by its lavish appointments.

Lurking under all that luxury is the strength to withstand an astounding degree of whatever particular automotive torture you choose to inflict.

Wade it through mud up to its bumpers.

Through snow higher than a husky.

Bounce it over boulders. With a massive frame and a remarkable suspension system, Range Rovers endure

punishment that would paralyze lesser 4-wheel drive vehicles.

In fact, Range Rovers endure, period.

Even 17 year old Range Rovers, some of the first ever built, are still on the road. And off it.

So call 1-800-FINE 4WD for a Range Rover dealer near you. In spite of its admittedly high price, it's one luxury car you don't have to coddle.

Not even if it's your own.

RANGE ROVER

Range Rover, 1988

We brake for fish.

Would you like to experience a Range Rover under optimum conditions?

Just add water.

A Range Rover can wade through depths that would immobilize a mere car.

And provide the added traction of 4-wheel drive in a downpour.

What's all the more extraordinary, though, is that a Range Rover isn't a vehicle you'll want to save for a rainy day.

Because on a dry road, it handles like a road car. And on a test track, it surges along at roughly 100 mph.

It even surrounds you with all the comfort and luxury of a luxury car.

So why not call 1-800-FINE 4WD for the name of a dealer convenient to you?

While a Range Rover is hardly inexpensive, it's well worth the price.

After all, when you buy one you're not simply buying an ordinary 4-wheel drive vehicle.

You're converting your money into a liquid asset.

RANGE ROVER

Range Rover, 1988

Jeep Wrangler, 1989

Isuzu Amigo, 1989

OUT-POWERS, OUT-ROOMS, OUT-TOWS EVERY OTHER WAGON!

FORD CLUB WAGON.

BEST-BUILT AMERICAN TRUCKS

POWERFUL CHOICE: SIX, DIESEL AND NEW MID-SIZE V-8!

For great outings, go with the wagon that outdoes all the rest —Ford's Club Wagon.

For starters, no other wagon, big or small, gives you such a power choice. V-8s headed by a new High Output 5.8L* with 4-barrel carburetor — and 27%

Get it together — Buckle up!

more power than Chevy's mid-size V-8. Ford's 4.9L I-6, the biggest Six in any wagon. The 7.5L,[†] most powerful V-8. And husky 6.9L diesel[†] that packs 35 more horsepower than Chevy diesel. (Dodge doesn't even offer one.)

And no other wagon gives you so much usable space —for people and/or

cargo. You can seat up to 12 in roomy comfort (15 in Ford's Super Wagon).

Ford Clubs are built tough, with strong body-on-frame construction. The bigger models are rated to tow as much as 10,000 lb.: 2,500 more than Dodge, 3,000 more than Chevy.

*Optional, not available in Calif. or with manual transmission.
[†]Optional, 4.9L I-6 standard

Quality is Job 1.

Ford's commitment to quality results in the best-built American trucks, based on a survey of owner-reported problems during the first three months of ownership of 1983 trucks. And the commitment continues in 1984. **BUILT FORD TOUGH**

Ford Club Wagon, 1984

Winnebago LeSharo, 1984

Ford Econoline, 1982

Dodge Grand Caravan, 1987

Make a radical departure.

Honda Scooters, 1985

Lou Reed New York City 1985

Don't settle for walking.

Honda Scooters, 1985

Rad Hot.

Katana 600

Paint the town red on a five-alarm beauty known as the 1989 Katana 600. Experience a fusion of optimum performance and maximum comfort. Here is a hot machine that will truly elevate your desire to a fever pitch. You'll forge new adventures through twisting roads and city streets. And every eye that is fortunate enough to catch you will be green with envy. The engine, based on the track-tough GSX-R750, is compact, potent, and tuned to deliver strong torque in the low and mid RPM ranges.

But comfort is what sparks the Katana. A comfortable seat and riding position help take the kinks out of long-distance trips. And the fairing vents engine heat away from the rider for greater comfort. Another example of ergonomic genius.

The '89 Katana 600. Sizzling looks, performance and total comfort that will have a lot of heads turning and saying,... *"Rad On, Suzuki."*

$ SUZUKI

Suzuki Katana, 1989

Introducing The Honda Passport. It fits your life as easily as it fits your budget.

Honda's remarkable new C70. The Passport. It gets up to 130 miles to the gallon.*

You also get an electric starter. An automatic clutch. That famous Honda reliability. And a brand new excuse to go somewhere.

It'll carry one or two of you comfortably.† And if you're wondering if you can afford it? Don't.

With the way gas prices are headed, you can't afford to be without it.

The Honda Passport. For all those trips that are too big for the feet and too small for the car.

The Honda Passport.

Get one. It'll take you almost anywhere.

Honda Passport, 1980

Our canyon cat and its cruisin' cousin.

Our agile GS-550 comes in two slick versions this year.

One is the E model. Better known as the canyon cat.

And the other is our L edition. Which we tabbed the Low Slinger. Outfitted for cruising, it sports extended forks, pull-back handlebars, teardrop tank and chopped megaphone pipes.

Both the Low Slinger and the canyon cat are powered by a smooth 4-stroke DOHC mill. And both come with disc brakes front and rear, mag-style wheels, 5-way adjustable shocks, transistor ignition and easy-grip power levers.

Also, like all 1980 GS models, these bikes are backed by a 12-month unlimited mileage warranty.*

Which means Suzuki is with you wherever you go. Canyons or cities.

$ SUZUKI 1980
The Performer.

1980 GS Model
TWELVE-MONTH UNLIMITED MILEAGE WARRANTY*

Clarion Car Audio, 1988 ◄   Suzuki Motorcycles, 1980

IT'S EVERYTHING OUR BIG SPECIALS ARE. EXCEPT BIG.

Our 1980 XS400 Special could easily be mistaken for one of our larger Specials. Not surprising, since the only real difference is its size.

The XS400 is smaller. Which certainly has some advantages. Like maneuverability. It's lightweight, agile and exceptionally stable.

Gas mileage is phenomenal. Over 60 miles per gallon.*

And to prove that mid-size doesn't have to mean mid-performance, the 400's tried-and-true 391cc, four-stroke engine is more than generous with power. While a six-speed transmission doles out the power precisely as you need it.

Like the bigger Specials, the XS400 sports all the extras considered standard on a Special: a redesigned frame and seat mounting system that lowers the seat height, giving you that feet-on-the-ground stability. Graceful, pullback handlebars. Tapered megaphone pipes. And one-piece cast alloy wheels.

It all adds up to the XS400 Special.

Big-bike styling. Big-bike performance. Mid-size price.

That's the special beauty of this beautiful Special.

YAMAHA
When you know how they're built.

Mileage figures based on EPA testing, for city riding. Your mileage may vary depending on the way you ride. Rear view mirror(s) standard equipment. Always wear a helmet and eye protection.

Yamaha XS400, 1980

THE MORE YOU KNOW ABOUT MOPEDS THE MORE YOU'LL WANT A VESPA.

For a rather enlightened group of people, mopeds have become one of the smartest ways to get around the problem of getting around.

While mopeds are a good idea, Vespa makes them even better. Vespa's two-passenger Grande, the new Si (say "see"), Bravo and Ciao (say "chow") give you more of what you're buying a moped for.

Zipping around town at up to 160 miles per gallon they add distinctive finesse to making your appointed rounds. You'll appreciate their stylish size and maneuverability whether motoring to your favorite sporting event or neighborhood merchant.

Vespa mopeds are superbly designed to take every ride in stride. Each features unitized frame construction for strength and comfort, separate belt and chain drive system for convenience and quiet dependability, forced-air rotary induction engine for durability and efficiency plus exclusive variable-ratio belt drive for extra power when you need it.

For extra confidence we offer an unlimited mileage 12-month warranty.

Over 30 years of engineering excellence and experience have supplied over 2 million Vespa mopeds and 6 million Vespa scooters to people all over the world.

We invite you to see the superior Vespa value for yourself. Visit your local Vespa dealer now for an insightful and delightful demonstration ride. Look in the Yellow Pages or write us for nearest location.

The more you know, the more you'll go for a Vespa moped.

Mileage is based on CUNA Standards. Yours may vary. The Vespa Grande is built for two persons. Two-passenger operation is not permitted in some states. Check local laws for operation and ownership. Ask Vespa Limited Warranty, Consumer Relations.

Check local laws about moped use. Vespa of America, 355 Valley Drive, Brisbane, CA 94005.

PIAGGIO GROUP

vespa®
THE UNCOMMON CARRIER

Vespa, 1980

Easy come. Easy go.

100 mpg. And air conditioning.

The Honda Express gives you fresh-air fun without driving you to the poorhouse. You can get up to 100 miles per gallon. And that rugged 49 cc Honda engine is built by the people famous for engine innovations.

There's no clutch lever, no gears to shift and no pedals to pump. Which leaves you free as a breeze to enjoy the wind in your face.

And starting an Express is as easy as riding one. Just turn on the ignition. Tap the starter a few times with your toe. And squeeze the rear brake lever.

Home economics.

The Honda Express fits nicely into your budget as an extra set of wheels for running all those household errands. And it also fits perfectly into that tiny, unused corner of the garage and just about any parking place you can find.

Of course, the Express isn't limited to working around the house. It's the right answer on college campuses where cars always outnumber parking places. And it's a great addition to a vacation home.

Choice seating.
With the Express you get some choices: The Standard Express. Or the Express II with a contoured bucket seat that lets you sit "in" it rather than "on" it. And whether to add the optional front and rear baskets. Then, there's the toughest choice of all. Yellow. Or blue.

Stop by your Honda dealer and let him show you how easy it is to own an Express.

ALWAYS WEAR A HELMET AND EYE PROTECTION. Designed for operator use only. Not available in Maryland. ©1980 American Honda Motor Co., Inc. For a free brochure, see your Honda dealer. Or write American Honda Motor Co., Inc., Dept FMRL, Box 50, Gardena, California 90247.
Based on tests conducted in normal city traffic with a top speed of 24 miles per hour. Your mileage may vary depending on speed, distance and weather.

HONDA EXPRESS
FOLLOW THE LEADER.

Honda Express, 1980

"HONEY, GUESS WHAT I JUST BOUGHT?"

Little by little, across America, people are bringing home a delightful accompaniment to the automobile. The Vespa scooter.

What is this two-wheel appeal? It's a totally unique kind of transportation that combines comfort, convenience and a stylish sense of sophistication.

The result is a vehicle with a low center of gravity that you ride with your feet on the floor.

You're protected by a welded, unitized body molded in graceful, almost voluptuous lines by Italian designers. Inside the top models lies an engine powerful enough for freeway driving and an automatic oil injection. There's electronic ignition and hydraulic front and rear suspension—even a hidden spare tire. Vespa scooters' ingenuous blend of style and over 30 years of engineering excellence and experience give you an excitingly different feeling of control and maneuverability.

You'll feel confident to know that more than 6 million Vespa scooters and 2 million Vespa mopeds have been sold so far and that

Vespa offers a 12-month, unlimited mileage warranty. When scooting along barely above a whisper, its 70-140 mpg consumption rating provides a true sense of value and efficiency. We urge you to see your Vespa dealer now to take a test drive. Look in the Yellow Pages or write us for nearest location. And see if your new Vespa scooter doesn't surprise you as much as it will surprise your friends.

Mileage is based on CUNA Standards. Yours may vary. Check with your Vespa dealer.
Vespa Limited Warranty. Wear helmet and eye protection. Check local laws.
Vespa of America, 355 Valley Drive, Consumer Relations, Brisbane, CA 94005.

PIAGGIO GROUP

vespa.
THE UNCOMMON CARRIER

© 1980 VESPA OF AMERICA

Vespa, 1980

And the winner is...

Big Hair, Big Plans, Big Bomb

Okay. You have this groovy little sports car ripe for an eighteen- to thirty-year-old demographic. Who do you call to help sell this hip, new automobile? Michael Jackson? Madonna? Prince? No, baby. Only the big hair and leather jackets of the original "Private Eyes" Hall & Oates would do. Compelled to lend their identity and their "Big Bam Boom" concert tour to the Pontiac Fiero, these pop sensations of the eighties would soon find out that both band and car were "Out of Touch."

Ihr habt wohl ´nen Fön

Da hat man einen tollen kleinen Sportwagen, der nur so nach 18- bis 30-jährigen Fahrern schreit. Und wen ruft man zu Hilfe, um diesen coolen Schlitten zu verkaufen? Michael Jackson? Madonna? Prince? Oh nein, Schätzchen. Nur die Fönfrisuren und Lederjacken des „Private Eyes"-Duos Hall & Oates waren gut genug. Diese Popgrößen der frühen Achtziger warben mit ihrer „Big Bam Boom"-Tournee für den Pontiac Fiero, mussten jedoch bald feststellen, dass sowohl Band als auch Auto mega out waren: „Out of Touch" eben.

Une coupe d'enfer, des plans d'enfer, le fiasco

Bon. Prenez une super petite voiture de sport, visant la tranche d'âge des dix-huit à vingt-cinq ans. A qui allez-vous faire appel pour faire vendre ce petit bijou dernier cri? Michael Jackson? Madonna? Prince? Tu te trompes, ma petite. A rien de moins qu'à l'authentique duo de « Private Eyes », Hall & Oates, avec leurs coupes d'enfer et leurs blousons de cuir. Ces deux popstars des années 80, contraints d'associer leur image et leur « Big Bam Boom » tournée à la Pontiac Fiero, comprendront assez vite que le groupe et la voiture n'étaient plus dans le coup.

Gran peinado, grandes planes... ¡una bomba!

De acuerdo. Te vienen con un súper deportivo destinado a un público objetivo con una edad comprendida entre dieciocho y treinta años. ¿A quién llamas para que venda este coche tan molón? ¿A Michael Jackson? ¿A Madonna? ¿A Prince? Nada de eso. Solo los tupés y las chaquetas de cuero de los originales Hall y Oates podrían hacerlo. Obligados a prestar su identidad y su gira de conciertos Big Bam Boom al Pontiac Fiero, este grupo de pop que causó sensación en los años ochenta no tardaría en descubrir que tanto el éxito musical como aquel vehículo eran inalcanzables...

でかい髪型、でかい計画、そして大失敗

オーケイ。君は18歳〜30代の年齢層のための、このいかした小さなスポーツカーを持っている。この最新流行の新しい自動車を売るために誰を呼べばいい マイケル・ジャクソン？マドンナ？プリンス？　ベイビー、違うよ。でかい髪型と革のジャケットの「Private Eyes」の元祖、ホール＆オーツだけができること さ。ポンティアック・フィエロのために強いて彼らのアイデンティティと「Big Bam Boom」コンサートツアーを借り、結果間もなくこの80年代の人気者たちに バンドと車の両方ともが「Out of Touch（事情に疎い）」だということを発見することとなった。

Pontiac Fiero, 1984

THE HENLEY COLLEGE LIBRARY

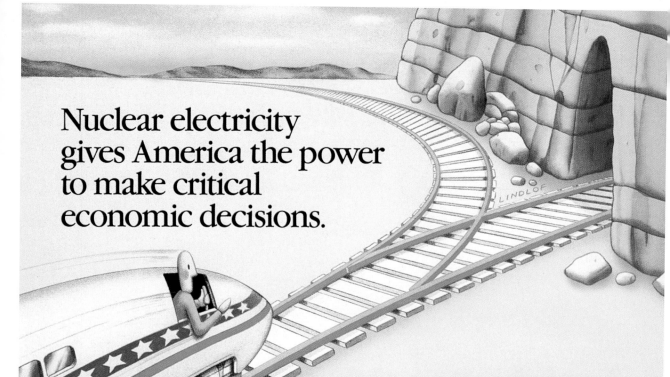

Nuclear electricity gives America the power to make critical economic decisions.

The 1973 Arab oil embargo gave America its first bitter taste of foreign oil dependence. To protect our economy, we turned to electricity. Using American resources and technology. As a result, nuclear energy has established itself as a cornerstone in rebuilding a strong economy.

The electrification of America

Electricity is the only major form of energy that has experienced overall growth since 1973. We are using 36% more now than we did then. It serves new uses in our factories and heats twice as many of our

© 1987 USCEA

homes. Nuclear energy's contribution to our electricity supply has more than quadrupled during that time, helping fuel a 34% growth in America's economy.

There are still no guarantees against becoming too dependent on foreign oil once again. Our economy continues to require increasing amounts of electricity for its growth. And that electricity must continue to come from nuclear energy, as well as coal and other domestic sources.

The growth of nuclear energy

American nuclear electricity was born in 1956. By 1973, it had become a technology America could turn to when faced with the oil crisis. And today, over 100 nuclear plants make nuclear energy our second leading electricity source, behind coal. In fact, nuclear energy and coal together have provided over 95% of all new electricity generated in America over the past decade.

Nuclear energy also saved Americans between 35 and 62 billion dollars from 1974 to 1985,

compared to the cost of non-nuclear-generated electricity. It has displaced over two billion barrels of oil. And its contribution continues to climb. The U.S. Department of Energy estimates that nuclear energy will provide 20% of our electricity by the early 1990s.

Nuclear energy for a secure future.

Nuclear energy has proven its worth to America's economy. Auburn University Dean of Engineering Dr. Lynn Weaver recently described nuclear energy as "…one of the basic props supporting the entire national economy." Yet, in spite of all we've accomplished, the threat of foreign oil dependence remains. Difficult choices will still need to be made. But one fact has made itself very clear: the more we develop our own energy sources like nuclear energy and coal, the more we control our own economic destiny.

For a free booklet on energy independence, write to the U.S. Committee for Energy Awareness, P.O. Box 1537 (ED07), Ridgely, MD 21681. Please allow 4-6 weeks for delivery.

Information about energy America can count on

U.S. COMMITTEE FOR ENERGY AWARENESS

The Prudential, 1987 ◄ *U.S. Committee for Energy Awareness, 1987*

Nuclear energy helps keep us from reliving a nightmare

The 1973 Arab oil crisis is a haunting reminder of the darker side of foreign oil dependence. Since then, America has turned more to electricity from nuclear energy and coal to help restore our energy security. As a result, these are now our leading sources of electricity and a strong defense against an increasing oil dependence that again threatens America's national energy security.

A dangerous foreign oil dependence

America imported four million barrels of oil a day in 1985. Last year that increased by another 800,000 barrels a day. The danger? Most of these new barrels come directly from OPEC. And the U.S. Department of Energy estimates that by year-end 1987, oil imports will be

©1987 USCEA

30% higher than the 1985 level—an ominous trend.

U.S. Interior Secretary Donald Hodel recently warned that "OPEC is most assuredly getting back into the driver's seat" and our increasing dependence will be "detrimental to the country's economic and national security and its financial well-being."

Nuclear electricity's contribution

America's electric utilities have helped diminish OPEC's impact. Today, over 100 nuclear plants make nuclear energy our second largest electricity source, behind coal.

And nuclear energy has helped cut foreign oil demand. It's saved America over two billion barrels of oil since 1973, and our nuclear plants continue to cut oil use. The energy analysts at Science Concepts, Inc. estimate that by the year 2000, nuclear energy will have saved us between seven and twelve billion barrels of oil.

Nuclear energy for a secure future

Nuclear energy is not just helping here in America. According to OPEC, nuclear energy has permanently displaced about six million barrels of oil a day in world markets.

The lessons we learned in 1973 are lessons we can't afford to forget. Nuclear energy and coal can't offer us guarantees against another oil crisis. But the more we hear about the return of OPEC dominance, the more we need to remember the critical role played by electricity from coal and nuclear energy in fueling America's economy and protecting our future.

For a free booklet on energy independence, write to the U.S. Committee for Energy Awareness, P.O. Box 1537 (OP26), Ridgely, MD 21681. Please allow 4-6 weeks for delivery.

Information about energy America can count on
U.S. COMMITTEE FOR ENERGY AWARENESS

U.S. Committee for Energy Awareness, 1987

▶ *Franklin Electric, 1980*

The Happy Truth About Tales Of The Unexpecte

Droughts. Water shortages. Deserts encroaching on once-fertile land.

It's about time America had some good news about water. It's about time we found a supply that could take the burden off the country's overtaxed and often polluted lakes, rivers and reservoirs.

Well, this'll be the best news you've heard about water in a long, long time. The happy truth is America has a virtually endless supply just waiting to be tapped.

All we have to do is look a little deeper.

AMERICA'S BEST WATER IS ALWAYS GETTING UNDERFOOT.

The earth has as much water today as it had in prehistoric times. The water may sometime change forms, but the supply itself is constant. So where is all the water today?

An amazing percentage is where it's always been. Underground.

An incredible 95% of all the fresh water on earth is ground water. In the United States, there's 20 or 30 times as much water underground as there is in all the lakes, streams and rivers *combined*.

What's more, it's a completely renewable supply: Although the rate of replenishing varies greatly, water is seeping into the ground constantly, every hour of the day, every day of the year.

WELL WATER IS A NATURAL DELIGHT.

The American public is using more than 90 *billion* gallons of well water a day.

Approximately 700,000 new wells are drilled every year. Wells now provide almost 35 percent of the water used by municipalities—and over 80% of the water used in rural areas for homes and livestock.

Why is it so incredibly popular now? Part of the reason is the very fact that it is so plentiful—and that once tapped, the water is available for as long as it's sensibly used.

But part of the reason, too, is that well water is part of America's healthy drive to get back to its roots. After all, wells tap America's purest supply of natural water.

Does that mean this water's 100% pure? Absolutely not. Although it rarely suffers from the pollution that so often afflicts surface water, nine times out of ten, well water is even better than totally pure water. It's enriched with dissolved natural minerals. Those minerals give well water in every part of the country its distinct, regional flavor. (If those minerals impart too strong a flavor, a simple filtering device can usually purify the water automatically.)

AMERICA'S MOST FERTILE FIELDS ARE ALL WET.

Many of the irrigation systems in the arid and semi-arid regions of the United States

It's called the hydrologic cycle. It means that billions of gallons of water are entering underground reservoirs e

rely exclusively on huge underground reservoirs that have been c lecting water for centuries. Withou those rich water supplies, many of most fertile fields in the country w soon become barren. In the 17 wes states, for example, about 70 perc the water used for irrigation comes from wells.

Is well water pure water? Usually it's better than pure.

Endless Well And Other from The Underground.

As long as that water isn't pumped aster than it's naturally replaced, there ill always be plenty for the fields—and or the factories, homes and entire cities hat rely on our underground resource.

WHY YOU SHOULD ALWAYS LOOK BELOW THE SURFACE.

et's say you're looking for a new water upply. Maybe you're building a new ome, factory or office building. Maybe ou're planning a multi-acre farm or a uarter-acre garden. Maybe you're on he board of a regional or municipal ater authority. Or maybe you'd just ke the secure feeling that comes with nowing that no one can turn off or limit our water supply.

The first place to look is your own ackyard.

Ground water in some quantity an be found under almost every tract

merica grows ground water.

f inhabitable land on earth. The cost f getting that water is almost always ower than the cost of relying on any other water supply.

If you have a professional, experienced water well contractor inspect your site to determine the feasibility of using ground water, you'll be doing yourself and your ocality a favor, because you'll be relying on a water storage ystem that doesn't drain the public reservoirs. A system that doesn't require major

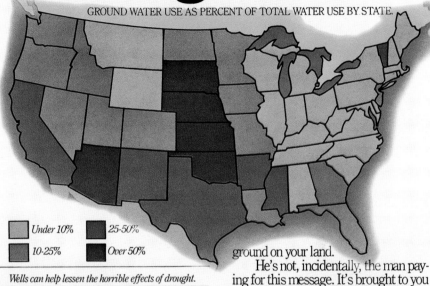

GROUND WATER USE AS PERCENT OF TOTAL WATER USE BY STATE.

Under 10%   25-50%
10-25%   Over 50%

Wells can help lessen the horrible effects of drought.

Bettman Archive

construction. A system that never becomes clogged with silt or weeds. One that never loses water by evaporation. One that doesn't remove productive land from other beneficial uses.

The fact is, ground water is a virtually untapped, unfailing resource. A priceless resource that's so vast, its potential has just begun to surface.

IT'S TIME YOU WENT TO THE PROS.

There's water under almost every inhabitable tract of land on Earth.

A professional water well contractor is a water specialist, an engineer and a craftsman all rolled into one. He knows the right techniques for finding the best site and building the best kind of well. He knows what equipment to use.

He's the man you should call to find out more about what's going on under-ground on your land.

He's not, incidentally, the man paying for this message. It's brought to you instead by Franklin Electric, the company that makes the motors for most of the submersible pump manufacturers.

We're doing it because we think it's time you knew the good news about one American resource that's not in trouble.

The story's been kept underground long enough.

Finding new energy. It's lining
up more support every day.

❝America may be running short of
gasoline, but we're not running out of
energy. We've got enough coal to produce twice as much energy as all the oil
in the Middle East. We have tar sands
and oil shale. We can burn our garbage
to produce electricity and we've experi-
mented with making oil from forest
waste products. We can turn coal into
gasoline for our cars or into natural gas
for our homes, and do it in an environ-
mentally responsible manner.

"There's nuclear and solar, the winds
and even the possible use of ocean
currents to generate electricity.

"Here at Bechtel, teams of energy
specialists have completed work in all
of these areas, and many are helping
meet our energy needs at this very
moment.

"As energy specialists, we know that
no single power source is the answer
to our energy problems. America needs
a balanced energy program . . . coal.

oil, nuclear, and geothermal as well as
solar, wind, biomass, nuclear fusion,
hydroelectric and synthetic fuels.

"Finding ways to meet our energy
needs is part of what we do at Bechtel.

"For more information about Bechtel,
please write Bechtel Information, P.O.
Box 3965, San Francisco, CA 94119.

We're Bechtel.❞

BECHTEL
Professional Engineers-Constructors
Division headquarters:
San Francisco • Los Angeles • Houston •
Ann Arbor, Mich. • Gaithersburg, Md. • London

Bechtel, 1981

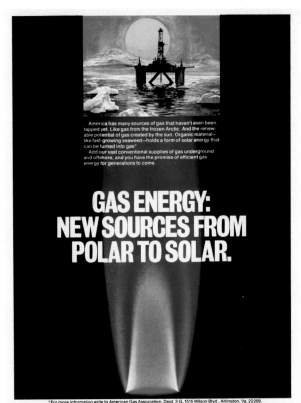

America has many sources of gas that haven't even been
tapped yet. Like gas from the frozen Arctic. And the renewable potential of gas created by the sun. Organic material—
like fast-growing seaweed—holds a form of solar energy that
can be turned into gas.*

Add our vast conventional supplies of gas underground
and offshore, and you have the promise of efficient gas
energy for generations to come.

GAS ENERGY:
NEW SOURCES FROM
POLAR TO SOLAR.

*For more information write to American Gas Association, Dept. 3-G, 1515 Wilson Blvd., Arlington, Va. 22209.

Gas: The future belongs to the efficient.

American Gas, 1980

Boise Cascade Corporation, 1984 ◀   *Champion International Corporation, 1980*

There are some marvelous benefits ahead for
mankind. But along with every benefit will come a
whole new set of problems.
Champion is a forward-looking forest products
company. We plant seeds for a living. Seeds that
take from 25 to 50 years to become mature trees.
Therefore, we think a lot about The Future of the forest. And of the people who will be around to buy our
products in the years to come.
So, during the coming year, in magazine ads like
this, we will continue our program of discussing
some of the potential cultural and sociological im-
pacts of future technology and change—to help you
make intelligent choices.
You might say, we're planting seeds of thought
for tomorrow.

The Future is
coming.
But only you
can decide
where it's going.

Lord Kelvin, the eminent nineteenth century physicist, once predicted: "X-rays will
prove to be a hoax"; "Aircraft flight is impossible"; and "Radio has no future."
Octave Chanute, an aviation pioneer said
in 1904: "The [flying] machines will eventually
be fast, they will be used in sport, but they are
not to be thought of as commercial carriers."
Henry L. Ellsworth, U.S. Commissioner of
Patents in 1844, a man who should have known
better, said: "The advancement of the arts [of
invention] from year to year...seems to presage
the arrival of that period when further improvement must end."
In a comment on this kind of "technological
pessimism," science writer Arthur C. Clarke,
in *Profiles of the Future*, said: "When a distinguished but elderly scientist states that something is possible, he is almost certainly right.
When he states that something is impossible,
he is very probably wrong."
Obviously, we can't leave The Future *just*
to the experts. As intelligent and well-informed
as they are, they are not infallible.
Collectively, we all have to take responsibility for the future. It doesn't just *happen* to
us. We must learn all we can from the past.
And use it to help us in the years to come.
The human race is now making choices

that may well determine our long-term future.
No one knows the precise nature of these
choices, but futurists agree that our actions
today will reverberate throughout the years
ahead.
As a company whose entire being is based
on the tree, a renewable resource that takes
from 25 to 50 years to mature, we have always
been particularly concerned about the pros-
pects of future generations of forests and of
future generations of people.
So it seems only natural for us to consider
some of the situations that futurists foresee for
the coming generations. And to discuss some
of the choices that will have to be made.
In magazine pages like this, we will continue to look at some of the major issues that
can affect us all in the years to come.
If you have any doubts about The Future
remember this: many of the supposedly "un-
solvable" problems of past generations have
been very successfully solved. For example, we
now have insulin for diabetics, ships that fly to
the moon and an effective polio vaccine.
If you agree that The Future consists of a
variety of alternatives, that choice is unavoid-
able and that refusing to choose is itself a
choice, you have taken the first step toward a
more active role in your own future. You can
learn more by sending for a free brochure
about the critical issues we face in The Future
and a bibliography for further reading. Write:
Champion International Corporation
Dept. 200N, P.O. Box 10140
Stamford, Connecticut 06921

**Champion—
a forest products company with
its roots planted firmly
in the future.**

We are in the forest products business.
We plant trees, grow trees, harvest
trees. And from trees we make wood
building products. Plus fine paper for printing
and business. And paper packaging for
shipping and selling.
Because we make our living from the
forest, our success depends, in one
way or another, on the future. And
we're planning—and planting—for it.

Champion
Champion International Corporation
Planting seeds for the future

165

The little fox and the coyote.

Across the twilight of a California desert, a kit fox hears the deadly footfalls of a coyote. Caught in the dangerous open, she can streak for safety to a curious mound at the edge of an oilfield. People who work there, consulting with wildlife experts, built it specially for her.

So now she can shoot through a pipe just big enough for her and into a cozy den that's designed to keep her snug and safe.

Do people think of things like this just to help an endangered species make it through the night?

People Do.

Chevron

For more information write: People Do-F, P. O. Box 7753, San Francisco, CA 94120

Chevron, 1988

▶ *Phillips 66 Petroleum, 1987*

Too pretty to get its feet wet.

Shaving by shaving, feather by feather, a wood block takes on life. The shaping of decoys has been a skill in Louisiana for as long as Cajun has been spoken. But this beauty will never flirt with a duck. Her charms are saved for the artistic, the art  collector, for all the admirers of things carved by hand. We at Phillips Petroleum are captivated, too. We try to take as much care when the work we do touches the habitats of wildfowl, as these artists take with their birds. To every last feather.

PHILLIPS 66

When You've Tried To "Just Say No" And Can't.

Let's face it. Catchy slogans alone aren't going to solve too many drug abuse problems. It requires hard work and plenty of understanding. We hit upon this successful combination over 19 years ago. And it's been helping people get off drugs and on with their lives ever since. So if you or someone you care about can't "just say no" give us a call at 212-247-4920. Our treatment programs can help.

ACI
500 West 57th Street,
New York, N.Y. 10019

ACI is a fully licensed and accredited private facility.

ACI, 1988

▶ *Metropolitan Life Insurance, 1988*

NO MUMBO JUMBO FROM MET LIFE.

When you get insurance and financial services from Met Life, your Met Life Rep
explains things clearly, right up front, so you know what you're getting.
For more information, call your Met Life Rep, or 1-800-MET-2677.

GET MET. IT PAYS.

 **Metropolitan Life**
AND AFFILIATED COMPANIES

The hands outlined below are of average size. Yours probably aren't a perfect match.

That's why we don't design IBM products for "average" people of "average" size. Rather, we design them to be flexible so they can contribute to the comfort and productivity of all the individuals who use them.

We make display screens that tilt and swivel.

We also make keyboards that can be angled as you wish and moved around your work area. IBM office furniture flexes and extends just as your body does.

We also make sure our products fit the job they have to do.

For example, IBM makes a wide selection of displays and keyboards: some used in offices, others at supermarket checkouts, in cash-dispensing machines or at airline ticket counters. Each must satisfy the demands of its work environment. Will people use it while sitting or standing? From what distance will people view it? What will the prevailing light source be? How many characters will be displayed?

Accommodating both the diversity of the human form and the kinds of work humans do is the job of IBM human factors specialists.

What difference does that make in an IBM product?

Just wait till you get your hands on one. **IBM**

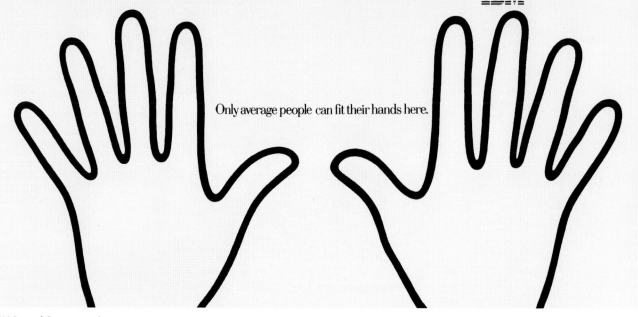

Only average people can fit their hands here.

IBM Personal Computers, 1984

There are rules for driving a computer, too.

Everyone knows that the rules of the road have to be taken seriously. So do the rules for using a computer.

Two of those rules are basic:

Everyone who uses a computer has a responsibility for the security of the information in that machine. No one who uses a computer has the right to violate anyone else's security.

To help people keep to those rules, we at IBM have developed a wide range of security systems.

For instance, IBM computers can require identification in any number of ways, including passwords, keys and magnetic

ID cards. Encryption devices can turn information into codes that are virtually impossible to crack.

But good security requires something from everyone involved with information systems.

Both the suppliers and users of computers, software and telecommunications have a responsibility to help ensure that such information systems are used conscientiously, and with the understanding that other people depend on these systems too.

Because when it comes to keeping information secure, each one of us is in the driver's seat. **IBM**

IBM Personal Computers, 1984

WITH IBM PC AT THE OFFICE AND PC*jr* AT YOUR HOUSE, YOU CAN TAKE WORK HOME ON YOUR LITTLE FINGER.

Many business people already know about the IBM® Personal Computer family.

Many are now hearing about its new member, the IBM PC*jr*.

And some have already discovered how PC and PC*jr* can work together.

THE JOY OF PERSONAL COMMUTING

PC*jr* bears a strong resemblance to the rest of the family.

If you know how to operate PC or PC/XT, you can operate PC*jr* easily. If you have programs for PC or PC/XT, you'll find many of them will run on PC*jr*.

Now, much of what you start at the office, you can finish at home, and vice versa.

And while you're at the office, your family will find plenty to do with PC*jr*.

THE BRIGHT LITTLE FAMILY ADDITION THAT CAN GROW UP FAST

PC*jr* is a powerful tool for modern times. With easy-to-follow new IBM Personal Computer programs, and with options like a printer and an internal modem for telecommunications, it can handle a great variety of jobs.

Children can learn new ways of learning, and make short work of homework. Adults can keep track of household expenses, write letters, file tax data, plug into information networks. And everyone can enjoy challenging new cartridge games.

IBM designed PC*jr* with lots of bright ideas to make computing easier.

The "Freeboard"—a keyboard that doesn't need a connecting cord—is easy to get comfortable with.

Built-in picture instructions can help the first-time user get started.

Diskette-drive systems include a program that allows users to explore computer fundamentals at their own pace. And to get PC*jr* up and running from the very first day, a sample diskette with eleven useful mini-programs is also included.

HOME ECONOMICS: IBM DISKETTE COMPUTING FOR ABOUT $1300

PC*jr* is the most affordable of the IBM personal computers. A diskette-drive model with a 128KB user memory is about $1300. An expandable 64KB cassette/cartridge model is about $700. (Prices apply at IBM Product Centers. Prices may vary at other stores.)

For a demonstration, visit an authorized IBM PC*jr* dealer or an IBM Product Center. And you can find the store nearest you with your little finger. Just dial 1-800-IBM-PCJR. In Alaska and Hawaii, 1-800-447-0890.

IBM Personal Computers, 1984

If you want to be in pictures,

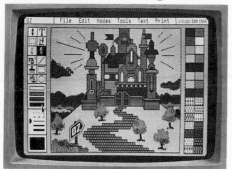

it's more fun in color.

Follow the yellow brick road. It sounds easy enough. But try "painting" on most computers and you'll have to settle for black-and-white pavement.

That's why IBM has just introduced PC*jr* ColorPaint—a $99* cartridge program that lets you paint with PC*jr*. In living, sparkling color.

It's sophisticated, yet extremely easy to use. (It works with a friendly little mouse!) So you can sit right down and paint just about anything you can think. Whether you're an artist or an accountant.

With PC*jr* ColorPaint, you can work with 16 colors—4 at a time—over 2,700 combinations of colors altogether. And there are all kinds of shortcuts to help you put together lines, shapes, patterns, even different size and style lettering.

Which makes it easy to draw and paint illustrations, charts, graphs, diagrams, whatever. For serious business. Or just a bit of funny business.

Of course, PC*jr* ColorPaint is only one program in a library of software that's growing by leaps and bounds.

PC*jr* now runs over a thousand of the best diskette programs that run on the IBM PC. Plus powerful new cartridge programs, like Lotus 1-2-3™ (available this fall) and Managing Your Money™ by financial expert Andrew Tobias.

And for all of its power, it costs less than $1,000*, without monitor.

PC*jr* and PC*jr* ColorPaint are both available now at authorized IBM PC*jr* dealers and IBM Product Centers.

Go see how well they work together. And draw your own conclusions.

For the name of the store nearest you, call 1-800-IBM-PCJR. In Alaska and Hawaii, call 1-800-447-0890.

More computer for your money.	
See how PC*jr* compares with other computers at its price.	
Memory	**Software**
User Memory (RAM): 128KB (expandable to 512KB) Permanent Memory (ROM): 64KB	Runs over 1,000 programs written for the IBM PC Runs both diskette and cartridge programs
Diskette Drive Double-sided, double density Capacity: 360KB	**Display** 40- and 80-column Resolution: 4-color 640 x 200, 16-color 320 x 200
Processor 16-bit 8088	**Expandability** Open architecture Optional 128KB Memory Expansion Attachment(s) 13 ports for add-ons, including built-in serial interface
Keyboard Typewriter style Detached, cordless	
Warranty 1-year limited warranty	

IBM PC*jr*
Growing by leaps and bounds.

*IBM Product Center prices. Computer price does not include monitor.
†Available from manufacturers other than IBM.
1-2-3 and Lotus are trademarks of Lotus Development Corporation.
Managing Your Money is a trademark of MECA.*

IBM Personal Computers, 1984

Why you should buy an Apple II-something instead of an IBM PC-anything.

Apple announces a breakthrough of incredible proportions.

The new Apple IIc Personal Computer.

It's 12" x 11½" x 2½."

It weighs less than 8 pounds. And costs less than $1,300.

Yet what it can do is all out of proportion to these proportions.

Because it's a direct descendant of the world's most popular computer, the Apple IIe.

It can run over 10,000 different programs. For business. For education. Or just for fun.

And it can do all that right out of the box.

The Apple IIc comes complete with everything you need to start computing. Including a free 4-diskette course to teach you how. An RF modulator that lets you use your TV as a monitor. And a gaggle of built-in features that cost extra on less senior machines:

128K of internal memory—twice the power of computers twice its size.

A built-in disk drive that could cost $400 if it weren't.

And built-in connections that let you add printers, phone modems and an extra disk drive without adding $150 goodies called "interface cards."

Two views of the IIc, shown here with its perfect match—the IIc 9" Monitor.

You can also plug in an AppleMouse—that little device that lets you tell a computer what you want simply by pointing.

In living color—SubLogic's Flight Simulator II. AppleWorks 3-in-1 advanced business software. MousePaint can draw out your artistic talents.

With 80-character capabilities, it can show you more than smaller-minded computers.

With 16 ultra high-resolution colors, it can bring a presentation to life—whether it's a quarterly report or a geography lesson.

In fact, the Apple IIc can run more educational and business software than any other computer save one: the Apple IIe.

Speaking of which, the Apple IIc is on speaking terms with the entire Apple II family of computers and accessories.

Including its very own Scribe Printer—Apple's first full-color text and graphics print-on-anything printer for under $300.

Small as it is, the Apple IIc is very easy to find—at over 3,000 authorized Apple dealers world-wide. So come in and get your hands on one.

You'll find it's a lot bigger than it looks.

*Don't asterisks make you suspicious as all get out? Well, all this one means is that the IIc alone weighs 7.5 pounds. The power pack, monitor, an extra disk drive, a printer and several bricks will make the IIc weigh more. Our lawyers were concerned that you might not be able to figure this out for yourself. **The FTC is concerned about price-fixing. So this is only a Suggested Retail Price. You can pay more if you really want to. Or less. © 1984 Apple Computer, Inc. Apple, the Apple logo and MousePaint are trademarks of Apple Computer, Inc. For an authorized Apple dealer nearest you, call (800) 538-9696. In Canada, call (800) 268-7796 or (800) 268-7637.*

Apple IIc Computers, 1984

---

10 reasons to buy an Apple IIc.

The newest member of the Apple II family has its own reasons for being.

It can run more software than any other personal computer in the world, save one—the Apple IIe.

But it offers some advantages the Apple IIe doesn't. And a whole passel of advantages the IBM PCjr can't touch.

For starters, it comes with everything you need to start computing, including a free 4-diskette course to teach you how—the most comprehensive how-to tutorial available with any personal computer.

Which makes it the most perfect computer for most of the people most of the time.

1) Expandability Theory 202

While the IIe has open-ended expandability, the IIc has *built-in* expandability—it's a complete computer solution.

The most popular interfaces are already built into the machine. So you can simply plug in a printer, an extra disk drive, a modem—in fact, any of the peripherals almost anyone would want—without adding interface cards.

(Not to alarm you, but adding interface cards does require some skill—if you do it wrong you could blow up your shiny new computer and perhaps ruin your carpet.)

And since interface cards can cost up to $200 each, that can save you up to $550 on the cost of a fully configured system.

2) 100% more brainpower.

The Apple IIc has 128K of internal memory—or twice the power of the basic Apple IIe system.

And while you can expand the IIe's memory all the way to four times that, 128K is more than enough power to handle sophisticated integrated business software like AppleWorks.

3) The drive within.

The Apple IIc comes with a built-in disk drive. Which would cost over $400 if it weren't.

But there's nothing to hook-up or connect—the IIc comes ready to run.

Built-in ports for making family connections.

Disk drives, as you may or may not know, are the most vulnerable components of any computer system. So it's nice to know that the IIc's is as close to fail-safe as a drive can be. It's a half-high version of one of the most reliable drives in the world—the Apple Disk II.

4) The drive without.

And you can easily add a second IIc disk drive. In tandem with its built-in drive, an external drive doubles the capability and capacity of the machine.

So you can run integrated business software like AppleWorks without doing the floppy disk shuffle.

And a 10-megabyte hard disk is available for the Apple IIc that can store reams and reams (20 of them, actually) of information.

An extra disk drive doubles the IIc's storage.

5) Other inner strengths.

To keep it compatible with the most software, the IIc has a built-in switchable 40/80 column display.

It also has a built-in switch that allows you to change the keyboard from its standard typewriter layout to DVORAK, an improved layout that lets you type 20-40% faster once you get used to it.

The IIc also features built-in color capability—it'll show you 16 ultra high resolution hues.

An Apple Modem gives the IIc phone privileges.

6) An improved School System.

The IIc is a more powerful, full-featured version of the most popular computer in schools —our very own Apple IIe.

Which means it works the same way as the computers your kids are probably using in school right now. And it can access the same huge library of educational software.

Everything from "Mother Goose Rhymes" to "Elementary Numerical Techniques for Ordinary Differential Equations."

An Apple Scribe can also make things perfectly clear in color.

7) The Hernia Factor.

At 7½ pounds, the IIc won't give you internal injuries when you move it from office to office or office to home. And its sleek, sexy body takes up just 12" by 11½" on a busy desktop.

Yet—thanks to its VLSI technology—it's still twice as powerful as computers twice its size.

*Not including monitor, power pack or jogger's bar bells.

8) An extended family.

The IIc can run a vast array of printers, plotters, modems and other accessories that are compatible with the Apple IIe.

But it also has its very own family of accessories that are aesthetically as well as technically compatible.

Including the Apple Scribe color/b&w text/graphics printer. An AppleMouse IIc that replaces complex keystroke commands with a simple point-and-click. And its standard matching 9" green phosphor monitor.

So buying an Apple IIc is just as easy as buying a matched component stereo system.

Independent manufacturers are extending the IIc's talents even further—with compatible accessories ranging from music synthesizers to home security systems.

The IIc carrying case for going on the road.

9) Travel Accessories.

The IIc can be a perfect travelling companion with a few simple additions. Like the first LCD Flat Panel Display** that can show you as much as a regular computer monitor—80 characters by 24 lines. And a carrying case with room for all of the above.

And a toothbrush.

10) And now, for our next number...

Unless you've been skimming this from back to front, you know by now that the IIc can run over 10,000 different programs.

But there are many new programs designed specifically to bring out the limitless talents of the IIc.

Like FlashCalc, a revised low-cost version of the popular spreadsheet program, VisiCalc.

And even as we write, famous software authors are writing new IIc programs. Including interactive educational software from leading textbook publishers.

Which means you'll never run out of things to do with an Apple IIc.

Or for that matter, reasons to buy one.

**Available early in 1985.

Apple IIc Computers, 1984 ◄ Apple IIc Computers, 1984

Introducing Automatic Art.

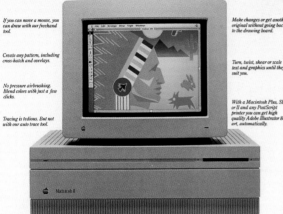

Adobe Illustrator, 1988

OK, what size would you like?

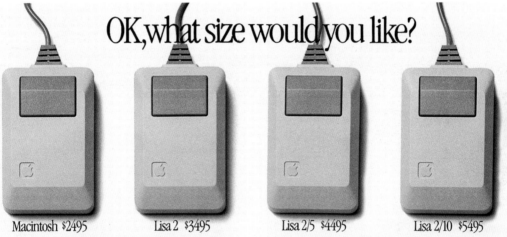

Apple Computers, 1984

In 1844, Morse established the first digital code, allowing the world to communicate in a universal language.

Samuel Morse's 1844 telegraph key – original constructed by Alfred Vail.

MANUFACTURING PLANTS: ANN ARBOR, MI • ATLANTA, GA • CONCORD, NH • CREEDMOOR, NC • MINNETONKA, MN • MARLTON, NJ • MORRISVILLE, NC   MORTON GROVE, IL • NASHVILLE, TN • RALEIGH, NC • RICHARDSON, TX • SAN DIEGO, CA • SANTA CLARA, CA • WEST PALM BEACH, FL

Today, Northern Telecom is doing more with that code than Morse ever dreamed possible.

Based on a binary code of dots and dashes, Morse's communication system was one the whole world could use. For years, it was the primary high-speed means for the transmission of information, and for personal and business messages.

From this earliest application of a digital system has emerged a new communications technology, with Northern Telecom leading the way as the world's largest manufacturer of fully digital tele-communications systems.

We're creating new, cost-effective networks that allow the communication of all forms of information—around the office, around the country, or around the world. They're responsive; they adapt to your requirements, not the other way around. They constantly evolve; they change with your changing needs and never become obsolete.

These Integrated Business Networks and Integrated Information Systems from Northern Telecom are fulfilling the great hope of Morse's invention: To make better, easier, efficient communications possible for everyone.

nt   northern telecom

*For further information write:
Northern Telecom Inc., Public Relations Dept.,
259 Cumberland Bend, Nashville, TN 37228.
Or call (615) 256-5900, Ext. 4264.
© Northern Telecom 1985*

Northern Telecom, 1985

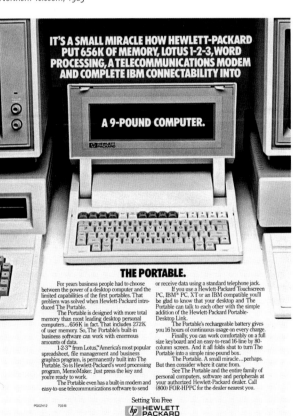

IT'S A SMALL MIRACLE HOW HEWLETT-PACKARD PUT 656K OF MEMORY, LOTUS 1-2-3, WORD PROCESSING, A TELECOMMUNICATIONS MODEM AND COMPLETE IBM CONNECTABILITY INTO

A 9-POUND COMPUTER.

THE PORTABLE.

For years business people had to choose between the power of a desktop computer and the limited capabilities of the first portables. That problem was solved when Hewlett-Packard introduced The Portable.

The Portable is designed with more total memory than most leading desktop personal computers...656K in fact. That includes 272K of user memory. So, The Portable's built-in business software can work with enormous amounts of data.

1-2-3™ from Lotus,™ America's most popular spreadsheet, file management and business graphics program, is permanently built into The Portable. So is Hewlett-Packard's word processing program, MemoMaker. Just press the key and you're ready to work.

The Portable even has a built-in modem and easy-to-use telecommunications software to send or receive data using a standard telephone jack.

If you use a Hewlett-Packard Touchscreen PC, IBM® PC, XT or an IBM compatible you'll be glad to know that your desktop and The Portable can talk to each other with the simple addition of the Hewlett-Packard Portable-Desktop Link.

The Portable's rechargeable battery gives you 16 hours of continuous usage on every charge.

Finally, you can work comfortably on a full size keyboard and an easy-to-read 16-line by 80-column screen. And it all folds shut to turn The Portable into a simple nine-pound box.

The Portable. A small miracle...perhaps. But then consider where it came from.

See The Portable and the entire family of personal computers, software and peripherals at your authorized Hewlett-Packard dealer. Call (800) FOR-HPPC for the dealer nearest you.

Setting You Free

hp HEWLETT PACKARD

PG02412   703 B

IBM is a registered trademark of International Business Machines Corporation. 1-2-3 and Lotus are trademarks of Lotus Development Corporation.

Hewlett-Packard Portable Computer, 1984

YOU'VE ALWAYS HAD A LOT OF COMPETITION. NOW YOU CAN HAVE AN UNFAIR ADVANTAGE.

Nobody ever said it was going to be easy. But it just got easier. Now there's Amiga.™ The first and only computer to give you a creative edge. Amiga makes you look better, sound better, work faster and more productively.

You can't buy a computer at any price that has all of Amiga's features. Nor can you find one that's easier to use. Amiga lets you point at symbols instead of learning complicated commands.

Amiga is friendly, but it's a powerhouse, too. It has twice the memory of Macintosh™ or IBM® PC. It costs less than either of them and can do everything they can do, better.

No other personal computer gives you over 4,000 colors, stereo sound and incredible dimension. Imagine the advantage of preparing business presentations with color graphics and sophisticated animation right on your computer.

Need to make creative use of your time? Amiga can do as many as four or five things at once in separate windows on the screen. Not just display them. Work on them. No other personal computer can.

Amiga is IBM-compatible, too. A simple piece of software teaches Amiga to emulate the IBM operating system, so you can run most IBM programs. You'll have instant access to the largest library of business software in the world, including favorites like Lotus® 1,2,3, and dBase®

And Amiga is endlessly expandable and adaptable. You can plug in printers (almost any kind), modems, musical keyboards, extra disk drives. You can even expand the memory to a whopping 8 megabytes with an optional expansion module.

See an Authorized Amiga Dealer near you. And don't wait. Your competition is gaining on you. Is that fair?

Amiga by Commodore.

Amiga's 4,096 colors give your business graphics a visible advantage.

Amiga makes telecommunications fast, easy and colorful.

Amiga's 4 channels of stereo give you a sound advantage.

✓AMIGA GIVES YOU A CREATIVE EDGE.

™ Amiga is a trademark of Commodore-Amiga, Inc. ™ Macintosh is a trademark licensed to Apple Computer, Inc. ® IBM is a registered trademark of International Business Machines, Inc. ® Lotus is a registered trademark of Lotus Development Corporation. ® dBase is a registered trademark of Ashton-Tate, Inc. ©1985, Commodore Electronics Limited.

Amiga Personal Computers, 1985   ▶ *Apple Computers, 1981*

175

Reddy Chirra improves his vision with an Apple.

Reddy is an optical engineer who's used to working for big companies and using big mainframes.

But when he started his own consulting business, he soon learned how costly mainframe time can be. So he bought himself a 48K Apple II Personal Computer.

And, like thousands of other engineers

and scientists, quickly learned the pleasures of cutting down on shared time and having his own tamper-proof data base.

His Apple can handle formulas with up to 80 variables and test parameters on 250 different optical glasses.

He can even use BASIC, FORTRAN, Pascal and Assembly languages.

And Apple's HI-RES graphics come in handy for design.

Reddy looked at other microcomputers, but chose Apple for its in-depth documentation, reliability and expandability.

You can get up to 64K RAM in an Apple II. Up to 128K RAM in our new Apple III. And there's a whole family of compatible peripherals, including an IEEE-488 bus for laboratory instrument control.

Visit your authorized Apple dealer to find out how far an Apple can go with scientific/technical applications.

It'll change the way you see things.

The personal computer.

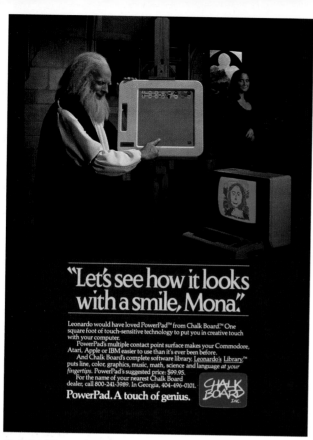

"Let's see how it looks with a smile, Mona."

Leonardo would have loved PowerPad™ from Chalk Board.™ One square foot of touch-sensitive technology to put you in creative touch with your computer.

PowerPad's multiple contact point surface makes your Commodore, Atari, Apple or IBM easier to use than it's ever been before.

And Chalk Board's complete software library, Leonardo's Library™ puts line, color, graphics, music, math, science and language *at your fingertips.* PowerPad's suggested price: $99.95.

For the name of your nearest Chalk Board dealer, call 800-241-3989. In Georgia, 404-496-0101.

PowerPad. A touch of genius.

CHALK BOARD INC.

Chalk Board PowerPad, 1983

"You Won't Find a Broader Line of Microcomputers Than Radio Shack's TRS-80."
— Isaac Asimov
Renowned Science
and Science-Fiction Author

From Computers That Fit In Your Pocket to Complete Business Systems, Radio Shack Has it All — at Affordable Prices!

"Radio Shack has taken the logical approach to computers." Instead of making one computer try to do everything, Radio Shack makes many computers. As Isaac Asimov notes, "You can pick just the model you need, without paying for features you may never use."

"One of these TRS-80's was designed with you in mind." If you're constantly on the move, you can choose from two pocket-size TRS-80® computers. Four personal desktop models are ideal for use at home or office. Three color computer versions let you play exciting computer games on your own TV. Our deluxe TRS-80 Model II business computer helps improve office efficiency at very low cost. And a new

state-of-the-art system will allow up to three people to use the same computer at the same time!

"A wide selection of ready-to-use software means I don't have to write programs unless I want to," adds Isaac. Off-the-shelf software is in stock at over 6,200 locations coast to coast. And Radio Shack offers leasing, training and service, too.

Stop by any Radio Shack for a hands-on demonstration. Or see the complete TRS-80 line at your nearest Radio Shack Computer Center or in the expanded computer department of selected Radio Shack stores and dealers nationwide.

Radio Shack
The biggest name in little computers™
A DIVISION OF TANDY CORPORATION

Send me a free TRS-80 Computer Catalog!
Mail to: Radio Shack, Dept 82-A-415
1300 One Tandy Center, Fort Worth, Texas 76102
NAME
ADDRESS
CITY_____ STATE_____ ZIP____

Radio Shack, 1982

How a dirty old sneaker made living rooms livable.

When 3M first developed fluorochemicals, they did everything we expected... and a bit more. The bonus came when some spilled onto a tennis shoe and tests showed that part of the shoe just *couldn't* be easily soiled. It was the birth of "Scotchgard" Protector...the world's finest soil and stain repellent for carpet and fabrics.

It was another case of 3M people stretching their minds. Sharing technologies, probing, exploring. To make small ideas big ones: to make big ideas better.

It's an environment we encourage at 3M. To promote innovation. To make our people eager and able to respond to your needs. And it works wonders.

Let us demonstrate. Tell us of a problem that you have. And then watch how quickly we respond. Because 3M hears you.

Call Terry Baker at 800-328-3234. In Minnesota call 612-736-6772.

3M hears you...

3M

3M, 1985

ADAM™
HELPS PREPARE KIDS FOR COLLEGE, AND HELPS PAY FOR IT TOO.

Buy an ADAM Family Computer System
between September 1 and December 31, 1984 and Coleco will provide
a $500 college scholarship for your child.

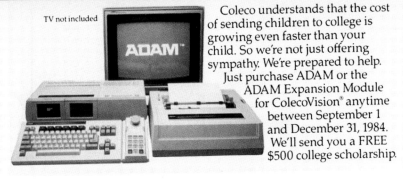

TV not included

Coleco understands that the cost of sending children to college is growing even faster than your child. So we're not just offering sympathy. We're prepared to help. Just purchase ADAM or the ADAM Expansion Module for ColecoVision® anytime between September 1 and December 31, 1984. We'll send you a FREE $500 college scholarship.

This scholarship offer applies to any individual child in your family who will be under 18 by September 1, 1985. Certain other restrictions apply, so see your store for details, or call 1-800-842-1225. © 1984 Coleco Industries Inc.

ADAM™
It's the smartest gift you can give your family.

Coleco ADAM Computer, 1984

IT RUNS THO PROGRAMS AS USANDS OF EASY AS 1-2-3.

If you have to plan, figure, write, organize, predict or communicate, the NCR PC 4 can help you do it easier and better.

Because the NCR PC is compatible with thousands of off-the-shelf programs available through your local PC dealers.

From the best-selling 1-2-3™ by the Lotus™ people to all sorts of other programs for business, education or just plain fun.

But besides getting more software to choose from you get more computer to work with.

For instance, you can get all the memory you need—all the way up to 640K.

An enhanced keyboard with separate cursor keys and separate numeric key pad that make it easier for you to work with spreadsheets and data base programs.

A special program called a RAM-DISK that acts as a super fast disk drive. It allows you to access information up to 15 times faster than a floppy disk.

And a rugged, compact cabinet that looks great on any desk.

Plus extras others charge extra for. Like built-in serial and parallel ports. Disk and video controller boards. Plus the standard operating system, GW™ BASIC and self-teaching programs to get you started.

The NCR PC is also compatible with industry standard hardware. So you can attach all kinds of fun options to it. Like a mouse, a modem, a printer, a hard disk, a graphics board, etc.

In short, the NCR PC is exactly the personal computer you'd expect

from a company that's been doing business with business for 100 years.

See your Authorized NCR Personal Computer Dealer. He'll be glad to show you how easily the NCR PC can make things easier for you.

For the name of your nearest dealer call toll-free 1-800-544-3333.*

A BETTER PERSONAL COMPUTER. IT'S EXACTLY WHAT YOU'D EXPECT FROM NCR.

© 1984 NCR Corporation
Lotus and 1-2-3 are trademarks of Lotus Development Corporation. GW-BASIC is a trademark of Microsoft Corporation.

*In Nebraska call 1-800-343-4300.

NCR Personal Computers, 1984

Introducing the Sinclair ZX81.

If you're ever going to buy a personal computer, now is the time to do it.

The Sinclair ZX81 is the most powerful, yet easy-to-use computer ever offered for anywhere near the price: only $149.95* completely assembled.

Don't let the price fool you. The ZX81 has just about everything you could ask for in a personal computer.

A breakthrough in personal computers.

The ZX81 is a major advance over the original Sinclair ZX80—the first personal computer to break the price barrier at $200.

In fact, the ZX81's 8K extended BASIC offers features found only on computers costing two or three times as much.

Just look at what you get:
- Continuous display, including moving graphics

THE $149.95 PERSONAL COMPUTER.

- Multi-dimensional string and numerical arrays
- Mathematical and scientific functions accurate to 8 decimal places
- Unique one-touch entry of key words like PRINT, RUN and LIST
- Automatic syntax error detection and easy editing
- Randomize function useful for both games and serious applications
- Built-in interface for ZX printer
- 1K of memory expandable to 16K
- 164-page programming guide and operating manual

The ZX81 is also very convenient to use. It hooks up to any television set to produce a clear 32-column by 24-line display. It comes with a comprehensive 164-page programming guide and operating manual designed for both beginners and experienced computer users. And you can use a regular cassette recorder to store and recall programs by name.

Order at no risk.*

We'll give you 10 days to try out the ZX81. If you're not completely satisfied, just return it to Sinclair Research and we'll give you a full refund.

And if you have a problem with your ZX81, send it to Sinclair Research within 90 days and we'll repair or replace it at no charge.

Introducing the ZX81 kit.

If you really want to save money, and you enjoy building electronic kits, you can order the ZX81 in kit form for the incredible price of just $99.95.* It's the same, full-featured computer, only you put it together yourself. We'll send complete, easy-to-follow instructions on how you can assemble your ZX81 in just a few hours. All you have to supply is the soldering iron.

A leader in microelectronics.

The ZX81 represents the latest technology in microelectronics. More than 10,000 are sold every week. In fact, the ZX81 is the fastest selling personal computer in the world.

We urge you to place your order for the ZX81 today.

To order.

To order, simply call toll free. Or use the coupon below. Remember, you can try it for 10 days at no risk.** The sooner you order, the sooner you can start enjoying your own computer.

Call toll free 800-543-3000.

Ask for operator #509. In Ohio call: 800-582-1364; in Canada call: 513-729-4300. Ask for operator #509. Phones open

24 hours a day, 7 days a week. Have your MasterCard or VISA ready.

These numbers are for orders only. If you just want information, please write: Sinclair Research Ltd., 2 Sinclair Plaza, Nashua, NH 03061.
*Plus shipping and handling. Price includes connectors for TV and cassette, AC adaptor, and FREE manual.
**Does not apply to ZX81 kits.

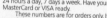

NEW SOFTWARE: Sinclair has published pre-recorded programs on cassettes for your ZX81. We're constantly coming out with new programs, so we'll send you our latest software catalog with your computer.

ZX PRINTER: The Sinclair ZX Printer will work with your ZX81. It will be available in the near future and will cost less than $100.

16K MEMORY MODULE: Like any powerful, full fledged computer, the ZX81 is expandable. Sinclair's 16K memory module plugs right onto the back of your ZX81. Cost is $99.95, plus shipping and handling.

sinclair

To order call toll free: 800-543-3000

Ad Code	06SA	Price*	Qty.	Amount
ZX81		$149.95		
ZX81 Kit		99.95		
16K Memory Module		99.95		
Shipping and Handling		4.95		$4.95
			TOTAL	

MAIL TO: Sinclair Research Ltd.,
One Sinclair Plaza, Nashua, NH 03061.

Name
Address
City_____ State_____ Zip_____
*U.S. dollars

Sinclair ZX81, 1982

The Texas Instruments Home Computer gives you a tutor, an accountant, a librarian, a file clerk and a pro football team in your own home.

Texas Instruments, 1980

"I love my new Panasonic. I designed it myself."

IT'S THE MODULAR OFFICE TYPEWRITER.

"I just got two things that changed my career for the better. A Panasonic® Modular Electronic Typewriter, and a promotion. Which came first? My Panasonic.

"Modularity means you select the features you want. I chose a large 40-character display to help me catch my typos, text editing features that make changes a snap, and the optional SpellScan Dictionary. It even has a built-in disk drive for unlimited memory. Exactly what I need to make my work easier.

"Panasonic Modular Electronic Typewriters offer over 1,000 different variations. If I keep moving ahead the way I intend to...I'll be using a lot of them!"

Call 1(800)255-2550 to find out how the Panasonic Modular Office Typewriter can help make *your* work easier. You'll agree: **THE EASIER, THE BETTER.**

I have designs on the new Panasonic Modular Typewriter.
☐ Please send the details to my office.
☐ Please have a dealer call to arrange a demonstration.

Name_____
Company Name_____
Address_____
City_____ State_____ Zip_____
Phone (   )_____

Panasonic Industrial Company,
1909 East Cornell, Peoria, IL 61604.
7CSM96

Panasonic
Office Automation

Panasonic Typewriters, 1986

COMMODORE MAKES SOFTWARE FOR EVERY MEMBER OF THE FAMILY.

ALMOST.

Commodore makes software for uncles, cousins, aunts who teach, nieces, nephews, brothers, sisters preparing for exams, fathers, mothers and brothers-in-law in roofing and tiling.

You see, Commodore makes software for fun, profit, homework, housework and office work.

Our Easy-Calc (upper left) is an electronic spreadsheet that's 63 columns x 254 rows with graphics and bar charting. And even with color options.

Fish Metic™ (upper right) is an educational math program in a game format. With our Manager program (lower left), you get a sophisticated database system with four built-in filing applications. Or you can design your own.

Why, in the lower right hand corner, there's even a...oh, we don't make that one yet.

But we're working on it. Incidentally, we also make the perfect place to use all these software programs (except the last one): the all purpose Commodore 64,™ the world's best selling computer.

COMMODORE 64

IT'S NOT HOW LITTLE IT COSTS, IT'S HOW MUCH YOU GET.

Commodore 64, 1984

Bound for glory.

The Epson® Line has a printer for all reasons.

Epson is the best-selling name in printers for small computers the world has ever seen.

Because we make the right printer for virtually every computer. And every job.

Something for everybody.
Our reliable, affordable RX™ Series printers, for instance, are perfect for the small business or home user. Our FX-80™ and wide-carriage FX-100™ provide all the speed, graphics capability and features anyone could ask

for. And our new LQ-1500™ is an astonishing breakthrough for business —it switches effortlessly between letter quality and high speed draft printing.

What's more, any printer you buy in the U.S. with the Epson name on it is guaranteed for a full year. Which is four times longer than the guarantee on most printers.

Get on board.
No matter what kind of computer you own, or what job you intend for it, your printer should be an Epson.

Because we build a better printer, price it fairly, guarantee it longer, and give you the one thing you don't always get from a printer company.

A choice.

Number one. And built like it.

EPSON
EPSON AMERICA, INC.

3415 Kashiwa Street, Torrance, California 90505 • Call (800) 421-5426 for the Epson dealer in your area. In California call (213) 539-9140.

This man has forgotten his computer system.

Deep at work as he is, the man behind this hand is oblivious to everything but his interactive artwork. His medium is Scitex's Response system, the first to prepare images by computer for color printing plates. The operator thinks of it as a movable window which lets his stylus through to paint and reshape, alter contrasts and colors, and generate color pages with text. For the printing industry worldwide, Response systems give better color and detail, in less time, than conceivable before.

This advertisement developed, like others in this magazine, as 20 megabytes in the memory of a Response system.

In America, Europe, and Japan, the talent to see through equipment into processes is common to operators of the Response. At Scitex in Israel, where Response systems are developed, the talent to see through processes into systems is the common factor. Here north of Tel Aviv, scientists whose backgrounds range from electro-optics to real-time software, and span many countries, have united to win leadership in color image processing with a product so responsive it can seem transparent.

For more information:
Scitex Corporation – P.O.B 330,
Herzlia B 46 103, Israel

scitex

Scitex Corporation, 1981

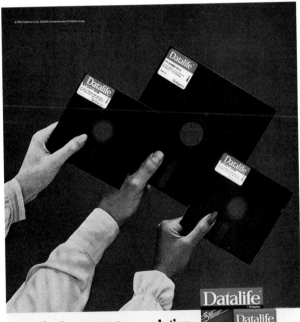

Datalife

To win the computer revolution, you need the right ammunition.

The computer revolution is changing the way we do so many things including the way we make mistakes.

But many computer errors aren't really the computer's fault. Often, it's the flexible disk that's become weak or worn out.

Problems like that won't happen if you use Datalife™ flexible disks. They're certified 100% error free and backed by a 5-year warranty, which means the information you put on one stays put.

So, if you're part of the computer revolution, make sure you always come out a winner. Use Datalife by Verbatim, the world's leading producer of flexible disks.

For your nearest Verbatim dealer, call toll-free 800-538-1793; in California or outside the U.S., call collect (408) 737-7771.

Epson Printers, 1984 ◄ *Datalife, 1983*

"Son, that's where the Statue of Liberty used to be."

Let's make sure this never happens. With our help, this 99-year-old lady can live forever. Please send what you can to: The Statue of Liberty/Ellis Island Foundation, P.O. Box 1992, Dept. F, New York, NY 10008.

This advertisement created as a public service by Saatchi & Saatchi Compton Inc.

Without us, the home of free speech could lose the power of speech.

In the communications industry, a leading buzzword for the future is fiber optics. At NYNEX, it's a word for yesterday. Because NYNEX has 50,000 miles of these hair-thin fibers in place now.

In the most information-hungry communities in the country: Boston, New York, and their surrounding areas.

It's one of the world's largest lightwave installations. It transmits calls, data, and saves space for the future in congested tunnels.

Water can't harm it. And neither can extreme temperatures.

In short, it's a network tough enough to make sure the home of free speech never loses the power of speech. It's what you get when you team New England determination with New York foresight.

NYNEX is the parent company of New York Telephone and New England Telephone, plus subsidiaries that offer mobile services, directory publishing and business communication equipment.

For information, call (800) 441-1919. In Utah, call (800) 453-9000. Or write T. Parra, Dir. Investor Relations, NYNEX, Box 2945, NY, NY 10185.

Tough demands breed tough minds.

© NYNEX Corporation 1985

NYNEX

The Statue of Liberty/Ellis Island Foundation, 1985 ◄ NYNEX Telecom, 1985

ARE YOU MAN ENOUGH TO DRINK LESS THAN THE REST OF THE BOYS?

Some people think the more a man can drink, the more of a man he is. However, it usually works the other way around.

Men who drink to build up their egos, end up putting themselves down.

The guy who claims he can drink everyone under the table looks pretty low. Especially if he gets there.

The hero who thinks it's macho to drink like a fish is regarded by sensible people as an animal.

That's why we, the people who make and sell distilled spirits, urge you to use our products with common sense. If you choose to drink, drink responsibly.

A real man has the strength to say no when he's had enough.

Distilled Spirits Council of the U.S. (DISCUS), 1300 Pennsylvania Building, Washington, D.C. 20004

IT'S PEOPLE WHO GIVE DRINKING A BAD NAME.

Distilled Spirits Council of the U.S., 1980

If you want to quit smoking for good, see your doctor

New knowledge about the smoking habit

Two major factors in cigarette smoking have long been recognized—psychological and social factors. Now research has clearly revealed a third important link in the habit—*physical dependence on nicotine*, which slowly but surely develops in many smokers. When people first start smoking, their bodies must get used to the nicotine. After smoking becomes a habit, their bodies may *depend* on getting nicotine.

Why a total program approach is needed to break the habit

When smokers try to quit, the body often reacts to the withdrawal of nicotine. This can result in craving for tobacco, restlessness, irritability, anxiety, headaches, drowsiness, stomach upsets, and difficulty concentrating.

Because these effects can defeat even a strong willpower, your chances of quitting successfully are greater with a program that provides an alternative source of nicotine to help alleviate tobacco withdrawal while you concentrate on breaking the habit.

How your doctor and Merrell Dow can help you succeed

If you are determined enough to sustain a strong effort, your chances of breaking the smoking habit are better than ever. Now your doctor can provide a treatment to help control nicotine withdrawal symptoms, materials to help you overcome the psychological and social factors, plus valuable counseling and follow-up. Merrell Dow has conducted extensive research into the smoking problem and is providing a wide range of support to health professionals.

QUIT

Merrell Dow

Dedicated to improving the health of Americans

© 1985, Merrell Dow Pharmaceuticals Inc., Cincinnati, Ohio 45242-9553.

Merrell Dow, 1986

Do you want a cigarette? Or do you need the nicotine?

Take this test, then take it to your doctor.

Most smokers are addicted to nicotine. Are you one of them?

If you're like most smokers, you have a physical dependence on the nicotine you get from smoking. That means when you quit smoking, you deprive your body of the nicotine it's become dependent upon, which can start a whole series of unpleasant withdrawal symptoms. Nervousness, headache, dizziness, and stomach upset can become so severe that even the most determined quitters start smoking again.

To get the help you need to quit for good, see your doctor.

LAKESIDE PHARMACEUTICALS
Division of Merrell Dow Pharmaceuticals Inc.
Cincinnati, Ohio 45242-9553
Dedicated to a smoke-free America

Merrell Dow Pharmaceuticals, 1988

Answers to the most asked questions about cigarettes.

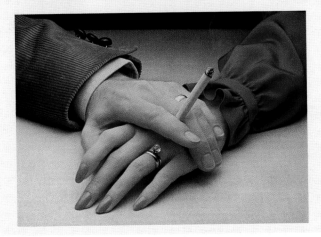

The Tobacco Institute, 1982

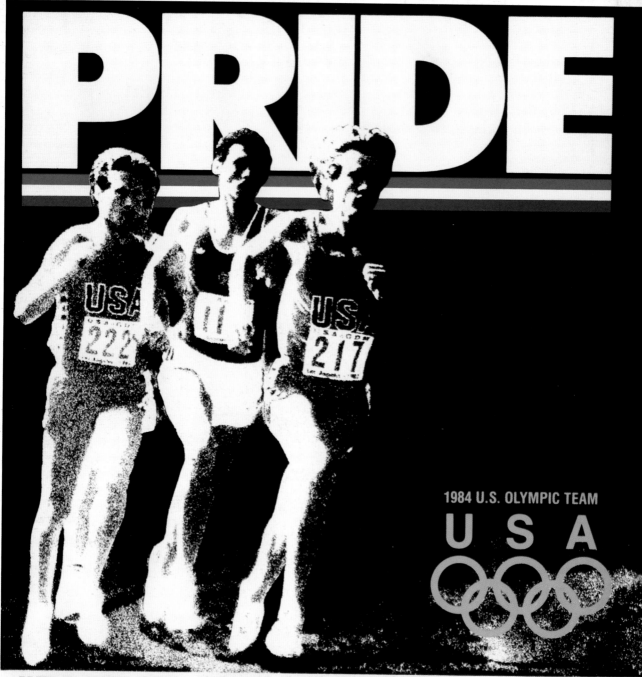

PRIDE

1984 U.S. OLYMPIC TEAM

USA

HELP THE RED, WHITE AND BLUE GO FOR THE GOLD

Only your dollars can help support an American tradition of excellence. It takes thousands of dollars and years of hard work to send each athlete to the Olympics. Your help is urgently needed NOW to help our 1984 U.S. Olympic team compete.

Be a part of the excitement. For every contribution of $10 or more, we'll send you an official United States Olympic team poster, button and bumper sticker.

Send contribution to:
UNITED STATES OLYMPIC COMMITTEE
P.O. Box 1984, Los Angeles, CA 90051

Support Our 1984
U.S. Olympic Team

USA

Poster (actual size 17"x22")

We need your support NOW!

Name _____

Address _____

City _____ State _____ Zip _____

Number of sets @ $10.00 ea. _____

Check enclosed for _____
Make checks payable to U.S.O.C.

Contributions to USOC are tax deductible. Prepared by CMCI, an official sponsor of the United States Olympic Committee.

Ad created courtesy of Dyer/Kahn, Los Angeles. Photography supplied by After-Image Stock Photo Company. Typography by Marchese Graphics.

United States Olympic Committee, 1984

▶ *Star Technologies, Inc., 1984*

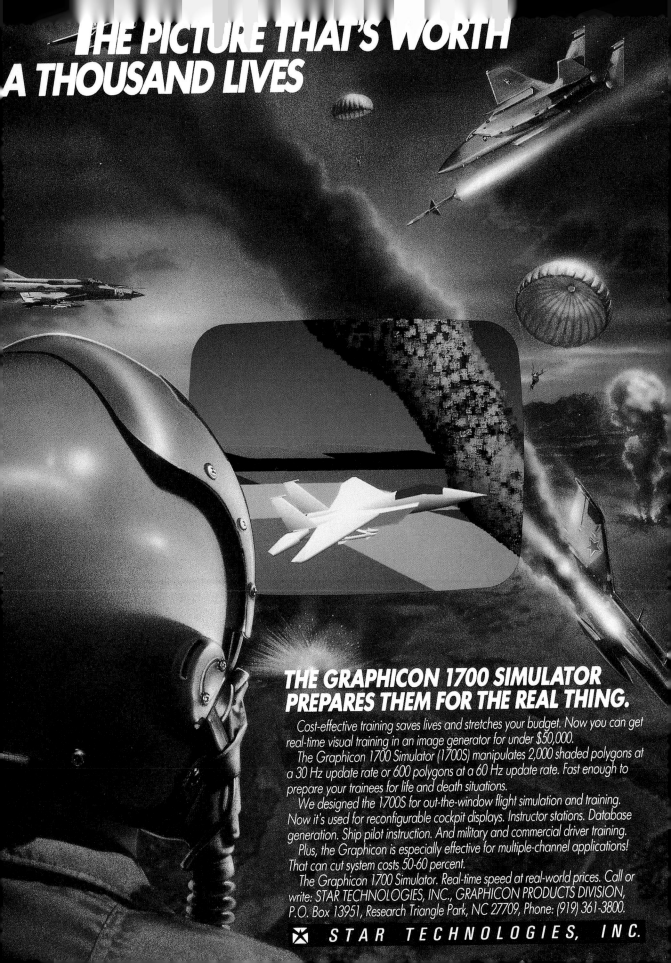

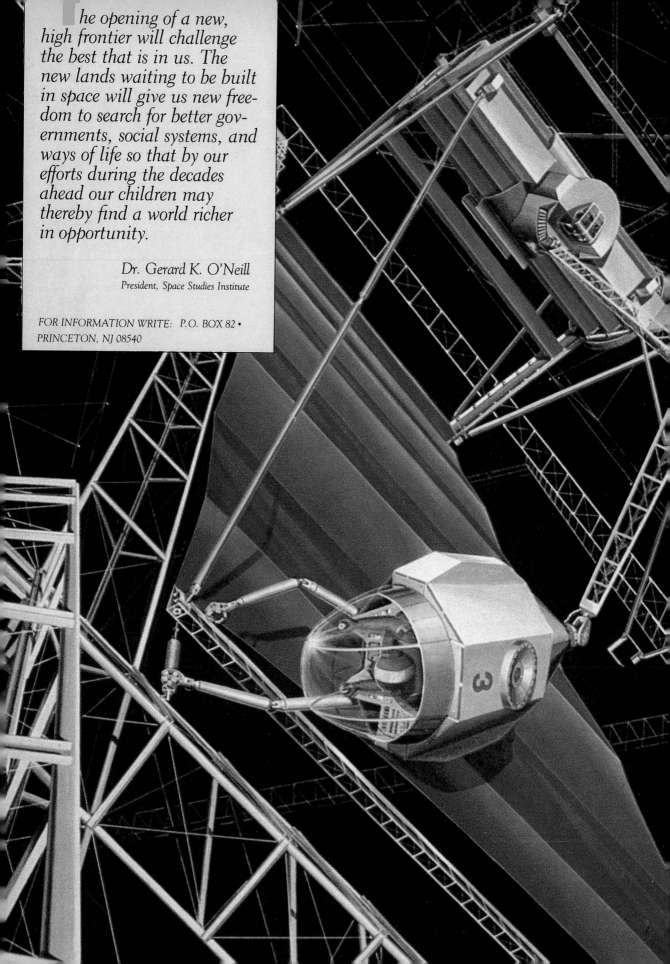

The opening of a new, high frontier will challenge the best that is in us. The new lands waiting to be built in space will give us new freedom to search for better governments, social systems, and ways of life so that by our efforts during the decades ahead our children may thereby find a world richer in opportunity.

Dr. Gerard K. O'Neill
President, Space Studies Institute

FOR INFORMATION WRITE: P.O. BOX 82 •
PRINCETON, NJ 08540

Will You Be Ready for the 21st Century?

Develop the high-tech skills that will be necessary to cope with tomorrow's world. Then share those skills with America's children. Support the *Young Astronauts.*™

For information on how you can prepare the younger generation for the 21st century, please write to:

YOUNG ASTRONAUT COUNCIL™
P.O. Box 65432 • Washington, D.C. 20036

Space Studies Institute, 1986 ◄ *Young Astronaut Council, 1986*

Army, 1984

Marines, 1984

Army, 1986

Marines, 1986

Northrop, 1984

Northrop, 1986

McDonnell Douglas, 1984

Harrier II, 1988

Left to right: NH 90, Airbus A340, JF-90/EFA, DFS-Kopernikus, MTFF (COLUMBUS), SÄNGER, ARIANE 5 with HERMES, PAH-2.

Nothing Is More Realistic Than Strong Visions.

In 1891 Otto Lilienthal made his first glider flights of up to 300 meters. But most of his contemporaries could only laugh at his "ridiculous attempts to fly." A few decades later, a 25-year-old American mailplane pilot climbed into his single-wing Ryan in May of 1927, taking off to stun the world with the first solo, non-stop flight from New York to Paris. Charles Lindbergh landed in Paris a gruelling 33 hours and 5,800 kilometers later. His record-breaking

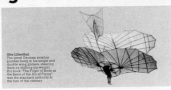

Otto Lilienthal. The great German aviation pioneer hung in his single and double wing gliders, steering them by shifting his weight. His book "The Flight of Birds as the Basis of the Art of Flying" was the standard authority at the turn of the century

flight was and is a sensation that is only comparable with the first manned moon landing 42 years later. Both extraordinary feats began with a vision. Visions which became reality by intelligence and determination.

Likewise, people could only shake their head at the first talk of a possible European cooperation in Aerospace. Visions like this did not fit into the times. And, still later, hardly anyone believed the possibility of an airplane being

built by four countries, and that it could ever go on to worldwide success.

Visions can only grow with long-term thought. Thought that goes beyond one's own lifetime, and certainly beyond the active span of a career.

MBB is a partner in international programs: A system company doing its part to make high-tech-world visions come true.

MBB Partner in international programs
Messerschmitt-Bölkow-Blohm GmbH

MBB, 1988

WHO DID WHAT?

(1) GTE (2) GRUMMAN (3) RCA (4) GE
(5) ITT (6) HUGHES (7) TRW (8) WESTINGHOUSE

Test your corporate I.Q. Look over the eight achievements pictured here and match each to the corporation responsible for it. Take your time; we'll wait.

Finished? O.K., let's review your answers. Who is building the first high-powered Direct Broadcast Satellite? Hughes? No, RCA.

Who supplied the video cameras, video equipment, and transmission services that sent back the stunning, live pictures from the Space Shuttle? Westinghouse? No, RCA.

Who developed and built AEGIS, the Navy's new seabome electronic defense system? Again, the answer, RCA. In fact, the correct answer to each of the questions is the same. RCA.

Surprised? If you're like most people, you aren't aware of what a major force RCA has become in many high-tech industries. Or that we invested over $200 million of our own money in R&D last year. A figure that compares with what many purely high-tech companies spend.

RCA ONE OF A KIND

If you'd like to learn more about RCA as a corporation, an investment or as a place to work, write to: This Is RCA, P.O. Box 91404, Indianapolis, Ind. 46291. We'll send you a few more surprises.

In electronics, communications and entertainment, RCA is one of a kind.

RCA Electronics, 1985

Because conditions are seldom ideal...

For more than 25 years, Control Data has been a leading supplier of reliable militarized information management systems and products you can rely on under all conditions. Ideal, or otherwise.

No matter what the environment, platform, or mission, Control Data's Government Systems Group has a unique ability for combining advanced technologies into systems for a wide range of defense-related applications. We have proved our ability to design and integrate information systems with an architecture flexible enough to meet the challenges of ever-changing environments.

Land-based systems. Control Data has designed and integrated the world's first digital fire control system for the Abrams main battle tank. Other land-based achievements include: CYBER computers and software used for the massive signal processing tasks in NORAD's Pave Paws Early Warning phased array radar network.

Airborne capabilities. Our Reconnaissance Management System (RMS) lets flight personnel study real-time information gathered from external sensors, then relay pertinent mission information to command centers. We've also designed the Navy's standard AN/AYK-14 airborne computer to be reconfigurable for a wider range of performance and memory capabilities.

Information at sea. Control Data's experience in integrating sophisticated data systems into even more sophisticated shipboard systems resulted in our being chosen to develop directed-fire systems such as the Phalanx Close-in Weapons System and the AEGIS Shipboard Air Defense. Our ASW capabilities include a fully-integrated system capable of handling sonobuoys or dipping sonar systems, or a mix of both—aboard ship or on airborne platforms.

The future. We intend to remain in the vanguard of advanced information management systems development. Regardless of the mission, environment or platform, experience is what makes Control Data's Government Systems Group one of the most reliable suppliers for systems, systems integration, hardware and software.

For information on any of these or other systems, call 612/853-5000. Or write Control Data's Government Systems Group, P.O. Box O, HQF500, Minneapolis, MN 55440.

Control Data, or your data will control you.

⊖⊕ CONTROL DATA

(Enter No. 57 on Inquiry Card for more data)

Control Data, 1988

Airbus Aircraftsmanship

Carbon fibre and composites in general signify state of the art materials to most people.

Yet Airbus has quietly become the acknowledged leader in their useful application in passenger aircraft production.

Our aircraftsmanship philosophy does not mean applying high-technology methods and materials simply for the sake of it. It means reducing weight, maintenance and holding down operating costs.

This realistic approach goes down well with our customers. And goes to prove we're a cut above the rest.

✈ AIRBUS INDUSTRIE

Airbus Industrie, 1989

NESP. It's the Navy's way of keeping its business among friends.

Suppose an American sub had just located hostile naval units. The last thing her captain would want would be to have his messages to other U.S. forces intercepted or jammed.

The Navy EHF Satcom Program (NESP), part of the MILSTAR joint-service program, was created to make secure and dependable communications a certainty.

Now, with Raytheon as prime contractor, NESP has reached the test stage. Ships and submarines are sending voice and teletype messages to each other and to a shore station

in San Diego, using AN/USC-38 (V) terminals developed and produced by Raytheon.

After testing is complete, these survivable terminals will be installed aboard hundreds of ships, submarines, and shore stations. At the same time, Raytheon will continue with its companion development of terminals for Air Force aircraft and ground stations.

Through its adherence to the fundamentals of EHF communications, computer technology, and systems management, Raytheon is helping make NESP a success.

For further information, write: Raytheon Company, Government Marketing, 141 Spring Street, Lexington, MA 02173.

NESP provides secure communications via satellite.

Raytheon
Where quality starts with fundamentals

Raytheon, 1988

Each SGT. YORK protects over ten times its own unit cost in other armored assets.

SGT. YORK is the only system with fire-on-the-move and all weather capabilities that can defeat the threat of maneuvering fixed-wing aircraft and stand-off helicopters in the forward battle area. It is the most effective air defense gun system in the world.

Every SGT. YORK unit meets demanding performance and reliability requirements and is backed by one of the most stringent warranties for any major weapon system.

SGT. YORK from Ford Aerospace — the first name in advanced air defense systems worldwide.

Ford

Ford Aerospace & Communications Corporation

Ford Sgt. York, 1984

And the winner is...

Zen for the Computer Age

Yes, the transition from DOS to Windows 2.0 and the wonders of floppy diskettes could bend the chakra of the early computer user to breaking point. But, thankfully, just as the New Age was hitting its stride, along came help in the form of Zen Master Rama (a.k.a. Frederick Lenz). Guiding yuppies (and their copious bank accounts) through an increasingly complex, computerized world to Enlightenment, his seminars promised freedom, self-control, balance, and power. The alleged detail he forgot to mention was that his cult let few members leave alive ... an ironic twist for a man who later died at his own hands.

Zen im Computer-Zeitalter

Ja, der Übergang von DOS auf Windows 2.0 und die Wunder der Floppy Disk haben dem Chakra des frühen EDV-Anwenders natürlich stark zu schaffen gemacht. Doch mit der neu aufkommenden Esoterik-Bewegung bot sich, Gott sei Dank, Hilfe in Gestalt von Zenmeister Rama alias Frederick Lenz. Seine Seminare, in denen Yuppies (mit ergiebigen Bankkonten) in der komplizierten, computerisierten Welt zur Erleuchtung geführt wurden, versprachen den Teilnehmern Freiheit, Selbstkontrolle, Ausgewogenheit und Macht. Leider vergaß die Anzeige zu erwähnen, dass nur wenige Mitglieder diese Sekte lebendig verließen – Ironie des Schicksals bei einem Mann, der später Selbstmord beging.

Zen à l'âge de l'ordinateur

Mais oui, le passage de DOS à Windows 2.0 et le miracle des disquettes pouvaient tordre le chakra des premiers utilisateurs d'ordinateur jusqu'à la cassure. Mais heureusement, au moment où le New Age arrivait en force, il apportait en même temps le remède sous la forme du maître zen Rama (alias Frederick Lenz). Il guidait les yuppies (et leurs comptes bancaires bien garnis) sur la voie de l'Illumination dans un monde à la technologie de plus en plus complexe, par des discours promettant la liberté, le contrôle de soi, l'équilibre et le pouvoir. Il oubliait de mentionner un petit détail : son culte laissait peu de membres quitter le groupe de leur vivant... Une ironie du destin pour un homme qui, plus tard, mettra fin à ses jours.

Zen en la era informática

Cierto, la transición del sistema operativo DOS a Windows 2.0 y las maravillas de los disquetes podían elevar el chakra de los primeros usuarios informáticos hasta límites insospechados. Por suerte, mientras la música *new age* ganaba terreno a pasos agigantados, vino a salvarnos el maestro zen Rama (alias Frederick Lenz). En sus seminarios guiaba a *yuppies* (y a sus copiosas cuentas bancarias) a través de un mundo cada vez más complejo e informatizado hacia la Revelación, con promesas de libertad, autocontrol, equilibrio y poder. El detalle que supuestamente se le olvidó mencionar es que su culto dejaría a pocos miembros con vida... Un giro irónico para un hombre que luego murió a sus propias manos.

コンピュータ世代の禅

そう、DOSからWindows 2.0への移行とフロッピーディスクの驚異が、初期のコンピュータユーザーのチャクラを極限までねじまげてしまった。しかし、ありがたいことに、新世代達は禅の指導者ラマ（別名はフレデリック・レンズ）の指導によって調子を取り戻していた。ますます複雑になりコンピュータ化する世界から、ヤッピー達（そして彼らのたくさんの銀行口座）を悟りへと導きながら、彼のセミナーは自由と、自己統制と、バランスと、力とを約束した。彼が言及し忘れたと言われている"ささいな事"は、彼のカルト教団はわずかなメンバーだけしか生かして残さないということ…後に彼自身の手により死んだ者にとっては反語的な隠し事であった。

THE STILL CENTER
OF THE TURNING WORLDS

There is a still center of Eternity. A place where all pasts, presents and futures meet. This intersecting point of knowledge and experience, pleasure and pain, mortality and immortality has been described and referred to in a variety of different ways by mystics, prophets and teachers who have experienced it.

Some have described it as God or Heaven. Others have referred to it as Nirvana or Tao. In Zen it is called Zen mind or Enlightenment.

While names, descriptions and methods for reaching the still center of being vary greatly, the ultimate worth of this awareness is agreed upon by all who have shared it. The experience of the still center of being brings freedom, self-control, balance and power to those who have attained their lives to it.

Zen is the study of the Ten Thousand States of Mind and of Enlightenment, the still center which lies beyond the Ten Thousand States of Mind. It is a highly personal study which brings clarity and purpose into the lives of those who practice it.

Zen Buddhist thought has had a profound influence upon Chinese and Japanese history and culture. A great deal of the current success of the Japanese corporate mind stems from the effect of centuries of Zen practice in Japan. Martial arts, dance, poetry, the tea ceremony and many other forms of personal, athletic and artistic expression have been given birth to by Zen mind.

Zen is a highly refined and artistic approach to the meaning of life. It isn't necessary to learn Oriental customs or to speak the Japanese language to successfully practice it. All that is required is an open mind, patience, a good sense of humor and an intense desire for self-improvement.

I have written a free booklet about Zen for the "computer age" called "Zen Mind and Enlightenment." In it I discuss Zen in more depth, and describe both contemporary and traditional methods I employ in teaching Zen at seminars and in private practice.

If you would like to learn more about Zen and the wonders of your own mind, call or write for this free booklet today.

Find the still center of your own being. Study Zen.

Zen Master Rama

Intensive Seminar In Zen Buddhist Meditation

WITH ZEN MASTER RAMA
Saturday, April 25, 1987
7:30 pm to 10:30 pm
Berklee Performance Center
136 Massachusetts Ave., Boston
Tickets $10 at the Door

Tickets available in advance at Berklee Box Office, all Ticketron Outlets, Out-of-Town (in Harvard Square), Strawberries Record Stores, Concertcharge (617) 497-1118, and Teletron (617) 720-3434

Please send me information about Rama Seminars ℗:

Name _____
Address _____
City _____
State _____ Zip _____

Zen Master Rama, 1987

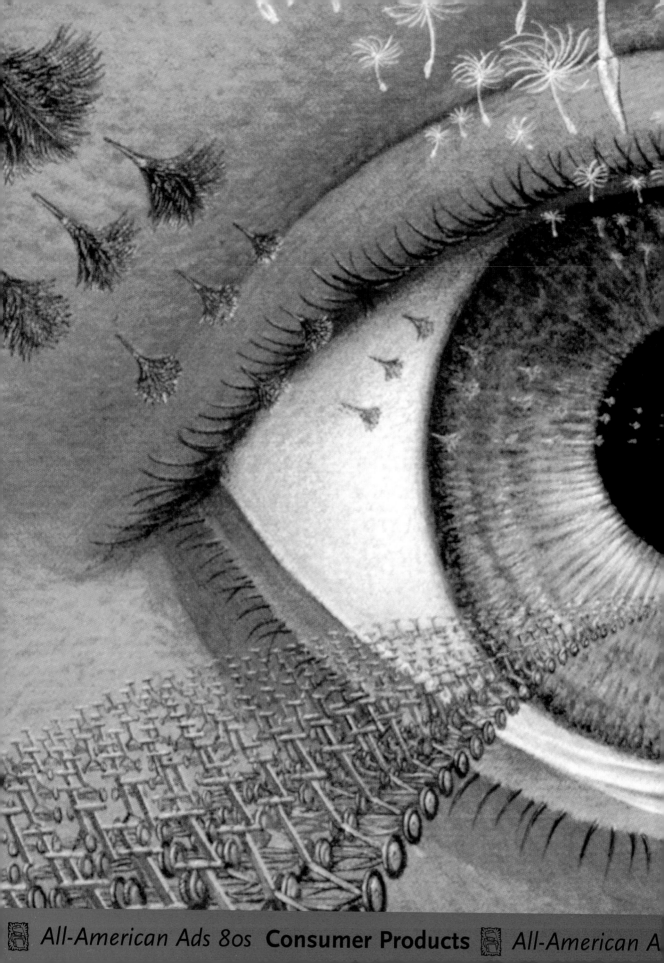

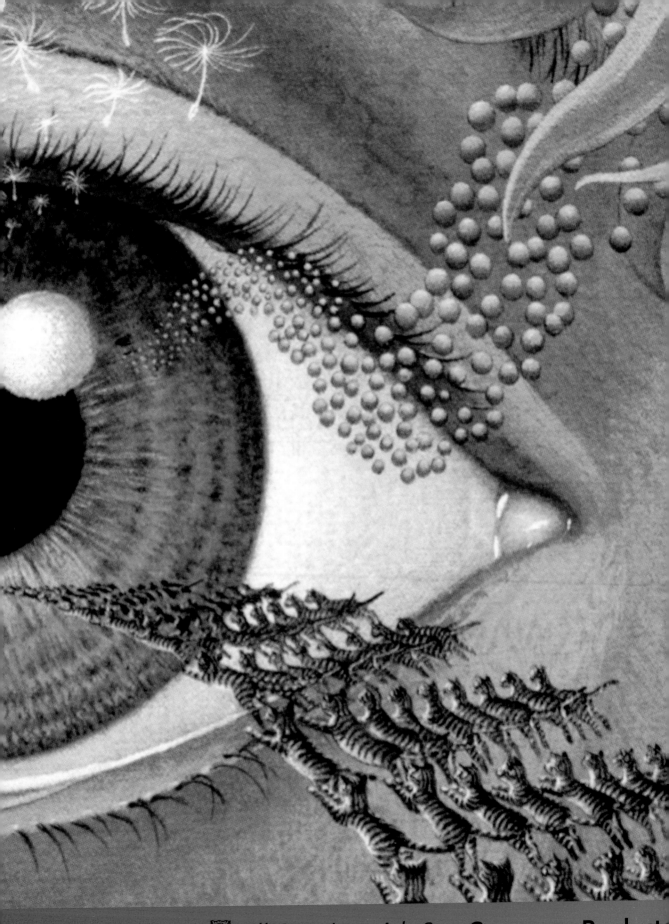

SWATCH® : STATE OF THE ART

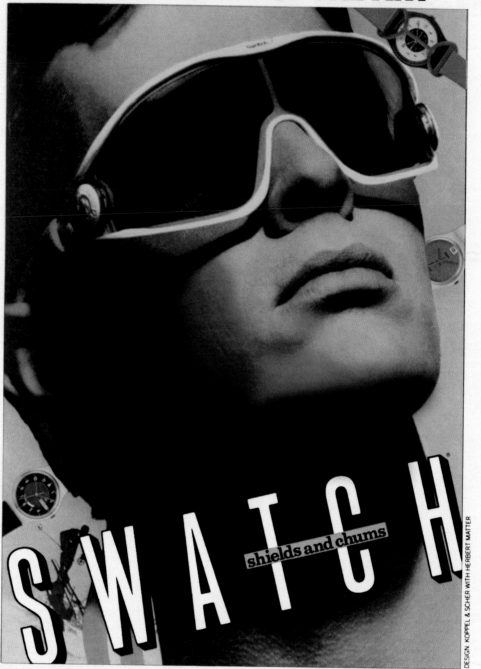

SWATCH shields and chums

DESIGN KOPPEL & SCHER WITH HERBERT MATTER

SWATCH SHIELDS · Innovative style and technology. Adjustable arms and temples for a perfect fit. Available in 10 great colors for both fashion and sport. Suggested retail $35.

SWATCH CHUMS · 100% Cotton sunglass retainers. Fun and functional, wear them casually around your neck or tightened up for action. Chums are the best friend your glasses will ever have. Suggested retail $5.

swatch✚
SWATCH WATCH, U S A INC
608 FIFTH AVE . SUITE 801
NEW YORK, N Y 10020

Available At **Robinson's**

OMEGA.
HEN YOU CAN HAVE
HATEVER YOU WANT.

Introducing The Omega Titanium.
A most remarkable blend of technology and craftsmanship. Its precis
Swiss quartz movement is encased in the space age metal Titanium.
So it's extremely light yet incredibly strong.
Water-resistant to 400 ft., the Titanium features 18K inlaid gold and
a scratch-resistant sapphire crystal.
To find out where you can acquire one, write us. We're at 301 East
57th Street, New York, N.Y. 10022.
Two floors above Rolls-Royce.

In Canada, write to: Omega Watch Company (Canada) Ltd./Ltée.,
70 Wynford Drive, Don Mills, Ontario M3C 1J9

Any true international traveller finds his Rolex invaluable.

Ever since 1937, Thor Heyerdahl has had a dream.

To find out if the ancient civilisations of Mexico, Peru, the Pacific Islands, Egypt and Mesopotamia could have had a common origin.

To prove that, long before the Europeans, the crossing of the world's three oceans could have been achieved.

In 1947, Heyerdahl set sail from the coast of Peru in the balsa log raft "Kon-Tiki." One hundred and one days later the "Kon-Tiki" made landfall in the Pacific Islands.

In 1970, Thor Heyerdahl's papyrus reed ship "Ra II" left Africa. Fifty-seven days later "Ra II" reached Barbados on the other side of the Atlantic.

During 1977-78, Heyerdahl built the reed ship "Tigris" in Iraq, and sailed it by way of Oman and Pakistan to the entrance of the Red Sea. Local war stopped further progress, but "Tigris" had shown that the three old-world civilisations of Sumer, the Indus Valley and Egypt could have communicated by sea.

"The oceans did not separate early

civilisations," says Heyerdahl. "They linked them together."

The success of Heyerdahl's expeditions is based on careful planning and strict accuracy in every detail.

"We have sailed precise replicas of the first ships built by early navigators," says Heyerdahl. "We have used their rigging and steering methods, survived on their food, and tested their simple navigation devices. But for accurate scientific plotting of our routes, and for obligatory radio contacts when entering modern ports and shipping channels, we needed what ancient man could do without: a thoroughly reliable, precisely accurate modern watch."

We are flattered to receive such a compliment especially from the world's number one international traveller.

The watches used by Thor Heyerdahl and his crew are made by Rolex.

ROLEX
of Geneva

Write for brochure. Rolex Watch, U.S.A., Inc., Dept.116H, Rolex Building, 665 Fifth Avenue, New York, NY 10022. World headquarters in Geneva. Other offices in Toronto and major cities around the world.

Rolex Watches, 1980

The new **TIMEX QUARTZ**

So accurate you may have to reset it only once this year. Thin, sleek, more beautiful than any watch you've owned before. Built and priced in the Timex tradition. 39 styles for men and women from $39.95 to $61.95, suggested retail prices.

TIMEX
We make technology beautiful.

Timex Watches, 1980

We make digital watches you don't have to watch out for.

The Casio Watersports

Time was, when most digital watches didn't dare go near the water. One dunk and they were junk.

Now Casio has changed all that, with a full line of men's and women's digitals that are water resistant. And when we say water resistant, we mean it. Our Watersports have been tested in considerable depth—to 50 meters (165 ft.) and more. So no matter how wet things get, they

won't put a damper on your fun.

Not only are our Watersports water resistant, they come in styles that are hard to resist. All have calendars; most come with chronograph displays. (Some even have alarms.) And of course, they all display the high quality and low price tags that Casio is known for.

Whichever of our Watersports you decide on, you can be sure, come hell or

high water, that you'll have a watch that can watch out for itself.

CASIO
Where miracles never cease

Casio, Inc. Timepiece Division: 15 Gardner Road, Fairfield, N.J. 07006 New Jersey (201) 575-7400, Los Angeles (213) 923-4564.

Casio Watches, 1982

Masterpieces of Technology Exclusively from Pulsar.

The One-Step Alarm

The world's easiest to use alarm watch. You set everything with the crown. Sport and dress models available from $85-150.

The 2001 Series
The world's first quartz watch powered by ordinary light. No battery required. Sport and dress models available from $95-165.

Pulsar
The world knows a great watch when it sees one.

Pulsar Watches, 1985　　　▶ *Digits Finger Watches, 1988*

Performing the art of self expression.

RADO
More Swiss buy Rado than
any other quality Swiss watch

Men's and ladies' Rado Anatom in 18 kt. solid gold with scratchproof sapphire crystal.
Convex shaped case hugs the wrist perfectly. Water-resistant to 150 ft.
and high quality Swiss quartz movement.

Petochi & Gorevic
FINE JEWELRY & ANTIQUES

635 Madison Avenue (corner 59th Street), New York, New York 10022 • (212) 832-9000
Petochi, 23 Piazza di Spagna, 2nd Floor, Rome • **Gorevic,** 660 Lexington Avenue, New York, New York 10022
• St. Maarten c/o La Romana

Petochi & Gorevic Watches, 1986

▶ *Ocean Pacific Watches, 1989*

AIR TIME

Analog Dial w/ Sweep-Second Hand •
LCD Display • 12-Hour AM/PM or
24-Hour International Time • Stop
Watch w/ Lap Feature • Day/Date
Function • Alarm w/ Chime • Lamp
Illumination • Programmable Bezel
• Black Oxidized Metal Finish
• Rustproof Brass Construction

PACIFIC

P.O. Box 2019, Tustin, CA 92680 800-672-3224

CONCEPT: SWATCH U.S.A., 1985 ■ ART DIRECTION: IRENE HILTPOLD ■ PHOTOGRAPHY: ERNST WIRZ ■ STYLING: DAWN CLEIS/MARIANNE LEBER

SWATCH – IT'S ABOUT TIME?

swatch®
PRODUCT DESIGNS © SWATCH WATCH USA, INC.

Swatch Watch, 1985

▶ *Swatch Watch, 1985*

IT'S TIME TO TRUST ME.

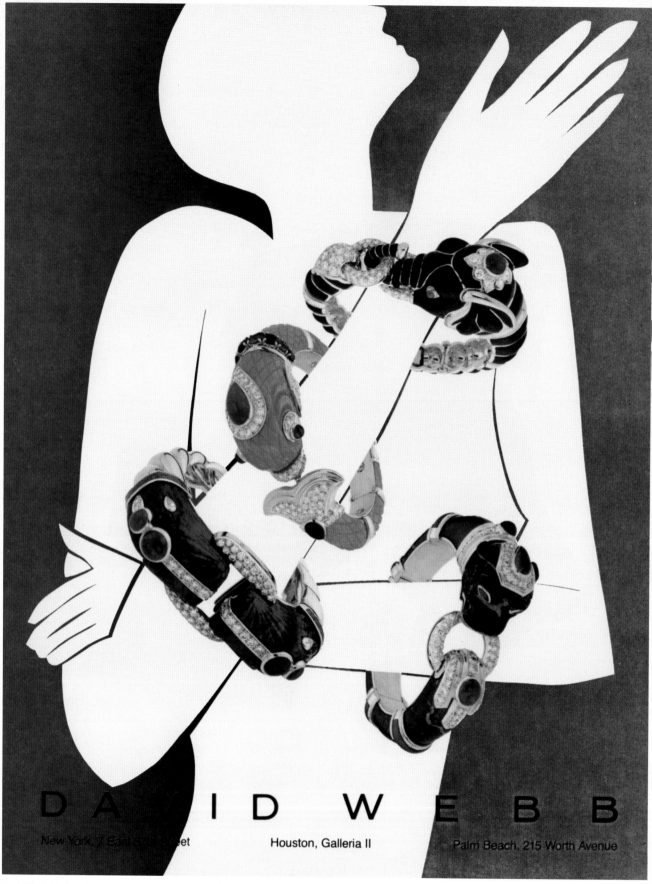

David Webb Jewelry, 1981

▸ *International Gold Corporation, 1984*

Gold.
Because I never want
her summer to end.

14K KARAT GOLD

Nothing else feels like real gold.

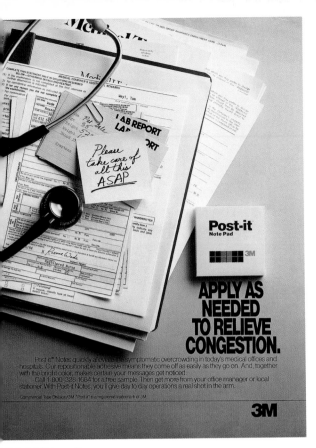

The Titanium Pen
Der Titanschreiber
Le Stylo en Titane
La Penna in Titanio
PORSCHE DESIGN

APPLY AS NEEDED TO RELIEVE CONGESTION.

Post-it™ Notes quickly alleviate the symptomatic overcrowding in today's medical offices and hospitals. Our repositionable adhesive means they come off as easily as they go on. And, together with the bright color, makes certain your messages get noticed.

Call 1-800-328-1684 for a free sample. Then get more from your office manager or local stationer. With Post-it Notes, you'll give day to day operations a real shot in the arm.

Commercial Tape Division/3M. "Post-it" is a registered trademark of 3M.

3M

3M Post-it Notes, 1984

Porsche Titanium Pen, 1984

The Gold Coins of Mexico

50 PESOS 37.5 GR ORO PURO 1821 1947

50 Peso "Centenario" Fineweight. 1.2057 troy ozs.

VEINTE PESOS GR ORO PURO

20 Peso "Azteca" Fineweight. .4823 troy ozs.

Once you know the story behind them, you'll know why so many Americans are purchasing them.

The Gold Coins of Mexico are official restrikes of the government of Mexico, minted by the Casa de Moneda de Mexico, the oldest mint in the western hemisphere, established in 1535. Exclusively minted for the Mexican Federal Reserve Bank, Banco de Mexico, The Gold Coins of Mexico have enjoyed a fine reputation throughout the world for many years.

Now, Americans who have made the decision to purchase gold coins have the opportunity to acquire The Gold Coins of Mexico in the United States at the following banks: Citibank, Swiss Bank Corporation and Republic National Bank of New York.

The Gold Coins of Mexico not only provide the convenience, portability and liquidity of owning gold in coin form, but they also offer more alternative choices for purchasers. Mexico's 50 peso gold piece, more commonly known as the "Centenario," is the heaviest of all high circulation gold bullion coins in the world—boasting a high gold content of 1.2057 troy ounces. The "Azteca," Mexico's 20 peso gold piece, features a .4823 troy ounce gold content for purchase on a small scale. A variety of Mexican gold coins of smaller denominations

ACTUAL SIZE

are also available.

Many people consider the value and purchasing power of gold as an alternative hedge against inflation. Of course, the decision to own gold is a highly personal one in which risks and advantages should be carefully considered in light of ones specific financial and investment goals. Since gold is a commodity, its value is subject to continual market fluctuations.

Over the years, The Gold Coins of Mexico have become among the most popular gold bullion coins in the world. Due to the careful craftsmanship of Casa de Moneda de Mexico and the wide distribution of these coins, you can usually avoid the cost and delay of determining their authenticity upon resale. As with all gold coins, your purchase price includes a premium above the then current market price of gold bullion to cover minting and distribution. Furthermore, purchases may be subject to state and local taxes.

Call any of the following toll-free numbers for up-to-the-minute prices. For additional literature, write: The Gold Coins of Mexico, Information Center, Grand Central Station, P.O. Box 1812, New York, N.Y. 10017.

THE GOLD COINS OF MEXICO

The Gold Coins of Mexico are exclusively supplied to:
Citibank, N.A. 800-223-1080   **Swiss Bank Corporation** 800-221-9406   **Republic National Bank of New York** 800-223-0840
N.Y. State call collect: 212-559-6041   N.Y. State call collect: 212-938-3929   N.Y. State call collect: 212-930-6338
The Gold Coins of Mexico are also available at coin dealers plus selected banks throughout the country.
The Gold Coins of Mexico is a Service Mark of Banco de Mexico, Mexico City.

Scripto Erasable Pens, 1984 ◄   The Gold Coins of Mexico, 1980

On Grandparents' Day, Spoil Them Rotten.

364 days a year, Grandparents have a grand old time spoiling the ones they love.

So it seems only fair that one day a year, the ones they love can spoil them back.

On Grandparents' Day, Sunday, September 13th. That's when you can send them a gift that not only makes their day special, but keeps on doing it for the rest of the year.

The Grandparents' Day Bouquet In A Frame by Teleflora. It arrives as a gift of fresh flowers nestled in a simulated carved oak frame container. Then later on, the container holds a plant, a 3x5 photograph and a whole bunch of memories.

The Grandparents' Day Bouquet is available for giving or sending anywhere in the U.S. Through one of 16,000 Teleflorists. Check the yellow pages for the one nearest you, or call toll-free 800-854-2003 or 800-522-1500 in California. Both extension 949.

And don't forget to order early. After all, this might be your only chance to give your grandparents the spoiling they deserve.

The Grandparents' Day Bouquet In A Frame By Teleflora

Teleflora, 1981

'The Grunt'

by Terry Jones

"I am an Infantryman . . .
A Grunt,
To so many, is the name . . ."
From "The Infantryman's Plead," folk poem,
Company C, 2d Battalion, 28th Infantry, Viet Nam.

"They struggled up the thin road to the helicopter
pad, tired but relieved, electric with anticipation,
looking forward to a promised four days turnaround
time in An Hoa before they beat the bush again.
Bagger, gaunt and hollow-eyed, but already starting
to unwind, walking with his sturdy yawing steps, his
rifle over one shoulder like a tramp's stick, held by
the barrel."

FIELDS OF FIRE
James Webb
Prentice Hall

10" in height,
in cold cast bronze
$250.00 plus $10 shipping
Public edition limited to
only 4500 worldwide

The American Print Gallery • 219 Steinwehr Ave., Gettysburg, PA 17325
America's foremost source of military art.
To Order, Call Toll Free: 1-800-448-1863
Send $2.00 for the latest full-color information.
Ask about our layaway plan.

The Grunt Figurine, 1989

RAPHAEL'S FINAL TRIUMPH

The most powerful portrait of
Christ by the genius of the
Renaissance. Now transformed
into hand-painted porcelain.

Commissioned in 1517 by Pope
Clement VII, it was the last and
most glorious achievement by
one of the greatest artists who
ever lived. A radiant portrait
of Christ rising to the sky.
Raphael's *Transfiguration.*
Now transformed into the
power of sculpture. To
capture the full depth
of Raphael's
divine vision.
Individually cast
in fine imported
porcelain. Hand-
painted in the rich
coloring of Raphael's
palette. And fired to
perfection to preserve
its spirit forever.

*In his final masterpiece,
Raphael most fully
reveals his inventive and
dramatic powers. The
original is still preserved
at the Vatican in Rome.*

Shown smaller
than actual size
of 11½" in
height, including
hardwood base.

The Franklin Mint
Franklin Center, PA 19091
Please send me Raphael's *Transfiguration,*
crafted in hand-painted porcelain. A handsome hardwood
pedestal will be provided.
I need send no money now. I will be billed in 5 monthly
installments of $39.* each, with the first payment due before shipment.
*Plus my state sales tax and a total of $3. for shipping and handling.

RESERVATION APPLICATION
Please mail by September 30, 1989.

MR./MRS./MISS _____
ADDRESS _____
CITY, STATE, ZIP _____
SIGNATURE _____
ALL APPLICATIONS ARE SUBJECT TO ACCEPTANCE

12212-00076

Franklin Mint Raphael Figurine, 1989

Presenting

Unicorn

THE MESSENGER OF LOVE

by David Cornell

*Handcrafted in Europe . . .
A beautiful sculpture in fine
bisque porcelain, embellished with
pure 24 karat gold.*

THE UNICORN. Fabulous creature of
myth whose elusive soul can only be
tamed by a maiden's magic power. And
whose eternal spirit is now portrayed
as never before—in a remarkable
sculpture crafted in porcelain and embellished with pure gold.
Created by an acclaimed British
sculptor, "Unicorn, The Messenger of
Love" is a triumph of artistry and imagination—a regal interpretation of a
wondrous creature.
Each sculpture will be *individually
hand-cast and hand-finished.* Each will be
crafted in fine European bisque—the
porcelain identified with many of
the world's most treasured works
of sculpture. And, finally, the
Unicorn's horn and collar
will be *hand-decorated with
pure 24 karat gold.*
This classic sculpture is
available exclusively from
The Franklin Mint and
only by direct order. The issue price is
$120, which is payable in four conven-
ient monthly installments of $30 each.
A Certificate of Authenticity will
be provided with your sculpture—
attesting to its status as an original
work by David Cornell. A specially-
prepared reference folder will also be
included, discussing the life and career
of the artist.
To acquire "Unicorn, The Messenger of Love"—as a fascinating conversation piece and an enchanting
addition to your home—simply mail
the accompanying order form directly
to The Franklin Mint, Franklin Center, PA 19091 by November 30, 1985.

Shown smaller than actual size.
Height: approximately 9 inches.

ORDER FORM

UNICORN, The Messenger of Love
The Franklin Mint
Franklin Center, Pennsylvania 19091

Please mail by November 30, 1985.
Limit: One sculpture per order.

Please accept my order for "Unicorn, The Messenger of Love," an original
sculpture by David Cornell, to be crafted for me in fine European bisque
porcelain and hand-decorated with pure 24 karat gold.
I need send no money now. I will be billed in four equal monthly
installments of $30.* each, beginning when my sculpture is ready to be
sent to me.
*Plus my state sales tax.

Mr./Mrs./Miss _____
Address _____
City, State, Zip. _____
Telephone No. (____) _____

Signature _____
ALL APPLICATIONS ARE SUBJECT TO ACCEPTANCE   IF YOU NEED TO CONTACT YOU ABOUT YOUR ORDER.

42

Franklin Mint Unicorn Figurine, 1985

LLADRÓ®
THE COLLECTORS CHOICE

Inspired by life, created by hand.

In the world of porcelain, Lladró has emerged unsurpassed. Handcrafted in Spain, with the prestige
and excellence our admirers have come to expect. Lladró...a timeless tradition.

Authenticity guaranteed by the distinctive Lladró trademark on the base.
For information about the Lladró Collectors Society, write to: Lladró, 225 Fifth Avenue, New York, NY 10010

"Here Comes the Bride" 14" With base (not shown)

Lladró Porcelain, 1985

The Buddha, 1982

THE VOYAGES OF THE STARSHIP ENTERPRISE

TO BOLDLY GO WHERE NO MAN HAS GONE BEFORE

The Hamilton Collection Presents...

MR. SPOCK

217

Carte Blanche Card, 1980

MasterCard Card, 1987

Discover Card, 1987

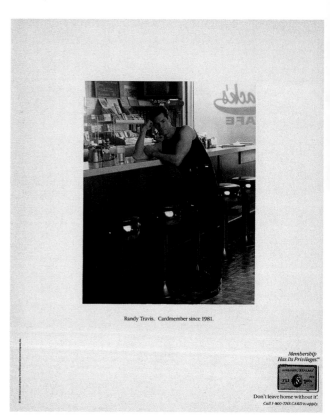

American Express Card 1989 ▶ *American Express Card, 1980*

All you need to get $75,000 travel accident insurance automatically.

Pass the lines at the insurance counter, skip filling out forms, just go to the gate. You're already protected. Every time you put your tickets (plane, train or ship tickets) on the Card you are automatically covered with $75,000 in Travel Accident Insurance. One ticket or a family's worth, they're all covered. The cost is included in your Cardmembership fee.* Charge your tickets in advance and you're covered on your way to and from the airport in a taxi, bus or airport limo. One more reason to carry the American Express® Card. Don't leave home without it.

*Underwritten by Firemen's Fund American Life Insurance Company.

AMERICAN EXPRESS

YOU'VE GOT TO WANT IT!

Start your summer r[...]
MTV™'s one-of-a-kin[...]
Each MTV SUMMER [...]
CAP has a "Hawaiia[...]
cool cotton; one size [...]

Then take it and stuff [...]
screamin' yellow MT[...]
BAG. Durable poly vi[...]
locking draw-string t[...]
adjustable shoulder [...]

Now you don't have to work at
MTV to own the MTV SATIN
JACKET. Here's a jacket with
an attitude! Embroidered logo.

This summer's hot item! Beat the
heat in this unisex MTV "HARLEY"
TANK TOP. 50/50 cotton/poly—
goes over very nice!

For rockin' on a sand[...]
this gigantic 34˝X64[...]
TOWEL is just what y[...]
It's 100% cotton.

Free MTV tumbler: order $30 worth of cool MTV stuff and get a plastic tumbler ($4.95 value) totally free!

☐ **OK! I want this MTV stuff!**

Please specify sizes for shirts and jacket: S, M, L, XL

Qty.		size(s)	each	
	(MS88A) **Big Beach Towel**		$24.95	
	(MS88B) **Summer Baseball Cap**		$ 7.97	
	(MS88C) **Beach Bag**		$17.95	
	(MS88D) **"Harley" Tank-T**		$ 9.97	
	(MS88E) **Satin Jacket**		$57.97	

SUBTOTAL
(MS88F) **Free MTV Tumbler** (with purchase of $30.00 or more)

SHIPPING: Add $3.00

TAX: CA, GA, IL, MI, NJ, NY, TX residents add local sales tax

TOTAL

Allow 4–6 weeks for deliv[...]

Name

Address   Zip

City

State

☐ Visa ☐ MC exp. date   Credit Card #

NL888   Signature

Hey! Limited time only on this offer. So really, don't delay—order today!

1-800-872-0600 Ext. 127

Hello, credit card types!
Prefer to order by phone?
To charge on Visa or
Mastercard call toll free
Or mail this order form,
with your check or
credit card number to:
MTV, Dept.   NL888,
C.S.B. 3173
Melville, NY 11747

Jessica Tandy and Hume Cronyn. Cardmembers since 1978.

Membership Has Its Privileges.™

Don't leave home without it.®
Call 1-800-THE CARD to apply.

American Express Card, 1989

The American Express® Card.
It's part of a lot of interesting lives.
Call 1-800-THE CARD for an application.

At Bret's Skysailing, you can't soar without a little daring, and you can't soar at all with American Express.

While most of his friends were just learning to drive, Bret Willat was already flying solo in sailplanes.

Now, almost 20 years later, his passion for soaring is greater than ever. And after one ride at his Skysailing School just south of San Francisco, you'll learn why.

Riding on invisible waves of rising air, Bret will bank your two-seater silently over the northern California countryside. And if that journey sparks a desire in you, Bret can teach you to soar alone. To catch a thermal above nearby Mission Peak and spiral upward in wide, lazy circles. Then to drift earthward, landing softly as a bird.

So if you go there, bring your sense of adventure and your Visa card. Because at Bret's, you can't soar above Mission Peak without a little daring, *and you can't soar at all with American Express.*

VISA
WORLDWIDE SPONSOR
1988 OLYMPIC GAMES

It's everywhere you want to be.®

©Visa U.S.A. Inc. 1987

MTV Products, 1988 ◄ *American Express Card, 1984*

Visa Card, 1987

221

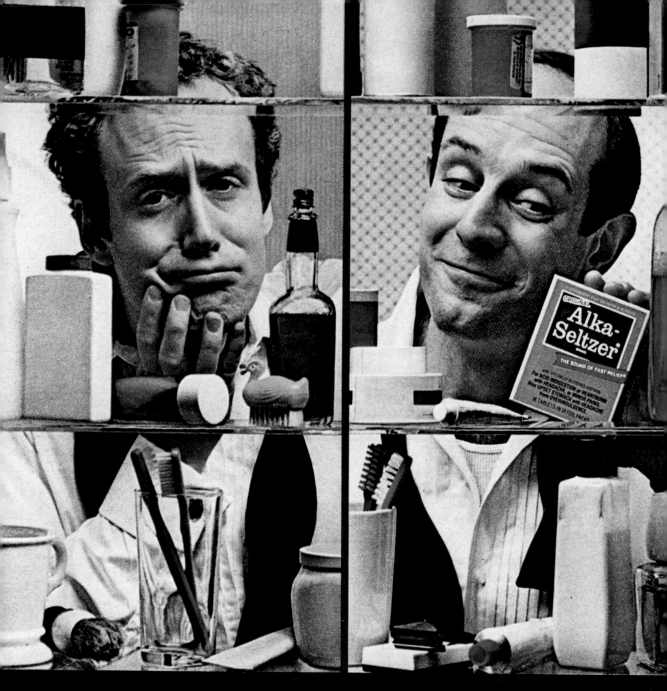

WILL IT BE THERE WHEN YOU NEED IT?

The man on the right has an aching head and acid indigestion. But he knows Alka-Seltzer® is there, waiting for him.

The man on the left also has an aching head and acid indigestion. And it isn't getting any better, because he forgot to buy Alka-Seltzer.

They both know nothing works better, nothing's more soothing.

The man on the left wishes he were the man on the right.

ALKA-SELTZER.® AMERICA'S HOME REMEDY.

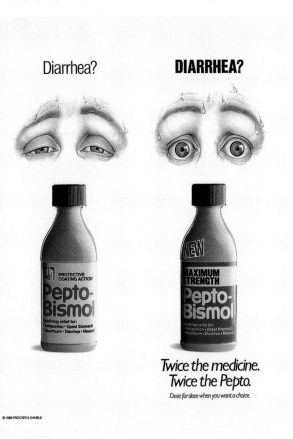

Diarrhea? DIARRHEA?

NEW MAXIMUM STRENGTH

PROTECTIVE COATING ACTION
Pepto-Bismol
Soothing relief for:
Indigestion • Upset Stomach
Heartburn • Diarrhea • Nausea

MAXIMUM STRENGTH
Pepto-Bismol
Soothing relief for:
Indigestion • Upset Stomach
Heartburn • Diarrhea • Nausea

*Twice the medicine.
Twice the Pepto.*

Dose for dose when you want a choice.

© 1988 PROCTER & GAMBLE

Pepto-Bismol, 1988

"I insist on relief."

Doris Jones, Assistant Bank Manager

"When you're responsible for thousands of dollars every day, you can't let a headache dull your thinking. So I take Extra-Strength TYLENOL. You can't buy a more potent pain reliever without a prescription."

Remember, no drug should be abused so follow label directions carefully.
TYLENOL is the registered trademark of the McNeil Consumer Products Co., identifying its brand of acetaminophen. © McNeil, 1980

Tylenol, 1980

"DID YOU PIVOT TODAY?"

You don't have to answer.
People can tell by the look on your face.
'Cause pivoting with the Gillette Atra twin blade razor gives you the best shave possible...the easiest...closest...most comfortable.

Gillette
We give you the edge.

GILLETTE ATRA
THE PIVOT MAKES IT BETTER.

Alka-Seltzer, 1982 ◄   Gillette Atra Razor, 1980

Alka-Seltzer®
If you need fast relief this winter, we'll be there.

Whether you're at the 1980 Olympic Games or watching them on TV, if acid indigestion and headache strike, you can depend on us. We'll instantly begin to neutralize stomach acid and speed relief to your aching head. Wherever or whenever you need us, we'll be there.

We'll sled you fast relief downhill.   **We'll skate you fast relief across the ice.**

We'll ski you fast relief anywhere.   **If you need us, we'll be there.**

Alka-Seltzer®
Plop Plop, Fizz Fizz. Oh, what a relief it is.®

© 1980 MILES LABORATORIES, INC. READ & FOLLOW LABEL DIRECTIONS. SUPPLIER TO THE U.S. OLYMPIC COMMITTEE.

Alka-Seltzer, 1980

223

TEETH AREN'T WHITE UNTIL THEY GLEEM.

GLEEM WHITENS TEETH

In lab tests, Gleem's whitening formula was proven superior to leading fluorides and was unsurpassed versus brands designed to fight smoking or coffee stains, control tartar, and protect sensitive teeth.

Gleem Toothpaste, 1988

Dressed to the Teeth.

Topol STAIN FIGHTING
Smoker's Toothpaste
ADVANCED FORMULA
WITH ZANTRATE
FLUORIDE   NET WT. 6.4 OZ

Coffee, tea, wine and tobacco stains on teeth just aren't your style. New whitening, brightening
Topol works more effectively...so you can wear a stain-free smile.

Topol Toothpaste, 1988

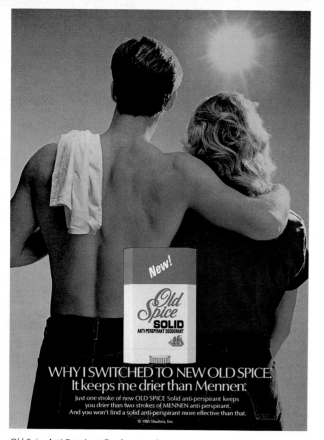

Old Spice Anti-Perspirant Deodorant, 1985

Clear Eyes Eye Drops, 1983

Dry Idea Deodorant, 1988

Superman III Flippy Flyer, 1983

▶ Visine Eye Drops, 1989

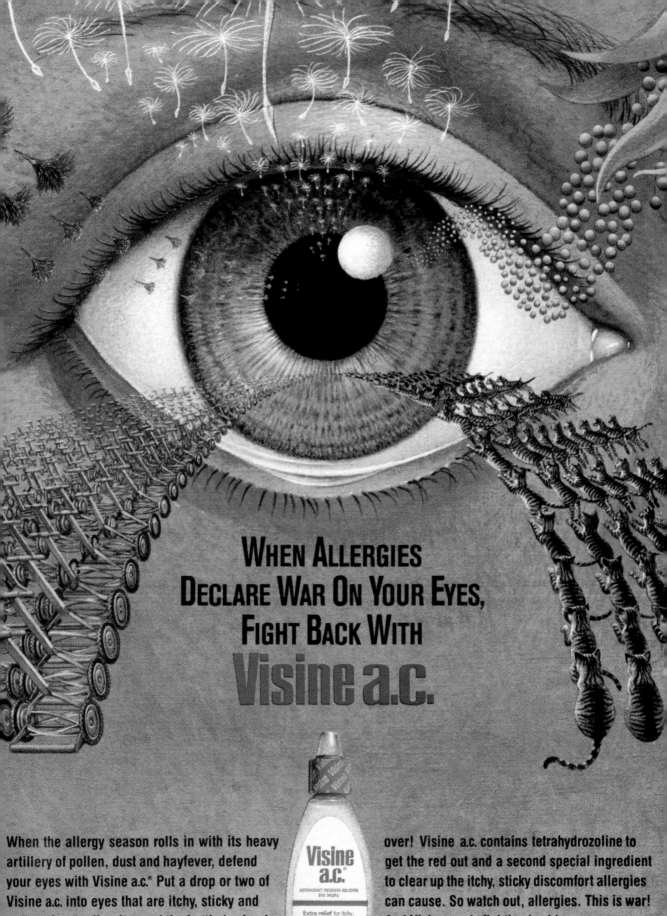

WHEN ALLERGIES DECLARE WAR ON YOUR EYES, FIGHT BACK WITH
Visine a.c.

When the allergy season rolls in with its heavy artillery of pollen, dust and hayfever, defend your eyes with Visine a.c.® Put a drop or two of Visine a.c. into eyes that are itchy, sticky and watery due to allergies, and the battle is clearly over! Visine a.c. contains tetrahydrozoline to get the red out and a second special ingredient to clear up the itchy, sticky discomfort allergies can cause. So watch out, allergies. This is war! And Visine a.c. is fighting back!

Tartar isn't sexy.

PRESENTING CLOSE-UP. TARTAR CONTROL PASTE

It helps prevent tartar from forming on teeth. Plus it gives you fluoride protection, and the whiter teeth and fresh breath you expect from Close-Up.

TARTAR CONTROL **CLOSE-UP**

Close-Up Toothpaste, 1988

RECENT CLINICAL STUDIES PROVE YOUR GRANDMOTHER WAS RIGHT.

Today it's known for a fact that Vicks' VapoRub not only relieves congestion like a pill, it also relieves coughs like a cough syrup. And nothing can match that warm, soothing VapoRub feeling. All of which goes to show that your grandmother did know what was best for you.

VapoRub. Relief with every breath.

© 1988 Richardson-Vicks Inc.

Vicks VapoRub, 1989

Mosquitoes love your kids too.

Protect them for 5 hours with Deep Woods OFF!

Deep Woods OFF! protects your family from mosquitoes for up to five hours. No leading repellent lasts longer. Try Deep Woods OFF! in the new pump spray. It's easy to use and sprays right where you want it. Also available in aerosol and lotion.

5 hour protection.

©1983 S.C. Johnson & Son, Inc.

Sea Breeze Cleanser, 1988 ◄ *Off! Bug Spray, 1983*

Suddenly, she's just "itching" to come home.

She isn't home sick. She has head lice.

Luckily, the only word you need to know about head lice is RID.

RID shampoo kills live lice completely, safely, and easily. And, the treatment includes the patented RID nit removal comb—proven 100% effective at removing the eggs lice leave behind. No wonder RID is the #1 recommended non-prescription lice treatment product by Pediatricians, Pharmacists and School Nurses.

RID is, now, available in a new 8 oz. size to treat more than one member of the family. And, to kill lice on furniture and carpeting, RID also has an effective household spray.

Remember…you can't buy anything more effective than RID to kill head lice.

Read label, use as directed.

Trust RID.
More parents choose RID than any other brand.

© 1989 Pfizer Inc.

RID Lice Elimination System, 1989

Banana Boat Skin Care, 1984

Tropic Sun Tanning Oil, 1982

Coppertone Suntan Lotion, 1986

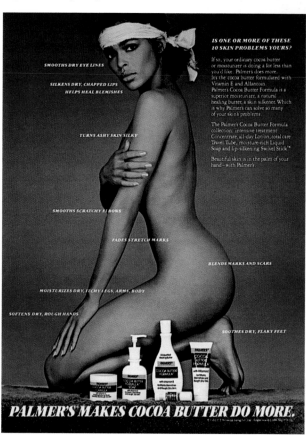

Palmer's Cocoa Butter, 1982

▶ *Tropical Blend Tanning Oil, 1983*

Capture
The Savage Tan.
Tropical Blend.

It's the deepest, darkest tan. The Savage Tan. And you get it fast with Tropical Blend. Tropical Blend has lush, tropical oils that soften your skin and keep it smooth. While the sun tans it wild! And Tropical Blend smooths on with the fragrance of fresh coconuts. Or choose exotic piña colada. The Savage Tan, from Tropical Blend. It makes other tans look tame.

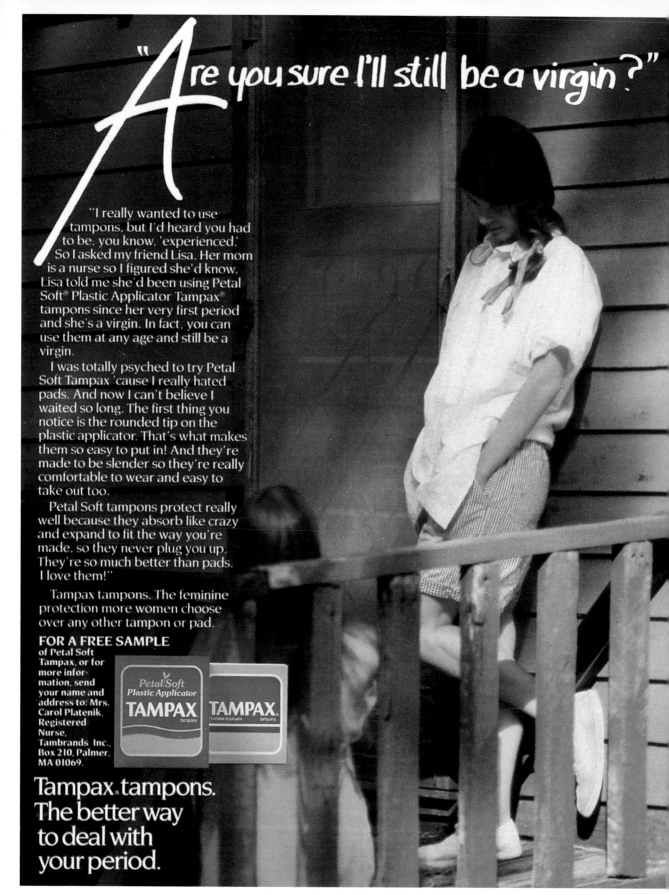

"Are you sure I'll still be a virgin?"

"I really wanted to use tampons, but I'd heard you had to be, you know, 'experienced.' So I asked my friend Lisa. Her mom is a nurse so I figured she'd know. Lisa told me she'd been using Petal Soft® Plastic Applicator Tampax® tampons since her very first period and she's a virgin. In fact, you can use them at any age and still be a virgin.

I was totally psyched to try Petal Soft Tampax 'cause I really hated pads. And now I can't believe I waited so long. The first thing you notice is the rounded tip on the plastic applicator. That's what makes them so easy to put in! And they're made to be slender so they're really comfortable to wear and easy to take out too.

Petal Soft tampons protect really well because they absorb like crazy and expand to fit the way you're made. so they never plug you up. They're so much better than pads. I love them!"

Tampax tampons. The feminine protection more women choose over any other tampon or pad.

FOR A FREE SAMPLE of Petal Soft Tampax, or for more information, send your name and address to: Mrs. Carol Platenik, Registered Nurse, Tambrands Inc., Box 210, Palmer, MA 01069.

Tampax tampons. The better way to deal with your period.

Tampax Tampons, 1988

One Alternative to Flossing Daily.

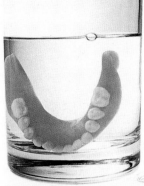

Daily flossing is the best way to prevent gum disease and tooth loss. That's why the American Dental Association recommends brushing *and* flossing every single day. In fact, millions of people wear dentures because of gum disease, *not* cavities. It's gum disease that causes the tooth loss that often means dentures. And since daily flossing is the best way to prevent gum disease, it helps you keep your teeth and avoid dentures.

Here's how gum disease can cause tooth loss: Every day a substance called plaque grows in places where a toothbrush can't reach, such as under your gums and between your teeth. If not removed by daily flossing, the live bacteria that make up plaque multiply, spread and travel under your gum line. Eventually you develop gum disease, which can destroy the very support structure of your teeth. That is exactly what has happened to millions of people who now wear dentures.

Johnson & Johnson Dental Floss is the dentists' choice. Johnson & Johnson Dental Floss is the floss most people use, and the one dentists recommend most. Because Johnson & Johnson Dental Floss offers the widest variety of flosses—it comes in the most flavors and widths—you can be sure there's one just right for you. Choosing the right kind of floss from the Johnson & Johnson line makes it easier to keep your teeth clean, healthy—and yours.

Johnson & Johnson DENTAL FLOSS

Your strongest line of defense against gum disease.

Johnson & Johnson Dental Floss, 1983

Free gift for the holidays! Your family portrait from

ADVANCED FORMULA
Centrum
HIGH POTENCY MULTIVITAMIN/MULTIMINERAL FORMULA

Free portrait at your *SEARS* Portrait Studio when you buy CENTRUM.

To get your free family photographic portrait (Regularly $15) take this form and proof of purchase (color band from CENTRUM package and cash register receipt) to your local *SEARS* Portrait Studio.

OFFER DETAILS:
1) Limit: One free 8 x 10 traditional background family portrait per family (POSES OUR SELECTION). You may purchase additional portraits and/or poses at SEARS regular low prices.
2) At least one family member photographed must be 18 years of age or older.
3) Families with more than seven members, please call in advance.
4) Does not include picture frame.
5) Portrait Studios located in most larger Sears retail stores.
6) Offer good until May 31, 1986. Please allow 4 weeks for processing (photography prior to December 7, 1985 for Christmas delivery).
7) Not combinable with other offers.

Name
Address
City _____ State _____ Zip
© 1985, Lederle Laboratories

From A to Zinc™

Lederle Laboratories, A Division of American Cyanamid Company, Wayne, New Jersey 07470

Centrum Multi Vitamins, 1985

Some days Jackie Joyner-Kersee's toughest race is for her next breath.

296

When world champion Jackie Joyner-Kersee has an occasional asthma attack, she relies on Primatene® Mist for the fastest kind of relief. In as fast as 15 seconds, Primatene restores free breathing. Primatene Mist. When speed of relief counts. For hours of relief, there's Primatene Tablets.

Primatene MIST

Primatene

USE AS DIRECTED. NOT FOR USE BEFORE OR DURING COMPETITION.

Primatene Mist, 1989

"DAILY PAK™ GIVES YOU VITAMIN POWER NO SINGLE TABLET CAN."
GEORGE BRETT, ALL-STAR THIRD BASEMAN

Just look at the difference. Each Daily Pak™ pak gives you more vitamin potency than Centrum®, Myadec®, Theragran-M® or One-A-Day® Including more B-Complex. More than twice the Vitamin C. And over six times more Vitamin E. Plus high potencies of nine essential minerals.

Take care of yourself like George Brett, and get the extra nutritional confidence you want most.

There's a personal Your Life® Daily Pak formula just for you. Try it today.

CALL TOLL-FREE 1 (800) 821-2280, EXT. 127, FOR THE DAILY PAK STORE LOCATION NEAREST YOU.

YOUR LIFE'S DAILY PAK

YOUR LIFE.

Daily Pak Vitamins, 1983

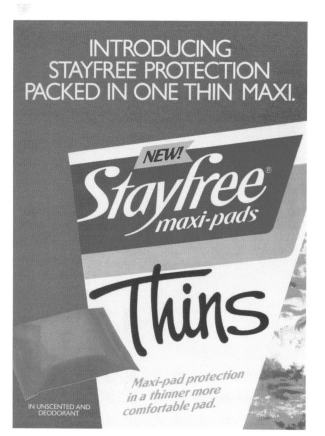

Stayfree Sanitary Pads, 1985

Sure & Natural Sanitary Pads, 1985

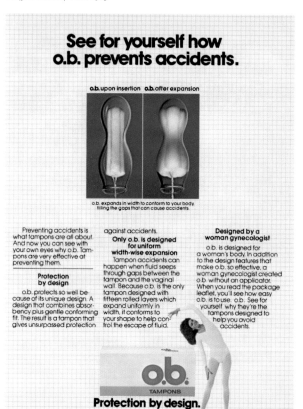

o.b. Tampons, 1983

Tampax Tampons, 1983

Sure and Natural.
We've got you covered.

The thin maxi
with a unique thin layer
of superabsorbents.

Sure & Natural Sanitary Pads, 1989

OVER 20 MILLION MEN & WOMEN SUFFER FROM . . .

HERPES

AND THERE IS NO CURE.
BUT THERE IS HELP . . .

HVS 1+2 Topical Solution™ has been laboratory tested and proven to inactivate 99.9% of human herpes virus. In clinical studies, 3 out of 4 sufferers found that HVS 1+2 Topical Solution. . .

- Relieves Pain and Discomfort
- Reduces Severity and Frequency of Outbreaks
- Promotes Faster Healing
- Is Effective on Subsequent, As Well As Initial Episodes
- Has No Side Effects

NOW AVAILABLE AT DRUG COUNTERS WITHOUT PRESCRIPTION

Call: 1-800-443-7737*
(in N.Y., call 516-454-9286)
If unavailable with your pharmacist, ask him to order through his wholesaler or ask him to call us at 1-800-443-7737.

© Chemi-Tech Labs, Inc. 1984
HVS 1+2 is registered with FDC - (NDC# on package)

HVS 1+2 Topical Solution, 1985

When insufficient lubrication interferes with sexual intercourse

Introducing

NEW

Lubrin™

Vaginal Lubricating Inserts

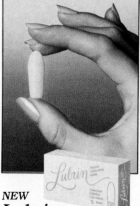

What is Lubrin?

New Lubrin is a vaginal lubricating insert specially formulated and designed for women when the lack of sufficient lubrication interferes with sexual intercourse. A problem that millions of women have but seldom talk about.

New Lubrin is an easy-to-use insert that is unscented, colorless and nonstaining. Because Lubrin liquefies within the vagina, it can be conveniently and discreetly inserted prior to intercourse to simulate your own body's natural lubrication.

Lubrin isn't messy like foams or jellies. It provides long lasting lubrication yet is easily washed off with water. Because each premeasured insert is individually foil-wrapped, Lubrin is convenient to carry in your purse or pocket.

Lubrin is gynecologist-tested, gentle and nonirritating. Use it with confidence.

NEW
Lubrin™

A product specifically designed for vaginal lubrication

Available without prescription at your pharmacy's feminine hygiene counter.

©1984 Upsher-Smith Laboratories Inc.
Minneapolis, Minnesota 55441. All Rights Reserved.

Lubrin Lubricating Inserts, 1985

"DO YOU USE CONDOMS?"

"Good! Because effective contraception, like condoms, is a great way to meet the responsibility that sex can bring. And, just as important, a wonderful way of showing how much you care for each other."

— Ruth Westheimer, Ph.D.

LifeStyles NUDA Made to feel natural

LifeStyles STIMULA Designed for her pleasure

LifeStyles NUDA PLUS™ with Spermicide

LifeStyles CONTURE Shaped to feel more

Lifestyles® Condoms. Because it isn't just about sex. It's about love.

© 1985 Warner-Lambert Company

Lifestyles Condoms, 1985

More and more women would. A condom means protection for both of you.

Try the Today Condom.® You'll be comfortable knowing it's safety-tested and from the contraceptive experts who make Today Sponge.® It's strong to help prevent pregnancy and sexually transmitted diseases.

What's more, you'll be

WOULD YOU BUY A CONDOM FOR THIS MAN?

comfortable with its extra-thin sensitivity.

Even buying is more comfortable. A question? Call the Today TalkLine, 1-800-223-2329.*

Look for the tasteful packaging. Lubricated, non-lubricated or with the spermicide Nonoxynol-9.

Today makes condoms more comfortable.

*In California 1-800-222-2329.

Today Condoms, 1988

One day late, and all I can think is, am I pregnant?

e.p.t. can tell you if you're pregnant, or not. All with a simple color change.

And now e.p.t. offers you two different test kits to choose from.

There's the e.p.t. stick test. It's simple to do and easy to read. If the stick turns pink, you're pregnant. If it stays white, you're not. It's that simple. Or, if you prefer, use e.p.t. plus. It's an easy-to-use color-change test that takes place with a single chemical step.

Whichever test you choose, e.p.t. is the fast and easy way to find out if you're pregnant. Or not. If you have any questions about e.p.t., call us toll free 1-800-562-0266. In New Jersey, call collect (201) 540-2458.

e.p.t. The first and most trusted name in pregnancy testing.

E.P.T., 1989

The touch of class.

Trojan brand Naturalamb condoms are the ultimate touch of class for those touching moments of intimacy. Made from a lamb membrane, they feel better and permit more pleasure. Unmatched for sensitivity, Naturalamb protects without presenting worrisome "side effects." Choose the touch of class. Choose Trojan Naturalamb from the Trojan display at your local pharmacy.

ψ **YOUNGS DRUG PRODUCTS CORPORATION**
Youngs® P.O. Box 385, Piscataway, New Jersey 08854 © Y.D.P.C. 1981

While no contraceptive is 100% effective, Trojan brand condoms, when properly used, are highly effective against pregnancy and venereal disease.

Trojan and Naturalamb are registered trademarks.

Trojan Naturalamb Condoms, 1982

IF YOU WANT
MASSIVE SIZE
& POWER
THERE'S ONLY ONE MAN
BIG ENOUGH TO SHOW YOU HOW!

Let The Incredible Lou Ferrigno, Bodybuilding's Most Massive Man, Unleash the Animal in You!

The Incredible Lou Ferrigno

The Courses

1. The Mind $5.00
2. Basic Principles $5.00
3. Intermediate & Advanced Principles $5.00
4. Legs $5.00
5. Abdominals & Serratus $5.00
6. Super-Wide Shoulders $5.00
7. The Back $5.00
8. Arms $5.00
9. Chest $5.00
10. Muscular Size & Power $5.00
11. Contest Training $5.00
12. Photo Album $5.00

The Products

13. New Lou Color Poster $7.95
14. Color Photo $5.00
15. Black & White Photo $2.00
16. T-Shirts S,M,L,& XL $8.95
17. Tank Tops S,M,L,XL $7.95
18. Lou Ferrigno Shorts $12.95
19. Lou Ferrigno Posing Trunks $16.95
20. Weight Lifting Belt $24.95
21. Seminar Tapes $19.95
22. The Incredible Lou Ferrigno Bodybuilding Book and Life Story $14.95

Your courses will come personally signed by Lou.

Lou Ferrigno is available for posing exhibitions and seminars. Write for details!

At Last! That incredible hulk of a man, the largest, most massively built bodybuilder in the world, is making all of his training secrets available to his fans. Learn how he built his incredible 58″ chest, his 22½″ arms, 29″ thighs, 20″ calves, 34½″ waist and his massively muscled 275-lb. body. This series of easy-to-follow courses will help you realize your bodybuilding potential faster! Every exercise is personally posed by Lou. If you're serious about building size and power, don't miss this once-in-a-lifetime offer to let the incredible Lou Ferrigno show you how.

YES, Lou! Please send me the items checked. I am enclosing $_____ in full payment. I understand you will autograph a course for me personally at no extra cost. Thanks.

Name _____ Age _____
Address _____
City _____
State _____ Zip _____

☐	1. The Mind	$ 5.00	☐ 13. Poster	$ 7.95
☐	2. Basic Principles	$ 5.00	☐ 14. Color Photo	$ 5.00
☐	3. Intermediate & Advanced Principles	$ 5.00	☐ 15. Black & White Photo	$ 2.00
☐	4. Legs	$ 5.00	☐ 16. T-Shirts ☐S ☐M ☐L ☐XL	$ 8.95
☐	5. Abdominal & Serratus	$ 5.00	☐ 17. Tank Tops ☐S ☐M ☐L ☐XL	
☐	6. Super-Wide Shoulders	$ 5.00	☐Yellow ☐Blue ☐Beige	$ 7.95
☐	7. The Back	$ 5.00	☐ 18. Shorts ☐S ☐M ☐L	
☐	8. Arms	$ 5.00	☐Black ☐Red ☐Gold	$12.95
☐	9. Chest	$ 5.00	☐ 19. Trunks ☐S ☐M ☐L	
☐	10. Muscular Size & Power	$ 5.00	☐Black ☐Red ☐Blue	$16.95
☐	11. Contest Training	$ 5.00	☐ 20. Weight-Lifting Belt	$24.95
☐	12. Photo Album	$ 5.00	☐ 21. Seminar Tapes	$19.95
			☐ 22. The Incredible Lou Ferrigno	
	☐ All 12 courses, Only $50.00		Bodybuilding Book and	
			Life Story (hardback)	$14.95

ORDER FROM:
Lou Ferrigno
P.O. Box 1671
Santa Monica, California 90406

All orders payable in U.S. dollars only. California residents add 6½% sales tax. U.S. and Canada add postage and handling as follows: $1.50 for orders up to $10.00, $2.50 for orders up to $20.00, $3.50 for orders up to $40.00. For orders over $40.00 add $4.50. Foreign orders: double the preceding charges.

Lou Ferrigno Bodybuilding, 1988

▶ *Jazzercise, 1985*

The Vertical Club, 1987

Bally Health Club, 1988

Victory Series Supplements, 1988

Hardware and Quicksilver Liquid Aromas, 1982

Eagle Fitness Systems, 1988

Diet Center, 1985

Soloflex, 1983

▶ Olympic Oil Stain, 1989

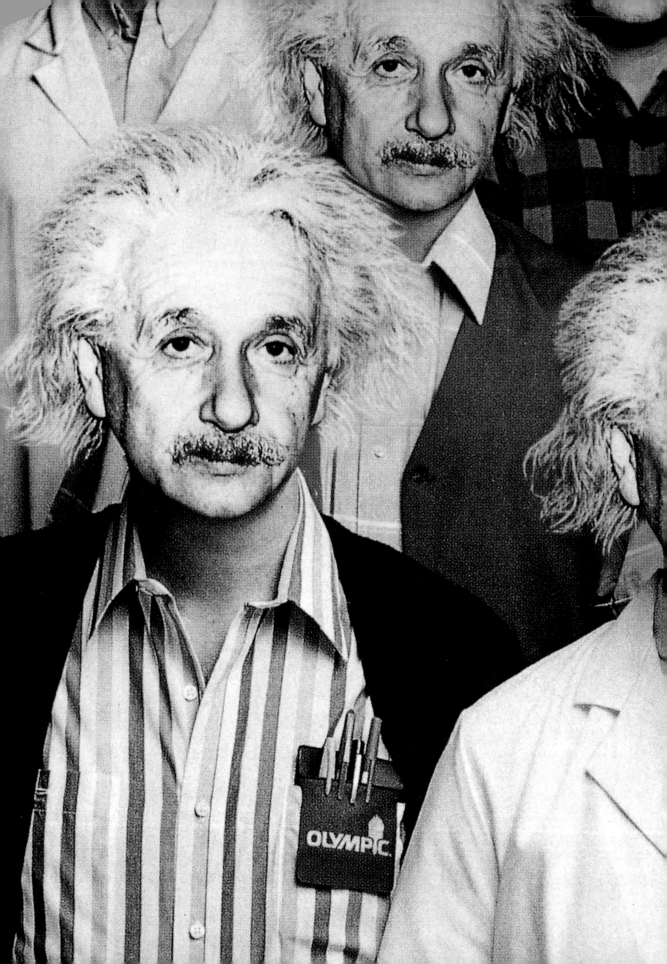

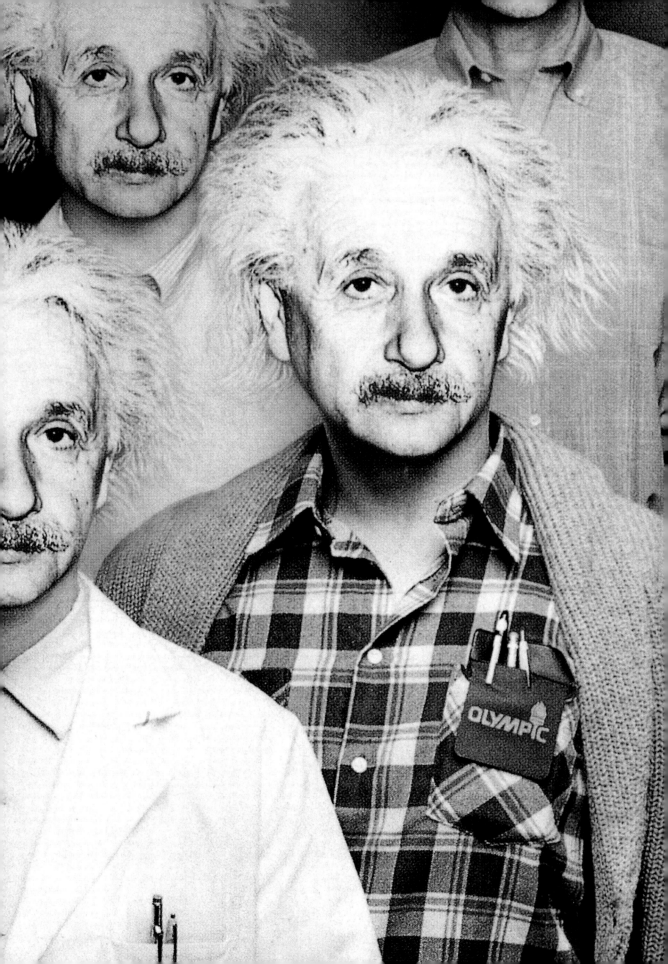

Parellex Corporation Products, 1985

THE NEW 9MM AUTOMATIC
Ruger P85

More Than World Class,
World's Best!

While other firearms companies tell of their history, Ruger is making history with new design, new technology, quality control and extensive testing.

Free instruction manuals for all Ruger firearms are available upon request.

 STURM, RUGER & Company, Inc.
31 Lacey Place, Southport, Connecticut 06490
Entire contents ©1987, Sturm, Ruger and Company, Inc.

Sturm, Ruger & Company Firearms, 1989

Get it off your chest! ©

Quality 50/50 Gray heather four color shirt. Please specify S,M,L,XL — $9.25 each ppd.

75¢ From each shirt sold will be donated to either the Nicaraguan Freedom Fund or the Afghan Rebel Fund.

Van's Military Surplus
P.O. Box 061146
Ft. Myers, 33906
please allow 4-6 weeks for delivery

Soldier of Fortune Magazine Ads, 1985

SURVIVAL

The Ultimate Survival Knife/Kit

This deluxe survival knife is the perfect companion for hunters, fishermen, campers and just to have around the house.

Quality features include 6" razor sharp blade, waterproof 4½" aluminum hollow handle, (available in camouflage or black) with liquid filled compass, leather sheath with sharpening stone.

Survival Kit includes: 10 matches, 20" wire saw, fishhooks, sinkers, nylon line for fishing, sewing, 2 large sewing needles can be used for medical use and to form a spear for hunting and fishing.

ONLY $19.95 EACH
SPECIAL $38.00 FOR TWO
SATISFACTION GUARANTEED
or your money back.

HOW TO ORDER INFORMATION:
TO ORDER BY MAIL, USE COUPON OR SEPARATE SHEET.
MAIL PAYMENT OR CREDIT CARD INFORMATION WITH
EXPIRATION DATE, CARD NUMBER AND SIGNATURE.

Knifeco P.O. Box 5271, Hialeah Lakes, FL 33014

Please send me:
☐ 1 Survival Knife @ $19.95 plus $3.00 for shipping & handling.
☐ 2 Survival Knives @ $38.00 plus $3.00 for shipping & handling.
Specify:
☐ Camouflage handle with green sheath & black coated blade.
☐ Black handle with black sheath & stainless blade.
Florida Resident add 5% sales tax.
Catalog only $2.00 ☐ Free with order
☐ Check enclosed ☐ Money Order
Charge my ☐ MasterCard ☐ Visa
Credit Card No.

Expiration Date

Authorized Signature _____
Name _____
Address _____
City _____ State _____ Zip _____
SF

Knifeco P.O. Box 5271, Hialeah Lakes, FL 33014

Knifeco Survival Knife Kit, 1985

Naugahyde® Brand Fabric works! On any furniture design. In any room. Because it comes in a myriad of colors, textures and patterns to complement any look, enhance any mood. Look for the tag that lets you know it's honest Naugahyde quality. On fine furniture in fine stores everywhere.

Naugahyde at work.

Naugahyde, 1981

Bielecky Brothers Furnishings, 1981

Century Furnishings, 1981

Karastan Rugs, 1984

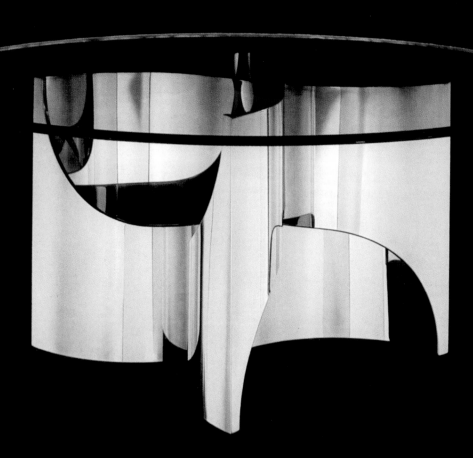

CASA BELLA.

NONSTOP

Stendig

Casa Bella Furnishings, 1981 ◄ *Stendig Furnishings, 1980*

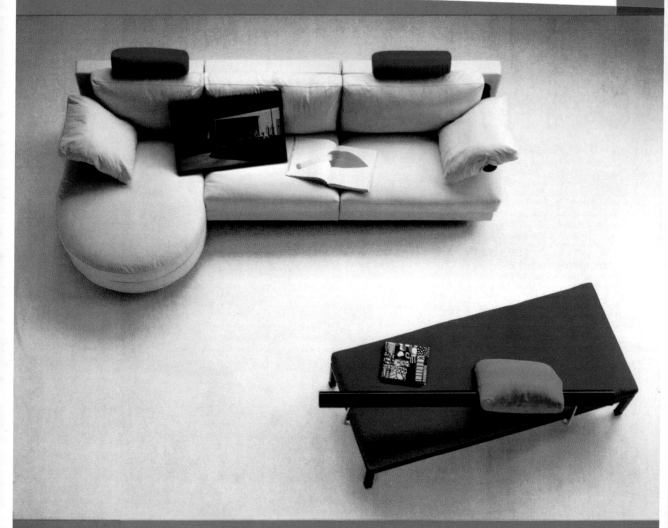

SITY:

The geometry of delight. Simple shapes, sizzling colors, playful yet serene. Artfully assembled by architect Antonio Citterio.

B&B ITALIA
AT

CASA BELLA.
INTERNATIONAL
215 E. 58 ST. NEW YORK 212-688-2020

Casa Bella Furnishings, 1980

▶ *Selig Furnishings, 1981*

Dream Pieces

White duck cushions on a tweed platform. Feels wonderful. Looks built in. We call it Stage One.
One, two and three-cushion pieces, with or without arms. You can arrange them in an L, or U-shape.
In any fabrics you want. After all, it's your dream.

SELIG

The Italian Tile Center, 1989

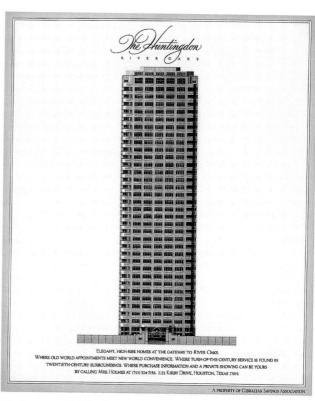

The Huntingdon High-Rise Homes, 1986

Wang Office Chairs, 1984

Mayline Drafting Furtniture, 1983

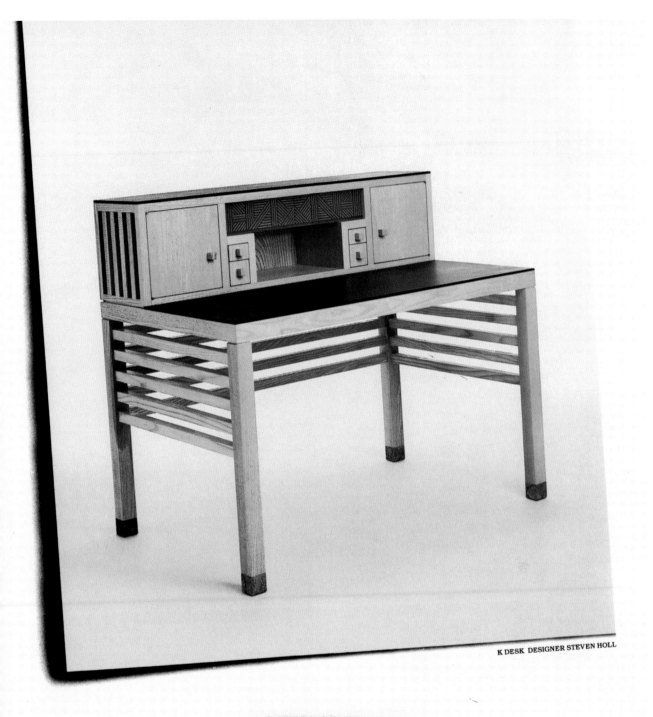

K DESK DESIGNER STEVEN HOLL

Pace Furnishings, 1989

Wamsutta Bedding, 1989

Springmaid Bedding, 1986

Martex Towels, 1981

▶ *Marimekko Bedding, 1982*

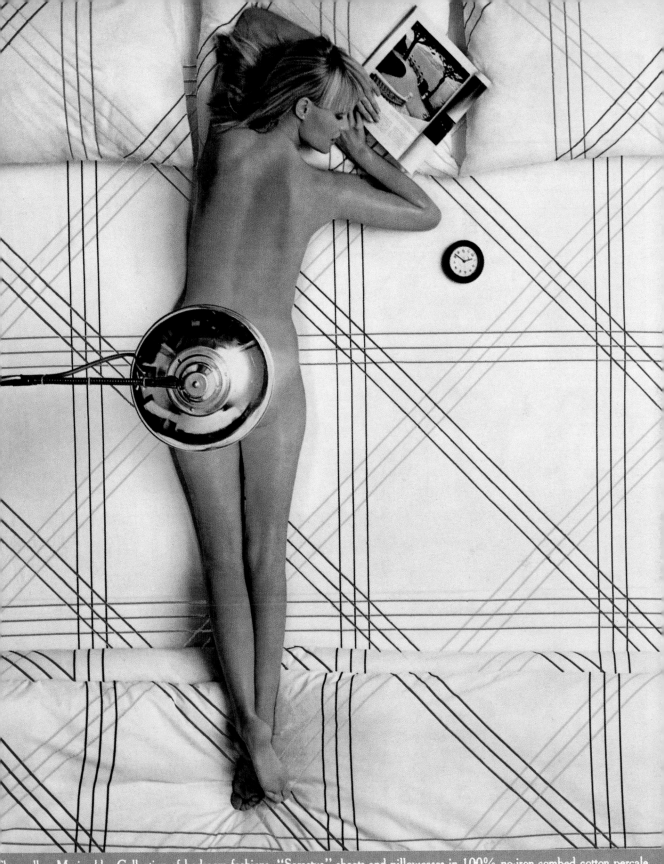

Eastpak Backpacks, 1989

WAS COOL IS

Eastpak Backpacks, 1989

"Take it from me, Mighty Dog® makes hash out of other dog foods."

Pure Beef.
That's what makes
Mighty Dog taste so good.

Beef Hash.
Other brands combine meat
with soy and by-products.

"Surprisingly, many dog lovers don't know the difference between Mighty Dog® Beef for Dogs and brands like Alpo, Kal Kan and Cycle.

"Mighty Dog, you see, is pure beef, (like a steak). Those others combine meat with other ingredients, (like hash). In fact, meat by-products and soy flour can make up to 75% of their weight.

"Check the ingredients list. You'll find only Mighty Dog lists beef as its number one ingredient.

"That's why, at dinnertime, my taste runs to Mighty Dog."

MIGHTY DOG®
The pure beef brand.

HOW I BECAME A HAPPY CAT.
(WITH A LITTLE HELP FROM MY FRIENDS)

"It all happened the day my mommy brought home Happy Cat® brand cat food. That's when I got to meet my little friends. They told me the taste of Happy Cat would make me happy. Boy, were they ever right! Happy Cat is so moist and meaty tasting, every little bite fills my tummy with joy. And Happy Cat stays moist in the bowl, too. So I stay happy until the very last piece is gone. And that's what I call a happy ending." **MAKE YOUR CAT A HAPPY CAT.**

Purina

Helping pets live longer, healthier lives™

® ©Ralston Purina Company, 1984

Your little gal will love our little Glamour Gals™

There's a little bit of glamour in every little girl. So yours will love this exciting new collection of fashion dolls.

Glamour Gals™ have the best of everything: luxurious hair that's fun to comb, exclusive designer-style outfits and poseable arms and legs.

Plus, there's a whole line

of exciting playsets and accessories that add to the fun. Yet Glamour Gals dolls and playsets cost less than you'd expect. So it's easy to help her collect them all.

Give your little girl a little glamour. Surprise her with the Glamour Gals Collection today.

Kenner

Glamour Gals, 1981

The fun of Strawberryland goes on and on, with new dolls, new fashions, new playthings.

Strawberry Shortcake, the "berry" little doll, just 5½" tall, who smells like her name, has five more friends. Raspberry Tart, Lemon Meringue, Orange Blossom and Apricot (with her little bunny Hopsalot), who smell like their names. Her friendly foe, Purple Pieman, smells like cinnamon apple pie. What fun to smell these tiny dolls, pose them, dress them in their Berry Wear™ Fashions and comb their "berry" soft hair with the strawberry-styled combs! Or give them a ride on "litter-Bit", the new Strawberry Shortcake Butterfly. Or have a pretend garden party with them in the pretty, new vine-covered Strawberry Shortcake Garden House. All the dolls, fashions and playsets are sold separately. This fun-filled playworld will tickle any little girl pink.

Kenner

Strawberry Shortcake, 1981

Look at the friends you can make with Play-Doh!

Play-Doh® brings its friends into the homes of kids everywhere. There's the world of Strawberry Shortcake®...all the Sesame Street® neighbors...the adventurous characters of Star Wars®*...and those comical Stone Age people, the Flintstones™. They all add to the fun children can make with Play-Doh Modeling Compound!

Play-Doh, 1981

Michael Jackson and Rainbow Brite. Gifts to keep children singing.

As long as there are songs to sing and nursery rhymes and ABCs to recite, children five and older will be enjoying their Vanity Fair phonographs. And you can give them their favorite this Christmas—with superstar Michael Jackson* or Rainbow Brite** and her magical flying horse, Starlite™. Be assured you're giving

the best quality children's phonograph. Vanity Fair builds them to handle a child's enthusiasm and to play any 45 or 33⅓ RPM record. Either phonograph has a kid-tough case, solid-state circuitry, child-tested safety plug, the nearly unbreakable Super Arm™ and a five-year warranty.

Your little star can even

sing along with the Michael Jackson phonograph on its remote microphone and hear his or her voice through the big four-inch speaker.

Give a Vanity Fair phonograph and you give years of fun. What a good idea!

VANITY FAIR by ERTL

THE ERTL COMPANY Dyersville, Iowa 52040 Subsidiary of Kidde, Inc.

Vanity Fair Phonographs, 1984

There were times when a little girl couldn't say how she felt.

But now, there's Poochie to help your little girl put it into words. On Poochie notepaper, with Poochie pencils and Poochie stamps that say all sorts of things.

There are Poochie stickers, Poochie combs, and mirrors, even Poochie purses.

With Poochie this and Poochie that, your Poochie girl will make quite an impression.

A Poochie girl says what's on her mind.

At one time, a little girl couldn't say what was on her mind. Now, she can say it with Poochie. **Give your little girl a style of her own.**

Poochie, 1983

My First Barbie®

The Barbie doll designed for younger girls

Remember how you played with your first Barbie doll? Changing her clothes, styling her hair—acting out every glamorous fantasy you could dream up?

It's the same with girls today. Except they start playing with Barbie dolls at a much younger age than you did. That's why Mattel made a doll called My First Barbie. She's specially designed to be your little girl's very first Barbie doll. Here's why My First Barbie is simply wonderful:

Her long hair is easy for uncertain little fingers to comb in simple styles. She comes with straight arms. And her straight legs have a special smooth skin—so she's easier for younger girls to dress.

My First Barbie comes with a complete easy-to-dress outfit of four fashion pieces to mix or match. And, of course, she has her own line of My First Barbie Fashions! They're all easy-to-dress fashions (each sold separately) that slip on, snap, wrap and tie.

Now, when your little girl is ready for a Barbie doll, there's My First Barbie. She's the Barbie doll that very little hands can handle.

MATTEL

B A R B I E
THE DOLL DREAMS ARE MADE OF

Barbie

Not so long ago, you played with Barbie® and dreamed of becoming all Barbie was. A career woman. A trend-setter. A sweetheart to someone special.

A mother now, you hold those dreams doubly dear—for you, and your daughter. And Barbie is still the doll to dream on. To grow on.

Bring Barbie into your little girl's life. Because when a girl has dreams, she can do anything. Right, Barbie?

Barbie®

My First Barbie, 1981 ◀   *Barbie, 1986*

Fisher-Price, 1980

Pop A Pom, 1982

Hasbro, 1983

K mart, 1984

Milton Bradley, 1983

Strawberry Shortcake, 1984

Etch A Sketch, 1985

Nerf, 1983

265

Imaginations take off with the Federal Express®Playset

New York. China. The Moon. With the Federal Express® Air Cargo Playset, a little aviator can speed packages to any place in the special world of his imagination.

At Playskool we know that the most creative playtimes often mirror real life situations. That's why we have included everything a real action-packed Federal Express delivery service would need. Lots of packages to load up. A delivery van with a courier. A plane complete with pilot and a flip-open door. Even a working conveyor to crank the packages inside the plane! Pretending has never been so real.

As the Federal Express plane soars, so will his imagination.

PLAYSKOOL

Still the standard.

Federal Express® is a registered service mark of Federal Express Corporation.

Playskool, A Milton Bradley Company.

Playskool, 1984

BASED ON THE TIME-HONORED NOTION THAT IT'S FAR BETTER TO GIVE THAN TO RECEIVE.

The rules of Gotcha are as simple as they are charitable: you see your opponent—you let him have it. For, given the opportunity, he'd surely return the favor. And because Gotcha delivers soft-shots of non-toxic washable color bursts, there won't be any hard feelings, win or lose.

Now, go out there and really do unto others. Goggles required. Minimum age 16. Follow guidelines. Available with accessories at toy and sporting goods departments.

GOTCHA! THE SPORT!

Gotcha!, 1987

Give your child all the fun in the Universe.

He-Man.® Orko.™ Castle Grayskull.® Skeletor.® Beast Man.® Snake Mountain.™ Battle Cat.®

What is this stuff?

This is the stuff of being a child. You know—that short period of life you left too soon.

And this is the stuff of Masters of the Universe.®

Millions of boys have discovered this limitless playground. It's filled with fun and excitement. With heroes and valor. And with colorful action toys that last as long as their imagination.

Here your child can be a hero, too. He can be brave and just. He can be anything he wants to be. But most of all, he'll be having fun.

While he's still a child.

He-Man Set, 1984

The Place Where Christmas Dreams Come True

STAR WARS RETURN OF THE JEDI

Kenner

Kenner Toys Are On Sale Nov. 13 Thru Nov. 19

A. Star Wars action play figures, including new heroes and villains from Return Of The Jedi Ages 4 and up....... Ea. 2.44
B. Jabba The Hutt and his pet, Salacious Crumb, await victims atop his switch-operated prison platform........ 11.96
C. Sit 'n Spin ride-on merry-go-round platform, featuring Care Bears. Light, rugged, self-operated, ages 1½–6...... 15.99

D. Strawberry Shortcake doll friends and pets, both old and new! Posable, scented, cute removable outfits....... Ea. 6.44
E. Strawberry Shortcake Baby Dolls, in dainty romper, cap and booties, blow fragrant little kisses........... Ea. 16.96

We've Got It And We've Got It Good!

Copyright 1983 by Kmart Corporation   Use Our Layaway Plan At **Kmart** The Saving Place®

Kenner Toys, 1983

The Place Where Christmas Dreams Come True

HASBRO

HASBRO Toys Are On Sale Nov. 20 Thru Nov. 26

A. G.I. Joe Mobile Strike Force Team Figures come equipped with weapons and accessories. Two-handed grip for exciting realism....... Ea. 2.47
B. Dragonfly XH-1 Assault Copter, with pilot "Wild Bill" in command, has spinning rotor and a canopy that really works!....... 9.88
C. SkyStriker XP-14F, with "Ace" as pilot, carries out G.I. Joe's most dangerous assignments with deadly accuracy........ 16.88

D. MOBAT Motorized Battle Tank, assigned to "Steeler", is the ultimate support vehicle in the ground assault arsenal....... 16.88
E. G.I. Joe Enemy Figures, with swivel grip, add more thrills to the peacekeeping missions of the Mobile Strike Force....... Ea. 2.47
*batteries not included

We've Got It And We've Got It Good

Copyright 1983 by Kmart Corporation   Use Our Layaway Plan At **Kmart** The Saving Place®

Hasbro, 1983

CHECK OUT THE ACTION AT K MART

Parker Brothers, 1983

Smurf Chewable Vitamins, 1984

New Strawberry Shortcake® Berry Happy Home.™
There's no place quite like it.

DOLL HOUSE

When your little girl sets eyes on this enchanting house, she'll do just what Strawberry Shortcake did... fall in love. How could she resist? There's so much fun under the big strawberry-red roof.

There are three floors to furnish and play in. A quaint kitchen where she can pretend to cook "berry" big meals, a living room and dining room that's perfect for entertaining, a restful bedroom and sparkling bath ... even an attic playroom with a secret fold-down stairway and pink skylight. She can put letters in the mailbox in front, push Strawberry Shortcake and Custard® on the bright yellow front porch

swing, and play with them on the sundeck off the bedroom.

The Berry Happy Home is simple to assemble, and can be purchased unfurnished or with a special selection of Berry Happy Home furniture. All of the furniture is specially designed for Strawberry Shortcake with opening doors, soft upholstery, rugs ...every detail is perfect. Your little girl will love collecting all the furniture sets and helping Strawberry Shortcake settle in.

The Strawberry Shortcake Berry Happy Home. There's no place quite like it.

Kenner

Dolls with Pets, and Furniture Sets, each sold separately.
Character names and trademarks (TM, ®):   © 1983 American Greetings Corp. Patent Pending.

Strawberry Shortcake, 1983

Now little kids don't have to wait for the bikes they've been waiting for.

New Huffy® First Bikes™ are just the right bikes in just the right sizes.

Huffy First Bikes are real little bikes that look like real big bikes. And with the extra magic of kid-pleasing colors and characters, they're the kind of bikes that little kids just can't wait to get on. Because First Bikes are specially designed with kids in mind, by Huffy, the largest selling brand.

Building bikes for little kids presents big challenges. Everything has to be just right, from the kid-sized pedals and grips to the durable frame. And First Bikes are adjustable, so they can grow as the rider grows. Even the chainguard is fully-enclosed, because you just can't be too careful. And, First Bikes have earned the Good Housekeeping Seal.

So if you know someone who just can't wait to be big enough for that first REAL bike, don't wait. Huffy First Bikes are the right size. Right now.

	For Boys	For Girls
	Thunder Road	Sweet Thunder
	Lightning	Fantasia
	Thunder MX	Teddy Bike
	G.I. Joe™	Herself the Elf™

HUFFY®
America's First Choice

Huffy Bicycles, 1983

SOME OF YOUR BEST CHILDHOOD FRIENDS HAVE NEVER GROWN UP.

Thumbelina.® You loved her then, your daughter will love her now. It's a feeling girls never outgrow.

Thumbelina.® Betsy Wetsy.® And Tiny Tears.® They're Ideal's Classic Dolls. As loved today as yesterday.

IDEAL CLASSIC DOLLS
IDEAL®

© 1983 CBS TOYS, A Division Of CBS Inc.

Ideal Classic Dolls, 1983

MOMMY. GIVE THIS AD TO DADDY.

You know why you should get me a Rainbow Brite™ bike from *Fit For Kids*™? 'Cause it fits me now, and even when I get more bigger, 'cause it's got an adjustable seat.

And it's got training wheels for when I'm learning how to ride, and you can take 'em off after I learn.

Daddy can put it together real easy 'cause they don't have lots of parts. The chain and the back wheel and lots of stuff are already attached. And anyway, I'll help.

Don't worry, Mommy. The man at the store says every Fit For Kids frame is fully welded. And they've got a coaster brake, and a chainguard that covers up the chain.

I really love this Rainbow Brite bike. And Fit For Kids has different kinds for little brother when he gets bigger. So give this ad to Daddy in time for Christmas, okay?

Available in 13" and 16" models. See your retailer for the complete line of Fit For Kids™ sidewalk bikes from Murray.

fit for kids
MURRAY

©1983 Hallmark Cards, Inc.

Murray Bicycles, 1984

Play for keeps.

She'll keep playing & playing & playing with her Power Wheels® Barbie® Corvette.®

Play cellular phone— essential for Barbie™ business calls and hours of chit chat.

More play! Power Wheels also makes road signs, and stoplights that really light.

Detailed dash, shift console with an ignition key, and glove compartment.

Play with confidence: Power Wheels patented safety braking system that stops the car the minute her sneaker leaves the pedal.

Real doors that open and close!

Runs on Power Wheels exclusive Super 6-volt system with rechargeable battery. Goes 3 mph forward and reverse.

Behind this symbol is a well-made toy: Power Wheels builds in quality with Corvette-perfect styling and super tough construction.

POWER WHEELS
FT. WAYNE, INDIANA

The world's leading maker of battery-powered vehicles.
Call toll-free 1-800-348-0751 *if you'd like our catalog, more information or help with a problem.*

BARBIE and associated trademarks are owned by and used under license by Mattel, Inc. ©Mattel, Inc. 1988. All Rights Reserved. CHEVROLET CORVETTE is a trademark of GENERAL MOTORS CORPORATION and is used under license.

Power Wheels Barbie Corvette, 1988

▶ *Univega Bicycles, 1985*

Tyco Golden Eagle, 1980

Hot Wheels, 1980

Märklin Model Railway, 1984

▶ *Gabriel Child Guidance Toys, 1980*

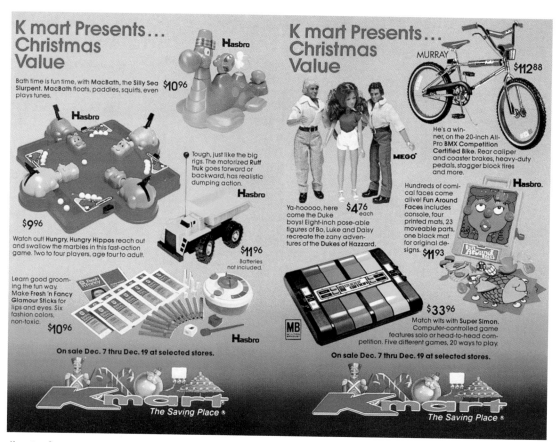

K mart, 1981

Gund Teddy Bears, 1984

BIG, FAT, FURRY GARFIELD

In person. Straight from the comic strip. The inimitable, lasagne-loving, one and only Garfield. Only from Dakin, and double-checked by Dakin for ⚡safety, and ⚡quality.

Make friends with Garfield, and dozens of other delightful Dakins. You'll find them at leading stores everywhere.

DAKIN
MAKIN'
FRIENDS

© 1981 R. Dakin & Company. GARFIELD:
© 1978 United Feature Syndicate, Inc.

Garfield by Dakin, 1981

"Grandpa, how'd your fur get that grey?"

"Too much playin' around."

Grandpa, the original Teddy bear (here, a replica) started a tradition of cuddly animals back in 1902. Even his cuddly son has been around since 1930. But his grandson is still wet behind the ears. All, made with the craftsmanship of Steiff, the original.

Steiff
BUTTON IN EAR

Steiff Teddy Bears, 1984

Holiday Wish Book

SOMEBODY YOU KNOW IS WISHING FOR SOMEBODY WE KNOW.

Where else could you find such a complete collection of cuddly characters than in the Sears Holiday Wish Book?

Rag dolls, baby dolls, bears and lots more. All huggable, all fun. And all ready to make a wish come true for somebody special on your Christmas list.

For toys or tennis togs, cordless phones or computer games, you'll find over 600 pages of giftable goodies in the Wish Book. It's the most complete Christmas catalog we have ever offered.

Sears prices are lovable, too. Look for our Early

Shopper Discount (through October 18). And specially priced Wish Book values. Sears Holiday Wish Book Catalog is now available at Sears Catalog Departments.

there's more for your life at Sears
CATALOG

Sears, 1983

FIND THE DAKIN SMILE.

These days Dakins are nearly everywhere. And so are the smiles. People can't ignore Dakin's colorful characters and cuddly creatures. Like GARFIELD and ODIE, Woolie Bear, Mary and Her Lamb, and Snow Leopard. The name Dakin on the label means highest quality—and lots of just plain good fun, at a surprisingly reasonable price. Most Dakins are under $10. And the smiles are free.

R. DAKIN & COMPANY
© 1983 R. Dakin & Company

Good Housekeeping PROMISES

(DAKIN)

GARFIELD Characters: © 1978 United Feature Syndicate, Inc.

Dakin Stuffed Animals, 1983

HACKY SACK® FOOTGAMES
YOU NEVER KNOW WHERE THEY MAY LEAD...

Just keep the pellet-filled leather footbag bouncing in the air using only your feet and knees. Look for Hacky Sack® footbags at your favorite sporting goods store or call **TOLL FREE 1-800-426-4791.**

M–F 8:00 AM–5:00 PM Pacific Time

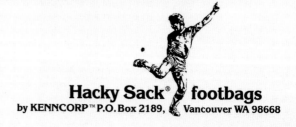

Hacky Sack® footbags
by KENNCORP™ P.O. Box 2189, Vancouver WA 98668

Hacky Sack Footbags, 1983

▶ *Frisbee, 1983*

FRISBEE
ou just can't do it alone.

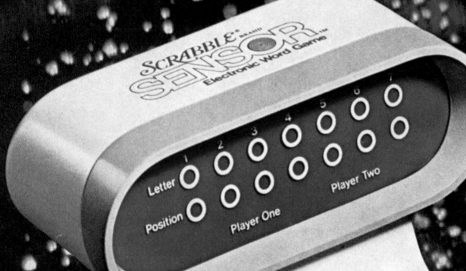

THE PURSUIT GOES ON. AND ON. AND ON.

Now there are six more card sets of Trivial Pursuit® to pursue:

- Baby Boomer® Edition—From Eisenhower to Flower Power.
- Silver Screen Edition—A ton of titillating Tinseltown trivia.
- All-Star Sports Edition—From Tinker to Evers to games of chance.
- Genus II™ Edition—Picks up where the Genus Edition™ laughed off.
- RPM™ Edition—Music, music, music! From Beethoven to Boy George.
- Young Players™ Edition —From the Brothers Grimm to the Brothers Gibb.

Get 'em all. Play 'em all. Have a ball!

Trivial Pursuit®
Every American is entitled to Life, Liberty & the Pursuit of Trivia.

ALSO COMES COMPLETE WITH GAME BOARD AND PLAYING PIECES.

Scrabble Sensor, 1980 ◄ *Trivial Pursuit, 1985*

Kemper Snowboards, 1989

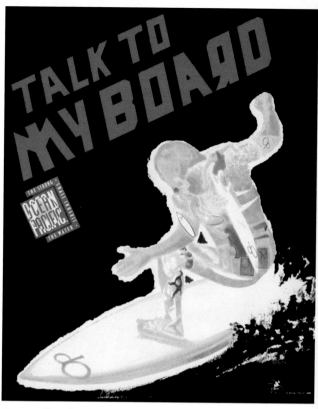

Ocean Pacific Surfboards, 1989

Pente Board Game, 1984

Sims Snowboards, 1989   ▶ ProLite Surfboards, 1989

SUBSCRIBE

WHO'S HOT?

WHO'S DOLLED UP?

WHO'S STUNNING?

WHO'S IN STYLE?

WHO'S LOVABLE?

WHO'S WINNING?

WHO'S SPUNKY?

WHO'S TEAMING UP?

WHAT'S SHAPING UP?

WHAT'S COOKING?

WHAT'S NEW?

WHO'S TOP CAT?

Surround yourself with a world full of PEOPLE. It's the picture-packed weekly that brings the stars into focus. It's wholesome entertainment, and habit forming fun. And it's all yours for just 79¢ a week when you

SUBSCRIBE

Paper Moon Greeting Cards, 1984 ◄ *People Magazine, 1983*

B. Dalton Books, 1983

HOW TO GET A LIFT FROM A FLYING SAUCER AND OTHER IMPORTANT TRAVEL TIPS.

FREE!

Written by Douglas Adams,
former hospital porter, chicken-shed
cleaner and contributing writer for "Monty Python",
The Hitchhiker's Guide to the Galaxy is a book no
interstellar voyager should be without.

Guided by The Hitchhiker's Guide to the Galaxy with
words DON'T PANIC written in nice friendly letters
on the cover, you'll discover answers to our most
pressing questions: Why are we born? Why do we
die? And why do we spend so much time in between
wearing digital watches? Write us or send in the
coupon and we'll send you a free copy. Providing
you're one of the first 3,000 people. And your reply
is postmarked before August 27, 1981. If not, DON'T
PANIC. The Hitchhiker's Guide to the Galaxy will be
on sale everywhere in October.

42 : ROLLING STONE, AUGUST 20, 1981

Name _____

Address _____

City _____

State _____ ZIP _____

Hyperspace Hitchhiking Club-Earth Div.
c/o Pocket Books
1230 Avenue of the Americas
New York, N.Y. 10020

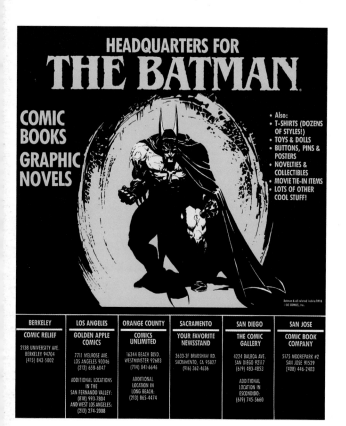

Batman Comics, 1989

The Hitchhiker's Guide to the Galaxy, 1981   ▶ The Dark Knight, 1986

"NEXT TO MY SOFTWARE, NOTHING'S MORE USER FRIENDLY THAN THE WALL STREET JOURNAL."

WILLIAM H. GATES III, CHAIRMAN, MICROSOFT CORPORATION

"I need a ton of information to stay the leader in computer software, but I have super limited time. Which is precisely why I read The Wall Street Journal.

"The way The Journal's organized, I can access a lot of information, valuable information, in practically no time. A quick scan of 'What's News' on the front page tells me what stories I should read. And the stories give you the most news in the fewest words.

"There are some things I don't have any way of finding out except by reading The Journal. Like which big companies are committing to what hardware. Information so important it influences the way we deal with our customers today and plan marketing strategies for tomorrow.

"It's really simple. If you're going to be a key decision-maker, you absolutely have to be keyed into The Wall Street Journal."

© 1984 Dow Jones & Company, Inc.

THE WALL STREET JOURNAL.

All the business news you need. When you need it.

Subscribe today, call 800-345-8540 except Hawaii or Alaska. PA 800-662-5180. Or write: 200 Burnett Rd., Chicopee, MA 01021.

The Wall Street Journal, 1984

Time Magazine, 1984

Newsweek Magazine, 1986

Heavy Metal Magazine, 1987

Heavy Metal Magazine, 1984

Interview Magazine, 1989

Newsweek Magazine, 1984

512 ISSUES LATER

ROLLING STONE turns twenty next month. That's when issue 512 hits the newsstand. We've spent over a year putting this special anniversary issue together, and it will be full of the things that you've always read ROLLING STONE for. You'll be getting more than 300 pages of the greatest photographs from the magazine's history and in-depth interviews with fifty of the most important and influential people of the last twenty years. Of course, that means some of the legends of rock & roll – Bob Dylan, Paul McCartney, George Harrison, Mick Jagger, Keith Richards, Stevie Wonder, Pete Townshend, John Fogerty, Tina Turner. And that's just the beginning. Issue 512 goes on sale October 20th. If you're not a subscriber, reserve a copy of ROLLING STONE now at your favorite newsstand.

Rolling Stone Magazine, 1987

SHOCKING PINK!

Other magazines may promise you the moon. HUSTLER delivers it. We aim for the stars and move heaven and earth to bring you a galaxy of entertainment in every issue. Subscribe now to HUSTLER, the magazine with universal appeal.

Penthouse Magazine, 1984 ◄ Hustler Magazine, 1980

293

And the winner is...

Tits and Aspen

Never underestimate the genius of Americans out to make a fast buck. The Colorado ski resort of Aspen was just beginning to catch the eye of jet setters when a clever merchandiser rose to the occasion with this brilliant idea. Get a tasty photograph of breasts and derrières to represent snow-clad mounds, add a miniature skier amidst the blossoming flesh, and, voilà! An instant winter fantasy for countless college lads, who could tape the poster to their dorm-room door and kick back dreaming of plunges down those virgin slopes.

Die Hügel und Täler von Aspen

Man unterschätze nie die Begabung der Amerikaner, wenn es darum geht, das schnelle Geld zu machen! Das Skigebiet Aspen in Colorado entwickelte sich gerade zum begehrten Ziel für Jetsetter, als ein Grafiker mit diesem cleveren Wortspiel reagierte. Man nehme ein leckeres Foto von Busen und Popos, gebe sie als schneebedeckte Hügel aus, platziere einen Miniaturskifahrer auf die prallen Rundungen und schon hat man die perfekte Winterlandschaft für zahllose Collegestudenten, die sich das Poster an die Wohnheimtür pinnen und von Abfahrten auf diesen jungfräulichen Pisten träumen.

Aspen et tétons

Ne sous-estimez jamais le génie des Américains à faire rapidement fortune. Aspen, une station de ski dans le Colorado, commençait tout juste à devenir populaire auprès de la jet-set, lorsqu'un commerçant habile eut une brillante idée. Prenez une photographie alléchante de bustes et d'arrière-trains pour représenter des montagnes enneigées, ajoutez un skieur miniature évoluant sur cette chair appétissante et voilà ! Un paysage d'hiver instantané à faire fantasmer des légions de collégiens qui pouvaient coller l'affiche sur la porte de leur dortoir et rêver à de belles descentes sur ces pistes vierges.

Paisajes corporales

Nunca subestime la capacidad de los estadounidenses para hacer dinero fácil. La estación de esquí de Aspen, en Colorado, empezaba a atraer la atención de la *jet set* cuando un promotor espabilado salió al paso con esta idea brillante... Obtén una exquisita fotografía de tetas y culos para representar montañas nevadas, añade un esquiador en miniatura en medio de tanta suculenta carne y ¡*voilà!*: una fantasía invernal instantánea para incontables estudiantes, que podían colgar el cartel en la puerta de su dormitorio y relajarse soñando con descensos por faldas vírgenes.

おっぱいとアスペン

簡単に金を稼ぎ出すアメリカ人の才能を決して過小評価してはならない。お利口な商品開発担当者がこの素晴しいアイディアをもって難局に対処したちょ
その頃、アスペンのコロラドスキーリゾートがジェット機族の目を惹き始めていた。雪に覆われた小山を表現した魅力的な胸と臀部の写真を入手して、花も
らう素肌の真ん中にミニチュアのスキーヤーを加えたら、ほーら! 寄宿舎の部屋の壁に貼って、"ヴァージン"スロープに突っ込んでいく夢を見ることもでき
それは無数の男子学生たちのための即席の冬のファンタジー。

Ski Asspen, 1982

295

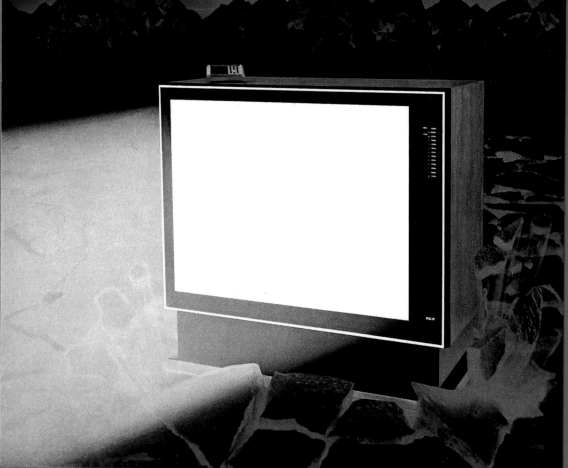

PROJECTION

PRESENTING THE END OF THE DARK AGES.

RCA INTRODUCES ITS BEST AND BRIGHTEST GENERATION OF BIG-SCREEN TV'S.

BIG, BRIGHT AND BEAUTIFUL. The picture you see on RCA's big 45-inch screen (measured diagonally) marks the beginning of a bright new era. Its remarkable 65% increase in peak brightness and 200% increase in contrast make it light-years ahead of earlier RCA projection sets. Watching projection television in the dark is a thing of the past.

Another improvement is a big, crowd-pleasing viewing angle that makes just about every seat in the house the best seat in the house.

VIDEO MONITOR CAPABILITY. Our high-performance giant is also a video monitor. Its convenient system of input/output jacks lets you hook up your video cassette recorder, videodisc player, and stereo for maximum enjoyment.

SIZE ISN'T EVERYTHING. RCA's best and brightest features our exclusive Digital Command Center. The total control remote control that enables you to switch from broadcast to VCR to videodisc viewing at the touch of a button.

All of this comes wrapped in the most compact cabinet in RCA big-screen history. To see our best generation of big-screen TV's ever, visit your RCA dealer.

It promises to be a most enlightening experience.

For more information and a free copy of "Living With Video" (a $2.50 retail value), write: RCA Consumer Electronics, Department 32-312P, P.O. Box 1976, Indianapolis, IN 46206.

WE'LL OPEN YOUR EYES. RC/I

TELEVISION

Panasonic Stereo, 1982 ◄   *RCA Projection Televisions, 1983*

C O L O R T R A K

PALE BY COMPARISON.

That's how a conventional 19-inch TV measures up against this ColorTrak 2000. RCA's remarkable new ColorTrak 2000 model #JR2020W puts 25" of picture (measured diagonally) into the same space as conventional 19" sets. And along with 70% more picture, this new ColorTrak comes with a combination of exclusive RCA features: 58-function Digital Command Center remote control, high-compliance speakers, 127-channel tuning (including cable) and RCA's advanced detail processor, which delivers a picture that appears almost 3-dimensional. See your RCA dealer for a demonstration. And see 25" of picture that sits in 19" of set. Beautifully.

For more information and a free copy of the "Living with Video" book ($2.50 retail value), write: RCA Consumer Electronics, Department 32-312L, P.O. Box 1976, Indianapolis, Indiana 46206.

WE'LL OPEN YOUR EYES.

RCA

T W O   T H O U S A N D

RCA Televisions, 1983

BASEBALL ON A SONY VIDEOSCOPE IS A WHOLE NEW BALL GAME.

Size alone isn't what makes Sony VideoScope™ so awesome. It's the quality of the picture. Our exclusive Coolant Sealed Picture Tubes and super-bright lenses offer the kind of bright, sharp picture you've come to expect from Sony.

And right now there's another big reason for buying our giant TV: the Sony World Series Sweepstakes!

WIN A FREE TRIP TO THE WORLD SERIES

Ask your Sony dealer for the brochure that explains why Sony VideoScope is so spectacular. Then answer the four simple questions on the entry form and send it to Sony. You could be among the first prizewinners to get an all-expenses-paid trip to the 1983 World Series.

For sports fans who don't like crowds, we're giving away twenty flat-screen Sony Watchmans™ as second prize. This truly personal TV is only 1¼" thin!

The big story, of course, is watching big league action on any of the wide range of Sony VideoScopes. There are one- and two-piece models, even rear-projection VideoScopes. The KP-5040 (50" measured diagonally) is a compact, single piece of furniture. It is fully cable-adaptable and comes with Express Commander™ wireless remote control.

Sony's two-piece units have a free-standing screen (that can also be mounted on a wall) and a projection unit that doubles as a coffee table. Or a peanuts and popcorn table.

The KPR-4600A rear-projection VideoScope completes Sony's winning line-up. It gives you a huge (46" diagonally) picture in the space of a console TV.

So get down to your Sony dealer before the Sweepstakes ends on September 1, 1983. Because once you've watched baseball on a Sony VideoScope projection TV, you'll never watch it on anything else.

No purchase necessary. See your Sony dealer for details. Void where prohibited.
© 1983 Sony Corporation of America. Sony is a registered trademark of Sony Corporation. VideoScope, Watchman and Express Commander are trademarks of Sony Corporation.

SONY
THE ONE AND ONLY   Simulated Pictures

Sony VideoScope, 1983

Not Evolutionary, Revolutionary.

Pioneer's Revolutionary Foresight System

Once you experience the glory of Pioneer's Foresight System, you can't help but pledge your allegiance to the finest audio/video system this country has ever seen. And no wonder. Because only Foresight gives your eyes and ears the thrill of LaserVision,® the only video format that delivers both digital sound and a video image 60% sharper than any VHS HQ in existence.

And that's just for starters. Because when you have Foresight, you have it all: easier operation due to a single "SR" system remote—three-dimensional surround sound—Pioneer's advanced audio technology—and Pioneer's 40" Projection Monitor, the best and the brightest ever made.

So if you're looking for the finest sight and sound show in America today, you have to look for your Pioneer dealer. Because no matter how exciting this ad may be, it doesn't even come close to the excitement of Foresight. For your nearest Foresight Dealer, call 1-800-421-1404.

PIONEER
CATCH THE SPIRIT OF A TRUE PIONEER.

©1986 Pioneer Electronics (USA), Inc., Long Beach, CA. LaserVision is a trademark of the LaserVision Association. Actual closed circuit picture shown.

Pioneer Home Entertainment System, 1987

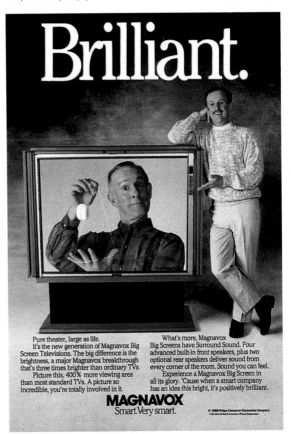

Brilliant.

Pure theater, large as life. It's the new generation of Magnavox Big Screen Televisions. The big difference is the brightness, a major Magnavox breakthrough that's three times brighter than ordinary TVs.

Picture this, 400% more viewing area than most standard TVs. A picture so incredible, you're totally involved in it.

What's more, Magnavox Big Screens have Surround Sound. Four advanced built-in front speakers, plus two optional rear speakers deliver sound from every corner of the room. Sound you can feel.

Experience a Magnavox Big Screen in all its glory. 'Cause when a smart company has an idea this bright, it's positively brilliant.

MAGNAVOX
Smart. Very smart.

© 1988 Philips Consumer Electronics Company
A division of North American Philips Corporation

Magnavox Televisions, 1988

Now Panasonic Hi-Fi VCRs can make your house sound better than most movie houses.

Experience the supernatural. An eerie presence seems to fill the room. This phenomenon is created by the picture and sound from the new Panasonic VHS Hi-Fi video recorder, PV-1742. In fact, it has the amazing ability to produce sound better than most movie houses.

This Panasonic VCR can do something else that's unbelievable. It can turn your ordinary TV into a stereo TV. Because its built-in MTS decoder lets you enjoy stereo TV broadcasts through your stereo.

Less sophisticated video recorders won't stand a ghost of a chance once you see what this VCR can do: Its HQ circuitry enhances the image. The Tech-4™ four-head system gives you virtually noise-free slow motion and freeze-frame. And its full-function wireless remote can even let you program it to record up to 8 shows over 3 weeks.

So create a supernatural presence in your home. Experience Panasonic VHS Hi-Fi.

Panasonic.
just slightly ahead of our time.

THE PANASONIC LAS VEGAS PRO-AM
APRIL 29-MAY 3, 1987. SEE IT ON NBC

Poltergeist II from MGM/UA Home Video November 1986.

© MGM Entertainment Co. 1986
TV picture simulated. Stereo where available.

Panasonic VCRs, 1986

WITH MAXELL VIDEO TAPE, EVEN AFTER 300 PLAYS YOU CAN STILL SAY...

"Play it again Sam"

Every Maxell video tape is destined to become an old favorite.

Because as well as delivering a great performance Maxell video tapes are designed to give you a lasting one.

So try Maxell VHS or Beta. The video tape you'll appreciate more and more...as time goes by.

maxell.
IT'S WORTH IT.

© 1983 Maxell Corporation of America, 60 Oxford Drive, Moonachie, N.J. 07074

Maxell Videotapes, 1983

▶ *Maxell Videotapes, 1986*

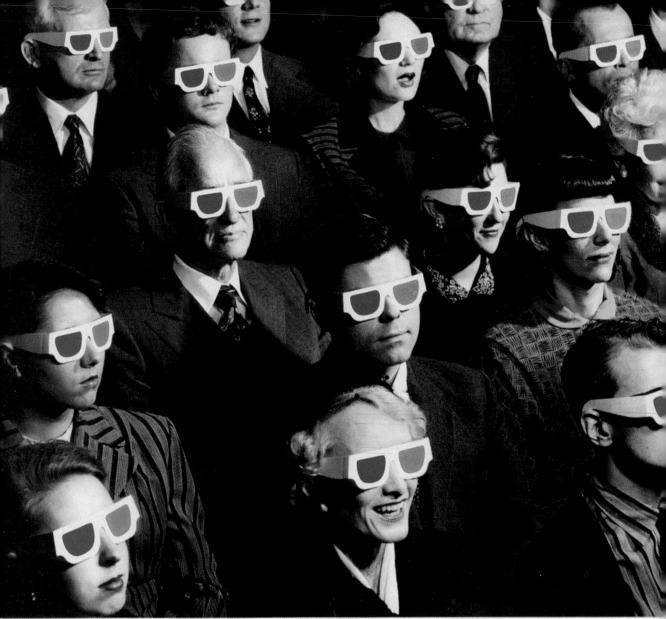

PRESENTING THE SAME THING ONLY FOR YOUR EARS.

What 3-D did for your eyes Technics can do for your ears.

Thanks to the virtues of our SA-R477 A/V receiver with Dolby Surround Sound.*

When hooked up to an extra pair of speakers and your VCR, it can make moving pictures a lot more moving. For instance, when the Orient Express crosses your TV screen, it will sound like it's crossing your living room. Or when you're watching a great war film, it will sound like the battle is taking place around your couch.

This incredibly life-like sound is brought to you in large part by a special digital delay circuit. Which allows you to decode the signal on many pre-recorded video tapes and acoustically shape

the size of the room to the sound of the movie.

Naturally, with 100 watts of pure power per channel (at 8 ohms, 20Hz—20Hz with 0.008% THD) it has the power to keep you on the edge of your seat. However, you certainly won't have to leave it. Because this receiver comes with a remote control that can control all compatible Technics audio components, and many TVs and VCRs, as well.

Hear the remarkable sound of the SA-R477 A/V receiver at a Technics dealer near you

You won't need a pair of those silly glasses to appreciate this type of 3-D. Just a good pair of ears.

Technics Surround Sound A/V Receiver.

Technics
The science of sound

Smart.

"It's the finest pocket color TV we've tested...
this set will give you a clear, sharp picture with
remarkably good color."
— Video Review, March 1988

Why does the Magnavox 3" LCD Color TV
deserve such rave reviews? See for yourself. Watch
it anywhere, anytime. Even outdoors. The picture
stays sharp. And bright. With rich, true color.

How? With the   most individual picture
elements in the world. Over 92,000. (But who's
counting?) What's more, Magnavox added
a new slant on pocket TVs, with an adjustable screen
angle for better viewing.

Magnavox has always made big advances
in TV technology. But putting them all into one little
package, now that's pretty smart.

MAGNAVOX

At last,
you can get it out of your system.

With Alpine's high energy, high technology car audio systems, at last there's equipment to give you the sensational sound of the groups you love live, accurately reproduced in your car.

With powerful, self-contained FM/AM tuner/cassette decks. Electronically superior pre-amps. Bi-level™ units with both power and easy add-on capability. High-powered amplifiers, equalizers, and component speaker systems. And features like Music Sensor™ and Cassette Glide™ that make it easy while driving. Specs like frequency response with metal tape on our 7307 FM/AM Cassette, 40 to 18,000 Hz. And dealers who not only know how to put a dynamite system together, but how to install it right. The first time.

So instead of driving around with only so-so sound, get the best. Get to an Alpine dealer. And get it out of your system. Once and for all. Alpine Electronics of America, Inc., 3102 Kashiwa Street, Torrance, California 90505.

ALPINE
car audio systems

Alpine Car Audio Systems, 1980

OWN THE FANTASY.

GET YOUR MUSIC FREE!

The new Spectrum Series from Kenwood. A collection of complete stereo systems. Everything you need. Already picked out. Matched to perform like no other. Branded with the one name that says you know a lot about sound.

And crafted with a look that says you also know a lot about style.

Buy any Kenwood Spectrum Series system. You'll get up to $100 worth of selected Columbia albums or tapes. Free.

See your participating Kenwood dealer before September 30, 1981.

Because with an offer like this, supplies won't last long.

For the Kenwood dealer nearest you, see your Yellow Pages, or write Kenwood, P.O. Box 6213, Carson, CA 90749.

This offer void where prohibited by law.

⊕KENWOOD® Spectrum series

Kenwood Spectrum Series, 1981

Yamaha. For the music in you.

"I love to play music that makes people feel good. But first it has to please me. I love sharing my music with an audience. That's when it really comes alive. And I love to hear it on a sound system that lets all those good feelings come through. Like Yamaha."
—Chuck Mangione

Yamaha. Because you want more than mere sound. You want to be moved. To be thrilled. You want the music.

And music is something we know a lot about.

Yamaha has been making musical instruments for almost one hundred years. So we know how music sounds. And we know how to make audio components that reproduce music accurately.

Every audio component we build must pass a final critical audition by the discerning ears of a Yamaha musical instrument designer. So it brings out what is most important. The music in you.

Yamaha Electronics Corporation, U.S.A.
P.O. Box 6660, Buena Park, CA 90622

Chuck Mangione's album "Tarantella" is available on A&M records and tapes.

YAMAHA

Yamaha, 1981

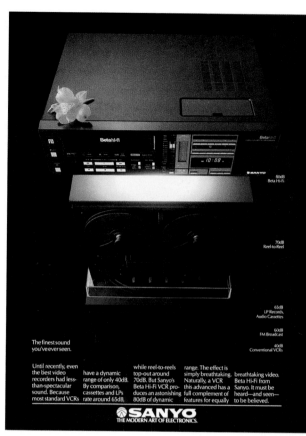

The finest sound you've ever seen.

Until recently, even the best video recorders had less-than-spectacular sound. Because most standard VCRs have a dynamic range of only 40dB. By comparison, cassettes and LPs rate around 65dB, while reel-to-reels top-out around 70dB. But Sanyo's Beta Hi-Fi VCR produces an astonishing 80dB of dynamic range. The effect is simply breathtaking. Naturally, a VCR this advanced has a full complement of features for equally breathtaking video. Beta Hi-Fi from Sanyo. It must be heard—and seen—to be believed.

80dB Beta Hi-Fi
70dB Reel-to-Reel
65dB LP Records, Audio Cassettes
60dB FM Broadcast
40dB Conventional VCRs

SANYO
THE MODERN ART OF ELECTRONICS.

Sanyo VCR, 1984

HI-FI FOR THE EYE.

Up until now, if you wanted music that was great to listen to, you often got a room that wasn't so great to look at. An amplifier here, a tuner there, bookshelves in rooms you didn't want them. The components took over your house.

In creating Syscom, Pioneer has solved this problem once and for all. Instead of components all over the place, they're in one lovely place. A cabinet that harmonizes with just about every decor.

Pioneer Syscom is more than beautiful furniture, however, it's beautiful sound. A truly complete component system put together by Pioneer engineers. Amplifier, tuner (or receiver), turntable, tape deck, speakers all perfectly matched.

There are 7 Pioneer Syscom groups to choose from. One is perfect for your music, your budget, your room.

Call us at **800-621-5199*** for the store nearest you. You should see Syscom. A lot of people buy it before they ever turn it on.

*(In Illinois 800-972-5855).

SYSCOM by PIONEER
Serious hi-fi. Finally made simple.

Headphone and matching turntable optional.

© 1980 U.S. Pioneer Electronics Corp.

Pioneer Syscom, 1980

Not for the meek

When you buy a Sanyo Digital Audio System, you have to be prepared.

The sound is so spectacular, so commanding, that it challenges your ability to take it all in. But if you're someone who appreciates breathtaking power and clarity, Sanyo has two new digital audio systems for you.

Each has the CP300 player. Its laser pickup system reads the computer-coded music on compact digital discs without touching the surface—so discs keep their sparkling sound forever.

It's easy to operate, and includes rapid access, automatic repeat, and programmable track memory.

To handle the enormous dynamic range of digital audio, you can choose from a crisp 50 or a superb 100 watt per channel* amplifier. A built-in graphic equalizer lets you "fine tune" the sound.

Other matched components include a computer-controlled digital AM/FM tuner that actually seeks out and programs up to 20 stations into its memory. Plus a high-performance Dolby** cassette deck. And 3-way high-efficiency speakers. There's even a semi-automatic direct drive turntable.

Contact your local Sanyo dealer to audition both of these impeccable performers.

If you dare.

*Minimum Continuous Average Power per channel, both channels driven into 8 ohms, 20—20,000Hz, no more than 0.3% Total Harmonic Distortion

**TM Dolby Laboratories
©Sanyo 1984

SANYO
The modern art of electronics.

Sanyo Digital Audio System, 1984

Panasonic introduces SoundScapes™. The sound of components. Without the complexity of components.

Escape to the world of extraordinary sound and beauty. Escape from the world of technical intimidation. Escape to SoundScapes from Panasonic.

SoundScapes give you the startling precision, clarity, and depth of components. But unlike components, SoundScapes are self-contained and matched, so they're easy to operate yet still technically sophisticated.

The SoundScapes P-9 (shown below), for example, has all this: A powerful amplifier. The world's most accurate AM/FM tuning system, a quartz synthesizer. A fully automatic turntable with linear tracking for virtually flawless sound reproduction. A microprocessor controlled cassette deck that's synchronized with the turntable, so you don't waste tape. And a 5-band graphic equalizer that lets you tailor the music to your taste. All this plus Turbo Thrusters™ speakers for an enhanced mid-range and an extra thrust of bass.

There are four different SoundScapes systems. All with the sound of components. But all without the complexity of components.

SoundScapes
Panasonic
High Fidelity Systems

Panasonic SoundScapes, 1981

▶ *Maxell Cassette Tapes, 1984*

309

CarryClip™

THE HIP WAY TO CARRY MUSIC.

The favorite cassette tape of serious audio enthusiasts is now ready to travel. Denon's new CarryClip™ lets you leave heavy, bulky cassette boxes at home, and still protect your music from dust and shock. Get two free with each DX-7 two-pack you buy.

DENON
THE MOST MUSICAL CASSETTE TAPE.

Denon Cassette Tapes, 1985

SONY TAPE. FULL COLOR SOUND.

There's more to Full Color Sound than meets the ear.

There is a story of experience and technical achievement that has made Sony a leader in its field. Sony produces both high fidelity audio and video tape and the high quality equipment that plays it. In fact, Sony pioneered magnetic tape recording, and has been producing tape and tape equipment for over 30 years.

What makes Sony audio tape so special is *balance*. The fine tuning of all the electrical and mechanical elements to match

each other, for a recording as close to perfect as is humanly and technically possible.

The more sophisticated your equipment, the more you'll appreciate Sony high quality audio tape.

Try Sony SHF (normal bias), EHF (high bias), FeCr or Metallic.

Listen to the balance. It's the secret of Full Color Sound. **SONY.**

Sony Cassette Tapes, 1981

Now Sony turns your living room, your car, and your backpack into a concert hall.

Since the invention of the phonograph player in 1877, there have been many technical refinements, but the basic concept hasn't changed a bit.

Until now.

Sony* has created a revolution in sound reproduction by bringing the world the first Compact Disc Player. A system that replaces the inaccuracy of the phonograph needle with the precision of the laser beam.

Imperfect record grooves with mathematically perfect computer codes.

Vulnerable records with durable discs.

A system that High Fidelity magazine called "the most fundamental change in audio technology in more than eighty years."

Today, while over 30 companies are joining the revolution, Sony is starting two others:

The Car Compact Disc Player.

And the Portable Compact Disc Player.

So people who want true concert hall fidelity never have to be without it.

You can audition these masterpieces of engineering at your Sony dealer now.

Or you can listen to everyone else's copy of them later.

THE ONE AND ONLY SOUND OF

Sony Stereos, 1984

NO OTHER AUDIO TAPE DELIVERS HIGHER FIDELITY.

maxell
The Tape That Delivers
Higher Performance.

Maxell Cassette Tapes, 1989

NEVER, NEVER CALL IT A BOOM BOX.

Panasonic Platinum Collection. From XBS Extra Bass System to CD sound that's worthy of the name "platinum."

You would never consider a house wine when there are great vintages. You would never settle for a print when you can have an original. And you would never, never even think about buying a boom box. That's why Panasonic created Platinum Collection portable stereos.

A sterling example is the RX-DS650 with its built-in CD player. The XBS Extra Bass System boosts low frequencies while helping minimize distortion. Detachable twin air suspension speakers with 6¼" woofers provide surprisingly powerful sound. It also sports 36-Step Random Access Programming and easy CD-to-tape editing.

The Platinum Collection includes three other models. One has remote control. Others feature dual cassette and digital tuning. All make a powerful statement anywhere you care to appreciate good music. The Panasonic Platinum Collection. As far removed from a boom box as you can get. ▪

Panasonic®
just slightly ahead of our time.®

Panasonic Portable Stereo, 1989

A clear case for Green: Green to be envied, Green that's the scene. Sonic sounds sound supersonic, fiery tones breathe fire, dazzling highs and lows razzle-dazzle. All in a case with a clear face. Sony, the Dean of Green. Being Green is being seen.

SOUND OF A DIFFERENT COLOR.

Sony Cassette Tapes, 1985

Aiwa Boombox, 1989

The Sony that broke the sound barrier.

Until Sony introduced the Walkman (a stereo cassette player about the size of a cassette), there was no way to hear quality sound reproduction this good unless you bought a ticket to Carnegie Hall, or sat home with an expensive component stereo.

Unfortunately, it was impossible to ski, jog, roller-skate or take a walk in a concert hall or your living room.

That is why on November 1, 1979, the Walkman took a historic step forward by combining incredible sound with total portability. What followed can only be described as a Sonic Boom. **THE WALKMAN**

BUY A WALKMAN 2 AT PARTICIPATING DEALERS AND GET MONEY-SAVING REBATES ON HEADPHONES AND ACCESSORY KIT UNTIL DEC 31, 1981.

SONY
THE ONE AND ONLY

Sony Walkman, 1981

CHOOSE YOUR ESCAPE ROUTE.

STEREO TAPE ESCAPE
Plan your escape with the Stereo Tape Escape. It's as simple as popping in a tape and putting on the featherweight (2-oz.) headphones. You get tone and channel controls to custom-shape the great stereo sound. And there's an extra jack so you can even escape with a friend. Model 3-5270

STEREO RADIO ESCAPE
Built-in auto-matic frequency control lets you escape with ease by locking in your favorite FM station. And just like its slightly bigger brothers, the ultra-light AM/FM Stereo Radio Escape has separate left and right channel controls, an extra jack for a friend, and, of course, incredible sound. Model 7-1000

STEREO GREAT ESCAPE
Turn on a tape or tune into the FM radio. How you choose to escape is entirely up to you when you have the Stereo Great Escape. Separate channel controls, an extra jack for a friend, and two escape routes make this one machine you shouldn't let get away. Model 3-5271

WE BRING GOOD THINGS TO LIFE.

GENERAL ELECTRIC

For more information, write to General Electric Co., E.P., Bldg. 3, Rm. 138, Syracuse, NY 13221.

General Electric Escape Stereos, 1981

And now a little traveling music from Casio.

It's a sizable achievement—creating a radio the size of a credit card. And the credit goes to Casio's advanced micro-electronics and film lamination technology.

The results speak for themselves, with reception that's loud and clear. In both AM and FM.

What's also clear is that these Radio Cards are so incredibly thin they'll go anywhere your travels take

you. So when you're out running, hiking, biking, fishing or whatever, you'll never have to miss out on your favorite sounds.

What's more, while Radio Cards come in AM and FM, they're so inexpensive, you'll want one of each.

Casio Radio Cards. They're for anyone who's on the run and doesn't want to run out of entertainment.

CASIO
Where miracles never cease

Casio, Inc. Audio - Video Division: 15 Gardner Road, Fairfield, N.J. 07006 New Jersey (201) 575-7400, Los Angeles (213) 803-3411.

Casio Radio Cards, 1985

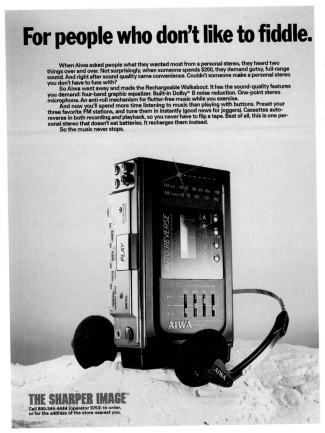

For people who don't like to fiddle.

When Aiwa asked people what they wanted most from a personal stereo, they heard two things over and over. Not surprisingly, when someone spends $200, they demand gutsy, full-range sound. And right after sound quality came convenience. Couldn't someone make a personal stereo you don't have to fuss with?

So Aiwa went away and made the Rechargeable Walkabout. It has the sound-quality features you demand: four-band graphic equalizer. Built-in Dolby™ B noise reduction. One-point stereo microphone. An anti-roll mechanism for flutter-free music while you exercise.

And now you'll spend more time listening to music than playing with buttons. Preset your three favorite FM stations, and tune them in instantly (good news for joggers). Cassettes auto-reverse in both recording *and* playback, so you never have to flip a tape. Best of all, this is one personal stereo that doesn't eat batteries. It recharges them instead.

So the music never stops.

THE SHARPER IMAGE®
Call 800-344-4444 (operator 9753) to order, or for the address of the store nearest you.

Aiwa Walkabout, 1988

Beyer Dynamic Audio Systems, 1985

Boss Digital Sampler, 1985

Casio Synthesizers, 1987

Technics Keyboards, 1989

▶ *Yamaha Synthesizers, 1986*

It has two wheels, two sources
[p]ower and can go from 0 to 192 in
[ ]one shift. But instead of riding it,
[ ]strap it over your shoulder. Be-
[cau]se this machine is so powerful, it
[can]take you places just standing still.
The DX100 synthesizer.
Anything's possible.

Knight Warrior

Aria Pro II Electric Guitar, 1985

▶ *Hamer Guitars, 1989*

Kip Winger

Hamer builds instruments of uncompromising quality, for musicians who are serious about their sound.

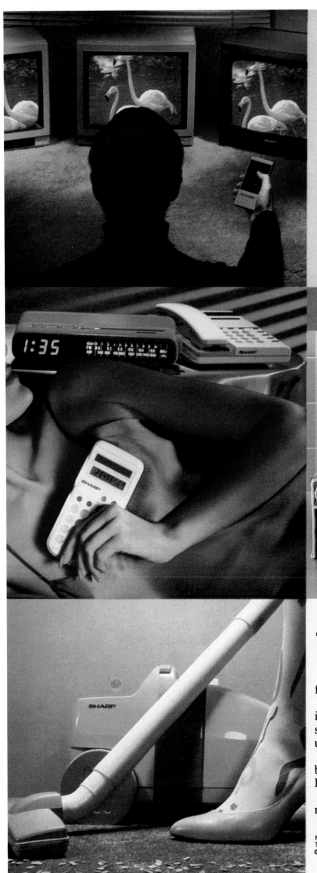

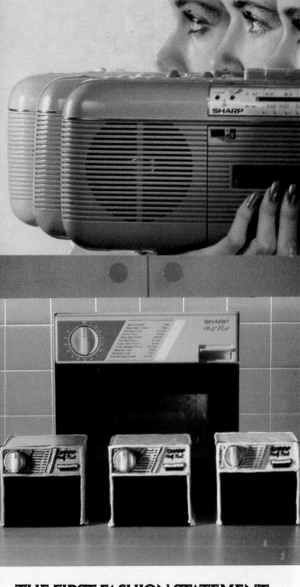

THE FIRST FASHION STATEMENT THAT TALKS, SINGS, BUZZES, HUMS, AND WHISPERS.

Suddenly, style is plugged into pastels. And Sharp is first with pastels you can plug in all around you.

Get ready for the shock of pulsating color in places it's never been before: microwave ovens, clock radios, stereo radio cassette players, telephones, calculators, vacuum cleaners, and TVs with color inside and out.

There are passionate pinks, greens, yellows, lavenders, blues, and other hues, all with the heat of a tropical sunset. It's lifestyle in living color. High tech turned hot tech.

Sharp Pastels. There is absolutely nothing neutral about them.

SHARP.
FROM SHARP MINDS
COME SHARP PRODUCTS™

Sharp Electronics, 1988 ◄ *Sharp Electronics, 1986* ► *Timex Computers, 1982*

TI's Home Computer Software.
Lets you use your head. Not just your hands.

Texas Instruments has some of the best arcade-quality games you can play on a computer. Our Parsec game, for example, combines fantastic graphics, speech, speed and machine intelligence to bring hours of excitement to the most demanding player.

But many of our games go beyond sheer excitement. We think games should give you the opportunity to learn something as well. That's why so much of our TI-99/4A Home Computer entertainment software consists of games of strategy and logic. Like Tunnels of Doom, or our 12-program Adventure series. Games so engrossing you'll never realize they're educational.

For children, we even have games that are obviously educational...but too much fun to seem like studying. This approach

makes addition, subtraction, multiplication and division come to life in our DLM Academics™ series.

And we also have plenty of traditional favorites, like Football, Blackjack, and Hangman — and arcade-quality action games: Parsec, TI Invaders, Munch Man and many more.

You can have a good time with the TI Home Computer. But there's no reason a good time can't be an education, too.

For more information about our entertainment software or our broad selection of other software applications, call toll-free (800) 858-4565.

Creating useful products and services for you.

TEXAS INSTRUMENTS

Copyright © 1983 Texas Instruments.

Texas Instruments Computers, 1983

Freeway Game, 1981

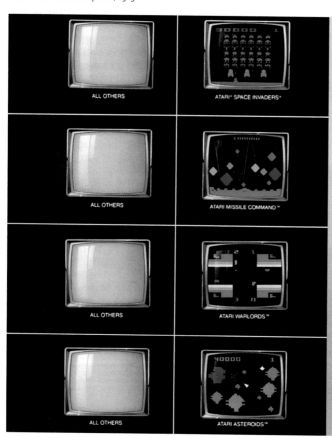

Atari Game System, 1981

▶ *Odyssey² Game System, 1981*

ON YOUR MARK, GET SET, MUNCH.

With new K.C. Munchkin from Odyssey², you don't destroy your enemies, you simply eat them.

Simulated TV picture.

How many Munchies can your Munchkin munch before your Munchkin's all munched out? Play K.C. Munchkin and see!

It's fun. It's exciting. It's challenging. Your whole family will love it!

A Munchkin, three Munchers and 12 Munchies float in a maze with a rotating center. The more Munchies your Munchkin munches, the more points you get. The more points, the faster the computer makes the game go. And the more skill you need to score and to keep your Munchkin from getting munched by one of the Munchers!

The better you play, the greater the challenge!

You can play a different maze every time by letting the computer generate them. Or use the Odyssey² keyboard and program your own. There's virtually no limit to the number of mazes you can create. There are even invisible mazes for when you're ready to turn pro.

Choose from more than 40 arcade, sports, education and new Master Strategy™ games. See Odyssey² today. It's waiting for you now at your video games or Odyssey² Magnavox dealer.

Odyssey²...video game fun, computer keyboard challenge. All for the price of an ordinary video game.

The excitement of a game. The mind of a computer.

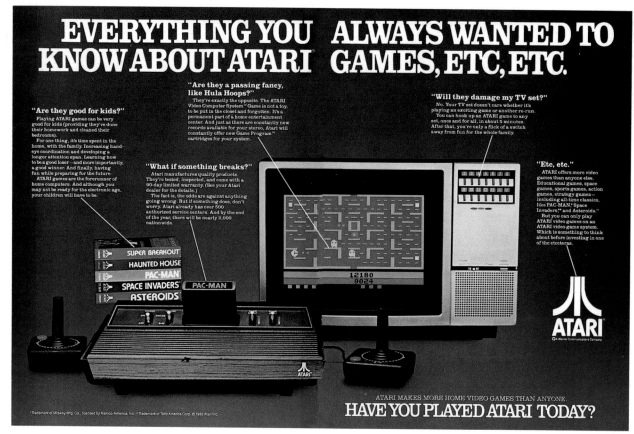

Atari Game System, 1982

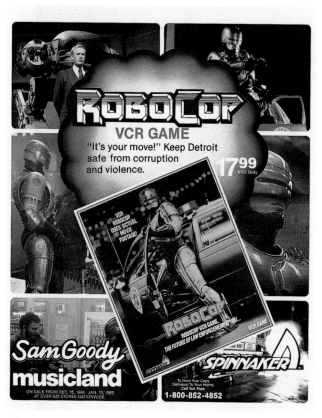

RoboCop Game, 1989

RoboCop Game, 1989

THE ONLY VIDEO GAME VOICE MODULE WITH AN UNLIMITED VOCABULARY.

The Voice from Odyssey² adds a whole new dimension to the fun of video games. With this optional module and its specially programmed cartridges, Odyssey² becomes the only video game system that can repeat any words typed into the keyboard, and much more!

Depending upon which cartridge you insert, The Voice can do a whole bunch of other exciting things. Like asking questions and demanding answers to math and spelling problems. It even enhances sound effects and warns of approaching enemies in certain arcade games!

A whole series of specialized arcade, educational and strategy voice cartridges is available for use with The Voice, with a lot more to come. But you can still play all other Odyssey video games through The Voice module.

So if you're on the lookout for greater challenge, listen to The Voice, from Odyssey.² The fun you will have will speak for itself. For your nearest dealer call (800) 447-2882. In Illinois call (800) 322-4400.

© 1982 N.A.P. CONSUMER ELECTRONICS CORP.
A NORTH AMERICAN PHILIPS COMPANY

ODYSSEY²

The keyboard is the key to greater challenge.

THE WIZARD OF ODYSSEY REVEALS THE KEY TO GREATER CHALLENGE.

The Keyboard!
It makes the fun go further with Odyssey² than any other video game. The keyboard lets you program mazes and grids. Type numbers and letters on the screen. Increase skill levels. It even lets you change opponents and fields of play!

And only Odyssey² offers—The Master Strategy Series™! Each game comes with its own game board. You use it to plan your strategy.

input that strategy through the keyboard, and play out the action on your TV screen.

Plus, Odyssey² offers over 50 games, including arcade, educational, sports and strategy games.

So take the word of the Wizard of Odyssey. If you're looking for greater challenge in a video game, look to Odyssey²! For your nearest dealer call (800) 447-2882. In Illinois call (800) 322-4400.

ODYSSEY²

The keyboard is the key to greater challenge.

© 1982 N.A.P. CONSUMER ELECTRONICS CORP.
A NORTH AMERICAN PHILIPS COMPANY

Award-Winning Hits for your Commodore   with a Free Software Bonus.

CHOPLIFTER*
For the Commodore VIC-20.
Sixty-four Americans are being held hostage behind enemy lines. You've got to shoot your way in there and bring them back alive. Sneak over the border, make your way through heavily fortified enemy fire, and blast your way back to safety. It may be a suicide mission, but somebody's got to do it. America is counting on you!

SERPENTINE*
For the Commodore VIC-20.
Three huge and evil red snakes are slithering through the corridors of a burnt-out city, closing in on your good blue serpent from all sides. Move fast, watch your tail, and try to survive long enough to let your eggs hatch into reinforcements. Swallow the magical frogs or your enemy's eggs and you get the strength to go on! Complex strategy-action and increasing levels of difficulty.

PIPES*
For the VIC-20 and Commodore 64.
Arlo is a hardworking plumber, but a touch absent-minded. Help him construct a water supply system for a whole neighborhood. Choose the right pipes from the factory, plan the most economical layout, and just hope Arlo has remembered to open and close the right valves! A marvelously entertaining and challenging exercise in planning, economics and spatial relationships for all ages.

SAVE NEW YORK™
For the Commodore 64.
Hordes of grotesque aliens are swooping down on the Big Apple, munching like mad and laying eggs in the subway tunnels that hatch and creep up from below. As the lone defender you will fight against incredible odds and a shrinking fuel supply, in the most challenging battle ever seen on the Commodore 64!

*SELECTED AS SOME OF THE "MOST INNOVATIVE COMPUTER PROGRAMS" 1983 CES SOFTWARE SHOWCASE AWARDS.

Now you can play some of America's hottest computer games on your Commodore, and get a FREE introduction to Home Management Software. It's our way of showing you that action-packed gaming is

only the beginning of your Commodore's capabilities. It can teach you. Manage your family finances. Even help you buy a new car. And now, for a limited time only, when you buy one of our specially-marked

games you'll receive a certificate good for one of our Home Management Programs absolutely free. See your Creative Software dealer for complete details. Get more out of your Commodore. Get Creative!

C R E A T I V E   S O F T W A R E

"CHOPLIFTER" AND "SERPENTINE" ARE VIC-20 TRANSLATIONS OF ORIGINALS BY DAN GORLIN AND DAVID SNIDER, RESPECTIVELY.   "CHOPLIFTER" AND "SERPENTINE" ARE LICENSED FROM BRODERBUND SOFTWARE, INC.   "VIC-20" AND "COMMODORE 64" ARE TRADEMARKS OF COMMODORE ELECTRONICS, LTD.   © 1983 CREATIVE SOFTWARE.

There's no match for WWF WrestleMania.

WWF WrestleMania

You've always dreamed of being Hulk Hogan.™ Or one of the other WWF Superstars. And now here's your chance. Challenge your opponent to a wild match of dropkicks, headlocks, bodyslams and more! Or create your own tournament and compete against your friends or the computer. Up to six can play. So step into the ring and experience WWF WrestleMania®... from the inside!

Look for our Wrestlemania® Nintendo® and Hand-Held games.

Official Nintendo Seal of Quality

Licensed by Nintendo for play on the

Nintendo ENTERTAINMENT SYSTEM

A⟨⟨laim™
entertainment, inc.
Masters of the Game™

WWF WrestleMania Game, 1989

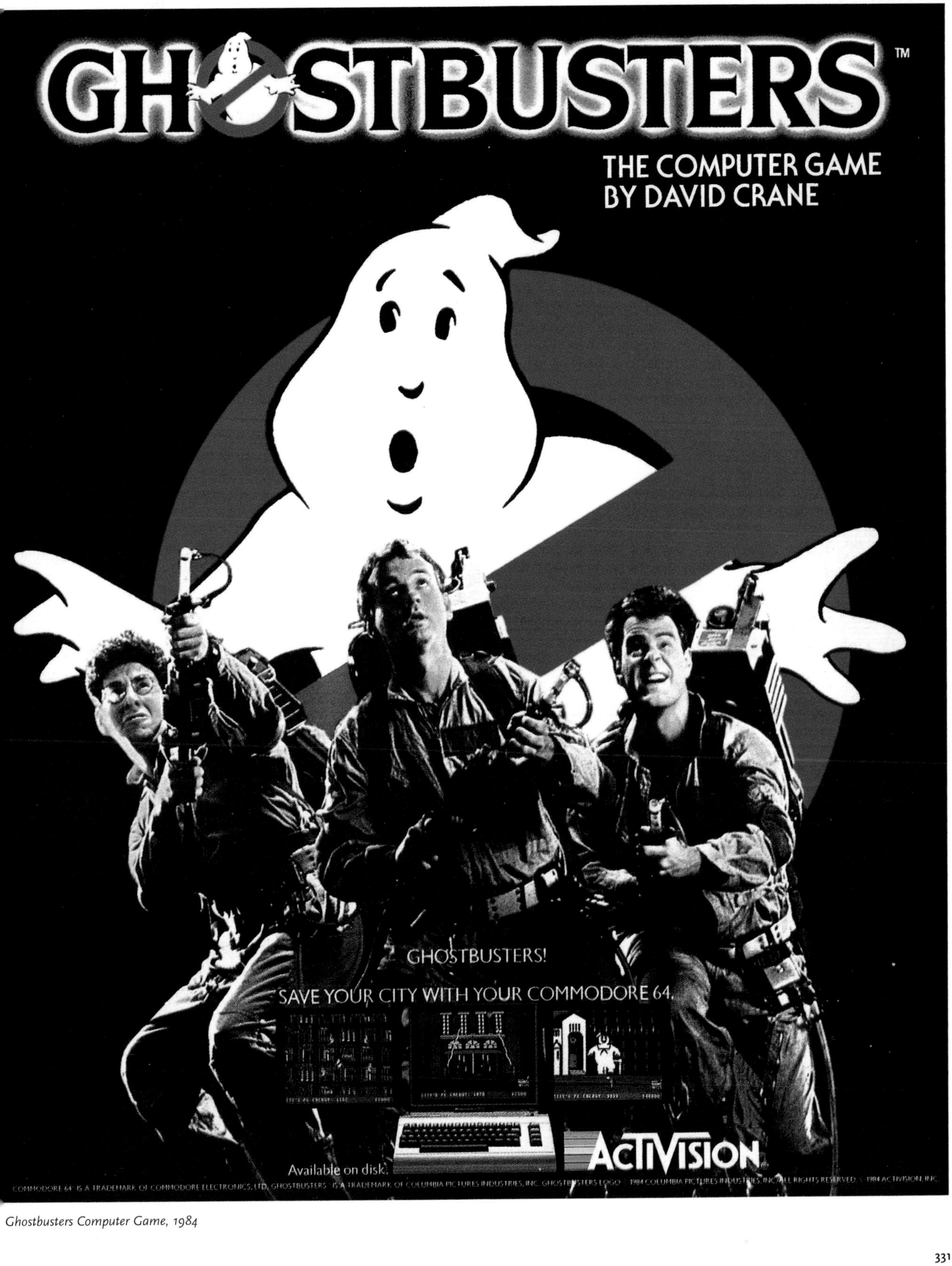

Ghostbusters Computer Game, 1984

Meet your kid's new teachers.

At first glance, they look like funny creatures right out of a computer game shoot 'em up. But underneath the funny surface, they represent one of the most serious approaches to home education you've ever heard of. INTRODUCING SPROUT™ SOFTWARE. GAMES THAT TEACH.

These amazing teachers are called Tink and Tonk. They come from Sprout. Software for kids 4 to 8.

The beauty of Sprout is how we balance entertainment with a healthy dose of education.

While kids are having fun at home, they're reinforcing what they've learned at school. Things like the alphabet, spell-

ing, vocabulary, counting, adding, and pattern recognition.

You'll also like how Sprout prevents boredom. Our games grow up, instead of wear out. As kids get older, the game gets harder—with many variations and many decisions to make.

Sprout didn't learn how to do all this overnight. You see, we've got a hundred years of experience to lean on. (Our parent company is SFN, the country's #1 text book publisher for

elementary and high schools.)

We've also got the experience of Mercer Mayer, who has written or illustrated 80 children's books. He dazzles kids with ideas and pictures that keep them coming back for more.

So let TINKITONK™ software teach your kids. And when they play at the computer, they won't be playing around. They'll be learning something.

sprout

Games that grow up. Instead of wear out.

Compatible with Atari,® Commodore,® Apple® and IBM.®

TINKITONK characters © 1983 TINK TONK, Inc. All rights reserved. TINKITONK is a trademark of TINK TONK, Inc. Sprout is published by Mindscape, Inc., Northbrook, IL 60062.

Sprout Software, 1984

Our bright idea for video games gives you a computer keyboard that's more than fun and games.

Simulated TV picture.

© 1980 MAGNAVOX CONSUMER ELECTRONICS CO.

buy additional hand controls or keyboard options and attachments with Odyssey.² With the others, add-ons can cost you up to hundreds of dollars extra.

Our computer keyboard lets you teach your children to spell and do math. And your entire family can have unlimited fun with Odyssey² cartridges like these:

Speedway, Spin-Out, Crypto-Logic, Las Vegas Blackjack, Armored Encounter, Sub Chase, Football, Bowling, Basketball, Math-A-Magic, Echo, Computer Intro, Match-Maker, Logix, Buzzword, Baseball, Computer Golf, Cosmic Conflict, Take The Money And Run, I've Got Your Number, Invaders from Hyperspace, Thunderball, Show-down in 2001 A.D., War Of Nerves, Alpine Skiing, Helicopter Rescue, Out Of This World, Hockey, Soccer, Dynasty.

Unlike most of the other video games in town, Odyssey² from Magnavox comes with a complete 49-character alphabet and number keyboard. And two, eight-position hand controls.

This means you don't have to

Volleyball, Electronic Table Soccer, Pocket Billiards, Pachinko, Blockout, Breakdown, Slot Machine.

Call 800-447-4700 toll free for the store nearest you.
In Illinois, call 800-322-4400.
See Odyssey² soon.

The brightest ideas in the world are here to play.

Odyssey² Game System, 1980

When it comes to your child's mind, we don't play games.

Texas Instruments, 1980

WHY ATARI IS #1.

The most games, the best games are only from Atari. Atari makes more video game cartridges than anyone else.
Adventure games, arcade games, educational games, our new RealSports™ games.
And they only work in the ATARI 2600 Video Computer System.™
No other system gives you nearly as much choice.
Or nearly as much fun.

DEFENDER
VAAS' REVENGE
HAUNTED HOUSE
CIRCUS ATARI
BERZERK
STAR RAIDERS
VIDEO PINBALL

Atari brings the arcade classics home. Only Atari has home versions of Space Invaders,* Pac-Man,* Missile Command,* Asteroids,* Breakout,* Defender† and Berzerk.††
The greatest arcade hits of all time.
If you have an ATARI system, you can play them at home.
If you have some other system, you can't.

You don't need two people to play ball with an ATARI 2600. All the best ATARI games can be enjoyed by a single player.
Including our new RealSports games.
To play any other system's sports games, you need another person.

Simple, straightforward controllers. With some systems' controllers, learning a new game is about as much fun as learning to type.
That's why Atari gives you easy-to-use joysticks and paddles.
Because it's the games you're out to master, not the controllers.

ATARI
A Warner Communications Company

All for about $100 less. For the price of other game-playing systems, you can buy an ATARI 2600 and still have about $100 left over.
Enough to start your ATARI video game library with hits like Pac-Man, Asteroids, and Defender.
Which, by the way, you can't play on other systems at any price.

© 1982 Atari, Inc. All rights reserved. *Trademark of Taito America Corp. *Trademark of Bally Midway Manufacturing Co. Licensed by Namco-America Inc. †Trademark of Williams Electronics Inc. ††Trademark of Stern Electronics Inc.

Atari Game System, 1982

Intellivision, 1983

Atari Video Games, 1983

Intellivision, 1981

Melbourne House Computer Software, 1989

▶ AMF Voit, 1983

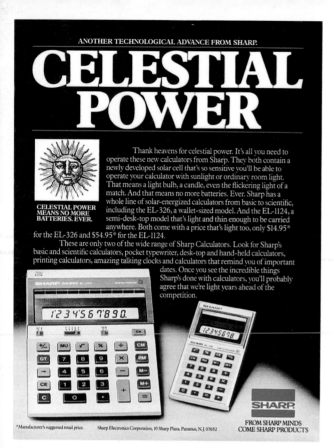

Sharp Calculators, 1982

Casio Calculators, 1984

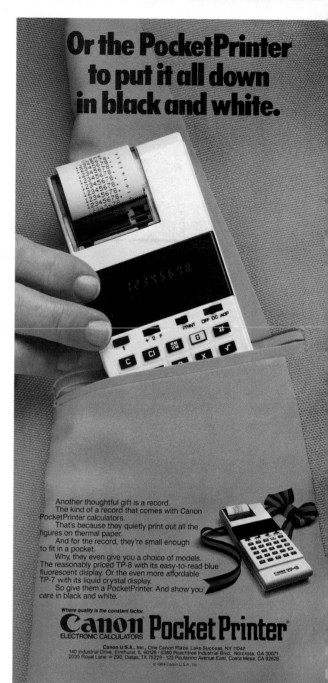

Canon Pocket Printer, 1984   ▶ *Casio Calculators, 1980*

Christmas gift giving solved in a flash!

Kodak Ektralite 10 camera. Built-in flash with aim-and-shoot convenience.

Who wouldn't love to receive a Kodak Ektralite 10 camera this Christmas? It's Kodak's most popular pocket camera—and no wonder. It gives you the convenience of built-in electronic flash in a slim, compact camera that's aim-and-shoot simple.

1880 **Kodak** *1980*

America's Storyteller

Kodak gifts make the giving easy.

©Eastman Kodak Company, 1980

Kodamatic Instant Cameras, 1982 ◄ *Kodak Ektralite 10 Camera, 1980*

Polaroid SX-70 Camera, 1981

Canon Sure Shot Cameras, 1987

Fuji Film, 1987

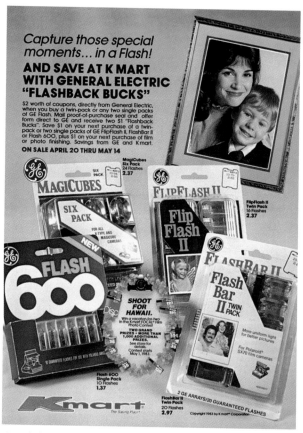

General Electric Flash Bulbs, 1983

► Polaroid Cameras, 1981

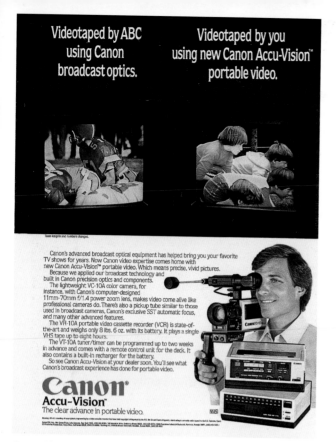

Nikon introduces the perfect camera for both.

You don't have to be a genius to use the Nikon N4004.

Even if your photographic IQ is near zero, this is one 35mm SLR you can take out of the box and begin using right away. Because it does everything for you.

It incorporates a remarkable Nikon innovation called the Decision Master System, which controls all camera, lens and flash functions automatically, even in difficult lighting situations.

The N4004 also loads, advances and rewinds the film automatically. It even focuses automatically.

When you need a flash, the N4004 will recommend that you use one. And you'll always have one, since the flash is built in.

But most important of all, as your photographic genius grows, and you want more creative freedom, the N4004 becomes less automatic. Allowing you to make all the settings yourself.

The Nikon N4004 is incredibly easy-to-use. At the same time, it's incredibly sophisticated.

That's not a contradiction. That's genius.

Nikon
We take the world's greatest pictures®

One year membership in the Nikon USA Club is free with every purchase when you submit the Nikon USA Club application. For further information write: Dept. 535, Nikon Inc., 19601 Hamilton Ave., Torrance, CA 90502-1309. © Nikon Inc., 1987.

Moe Howard © 1987 Norman Maurer Productions, Inc. Columbia Pictures Industries, Inc. Einstein licensed by The Roger Richman Agency, Inc., Beverly Hills, CA.

Nikon N4004 Cameras, 1988

PENTAX

The freedom to be your best.

Is it the setting sun? Maybe. Or perhaps the sight of some enchanted vessel that appeared out of nowhere. Well, the opportunity for a sensitive photograph is everywhere.

And the Pentax Program Plus gives you the freedom to catch this special moment. Even if your light is rapidly changing.

One turn of the dial offers you four programmed exposure modes. And that includes a metered manual mode for maximum creativity. Whether it's dawn or dusk. Or any time in between.

See your Pentax dealer now. Or write Pentax Corporation, 35 Inverness Drive East, Englewood, CO 80112.

PENTAX

© 1984 Pentax Corporation

Pentax Cameras, 1984

See beyond the ordinary.

The Canon A-1 is no ordinary camera. It is a creative tool. Conceived as the ultimate in automatic SLR's, the A-1 is unsurpassed in providing exposure control options. There are six, to be precise, allowing you to select the one best suited to your subject. Choose a shutter speed to control and interpret action. Select a lens opening and blur away a background.

In the programmed mode, the A-1 makes both of these decisions for you so you can really concentrate on your subject. You just focus, compose and shoot.

And create. A bright digital display in the viewfinder shows the speed and aperture being selected in any automatic mode.

The A-1 provides the versatility to match your imagination. Add any of over fifty Canon FD lenses. A Canon Speedlite for automatic flash. You can shoot at up to five frames-per-second with the optional Motor Drive MA. But most important, the A-1 does everything automatically. Freeing you to shoot a special subject in your own special way, and make a picture that nobody else saw.

The Canon A-1. It's half of what you need to turn photography into fine art.

Canon A-1

Canon USA, Inc., One Canon Plaza, Lake Success, NY 11042 / 140 Industrial Drive, Elmhurst, IL 60126 / 5360 Peachtree Industrial Blvd., Norcross, GA 30071 / 3035 Royal Lane, Suite 290, Dallas, TX 75229 / 123 Paularino Avenue East, Costa Mesa, CA 92626 / 4000 Burton Drive, Santa Clara, CA 95050 / Bldg. B-2, 1050 Ala Moana Blvd., Honolulu, HI 96814 / Canon Canada, Inc., Ontario
© 1983 Canon U.S.A., Inc.

Canon A-1 Camera, 1985

RCA Video Camera, 1983

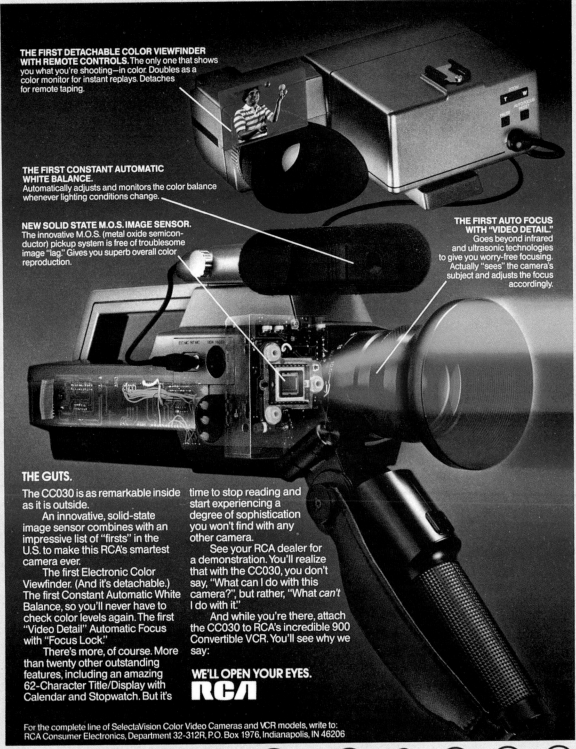

THE FIRST DETACHABLE COLOR VIEWFINDER WITH REMOTE CONTROLS. The only one that shows you what you're shooting—in color. Doubles as a color monitor for instant replays. Detaches for remote taping.

THE FIRST CONSTANT AUTOMATIC WHITE BALANCE. Automatically adjusts and monitors the color balance whenever lighting conditions change.

NEW SOLID STATE M.O.S. IMAGE SENSOR. The innovative M.O.S. (metal oxide semiconductor) pickup system is free of troublesome image "lag." Gives you superb overall color reproduction.

THE FIRST AUTO FOCUS WITH "VIDEO DETAIL." Goes beyond infrared and ultrasonic technologies to give you worry-free focusing. Actually "sees" the camera's subject and adjusts the focus accordingly.

THE GUTS.

The CC030 is as remarkable inside as it is outside.

An innovative, solid-state image sensor combines with an impressive list of "firsts" in the U.S. to make this RCA's smartest camera ever.

The first Electronic Color Viewfinder. (And it's detachable.) The first Constant Automatic White Balance, so you'll never have to check color levels again. The first "Video Detail" Automatic Focus with "Focus Lock."

There's more, of course. More than twenty other outstanding features, including an amazing 62-Character Title/Display with Calendar and Stopwatch. But it's time to stop reading and start experiencing a degree of sophistication you won't find with any other camera.

See your RCA dealer for a demonstration. You'll realize that with the CC030, you don't say, "What can I do with this camera?", but rather, "What *can't* I do with it."

And while you're there, attach the CC030 to RCA's incredible 900 Convertible VCR. You'll see why we say:

WE'LL OPEN YOUR EYES.
RCA

For the complete line of SelectaVision Color Video Cameras and VCR models, write to: RCA Consumer Electronics, Department 32-312R, P.O. Box 1976, Indianapolis, IN 46206

RCA Video Camera, 1983

Gucci Telephone, 1980

Trimline Telephone, 1980

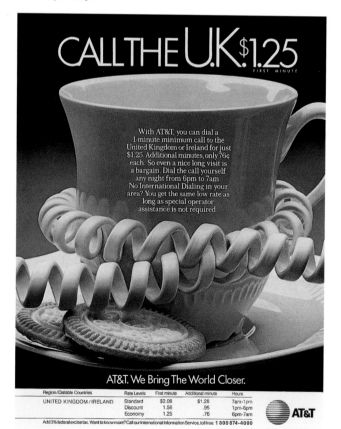

AT&T Telecom, 1984

General Electric Telephone Answering Machines, 1984

The Garfield Telephone

What a fun phone! Lift the receiver, and Garfield's eyes open.
All the latest features: last number re-dial and mute button for privacy.
Compatible with rotary and tone systems; one year limited warranty.

Real Phones for Real Fun
By Tyco

Tyco Industries, Inc. 540 Glen Avenue, Moorestown, NJ 08057 GARFIELD: © 1978 United Feature Syndicate, Inc.

Garfield Telephone, 1984

Panasonic Cordless Telephone, 1985

Cobraphone, 1983

Cobra Telephone-Clock Radios, 1983

Uniden Extend-A-Phone, 1982

Pocketful of miracles.

For those times you want to stay close to your phone there's a small wonder that goes with you wherever you go. It's the Extend-A-Phone EX 2600. The amazing cordless telephone from Uniden.

The handset of this technical miracle is so slim, so compact it fits right in your pocket. And it's so powerful you can make and take calls up to 1000 feet* from the base station.

Cordless convenience that fits in your pocket is just the beginning because, unlike a lot of small phones, you don't have to take the EX-2600 away from your ear to talk. A feathertouch electronic keypad makes dialing easy, and there's a one-touch button that automatically redials the last number called, even a long-distance number. Other features of the EX-2600 include base-to-handset paging, a selectable privacy code, AutoSecure™ to protect your phone line from outside access, and a replaceable nickel cadmium battery pack. And for truly hands-free conversation there's an optional lightweight headset and a belt holster for the handset.

The wonders never cease. There are Extend-A-Phone

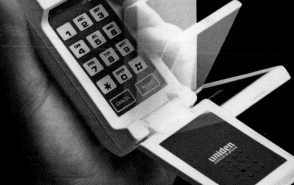

models that memorize numbers, redial them for you, tell time, give you the news, play music and wake you up.

That's why Extend-A-Phone is the number one selling cordless telephone in America.

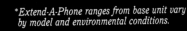

*Extend-A-Phone ranges from base unit vary by model and environmental conditions.

uniden
extend·a·phone®
Why not Number One?

Black & Decker Stowaway Travel Series, 1985

We measure up
in every way but one.

Fly wrinkle-free on your next trip with the travel iron that's full service, not full size.

The Small Wonder™ comes with elegant travel pouch and a dual voltage adaptor for jaunts overseas.

Its powerful steam performance knocks out wrinkles that regular travel irons aren't big enough to handle. Yet it's small and stream-lined and weighs only 1.7 lbs. So it's just the ticket for travelers.

The Small Wonder Travel Iron

General Electric Travel Iron, 1984

Merry crispness!
The present with a delicious future.

Presto made deep frying easy, simple and convenient, time after time.

No wonder Presto® FryDaddy® deep fryer is the season's most welcome gift idea.

Because it's Presto FryDaddy just four cups of oil give you four big servings.

Because it's Presto FryDaddy there's no control to bother with. Maintains ideal temperature automatically for perfect fried foods—crisp, cracklin', crunchy.

Because it's Presto FryDaddy there is a nonstick, no-scour surface inside and out. Just wipe clean.

Because it's Presto FryDaddy there's the famous Presto® scoop instead of a messy basket. And the snap-on lid helps save oil to use again and again. No spills, no odor.

Because it's Presto you choose the size you need from FryBaby®, FryDaddy® or GranPappy® deep fryers.

Because it's Presto you know you are giving the best—and so does the lucky person who gets one.

PRESTO®
...innovation to make it first
quality that makes it last and last!™

Presto FryDaddy, 1980

IT COVERS MORE GROUND.

Now there's a cordless vac that goes the extra distance—Black & Decker's DUSTBUSTER PLUS.™

DUSTBUSTER PLUS has the longer running time you need to do stairs, drapes, upholstery, or any of the bigger little messes you've got around the house. And DUSTBUSTER PLUS is more versatile. It even comes with an attachment for cleaning crevices and an upholstery brush.

Black & Decker's DUSTBUSTER PLUS™ vac, from the people who created DUSTBUSTER™, the leading cordless vac. It covers more ground, because you've got a lot of ground to cover.

B•D Black & Decker

Black & Decker Dustbuster, 1983

Sunbeam
Mixers

"Sunbeam has a Mixmaster Mixer for any and all foods you'd like to whip up."

Shirley Jones

Sunbeam makes a complete line of excellent mixers. Complete with the features to help you make it right.

Just look at the Power Plus Mix-master Mixer.

It's one of the most powerful mixers ever to wear the Sunbeam name, thanks to a 335 watt motor with precision controls.

It can help you prepare anything from fluffy egg whites to heavy yeast dough.

It comes with deep, tapered stainless steel bowls to concentrate the ingredients into the beaters. So it mixes like no ordinary mixer can.

The Power Plus dough hooks and beaters are larger and heavier than standard mixers. So it can knead enough dough for three 1-lb. loaves of bread at the same time.

All Sunbeam mixers are made with the same kind of quality.

From the Burst of Power Hand Mixer right up to the Infinite Speed Mixmaster Mixer, Sunbeam just can't be beat...

So take a look at our complete line of mixers soon.

Sunbeam

Quality you can count on.

Sunbeam Mixers, 1980

And the winner is...

Maxed Out

Going the way of the Edsel and the eight-track, the beta video format was one of the decade's biggest consumer electronics failures. In head-to-head competition with the VHS market, Sony® was unable to license Betamax to other companies. Seems no one gave a damn about its superior quality — the customer wanted double, even triple the recording time offered by the rival. The unavailability of the Betamax format in video rental stores secured its demise. The only legacy of Sony®'s flop is the phrase "to Betamax;" in other words, to be overwhelmed by competing, licensed manufacturers. A "fish story" no one at Sony® wants to tell.

Betamax, Pipifax

Das Beta-Videoformat war einer der größten Flops des Jahrzehnts im Bereich Unterhaltungselektronik und fiel dem gleichen Schicksal wie der Edsel und der Achtspurrekorder anheim. Im Kopf-an-Kopf-Rennen mit dem VHS-Markt schaffte Sony® es nicht, die Betamax-Lizenz an andere Firmen zu verkaufen. Niemand interessierte sich für die bessere Qualität – der Kunde wollte die doppelt oder dreifach so lange Aufnahmezeit, die von der Konkurrenz geboten wurde. Dass in den Videotheken keine Betamaxkassetten zu haben waren, besiegelte den Untergang des Formats endgültig. Dieser Haifisch hatte keine Zähne, eine Peinlichkeit, über die Sony® lieber schweigt.

Ejecté

Ayant subi le même sort que la Edsel et la bande à huit pistes, la vidéo de format Betamax a été l'un des échecs les plus retentissants du marché de l'électronique de la décennie. Dans une compétition au coude à coude contre le VHS, Sony® refusa d'accorder les licences d'exploitation du Betamax aux autres compagnies. On aurait dit que tout le monde se fichait de la qualité – le client voulait le double, voire le triple du temps d'enregistrement offert par la concurrence. Le fait qu'il était impossible de trouver des Betamax dans les magasins de location de vidéos a contribué à leur disparition. Tout ce qu'il nous reste du flop de Sony® c'est l'expression to betamax, qui signifie : être dépassé par la concurrence des fabricants sous licence. Une histoire incroyable dont personne chez Sony® ne veut entendre parler.

Betamenos

Siguiendo la estela de los Edsel y los ocho pistas, el formato de vídeo beta fue uno de los mayores fracasos electrónicos de la década, al menos en cuanto a público se refiere. En un mano a mano con el mercado del VHS, Sony® no otorgó la licencia a otras empresas para usar Betamax. A nadie parecía importarle que ofreciera una calidad mejor... Al cliente le interesaba más que su rival multiplicara por dos o por tres el tiempo de grabación. La escasa oferta de formato Betamax en los videoclubs no hizo más que garantizar su desaparición. El único legado de este fracaso estrepitoso de Sony® es el brindis «Por Betamax», el reconocimiento de la victoria de sus competidores, que sí ofrecían licencias. Una leyenda que nadie en Sony® osa contar.

全力を尽くしました

Edsel（数年で消えたフォードの一部門の自動車メーカー）や8トラックテープの轍を踏み、ベータ形式のビデオはこの十年期における消費者向けエレクトロニクス製品の最大の失敗であろう。VHS市場との接戦の中で、ソニーは他社にベータマックスをライセンスすることができなかった。誰一人その優れた品の値打ちを全く認めていないようだった…顧客はライバルが提供した2倍、それどころか3倍もの録音時間の方を欲しがった。レンタルビデオ店でベータマクス方式のビデオが借りられないということもその終了を確実にした。ソニーの大失敗の唯一の遺産は、「ベータマックスへ」というフレーズで、別の言い方言うと、「ライセンス認可を受けた競合会社に圧倒される」という意味だ。ソニーの誰もが話したがらない「ほら話」である。

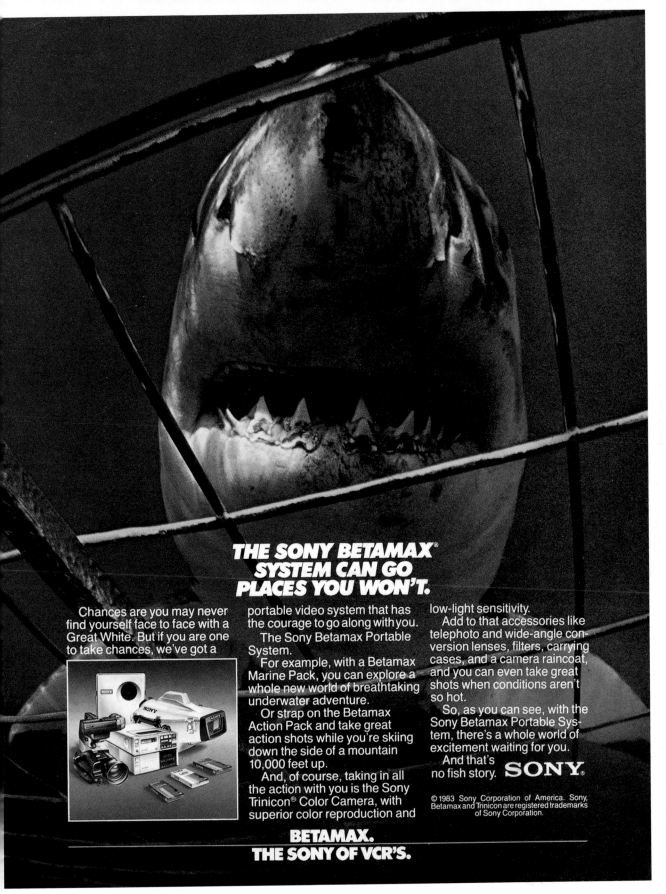

THE SONY BETAMAX® SYSTEM CAN GO PLACES YOU WON'T.

Chances are you may never find yourself face to face with a Great White. But if you are one to take chances, we've got a portable video system that has the courage to go along with you.

The Sony Betamax Portable System.

For example, with a Betamax Marine Pack, you can explore a whole new world of breathtaking underwater adventure.

Or strap on the Betamax Action Pack and take great action shots while you're skiing down the side of a mountain 10,000 feet up.

And, of course, taking in all the action with you is the Sony Trinicon® Color Camera, with superior color reproduction and low-light sensitivity.

Add to that accessories like telephoto and wide-angle conversion lenses, filters, carrying cases, and a camera raincoat, and you can even take great shots when conditions aren't so hot.

So, as you can see, with the Sony Betamax Portable System, there's a whole world of excitement waiting for you.

And that's no fish story. **SONY.**

© 1983 Sony Corporation of America. Sony, Betamax and Trinicon are registered trademarks of Sony Corporation.

BETAMAX.
THE SONY OF VCR'S.

Sony Betamax, 1983

Stir Crazy, 1980

Nine to Five, 1980

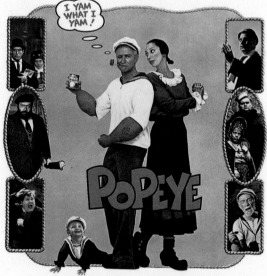

The Empire Strikes Back, 1980 ◄ *Popeye, 1980*

When Harry Met Sally, 1989

► *Private Benjamin, 1980*

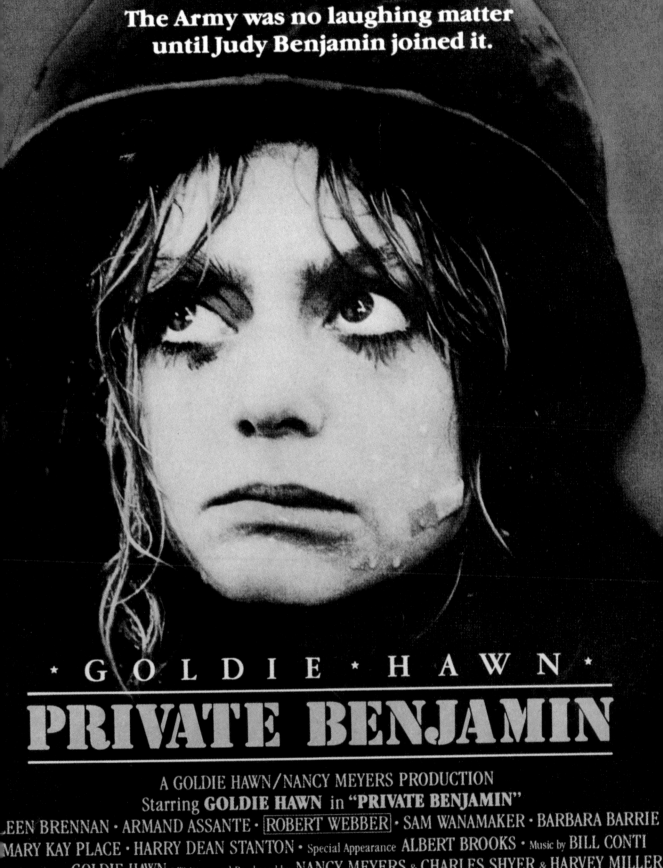

Bill & Ted's Excellent Adventure, 1989

Three Men and a Baby, 1989

Mr. Mom, 1983

Raising Arizona, 1987

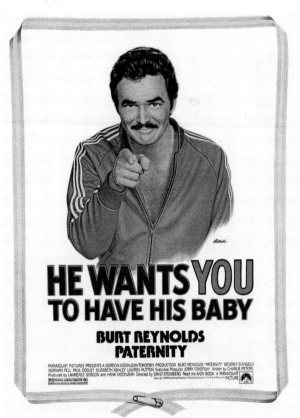

Paternity, 1981

National Lampoon's Christmas Vacation, 1989

Dragnet, 1987

Planes, Trains and Automobiles, 1987

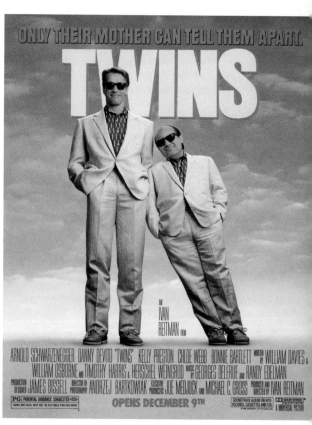

Twins, 1988

▶ *Ghostbusters II, 198*

BILL MURRAY   DAN AYKROYD   SIGOURNEY WEAVER
HAROLD RAMIS   RICK MORANIS

An IVAN REITMAN Film

GHOSTBUSTERS II

COLUMBIA PICTURES Presents
"GHOSTBUSTERS II" · ERNIE HUDSON · ANNIE POTTS MUSIC BY RANDY EDELMAN SPECIAL VISUAL EFFECTS BY I.L.M.
EXECUTIVE PRODUCERS BERNIE BRILLSTEIN · JOE MEDJUCK · MICHAEL C. GROSS WRITTEN BY HAROLD RAMIS AND DAN AYKROYD PRODUCED AND DIRECTED BY IVAN REITMAN
DOLBY STEREO IN SELECTED THEATRES ORIGINAL SOUNDTRACK ALBUM AVAILABLE ON MCA RECORDS AND CASSETTES READ THE DELL BOOK A COLUMBIA PICTURES RELEASE

OPENS JUNE 16TH AT THEATRES EVERYWHERE

Trapped in a world he never made.

Rolling Egg

EXCLUSIVE
BEVERLY
SIZZLES!
The Rolling
Egg Interview
WHATEVER
HAPPENED
TO QUACK?

GEORGE LUCAS Presents

HOWARD
THE DUCK

A WILLARD HUYCK Film
A GLORIA KATZ Production

More adventure than humanly possible.

Starring LEA THOMPSON · JEFFREY JONES · TIM ROBBINS "HOWARD THE DUCK" Written by WILLARD HUYCK & GLORIA KATZ Based on the Marvel Comics Character "HOWARD THE DUCK" Created by STEVE GERBER Music Score by JOHN BARRY
Original Songs Produced by THOMAS DOLBY Director of Photography RICHARD H. KLINE A.S.C. Co-Producer ROBERT LATHAM BROWN Executive Producer GEORGE LUCAS Produced by GLORIA KATZ Directed by WILLARD HUYCK
Soundtrack available on MCA Records & Cassettes   Read the BERKLEY Book   Visual Effects by INDUSTRIAL LIGHT & MAGIC   DOLBY STEREO   Rolling Egg is used under license from Rolling Stone
© 1986 UNIVERSAL CITY STUDIOS INC.   From Lucasfilm Ltd. and Universal Pictures

Now Playing

Howard the Duck, 1986

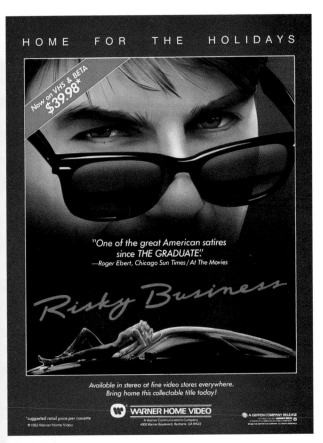

Risky Business, 1983

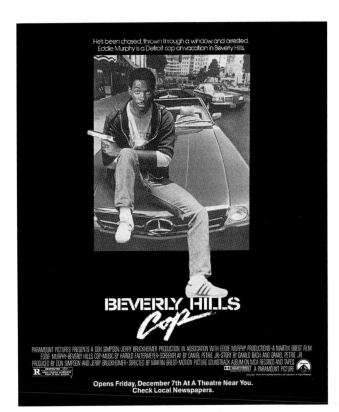

Beverly Hills Cop, 1984

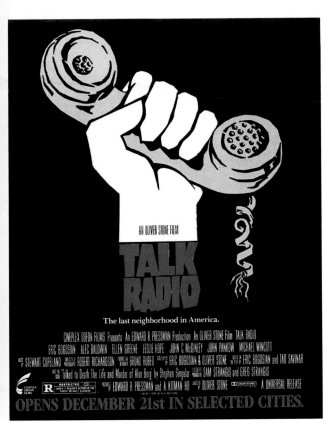

Talk Radio, 1988

The Karate Kid Part II, 1986

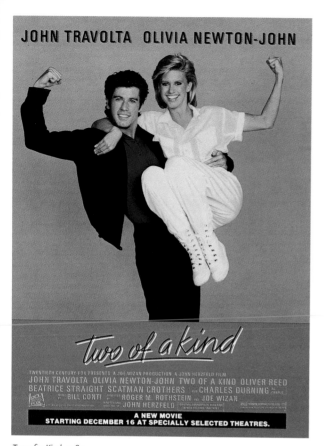

Two of a Kind, 1983

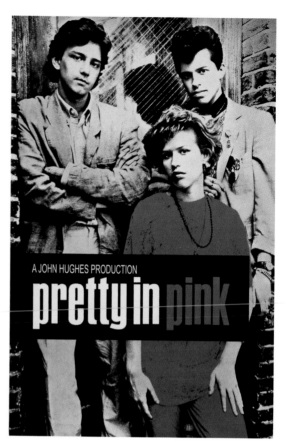

Pretty in Pink, 1986

Sixteen Candles, 1984

The Big Chill, 1983

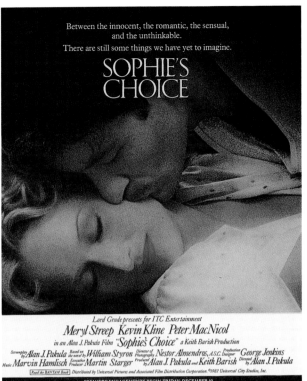

Sophie's Choice, 1982

Silkwood, 1983

Something Wild, 1986

She-Devil, 1987

They'll never get caught.
They're on a mission from God.

JOHN BELUSHI DAN AYKROYD
THE BLUES BROTHERS

JAMES BROWN · CAB CALLOWAY · RAY CHARLES · CARRIE FISHER
ARETHA FRANKLIN · HENRY GIBSON · THE BLUES BROTHERS BAND
Written by DAN AYKROYD and JOHN LANDIS
Executive Producer BERNIE BRILLSTEIN
Produced by ROBERT K. WEISS · Directed by JOHN LANDIS

OPENS FRIDAY, JUNE 20 AT A THEATRE NEAR YOU.

The Blues Brothers, 1980

▶ *Xanadu, 1980*

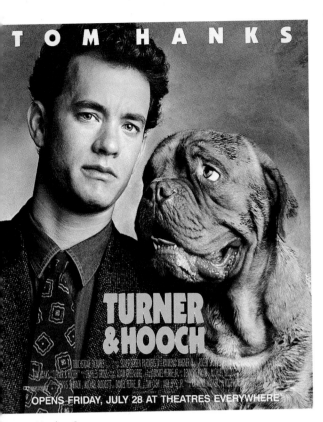

Turner & Hooch, 1989

Bull Durham, 1989

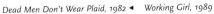

Dead Men Don't Wear Plaid, 1982 ◄ *Working Girl, 1989*

Married to the Mob, 1989

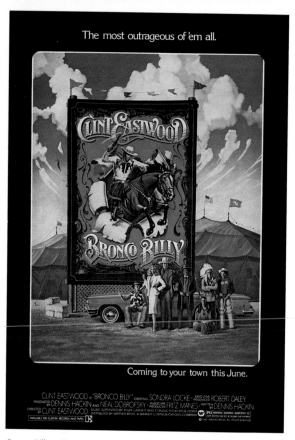

Bronco Billy, 1980

Time Bandits, 1981

Cocoon: The Return, 1989

True Stories, 1987

Field of Dreams, 1989

Fatal Attraction, 1987

▶ *The Howling*, 1981

Imagine your worst fear a reality.

THE HOWLING

A DANIEL H. BLATT PRODUCTION "THE HOWLING" Starring DEE WALLACE · PATRICK MACNEE
DENNIS DUGAN · CHRISTOPHER STONE · BELINDA BALASKI · KEVIN McCARTHY · JOHN CARRADINE
SLIM PICKENS And introducing ELISABETH BROOKS Executive Producers DANIEL H. BLATT and STEVEN A. LANE
Screenplay by JOHN SAYLES and TERENCE H. WINKLESS Based on the novel by GARY BRANDNER
Music by PINO DONAGGIO Produced by MICHAEL FINNELL and JACK CONRAD Directed by JOE DANTE
Presented by AVCO EMBASSY, INTERNATIONAL FILM INVESTORS and WESCOM PRODUCTIONS READ THE FAWCETT PAPERBACK
ORIGINAL MOTION PICTURE SOUNDTRACK ALBUM AVAILABLE ON VARESE SARABANDE RECORDS Prints by CFI

R RESTRICTED
UNDER 17 REQUIRES ACCOMPANYING
PARENT OR ADULT GUARDIAN

AVCO EMBASSY PICTURES Release
© 1980 AVCO EMBASSY PICTURES CORP

SOON AT THEATRES EVERYWHERE.

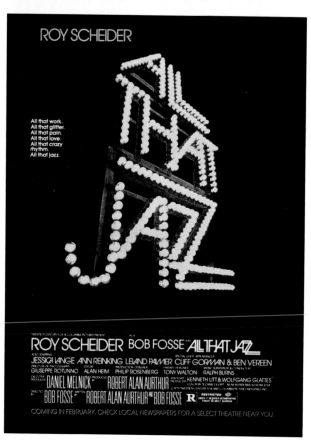

All That Jazz, 1980

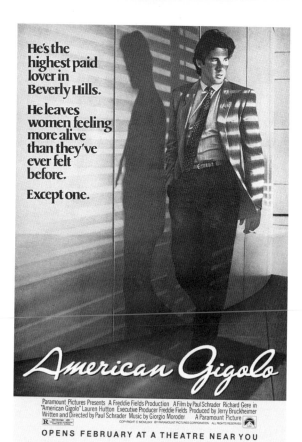

American Gigolo, 1980

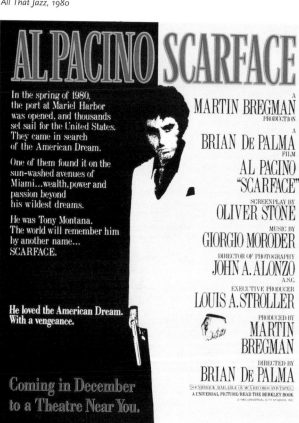

Scarface, 1983

Mommie Dearest, 1981

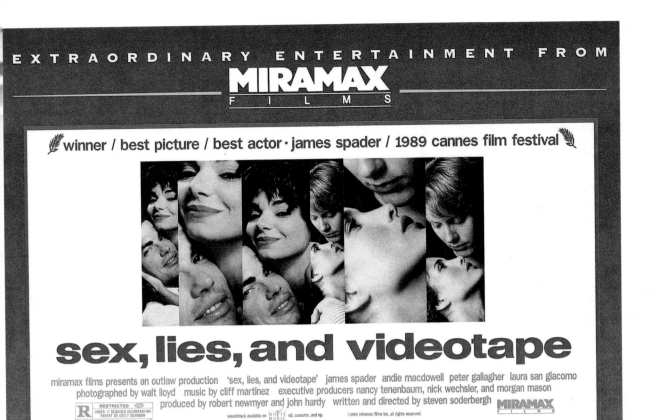

sex, lies, and videotape, 1987

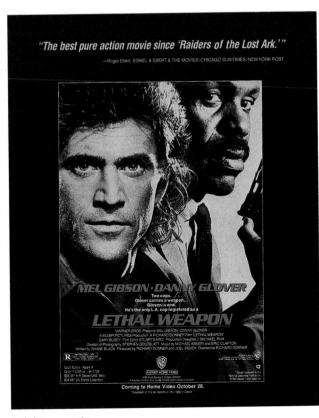

Lethal Weapon, 1987

Breathless, 1983

Do the Right Thing, 1989

▶ *Moonstruck, 1988*

MOONSTRUCK

CHER · NICOLAS CAGE

METRO-GOLDWYN-MAYER PRESENTS A PATRICK PALMER-NORMAN JEWISON PRODUCTION

A NORMAN JEWISON FILM

"MOONSTRUCK" STARRING VINCENT GARDENIA OLYMPIA DUKAKIS AND DANNY AIELLO MUSIC COMPOSED AND ADAPTED BY DICK HYMAN

PRODUCTION DESIGNER PHILIP ROSENBERG COSTUME DESIGNER THEONI V. ALDREDGE DIRECTOR OF PHOTOGRAPHY DAVID WATKIN FILM EDITOR LOU LOMBARDO

ASSOCIATE PRODUCER BONNIE PALEF WRITTEN BY JOHN PATRICK SHANLEY PRODUCED BY PATRICK PALMER & NORMAN JEWISON

DIRECTED BY NORMAN JEWISON

OPENS NATIONWIDE JANUARY 22nd

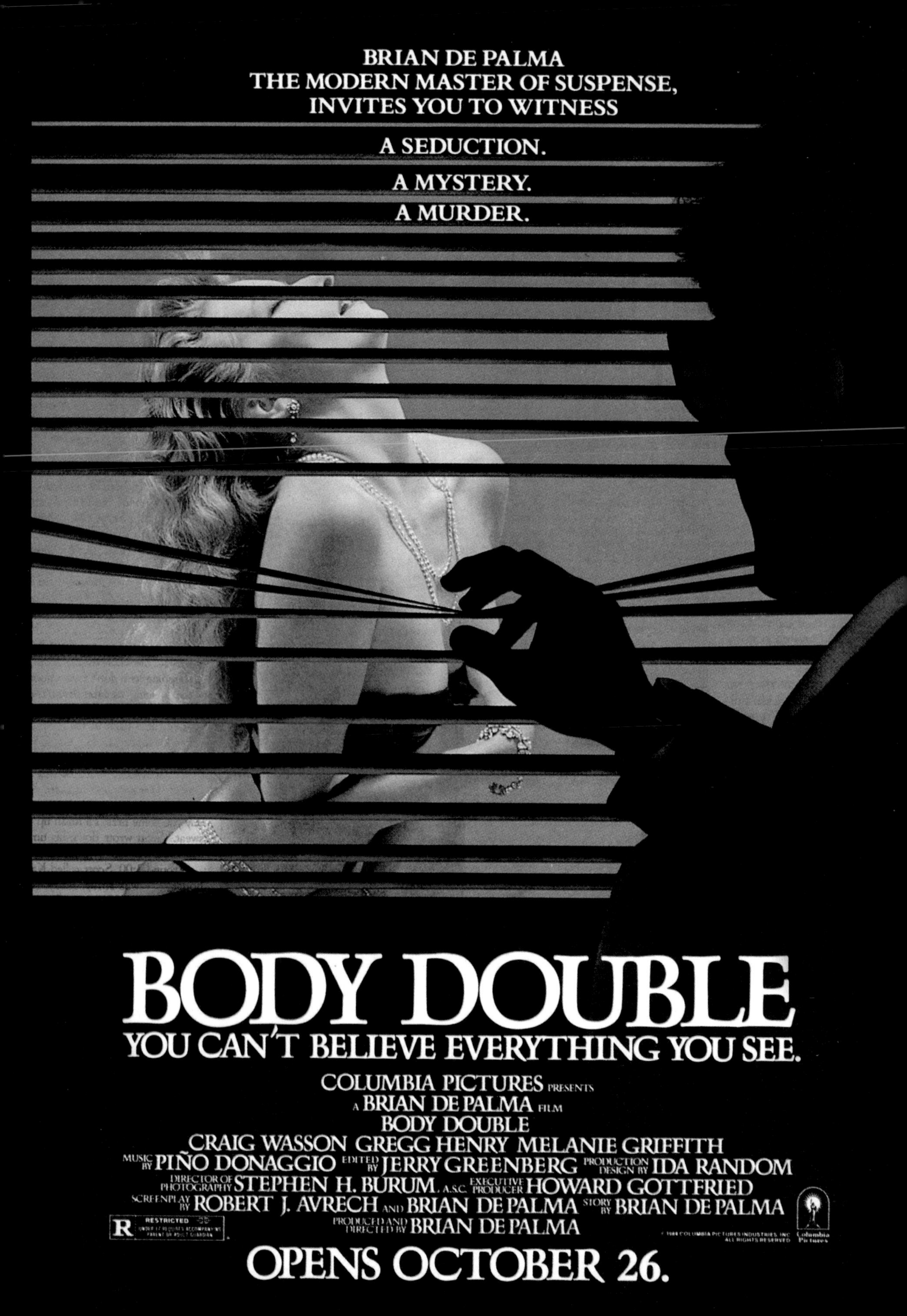

BRIAN DE PALMA
THE MODERN MASTER OF SUSPENSE,
INVITES YOU TO WITNESS
A SEDUCTION.
A MYSTERY.
A MURDER.
BODY DOUBLE
YOU CAN'T BELIEVE EVERYTHING YOU SEE.
COLUMBIA PICTURES PRESENTS
A BRIAN DE PALMA FILM
BODY DOUBLE
CRAIG WASSON GREGG HENRY MELANIE GRIFFITH
MUSIC BY PIÑO DONAGGIO EDITED BY JERRY GREENBERG PRODUCTION DESIGN BY IDA RANDOM
DIRECTOR OF PHOTOGRAPHY STEPHEN H. BURUM, A.S.C. EXECUTIVE PRODUCER HOWARD GOTTFRIED
SCREENPLAY BY ROBERT J. AVRECH AND BRIAN DE PALMA STORY BY BRIAN DE PALMA
R RESTRICTED
PRODUCED AND DIRECTED BY BRIAN DE PALMA
Columbia Pictures
OPENS OCTOBER 26.

AMADEUS

...EVERYTHING YOU'VE HEARD IS TRUE

The SAUL ZAENTZ Company Presents A MILOS FORMAN Film PETER SHAFFER'S AMADEUS
F. MURRAY ABRAHAM   TOM HULCE   ELIZABETH BERRIDGE
SIMON CALLOW   ROY DOTRICE   CHRISTINE EBERSOLE   JEFFREY JONES   CHARLES KAY
Executive Producers MICHAEL HAUSMAN and BERTIL OHLSSON   Director of Photography MIROSLAV ONDRICEK
Music Conducted and Supervised by NEVILLE MARRINER   Production Designer PATRIZIA VON BRANDENSTEIN   Choreographer TWYLA THARP
Screenplay and original stage play by PETER SHAFFER   Produced by SAUL ZAENTZ   Directed by MILOS FORMAN

An ORION PICTURES Release
© 1984 THE SAUL ZAENTZ COMPANY. ALL RIGHTS RESERVED
Filmed in PANAVISION®   Prints by TECHNICOLOR®   70 mm   DOLBY STEREO ®   ORIGINAL SOUNDTRACK ALBUM AVAILABLE ON FANTASY RECORDS AND TAPES   PG PARENTAL GUIDANCE SUGGESTED ◄► SOME MATERIAL MAY NOT BE SUITABLE FOR CHILDREN

NOW PLAYING AT SELECT THEATRES

Body Double, 1984 ◄ *Amadeus, 1984*

Somewhere under the sea
and beyond your imagination
is an adventure in fantasy.

THE LITTLE
MERMAID

The Little Mermaid, 1989

▶ *E.T., 1982*

He is afraid.
He is totally alone.
He is 3 million light years from home.

A STEVEN SPIELBERG FILM

E.T.
THE EXTRA-TERRESTRIAL

in his adventure on earth

COMING THIS SUMMER TO A THEATRE NEAR YOU

ERSAL PICTURES PRESENTS   A STEVEN SPIELBERG FILM   E.T. THE EXTRA-TERRESTRIAL   DEE WALLACE
THOMAS   ROBERT MAC NAUGHTON   DREW BARRYMORE   PETER COYOTE   MUSIC BY JOHN WILLIAM
ITED BY CAROL LITTLETON   WRITTEN BY MELISSA MATHISON   PRODUCED BY STEVEN SPIELBERG &
KATHLEEN KENNEDY   DIRECTED BY STEVEN SPIELBERG   READ THE BERKLEY BOOK   DOLBY STEREO

©1982 UNIVERSAL CITY STUDIOS, INC.

Discover John...the angry youth, the musician, the radical, the husband, the father, the lover, the idealist...through his own words and personal collection of film and music.

IMAGINE
John Lennon

WARNER BROS. Presents

A DAVID L. WOLPER Production An ANDREW SOLT Film "IMAGINE: JOHN LENNON" Narrated by JOHN LENNON   Supervising Film Editor BUD FRIEDGEN, A.C.E.
Co-Producer SAM EGAN   Written by SAM EGAN and ANDREW SOLT   Produced by DAVID L. WOLPER and ANDREW SOLT   Directed by ANDREW SOLT

STARTS OCTOBER 7th AT SELECTED THEATRES

Imagine, 1988

► *Bird, 1988*

FILM BY CLINT EASTWOOD

are no second acts in American lives." F. Scott Fitzgerald

WARNER BROS. PRESENTS A MALPASO PRODUCTION "BIRD"
OREST WHITAKER DIANE VENORA MUSIC SCORE BY LENNIE NIEHAUS
WRITTEN BY JOEL OLIANSKY EXECUTIVE PRODUCER DAVID VALDES
PRODUCED AND DIRECTED BY CLINT EASTWOOD

CHECK LOCAL LISTINGS

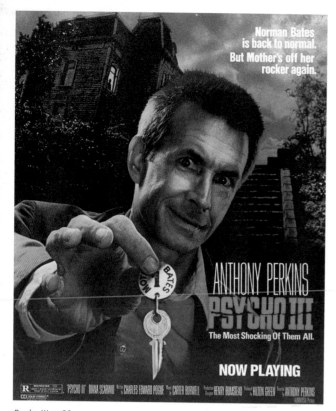

Psycho III, 1986

Fright Night, 1986

Black Widow, 1987

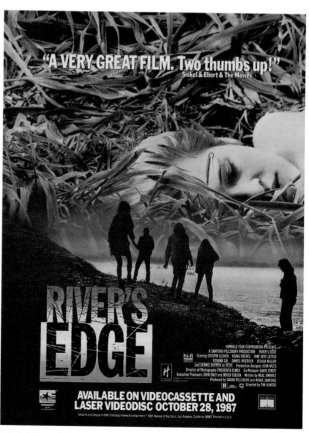

River's Edge, 1987

▶ *Killer Klowns from Outer Space*, 1988

Alien Klowns With A Killer Sense Of Humor.

Get ready to die laughing! This invasion of carnivorous klowns from outer space is a three-ring-circus of sci-fi comedy thrills.

The Killer Klowns are attacking with popcorn ray guns and deadly cotton candy. Will John Vernon ("Animal House") and Grant Cramer ("Hardbodies") stop them before they turn our population into Klown cuisine? The Killer Klowns have landed, and they're at your video store now!

On Videocassette

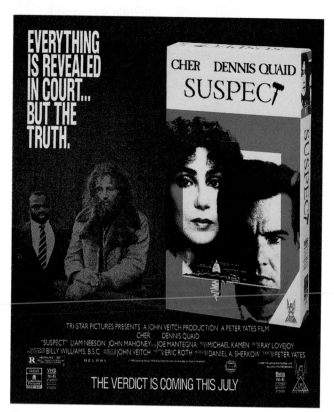

Suspect, 1988

The Clan of the Cave Bear, 1986

The Color Purple, 1989

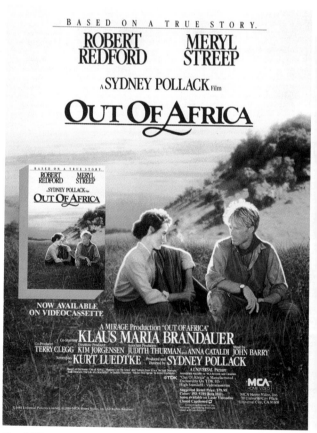

Out of Africa, 1986

Betrayed, 1989

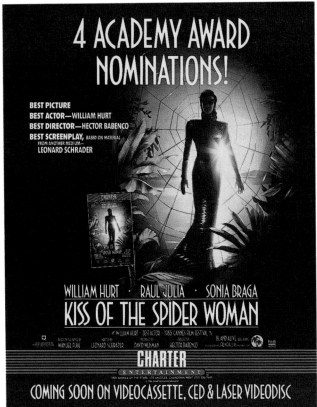

Kiss of the Spider Woman, 1985

Blue Velvet, 1987

Beach Blanket Babylon, 1984

Die Hard, 1989

Vestron Video, 1988

Indiana Jones and the Temple of Doom, 1986

A Nightmare on Elm Street, 1988

Porky's Revenge, 1985

Beetlejuice, 1988

Honey, I Shrunk the Kids, 1989

Monty Python, 1983

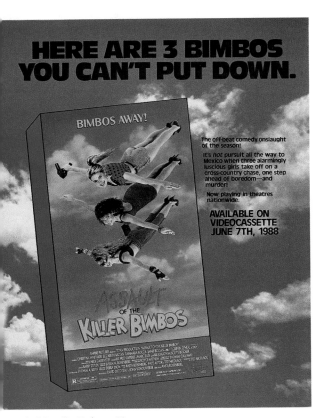

Assault of the Killer Bimbos, 1988

Who's That Girl, 1987

Good Morning, Vietnam, 1988

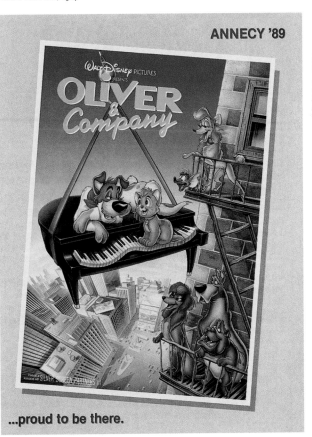

Oliver & Company, 1989

Tahitia, 1980

Hanky-Panky, 1984

FOLLOW THE LEADER.

Jane Fonda, naturally. Now join the millions of active women who work out with her every day. With Jane Fonda's new COMPLETE WORKOUT video you've got it all—the aerobics, conditioning and stretching routines that *you* combine to match your own fitness level and personal goals. From the 70-minute "whole-body" workout to shorter routines for spot toning and shaping, create a program that suits your busy day. And let Jane Fonda's COMPLETE WORKOUT lead you through a New Year of feeling better and looking healthier than ever before!

Jane Fonda's COMPLETE WORKOUT. Now in video stores everywhere.

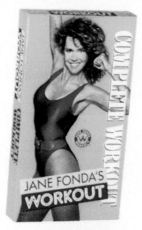

$29⁹⁸*

Now on
videocassette.

*Suggested List Price per Cassette. Higher in Canada.
Program Content: © 1988 Jane Fonda. Artwork: © 1988 Warner Home Video Inc.

INSIDE EVERY SUPERSTAR THERE'S SOMEONE WAITING TO BE HEARD.

Everyone knows Michael Jackson the performer. But, earlier this year, Spotlight Specials featured Michael Jackson the person. Michael offered many insights into his family life, his childhood and his relationship with the public.

Of course, this shouldn't be too surprising because many of the legends of music have opened up on Spotlight Specials. Interesting people like Rod Stewart, Olivia Newton-John, Dan Fogelberg, The Rolling Stones, and more. To check out the best 90 minutes of music and artists' insights, call your favorite radio station and ask about Spotlight Specials.

SPOTLIGHT SPECIALS
ABC CONTEMPORARY RADIO NETWORK

Jane Fonda's Workout, 1989 ◄   *ABC Radio, 1984*

DYNASTY

abc WEDNESDAYS

The Thorn Birds, 1983

All My Children, 1988

Dynasty, 1983 ◄   The Winds of War, 1983

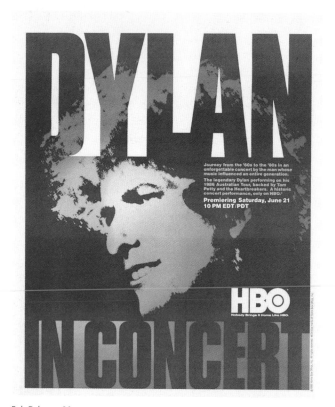

Bob Dylan, 1986

Barbara Mandrell, 1983

Liberace, 1988

Kenny Rogers, 1983

Bette Midler, 1984

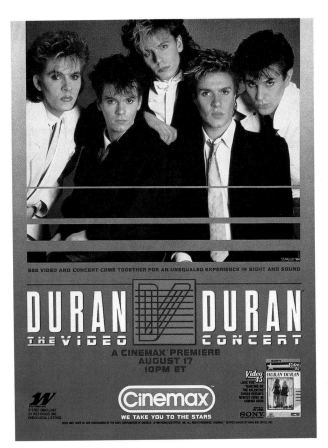

Duran Duran, 1984

Culture Club, 1984

Linda Ronstadt, 1983

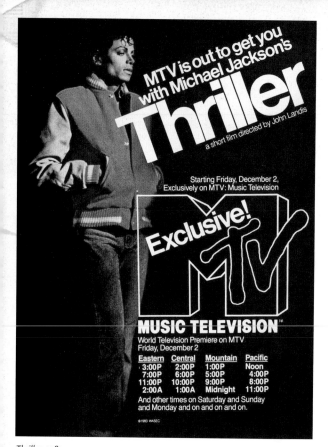

Thriller, 1983

Max Headroom, 1986

Farm Aid II, 1986

Once in a while we'll lose a viewer or two.

It's bound to happen.
Even though our audience loves to watch their music–hit music–
they have other things to attend to.
That's why over 25 million viewers make love, soothe their
infants, and pay their bills with us in their lives.
So turn on VH-1.
Or ask your cable operator to turn us on.
We've got exactly what you're looking for.
Even if you're not watching.

THE OTHER MUSIC TELEVISION **VH-1** VIDEO HITS ONE™

VH1, 1988   ▶ *MTV, 1988*

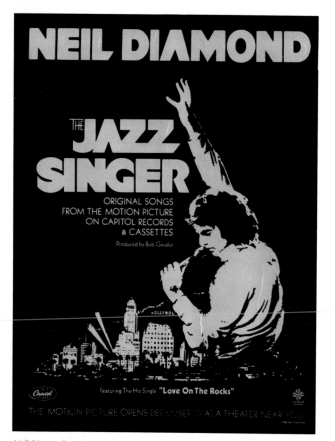

Neil Diamond, 1980

Barbra Streisand, 1981

Placido Domingo, 1985

Julio Iglesias, 1983

Lionel Richie, 1986

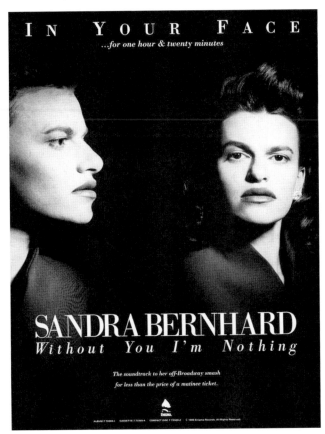

Sandra Bernhard, 1989

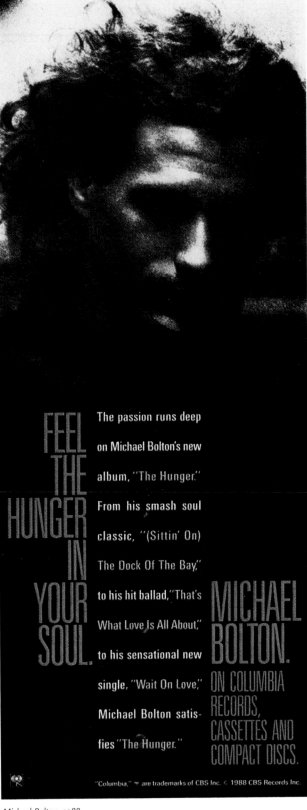

Michael Bolton, 1988

Thompson Twins, 1985

▶ *Blondie, 1981*

THE BEST OF
BLONDIE

THERE'S NOTHING LIKE THE BEST

"THE BEST OF BLONDIE" includes 12 exciting songs
featuring their 4 #1 singles
"Heart Of Glass," "Call Me," "The Tide Is High" and "Rapture"
plus special remixes.

Chrysalis
Records and Tapes
The album CHR 1337

R.E.M., 1987

Ted Nugent, 1980

Guns N' Roses, 1989

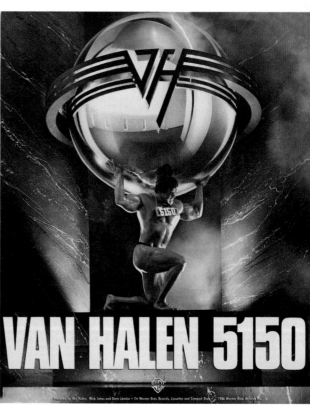

Van Halen, 1986

David Lee Roth, 1986

PRINCE AND THE REVOLUTION/PARADE
FEATURING THE HIT SINGLE "KISS"
MUSIC FROM THE 4THCOMING WARNER BROS. MOTION PICTURE UNDER THE CHERRY MOON
PRODUCED, COMPOSED, ARRANGED AND PERFORMED BY PRINCE AND THE REVOLUTION · MANAGEMENT: CAVALLO-RUFFALO-FARGNOLI · © 1986 WARNER BROS. RECORDS INC.

Prince, 1986

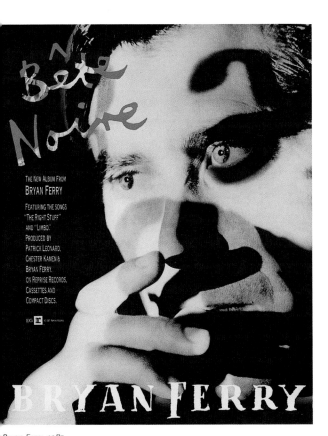

Bryan Ferry, 1987

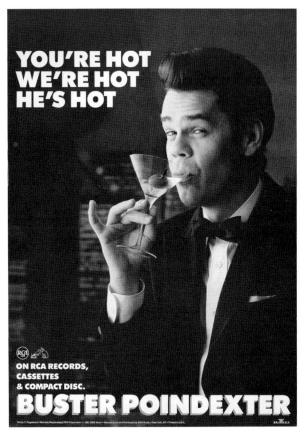

Buster Poindexer, 1987

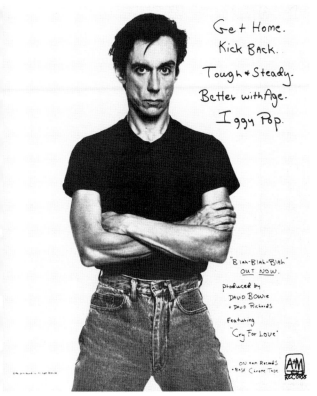

Iggy Pop, 1986

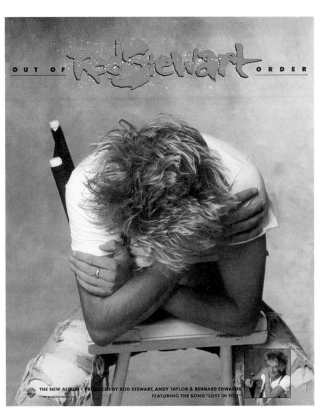

Rod Stewart, 1988

K.D. Lang, 1989

Sade, 1988

Diana Ross, 1982

MADONNA

true blue

THE NEW ALBUM

"PAPA DON'T PREACH"

"OPEN YOUR HEART"

"WHITEHEAT"

"LIVE TO TELL"

"WHERE'S THE PARTY"

"TRUE BLUE"

"LA ISLA BONITA"

"JIMMY JIMMY"

"LOVE MAKES
 THE WORLD GO ROUND"

ON SIRE RECORDS, CASSETTES AND COMPACT DISCS
©1986 Sire Records Company

Madonna, 1986

BENATAR ROCKS.

PHT BENATAR
WIDE AWAKE IN DREAMLAND

Pat Benatar's "Wide Awake in Dreamland,"
featuring the new single "All Fired Up." OUT NOW.

Produced by Peter Coleman & Neil Geraldo
"All Fired Up" Produced by Keith Forsey & Neil Geraldo/Management: Rick Newman/New Star Enterprises

Chrysalis.

Pat Benatar, 1988

Pet Shop Boys, actually.

New.
Includes the worldwide hit,
"It's A Sin,"
"What Have I Done To Deserve This?"
and more.

Eurythmics, 1986

Pet Shop Boys, 1987

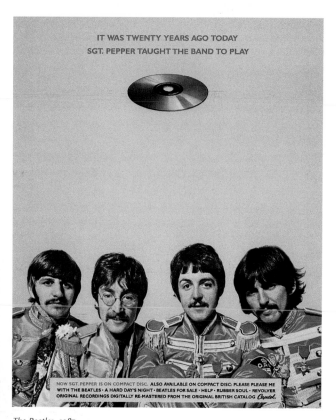

The Beatles, 1987

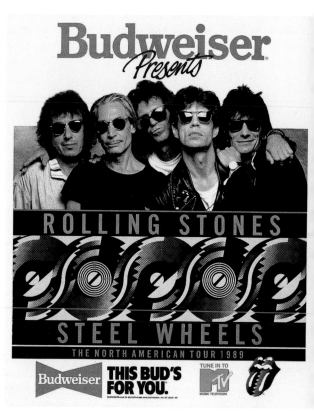

Rolling Stones, 1989

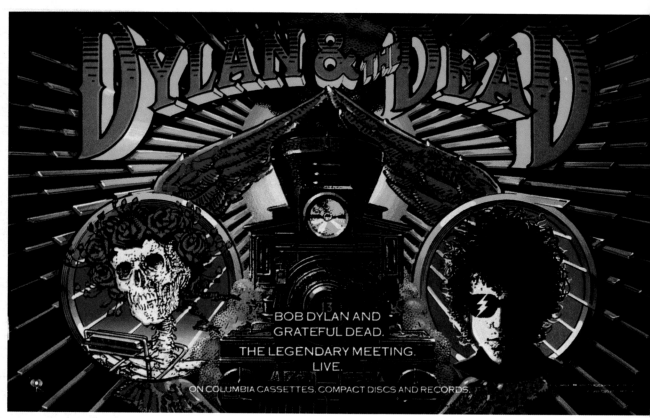

Bob Dylan & Grateful Dead, 1989

▶ *Tina Turner, 1986*

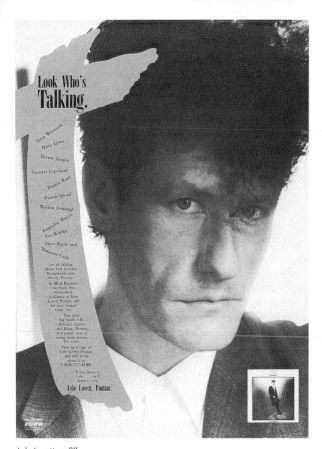

Lyle Lovett, 1988

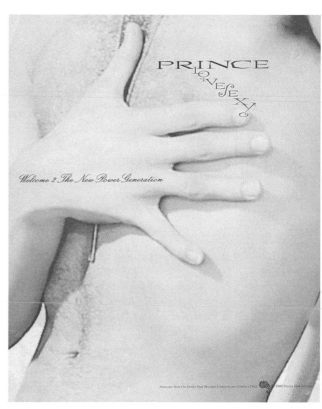

Prince, 1988

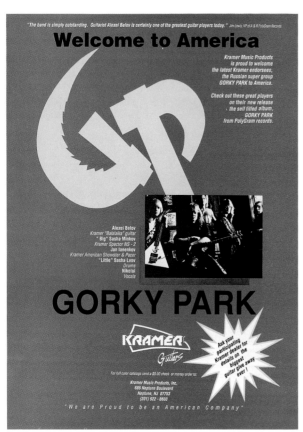

Gorky Park, 1989

Pink Floyd, 1988

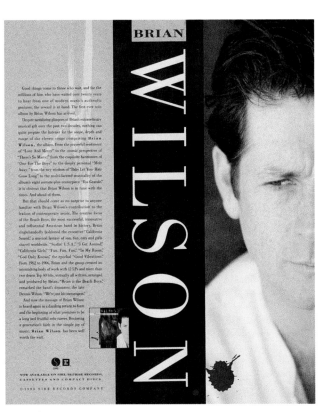

Brian Wilson, 1988

A Very Special Christmas, 1987

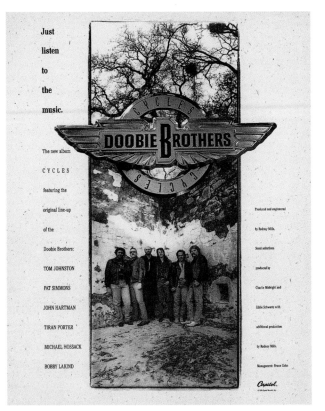

Doobie Brothers, 1989

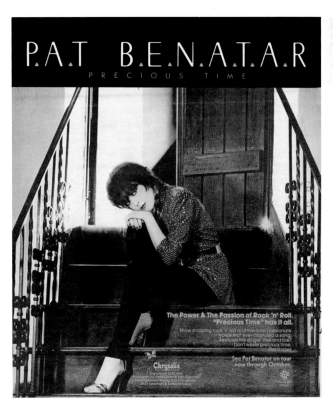

Pat Benatar, 1981

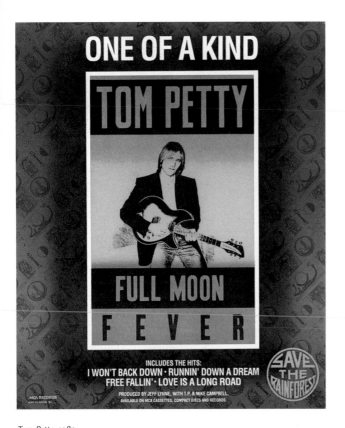

Tom Petty, 1989

Huey Lewis & the News, 1988

Duran Duran, 1989

Red Hot Chili Peppers, 1989

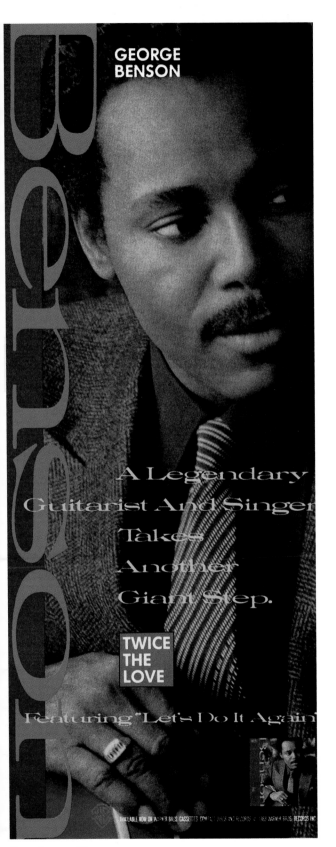

George Benson, 1988

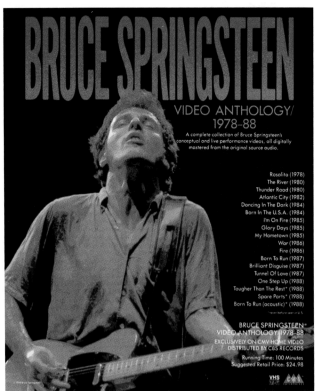

Bruce Springsteen, 1989

Quincy Jones, 1989

You'll never forget her for this

A Night
TO REMEM[ber]
The strongest music
statement from
Cyndi Laup[er]
Featuring the single,
"I Drove All Night"
On Epic Cassette[s,]
Compact Discs an[d]
Records.

Produced by Cyndi Lauper and Lennie Petze. Management: David Wolff

"Epic," "®" are trademarks of CBS Inc. © 1989 CBS Records Inc.

FAITH
GEORGE MICHAEL

"Faith." The Debut Solo Album
Featuring The No. 1 Single,
"I Want Your Sex," Plus "Hard Day"
And His New Smash Single,"Faith."
Written, Arranged And
Produced By George Michael.

ON COLUMBIA RECORDS,
CASSETTES AND COMPACT DISCS.
"Columbia," ♥ are trademarks of CBS Inc.   1987 CBS Inc.
MANAGEMENT: LIPPMAN KAHANE ENTERTAINMENT

Cyndi Lauper, 1989 ◄   *George Michael, 1987*

And the winner is...

Politician in Training

From his humble beginnings pumping iron, who would have guessed this hunk of Austrian flesh would be governor of California a mere two decades later? And what better preparation to run the world's fifth largest economy than *Terminator, Total Recall*, and *Kindergarten Cop*. But kicking around some Visigoth ass as Conan the Barbarian was Arnold's first super-hero step in working his way toward the American dream. Watch out, America, this is one Hun who is ready to pillage his way to the White House.

Politiker in spe

Wer hätte geglaubt, dass dieser österreichische Muskelprotz nach seinen bescheidenen Anfängen als Gewichtheber nur zwei Jahrzehnte später schon Gouverneur von Kalifornien sein würde? Eine bessere Vorbereitung auf die Führung der fünftgrößten Wirtschaftsmacht der Welt als *Terminator, Die totale Erinnerung* und *Kindergarten-Cop* kann es kaum geben. Und als Conan der Barbar ein paar Westgoten ordentlich in den Hintern zu treten, war Arnolds erster donnernder Schritt auf dem Weg zum amerikanischen Traum. Pass auf, Amerika, dieser Hunne wird noch mit Sengen und Brennen ins Weiße Haus einziehen!

Un entraînement de champion

A ses débuts modestes dans l'haltérophilie, qui aurait pu deviner que ce demi-dieu autrichien deviendrait le gouverneur de la Californie en seulement deux décennies ? Pas de meilleur entraînement que *Terminator, Total Recall* et *Kindergarten Cop* pour diriger la cinquième plus grande puissance économique mondiale. Mais botter le cul des Visigoths dans *Conan le Barbare* n'était que la première étape pour ce super-héros en route vers la réalisation du rêve américain. Attention l'Amérique, ce Hun est prêt à tout pour arriver à la Maison Blanche.

Político en formación

¿Quién habría imaginado que, desde sus humildes inicios como hombre de hierro, esta mole de carne austriaca acabaría por convertirse en gobernador de California poco más de dos décadas después? ¿Qué mejor preparación para gobernar la quinta mayor economía del mundo que *Terminator, Desafío Total* y *Poli de guardería*? Allí estaba Arnold, enfundado en su papel de Conan el Bárbaro, reduciendo con su fuerza a los visigodos, abriéndose paso en la piel de un superhéroe hacia el sueño americano. ¡Cuidado, América: ahí va un huno dispuesto a saquear la Casa Blanca!

訓練中の政治家

バーベルを挙げていた彼の卑しい過去を思うに、いったい誰がこのたくましいオーストリア人がたった20年後にカリフォルニア州知事になると予想したことだろう？そして世界で5番目に大きな経済組織を経営するために、『ターミネーター』や『トータルリコール』や『キンダーガートンコップ』以上に良い準備があるだろうか？しかし野蛮人コナンのように西ゴート人の尻を蹴り飛ばしたのは、アメリカンドリームへと突き進むアーノルドのスーパーヒーローとしての初めの一歩だった。アメリカさん、ご用心、これはホワイトハウスへの道を略奪する準備ができた一人のフン族ですよ。

THIEF.
WARRIOR.
BARBARIAN.
KING.

THE BARBARIAN

DINO DE LAURENTIIS PRESENTS
AN EDWARD R. PRESSMAN PRODUCTION
ARNOLD SCHWARZENEGGER · JAMES EARL JONES IN
"CONAN THE BARBARIAN"
STARRING
SANDAHL BERGMAN · BEN DAVIDSON · GERRY LOPEZ · MAKO · WILLIAM SMITH AND MAX VON SYDOW AS KING OSRIC
WRITTEN BY JOHN MILIUS AND OLIVER STONE MUSIC BY BASIL POLEDOURIS ASSOCIATE PRODUCER EDWARD SUMMER EXECUTIVE PRODUCERS D. CONSTANTINE CONTE AND EDWARD R. PRESSMAN
PRODUCED BY BUZZ FEITSHANS AND RAFFAELLA DE LAURENTIIS DIRECTED BY JOHN MILIUS A UNIVERSAL RELEASE
© 1982 UNIVERSAL CITY STUDIOS INC
RESTRICTED **R** UNDER 17 REQUIRES ACCOMPANYING PARENT OR ADULT GUARDIAN

COMING MAY 14th TO A THEATRE NEAR YOU

Conan the Barbarian, 1982

OPIUM

Yves Saint Laurent

conquer your heroes

gown: arnold scaasi necklace: arthur koby

without killing your budget. NINJA

If you like Opium or Cinnabar, you'll *love* Ninja® from Parfums de Coeur. $7.00 $3.95

Opium Perfume, 1981 ◄   *Ninja Perfume, 1983*   ► *Gianni Versace, 1985*

Gianni Versace

MACY'S

© 1989 Cher Beauty, a division of Parfums Stern, Inc.

UNINHIBITED BY CHER. *BOTTLED, BUT NOT CONTAINED.*

Coco Perfume, 1985 ◄ *Uninhibited by Cher Perfume, 1989*

Elizabeth Taylor's Passion Perfume, 1989

Fendi Cologne, 1989

Rive Gauche Perfume, 1981

CHANEL

CHANEL BOUTIQUES: NEW YORK, BEVERLY HILLS, CHICAGO, DALLAS, PALM BEACH, HONOLULU
OPENING SAN FRANCISCO, DECEMBER 1988

Chanel, 1988

Magical Musk Perfume, 1984

▶ *Camp Beverly Hills Perfume, 1987*

Sexy Hair

Sexy is the only word to describe hair
this shiny, this rich with body.
And now sexy hair is just a shampoo away
thanks to Farrah Fawcett Shampoo and
Farrah Fawcett Creme Rinse Conditioner.
Both with vitamins, minerals, protein
and herbs. From Fabergé.

L'Oréal Hair Color, 1988

Fabergé Haircare, 1982 ◄ *Clairol Hair Color, 1985*

JAZZING

**CLAIROL
FOR A NEW
GENERATION**

Hey listen! Jazzing is playing.
It's the most excitement
since haircolor first stepped on stage.
Color vibrant as trumpets;
shining like a night full of stars.
Color with no peroxide or ammonia.
Color you can play hot or subtle.
Color you can have for just a night or two.
Or have it linger on and on.
That's Jazzing.
Ask for it. And become
an overnight sensation.

AT SALONS ONLY

Clairol Hair Color, 1984

Dep**ortment**

*Learning all the
rules? Great idea.
It'll be much more
fun... when you break
them!
You can start with
breaking your dependence
on those aerosol mousses
with harmful alcohol that
dries your hair.
And get to know non-
alcohol Dep.
Because if you want your
hair to stay in lustrous,
healthy shape,
Dep will make sure
your hair is always on its
best behavior... even when
you're not.
Now you've got style!*

Dep Styling Gel, 1986

Cheryl's
a Dimensional
Woman.

with Clairesse®
**the Natural-Looking
Dimensional Hair Color**

Clairesse shades your hair the way nature does.
That's The Dimensional Look.
Each strand of hair is colored individually,
so your hair comes up lighter where your own light hair is,
richer and deeper where you have dark tones.
It looks almost the way it did when you were a child.
And no-ammonia Clairesse makes
The Dimensional Look even better because
exclusive extra conditioners are built into the color.
So Clairesse primes your hair for The Look you see,
then leaves it soft and touchable for The Look you feel.
Clairesse by Clairol is different
from any other shampoo-in haircoloring.

Clairesse...
because I Love The Look.

Oggi Haircare, 1988 ◄   *Clairesse Hair Color, 1981*

Clinique Men's Skincare, 1984

Quencher Nail Polish, 1983

Cover Girl Nail Polish, 1984

▶ *Almay Eyeshadow, 1981*

CHANEL

NEW FROM PARIS. TURBULENT, SEDUCTIVE COLOURS FOR LIPS AND NAILS.

hanel Cosmetics, 1985

CHANEL BEAUTY

Les Laques de Chanel. Brilliant new colors from Paris.

Chanel Cosmetics, 1981

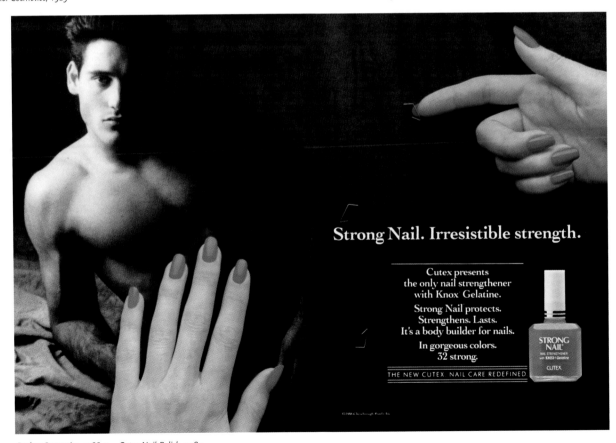

Strong Nail. Irresistible strength.

Cutex presents
the only nail strengthener
with Knox Gelatine.

Strong Nail protects.
Strengthens. Lasts.
It's a body builder for nails.

In gorgeous colors.
32 strong.

THE NEW CUTEX NAIL CARE REDEFINED

Revlon Cosmetics, 1988 ◄ *Cutex Nail Polish, 1989*

The essence of animal attraction.

Man and woman discovered musk together centuries ago.
They used its primal power to tease and please, to taunt and haunt.
Now Coty has bottled this mysterious essence of animal attraction.
Wild Musk for Women. Coty Musk for Men.

Caution: **Only Coty bottles the wild Wild Musk. Use it before you stalk.**

Coty Wild Musk Cologne, 1985

▶ *Aviance Night Musk, 1987*

Aviance Night Musk. Put it on...

Night Musk

Aviance

COTLER'S PANTS FOR THE RIGHT STANCE.

COTLER

STONE-WASHED DENIM PANTS

Cotler Pants, 1981

Gianni Versace

GianniVersace BOUTIQUE
MAYFAIR IN THE GROVE COCONUT GROVE, FLORIDA 33133
305·446·8405

Gianni Versace Boutique, 1981

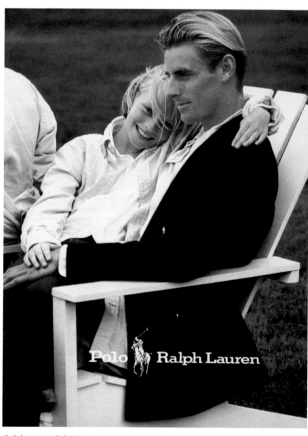

Modern Clothes For Men And Women

ESPRIT

Esprit Sportswear, 1985

Polo Ralph Lauren

Ralph Lauren Polo Menswear, 1986

GIORGIO ARMANI
PARFUMS

ARMANI
eau pour homme

Armani Cologne, 1988

449

Put chills down the ladies' spines when they reach out to touch your "thriller" curls.

Thrill them with the softness, fullness, silkiness and sexiness only Sta-Sof-Fro® Curl Activator gives your curls.

Thrill them with the non-whiting formulation that reduces build-up so you can maintain your cool, every day.

Thrill them with "Squalene," that keeps your curls locked in shape, so your curls look fresh, alive — and thrilling to the touch.

Thrill them with the non-greasy formulation that leaves your curls grease-free day after day.

And thrill yourself, everyday with Sta-Sof-Fro Curl Cream or Gel Activators. They keep your curls looking *so* natural, they'll put chills down *your* spine too!

THRILL YOUR CURLS WITH STA·SOF·FRO® CURL ACTIVATORS

FROM THE PEOPLE WHO KNOW YOUR HAIR... AND CARE.

© 1983 M&M Products Company

Sta-Sof-Fro Haircare, 1983

Classy Curl Haircare, 1982

Sta-Sof-Fro Haircare, 1982

Care Free Curl Haircare, 1984

▶ Obsession for Men, 1987

OBSESSION
FOR MEN
FOR THE BODY

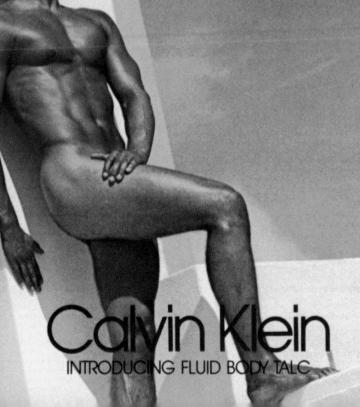

Calvin Klein
INTRODUCING FLUID BODY TALC

Calvin Klein Underwear

Calvin Klein Underwear, 1983

► Calvin Klein Underwear, 1985

Calvin Klein Underwear

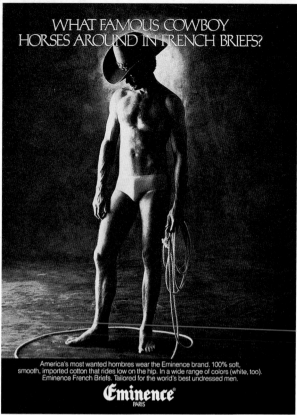

America's most wanted hombres wear the Eminence brand. 100% soft, smooth, imported cotton that rides low on the hip. In a wide range of colors (white, too). Eminence French Briefs. Tailored for the world's best undressed men.

Eminence PARIS

Available at Saks Fifth Avenue, Neiman Marcus, Mr. Guy, Fred Siegels, Ahmen

Eminence French Briefs, 1980

Christian Dior Underwear, 1983

Speedo Swimwear, 1982

▶ *Chess King, 1986*

chess king

BORiS ©86

Valentino Menswear, 1984

Missoni Menswear, 1983

Calvin Klein Jeans, 1981

Sergio Valente Jeans, 1984

The Gap, 1989

The Gap, 1989

Dickies Apparel, 1981

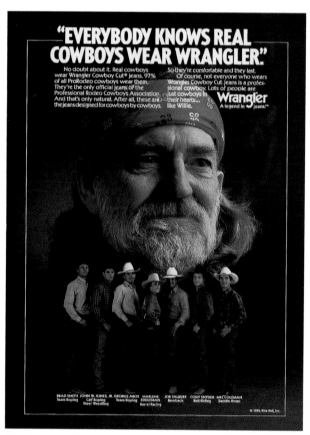

Wrangler Jeans, 1986

Levi's 501 Jeans, 1984

Man, I need VANS™

STYLE 439

STYLE 438

Breakers
Only For The Elite!

Vans Breakers, 1984

461

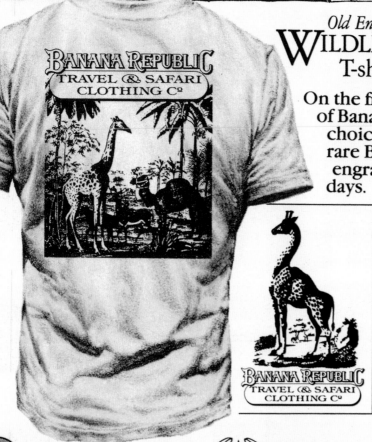

Banana Republic Sportswear, 1984

If you like our Nasty Boots...

STYLE & COMFORT
Hidden folds give when you lean for the bars. Snap-off fur collar is included.

PROTECTION
Built-in kidney support; forget those old clumsy, uncomfortable kidney belts.

WIND & WINE PROOF
Leather-laced ties ensure perfect before- and after-dinner fit, keep wind out.

EXTRA MACHO
Optional Sam Browne-type diamond-pattern belt, $30, including belt loops.

... You'll love our Nasty Leathers

We proudly present the NASTY jacket. Made best, for the best. A sleek-fitting, macho statement of who you are and what you believe. Black, bold, and 100% made in America. Fully lined. Tough leather reinforcing at every wear point ensures years of great looks and full protection. A biker-sized nylon zipper glides easily in all weather, and a large flap keeps the wind out and the warmth in. Leather-laced side ties mold it to your body. The NASTY jacket, for the travelin' *man* who wants it *all*.

Nasty Leathers, 1983

463

KENZO:
JAPANESE
BY ORIGIN.
PARISIAN
BY CHOICE.
INTERNATIONAL
BY NATURE.
AND
UNDEFINABLE

Kenzo, 1985

Swatch Sportswear, 1986

▶ *Georges Marciano Guess Jeans, 1986*

GUESS

Saks Fifth Avenue

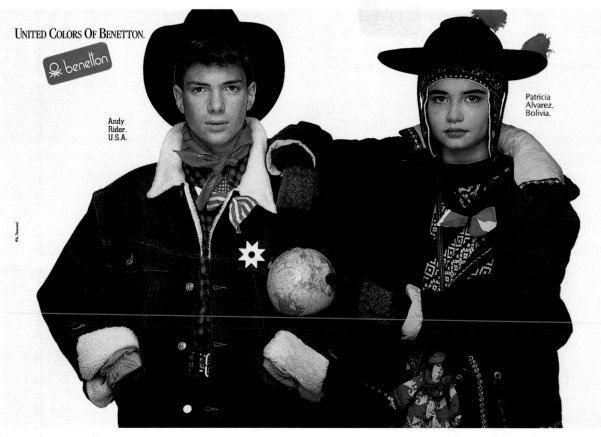

UNITED COLORS OF BENETTON.

Ⓡ benetton

Andy
Rider.
U.S.A.

Patricia
Alvarez.
Bolivia.

Benetton Sportswear, 1986

THE NEW BOTTOM LINE

MERRY
GO
ROUND®

FASHION BOUTIQUES
FOR MEN AND WOMEN

Marry Go Round Sportswear, 1989

JORDACHE®

Millers
Outpost

Jordache Jeans, 1988

MEMBERS ONLY®

"When you put it on...something happens to you."

Larry Gatlin and the Gatlin Brothers

Take a tip from the Gatlin Brothers.
Get into MEMBERS ONLY.
You'll look good and feel different.
But remember, it's only MEMBERS ONLY
if it says so on the pocket.

Members Only Jackets, 1983

Nike Sportswear, 1989

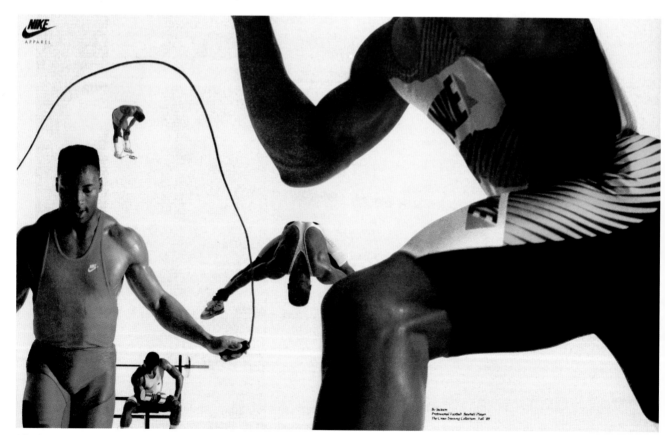

Nike Sportswear, 1989

Kenny Scharf Sportswear, 1987

Nike Sportswear, 1984

Nike Sportswear, 1988

© 1982 HANG TEN INTERNATIONAL

HANG TEN

You didn't buy your bike to cruise to the grocery store.
But eat it on one of these flat out mystery leaps, and you'll look like something from the meat department. That's part of the game. Only the strong survive, and only the crazed start out in the first place.

But when you know what you're doing, crazy is just a non-existent state of mind. Or in our case, a state of feet. The ones on our sportswear, sports gear and fun stuff. So keep that wrist locked wide open. Only ten more miles of torture—and you'll be half way home.

For Hang Ten poster information, or a free catalog of other Hang Ten fun stuff write: Hang Ten, Dept. **DBPB**, P.O. Box 2992, San Diego, CA 92101.

Hang Ten Sportswear, 1982

Lois
SPORTSWEAR

GQ/SEPTEMBER 95

Lois Sportswear, 1983

Gotcha Swimwear, 1989

WELCOME TO THE UNEXPECTED

CATALINA
JUNIORS

Catalina Swimwear, 1985

TOO HOT
BRAZIL

For the store nearest you call toll-free 1-800-421-5731

Contempo Casuals

Too Hot Brazil Swimwear, 1987

Nordica Ski Boots, 1989

Nike Hiking Boots, 1988

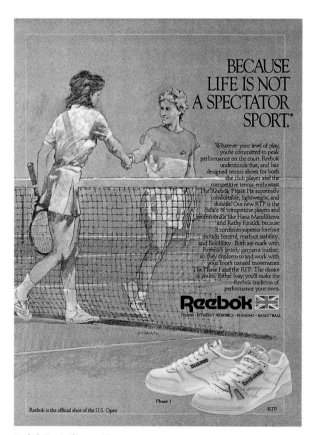

Reebok Tennis Shoes, 1986

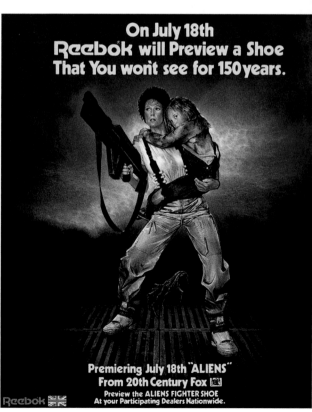

Reebok Aliens Fighter Shoes, 1986

Puma Athletic Shoes, 1985

YOU'LL NEVER CATCH THEM IN OUR SHOES.

Mizuno
ATHLETIC FOOTWEAR

Mizuno Athletic Shoes, 1987

Puma Athletic Shoes, 1985

CHOOSE YOUR WEAPON.

Larry Bird and Magic Johnson. When they play, they push themselves to the limit. And they trust their performance to Converse. The shoe they choose to do battle in is the Converse® Weapon™ – a shoe biomechanically designed to help players play their best.

These shoes offer superior traction because of their natural rubber outsoles. They're incredibly cushioned as well, due to the Center of Pressure outsole and a shock absorbing EVA midsole. And for the strong ankle support that Bird, Magic and every other ballplayer needs, there's the unique Y-Bar Ankle Support System.

Besides all these features, the Converse Weapon has a comfortable, removable insole and an extra padded collar that combines with the Y-Bar System for enhanced ankle support and comfort. Bird and Magic have chosen their weapons. Now choose yours.

The Converse Weapon. One more reason why athletes like Bird and Magic depend on Converse for the best possible performance.

THE CONVERSE®
WEAPONS™

CONVERSE
Reach for the stars.

©1986 Converse, Inc.

Converse Athletic Shoes, 1986

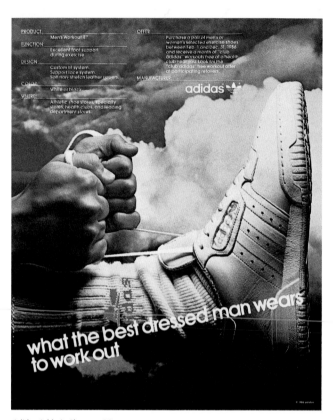

Adidas Athletic Shoes, 1986

Pony Athletic Shoes, 1988

Adidas Athletic Shoes, 1986

Converse Athletic Shoes, 1988

AND YOU THOUGHT YOU'D WORN EVERYTHING.

The Nike Aqua Sock comes in an array of colors, and sizes to fit both men and women.

You wear it as you would any other shoe. With one exception.

Instead of taking it off before you go in the water, you leave it on.

Now, this is going to feel a little strange the first time you try it. But once you

start thinking about the possibilities, you'll adjust.

To find the Nike Aqua Sock, call 1-800-344-NIKE.

Nike Aqua Socks, 1988

YOU KNOW WHAT THEY SAY ABOUT MEN WHO KEEP THEIR SOCKS ON.

They say they like it wet. They say that to hit the surf, dive the depths, soak the sand, a man's gotta wear what a

man's gotta wear. And so does a woman. The new Nike Aqua Sock, Aqua Sock Too and Aqua Boot. By land, or

by sea, this is how to make waves.

To find the Nike Aqua Socks and Boot, call 1-800-344-NIKE.

Nike Aqua Socks, 1989

Before.

After.

Reebok Athletic Shoes, 1989

Introducing the Cross-Training System by Reebok. Three shoes designed for any kind of workout, starting with what you do best.

AXT. The first shoe for runners who also want to lift weights and play court sports. Leather and mesh uppers for lightness. Forefoot sidewall wrap for stability. Dedicated to runners who would sometimes rather stand and fight.

CXT. The first shoe for court players who also want to run and lift weights. Midfoot strap for medial support. Midfoot sidewall for lateral support. Good for adjusting the attitude of the geek that beat you in tennis last week.

SXT. The first shoe for weight lifters who also want to run and play court sports. Midfoot and ankle straps for maximum support. Wide base ensures maximum stability for you and guarantees total insecurity for everyone around you.

The physics behind the physiques. **Reebok**

477

Adidas Sportswear, 1982

British Knights Athletic Shoes, 1988

JUST DO IT.

Nike Athletic Shoes, 1988

Just Doing It Doesn't Do It.

Introducing The ASICS' GEL-Trainer. No matter which sport you're training for or which surface you're training on, you can now do it better.

With the incredible shock absorption of ASICS' GEL.

Because now, the heart and sole of our running shoes is available in our new GEL-Trainer.

The difference: space age silicon GEL permanently encapsulated in pads at points of maximum biomechanical impact.

Which not only reduces workout fatigue, but offers you outstanding injury protection and stability.

So try on a pair of our low or mid-top GEL-Trainers.

The all-terrain vehicles for people who *don't* just do it.

asics
Don't Just Do It. Do It Better.

Nike Athletic Shoes, 1988 ◀ Asics Athletic Shoes, 1989

FOR A MEASLY $35, YOU CAN RUN IN A BREAKTHROUGH.

When it comes to technological savvy, no other running shoe company comes close to New Balance. The New Balance 375 is proof of that.

For all-out support, New Balance's all-leather sway bar. When you run your feet tend to roll in an inward or outward direction. Excessive roll or in either direction can result in injury. The 375 has leather side supports for exceptional side-to-side stability.

The New Balance outersole is so durable, you'll wear out before it does. When you're paying good money for a running shoe, it ought to be tough. The sole of the 375 is made from Goodyear Indy 500 rubber, the same material racing car tires are made from. Enough said?

New Balance stands for comfort, even in the achilles area. The 375 has a soft innersole that cradles your foot. A lightweight, shock-absorbing polyethylene mid-section. A padded heel area. Comfortable? Like you won't believe.

Only New Balance makes running shoes in a variety of widths. Feet come in different widths, and so does the 375. Because proper fit is the most critical feature of a running shoe.

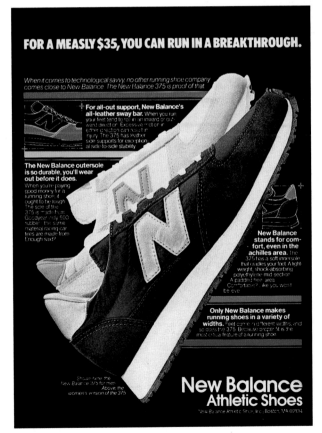

Shown here, the New Balance 375 for men. Above, the women's version of the 375.

New Balance Athletic Shoes
New Balance Athletic Shoe, Inc., Boston, MA 02134

New Balance Athletic Shoes, 1981

481

Puma Athletic Shoes, 1988

Reebok Athletic Shoes, 1988

Avia Athletic Shoes, 1989

IRREVERENCE. JUSTIFIED.

Nike Athletic Shoes, 1989

SHOTS Dazzling, Different, Awsome. The hottest new look
in high and low basketball shoes. Built to perform. With sizzling colors
that make Shots the toast of the town.

Available at:

**Footlocker · Lady Footlocker · Wild Pair · Macy's
Emporium Capwell · Nordstrom's · Carson Perie Scott · The Jones Store**

L.A. GEAR™
FASHION ATHLETIC FOOTWEAR™

4221 Redwood, Los Angeles, California 90066, 213-822-1995 • For Canadian distribution contact: Indeka Imports Ltd., Mississauga, Ontario, Canada L5L - 1X1 416-828-6800 • © 1988 L.A. Gear

L.A. Gear Athletic Shoes, 1988

▶ *Reebok Athletic Shoes, 1989*

MILLIONS OF GIRLS WANT TO BE IN HER SHOES.

BUT SHE WANTS TO BE IN OURS.

Paula Abdul is wearing shoes from the Dance Reebok® Collection. Available at department and fine specialty stores. Call 1-800-843-4444 for locations nearest you.

L.A. Gear Athletic Shoes, 1986

Reebok Athletic Shoes, 1987

Travel Fox Shoes, 1986

Foot Locker, 1988

Reebok Athletic Shoes, 1985

IT'S LIKE A JUNGLE OUT THERE.

Introducing the camouflage Converse All Star. It's the most hunted canvas shoe around. Look for the Converse All Star in pink and lilac, too. You can track them down everywhere.

Reach for the stars. Reach for Converse.
The Official Athletic Shoe of the 1984 Olympic Games

© 1984 Converse Inc.

Converse All Star Athletic Shoes, 1984

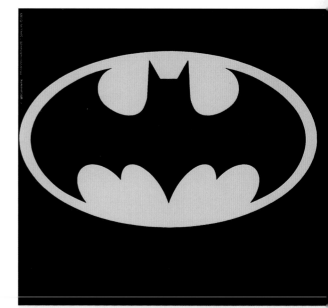

CONVERSE REINTRODUCES WINGTIPS.

They're back. Batman™ and his arch enemy, the Joker™ From Converse. At select stores for a limited time only. Call 1-800-545-4323 for the store nearest you.

Converse Batman and Joker Shoes, 1989

© 1985 Converse Inc.

LIMOUSINES FOR YOUR FEET.

Converse All Stars.® The original canvas high tops and oxfords in eighteen fun and flashy colors and prints for people who want to go places in style.

Reach for the stars.

26 ROLLING STONE, JULY 18/AUGUST 1, 1985

Converse All Star Athletic Shoes, 1985

Travel Fox Shoes, 1988

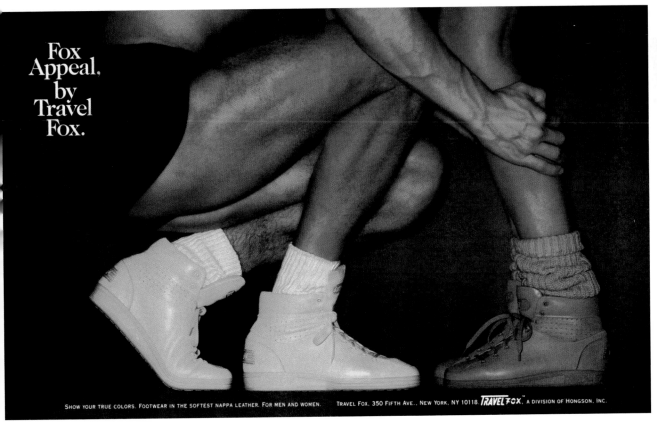

Travel Fox Shoes, 1987

Turtles Shoes, 1982

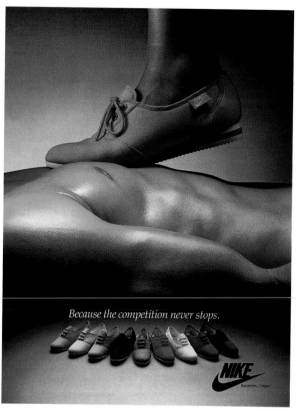

Nike Shoes, 1984

Cherokee Shoes, 1983

Hush Puppies Shoes, 1982

Sorels Boots, 1983

KangaRoos Athletic Shoes, 1983

KangaRoos Athletic Shoes, 1983

KangaRoos Athletic Shoes, 1984

"GENUINE DR. MARTENS ARE NEVER OUT OF STYLE"

NA NA

CLOTHING	SHOES	ACCESSORIES
NEW YORK	SANTA MONICA	SAN FRANCISCO
414 AMSTERDAM	631 SANTA MONICABLVD.	1108 & 1124 POLK
213.496.2955	213.394.9690	415.771.7400

FOR MAIL ORDER CATALOG WRITE: NA NA DEPT. D 631 SANTA MONICA BLVD.
SANTA MONICA, CA. 90401 FOR WHOLESALE ENQUIRIES,
PLEASE PHONE: 213.394.5305

PHOTO BY CYNTHIA LEVINE

Na Na, 1989

Definitely
PLAYBOY

Playboy Footwear, 1985

Crayons⁻, packed one color to the box

CRAYONS™ FOR MEN AND WOMEN
OVER 70 STYLES AND 350 COLOR COMBINATIONS TO CHOOSE FROM
AT SHOE CLOTHING AND DEPT STORES EVERYWHERE

Crayons Shoes, 1980

Why Frye?

Frye boots
give you
a great
new
feeling.

Rugged leathers.
Richer colors.

Quality you can
see and touch.
Styles with real
staying power.

You can always
count on Frye.

And that's why.

FRYE

120 GREAT YEARS FROM FRYE.

JOHN A. FRYE SHOE CO. IS A SUBSIDIARY OF ALBERTO-CULVER CO.

Frye Boots, 1983

Clicks Shoes, 1985

Spiegel Catalog, 1988

Ciao Womenswear, 1987

Treat 'Em Good and They'll Treat You Good.

In the Old West, it's said, some men took better care of their boots than their women. Not altogether admirable, but certainly understandable. Texas Brand® Boots are handsome, comfortable, rugged and dependable. Whenever and wherever you wear them, that's just the way they make you feel. As with any good friend, you take care of them and they take care of you.

For nearest retailer call toll free 1-800-251-3208, except in Tennessee call 1-615-444-5440.

© Texas Boot Company 1981

TEXAS TEXAS BRAND® BOOTS

THE LONGER YOU WEAR 'EM, THE BETTER THEY GET.

Texas Boots, 1981

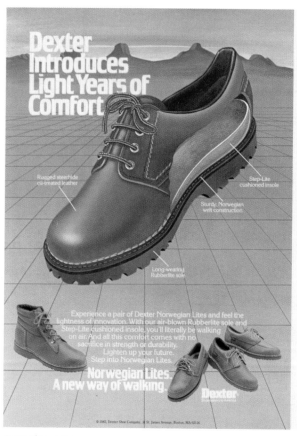

Dexter Introduces Light Years of Comfort

Rugged steerhide oil-treated leather

Step-Lite cushioned insole

Sturdy, Norwegian welt construction

Long-wearing Rubberlite sole

Experience a pair of Dexter Norwegian Lites and feel the lightness of innovation. With our air-blown Rubberlite sole and Step-Lite cushioned insole, you'll literally be walking on air. And all this comfort comes with no sacrifice in strength or durability. Lighten up your future. Step into Norwegian Lites.

Norwegian Lites. A new way of walking.

Dexter

© 1982. Dexter Shoe Company, 31 St. James Avenue, Boston, MA 02116.

Dexter Shoes, 1982

MONTANA DINGO

When "Super Bowl" Joe Montana plays the game, he does it in his Dingos. Because he loves the way Dingo® leather looks and the way Dingo leather feels. So put yourself in a pair of Dingos like Montana Joe. Because Dingo's the only way to play the game.

dingo®

Acme Boot Co., Inc., P.O. Box 749, Clarksville, Tenn. 37041-0749. A subsidiary of Northwest Industries, Inc. Call toll-free 1-800-251-1382. In Tenn. call 615-552-2000

15

Dingo Boots, 1983

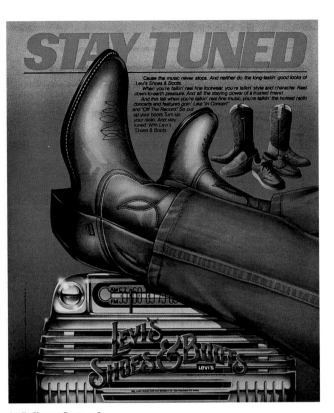

Levi's Shoes & Boots, 1981

Levi's Shoes & Boots, 1981

Northlake by Georgia Boots, 1984

Nasty Feet Boots, 1983

Pancaldi for Delman Shoes, 1985

THE SURVIVOR INSTINCT

With nothing but a few provisions, perfect teamwork
and the sheer comfort of our Herman Survivors,
we managed to survive. In style.

HERMAN SURVIVORS®

Joseph M. Herman Shoe Company, Millis, MA © 1982

Herman Survivors Shoes, 1982

▶ *Connie Shoes, 1982*

THE HENLEY COLLEGE LIBRARY

497

L'Eggs Hosiery, 1981

L'Eggs Hoisery, 1985

Round the Clock Pantyhose, 1985

Hanes Hoisery, 1985

Bass Footwear, 1984

Mammrae-9000, 1988

Improved Right Places, 1980

Bali Bras, 1981

Playtex Bras, 1981

Ce Soir Lingerie, 1980

Jockey Underwear, 1988

Playtex Bras, 1984

Maidenform Lingerie, 1989

Bill Blass

Bill Blass, 1985

NOLAN MILLER DYNASTY COLLECTION · A DIVISION OF THE LESLIE FAY COMPANIES · 530 SEVENTH AVENUE, NY, NY 10018 · (212) 221-2017

Nolan Miller
Dynasty Collection™

Nolan Miller Womenswear, 1985

Ralph Lauren Polo Womenswear, 1984

Blackglama Furs, 1981

Saint Laurent, 1985

Blackglama Furs, 1982

Pendleton Wools, 1986

Valentino, 1985

Levi's Jeans, 1984

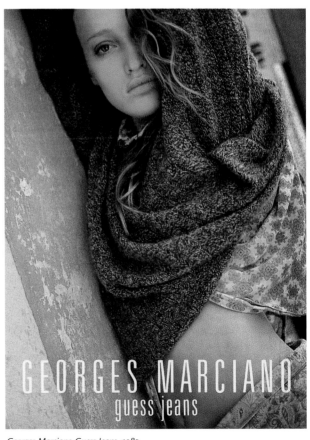

Georges Marciano Guess Jeans, 1985

For the first time since 1850...

WHAT MUST BE THE STRANGEST PAIR OF JEANS EVER MADE ARE FINALLY MADE TO FIT WOMEN.

Levi's® original button fly blue jeans-in a denim that shrinks so much, you'll need real faith to buy them. But, oh, what a fit!

The jeans that won the West have discovered women.

For over a century, the only way a woman could get authentic Levi's 501™ Blue Jeans was to buy a pair made for men. But now, at long last, we've started making those same rugged shrink-to-fit jeans for junior sized women.

Same metal buttons on the fly. Same copper rivets on the front pockets and red

Levi's "tab" on the back pocket. Nothing has been changed but the fit. To fit you perfectly.

Your washing machine "tailors" the 501™ to hug every curve.

What separates 501's™ from the jeans you're accustomed to wearing is our exclusive shrink-to-fit "XXX" all cotton denim. In the store, you'll find that the jeans feel stiff, look dark, and are much bigger than the size indicated.

But trust what we tell you: after just three washings, the length, waist, hips — everything —

shrinks permanently to fit like no jeans you've ever worn. A few more washings, and the fabric "breaks in" to become softer, lighter in color, and extraordinarily comfortable.

The older they get the better they look.

In many parts of the world, a washed-down and broken-in pair of 501™ jeans are more desirable than a brand new pair. Because despite

their after-washing softness, a good old pair of 501's™ is still as tough as nails. (Rumor has it that 501's™ never really die. They just sort of "fade away.")

With their button fly and shrink-to-fit fabric, Levi's 501™ Blue Jeans probably are a little strange.

Look for 501's™ in The Junior Department

But try a pair for yourself. After you've worn the very first blue jeans ever made, you may find everything else running a distant second.

501 **LEVI'S® WOMENSWEAR**

QUALITY NEVER GOES OUT OF STYLE ®

Levi's 501 Jeans, 1982

ZENA®
MADE IN THE U.S.A.
JEANS

Zena Jeans, 1986

BRITTANIA

"I BELIEVE IN BRITTANIA"

Total BRITTANIA® The Denim Jacket. The Vienna Jean. For the store nearest you, call 1-800-227-5600.   ©1988 Brittania® Sportswear Ltd.

Brittania Jeans, 1988   ▶ *Calvin Klein Jeans, 1980*

Calvin Klein Jeans

Betsey Johnson Womenswear, 1985

Koala Blue Sportswear, 1987

Esprit Sport, 1986

Neo Max Sportswear, 1987

Gap pocket-t as worn by
KIM BASINGER, actress

GAP

POWER.

The Gap, 1989

Benetton Sportswear, 1984

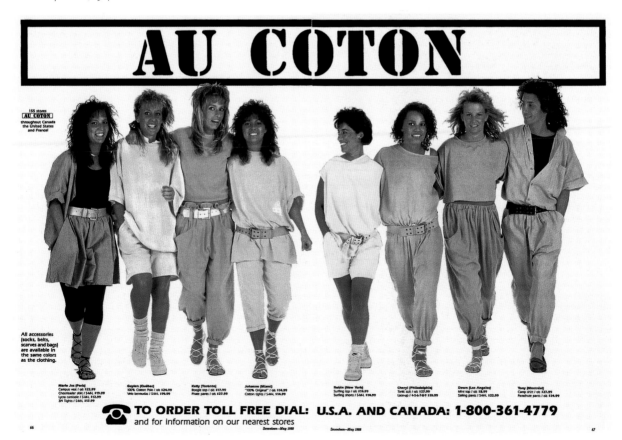

Au Coton Sportswear, 1988

Osh Kosh B'Gosh Kidswear, 1985

Carter's Sleepwear, 1981

Our Girl Apparel, 1983

Carter's Sleepwear, 1983 ▶ *Dobie Kidswear, 1984*

Guess who's having fun with Dobie?

Care Bears™ Kidswear.
by dobie
from Cluett
Makers of SuperTex™ 2000

Underoos Underwear, 1981

Underoos Underwear, 1980

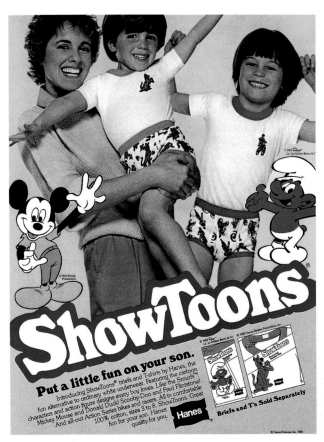

Show Toons Underwear, 1983

Winnie-the-Pooh Clothes, 1980

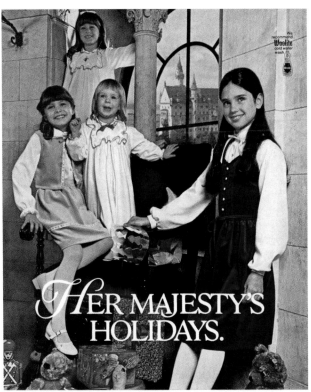

Her Majesty, 1981

WHEN HE GETS A LITTLE EDGES, REMEMBER THAT

His hair resembles nothing that occurs in nature. And his shoes look like protective packaging for radioactive materials. So how do you explain why he's

WEIRD AROUND THE HE LOVES LEVI'S JEANS.

so crazy about something as sturdy and sensible as Levi's jeans? Don't even try. To find out where to get Levi's jeans for boys, call **LEVI'S** 1-800-227-5600.

Levi's Jeans, 1988

Do you know why Dickies boy's wear wears so well?
Because Dickies makes the work sets most working men wear.
And boys are only slightly harder on clothes.

Dickies

Williamson-Dickie Apparel Manufacturing Company, Fort Worth, Texas

Dickies Boy's Wear, 1983

Calvin Klein Jeans for Girls

Calvin Klein Jeans, 1983 ▸ *Calvin Klein Jeans, 1983*

Calvin Klein Jeans for Boys

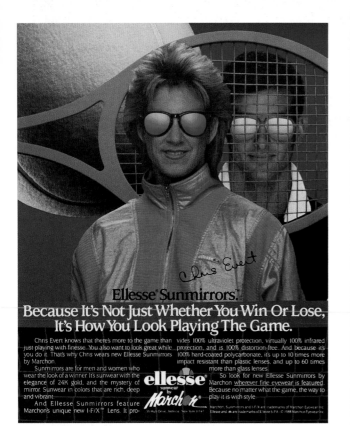

Ellesse Sunmirrors, 1988

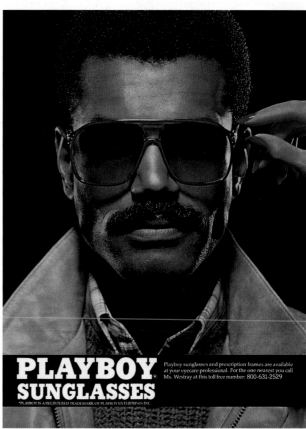

Playboy Sunglasses, 1982

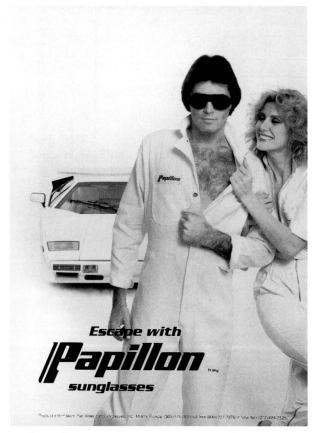

Papillon Sunglasses, 1982

Dobie Kidswear, 1984

A face is like a work of art. It deserves a great frame.

There has never been a frame quite like "The Beat." It was designed by l.a. Eyeworks, made in France and comes in dozens of textures, patterns and colors. Everything from matte crystal to buffalo horn to pink and black rayure (shown above). "The Beat" is available with many colored lenses and all prescriptions are filled in our own laboratory. Send $1 for a color catalog featuring "The Beat" and other designs by l.a. Eyeworks.

l.a. Eyeworks
7407 MELROSE, LOS ANGELES, CA 90046

Glasses shown: The Beat. Designed by l.a. Eyeworks. Face: Pee Wee Herman. Photographer: Greg Gorman. © 1984, l.a. Eyeworks, Los Angeles, CA 90046. Available at Barneys New York; Bendel's; Bergdorf-Goodman; Bullock's; Carson, Pirie Scott; Charavari; Foley's; I. Magnin; Jerry Magnin; McInerny; Neiman Marcus; Robinson's; Sointu; Theodore; Ultimo; Wilkes Bashford. For wholesale inquiries contact Three, 7407 Melrose Avenue, Los Angeles, CA 90046. 213/653-8176.

L.A. Eyeworks, 1984

And the winner is...

A Little Squirt Will Do You

What were the folks at Chanel® thinking of? Perhaps their advertising team was caught up in the last gasps of the sexual revolution. Whatever their strategy, the phallic-shaped bottle with its stream of white liquid jettisoned across the page was a wet dream of excess. Attempting to express masculinity at its virile best, this effort to sell an all-purpose lubricant "to attend to the needs of modern man" was one advertisement to make the porn industry green with envy.

Nur ein kleiner Abspritzer

Was haben sich die Leute bei Chanel® bloß dabei gedacht? Vielleicht war die sexuelle Revolution im Kreativteam ja noch nicht ganz außer Puste. Jedenfalls schießt die phallisch geformte Flasche mit der quer über die Seite spritzenden weißen Flüssigkeit über's Ziel hinaus. Diese Anzeige will Männlichkeit von ihrer besten Machoseite zeigen und verkauft ein Rundum-Gleitmittel für die „Bedürfnisse des modernen Mannes" – die Pornobranche wurde grün vor Neid.

Une petite giclée vous suffira

A quoi ont-ils pensé chez Chanel® ? Se pourrait-il que leur équipe de publicité ait été rattrapée par les derniers sursauts de la révolution sexuelle ? Quelle que fût la stratégie, le flacon phallique et son jet de liquide blanc en travers de la page témoigne d'une imagination débordante. Essayer de vendre un lubrifiant tous usages, qui «répond aux besoins de l'homme moderne» en suggérant la virilité dans toute sa puissance, fut l'une de ces publicités à faire pâlir d'envie l'industrie du porno.

Con un chorrito basta

¿En qué estarían pensando los directivos de Chanel®? Quizá su equipo publicitario se había quedado atascado en los últimos jadeos de la revolución sexual... Fuera cual fuera su estrategia, aquel envase con forma fálica que lanzaba un chorrito de líquido blanco a la página siguiente era un sueño húmedo excesivo. En un intento por expresar la virilidad en su estado más puro, este anuncio de un bálsamo multiuso «que cubre las necesidades del hombre moderno» seguramente tiñó de envidia a la industria pornográfica.

ちょっとの噴射であなたもご満足

シャネルの人々は何を考えていたのだろう？おそらく彼らの広告担当チームはセックス的変換期における臨終の局面にあったのかも知れない。彼らの戦略何であれ、男性性器の形をしたボトルと、ページを横切って発射された白い液体の流れは夢精過多のようだ。精力的最盛期の男性らしさを表現しようと試みつ、"現代の男性のニーズに応える"この多目的な潤滑剤を売ろうとする努力は、ポルノ産業に嫉妬の色を浮かべさせる広告となった。

ANTAEUS: SOOTHING MOISTURE BALM.
DEODORANT. BATH SOAP.
PROTECTIVE SKIN CONDITIONER.

ANTAEUS
POUR HOMME

CHANEL

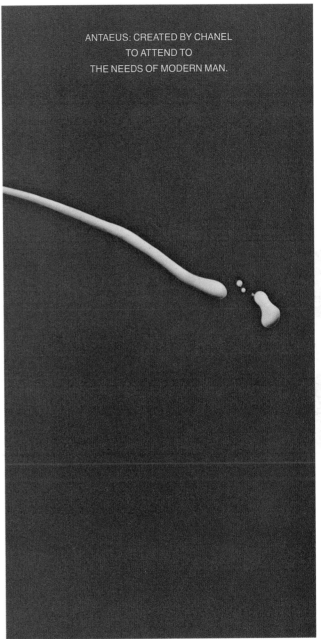

ANTAEUS: CREATED BY CHANEL
TO ATTEND TO
THE NEEDS OF MODERN MAN.

Chanel Antaeus Skincare, 1984

Light up your Jack-O'-Lantern Treats with new Marshmallow Krispies cereal.

Jack-O'-Lantern Treats

¼ cup margarine or butter
1 pkg. (10 oz., about 40) regular marshmallows or 4 cups miniature marshmallows
5 cups Kellogg's® Marshmallow Krispies™ cereal

1. Melt margarine in large saucepan over low heat. Add marshmallows and stir until completely melted. Cook over low heat 3 minutes longer, stirring constantly. Remove from heat.
2. Add Marshmallow Krispies cereal. Stir until well coated.
3. To make five Jack-O'-Lanterns, divide cereal mixture into five equal parts. Form pumpkin-shaped balls and stems. Decorate with frosting and Halloween candies.
Yield: 5 Jack-O'-Lantern Treats
NOTE: Best results are obtained when using fresh marshmallows.

Kellogg's®

® Kellogg Company
© 1982 Kellogg Company

Crystal Light Diet Drink Mix, 1986 ◄   *Marshmallow Krispies, 1982*   ► *Peanuts Easter Egg Kit, 1988*

This Easter, your kids can decorate and hunt Easter eggs with Snoopy

The PEANUTS Kit—just 60¢ with any $5.00 Hallmark purchase

Bring SNOOPY, WOODSTOCK, and the fun of decorating and hunting Easter eggs home to your family. The easy-to-use PEANUTS Kit comes complete with color tablets, egg dipper, drying tray, PEANUTS stickers, award stickers, and egg display stand. You'll even find Easter Beagle paw

prints to guide your children along the egg hunt trail. The PEANUTS Easter Egg Decorating and Hunt Kit—just add eggs and kids...and spring into Easter at Hallmark! Available March 7 only at participating Hallmark stores while supplies last. Limit one per customer.

Hallmark

When you care enough to send the very best

Morning is your time

For you, Grape-Nuts® is as natural as the morning.
No added sugar. No preservatives.
Just a nutty taste. And a rugged crunch.

Grape-Nuts® Cereal.
You know when you've got it good.

GENE
FOO

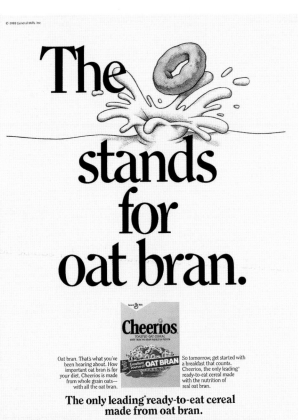

Cheerios Cereal, 1988

Fruit & Fibre Cereals, 1986

Grape Nuts Cereal, 1986 ◄ Burberrys Fine Foods, 1986

Grape Nuts Flakes Cereal, 1987

Hormel Sausages, 1986

Plume de Veau Veal, 1983

Steak-Umm Beef Product, 1983

Beef, 1989

ZESTY. MEATY. CHEESY. SAUCY. SPICY.
QUICKLY.

Five minutes.
That's all the time it takes
to cook a Weight Watchers Pizza.
Our new crisper board, built into every package,
makes them all microwaveable.
The cheese pizzas. The sausage pizzas.
The pepperoni pizzas. Even the French Bread Pizzas.
Five minutes. Why it's
barely enough time to work up an appetite.

Weight Watchers®
This is living!

Weight Watchers, 1988

"BURRITOS! ENCHILADAS! ESTO ES VIVIR!"

"This is eating with gusto! Weight Watchers
new zesty Mexican entrees. Two kinds of burritos:
lean beefsteak or juicy chicken with beans and
spices wrapped in tender flour tortillas. Three
kinds of enchiladas: shredded beef or tasty
cheese or chicken in hearty corn tortillas topped
with splendid south of the border sauces. As I said
above: 'This is living!'" Lynn Redgrave.

Weight Watchers®

Weight Watchers, 1986

Zucchini Lasagna
240 calories

Oriental Beef
280 calories

Chicken and Vegetables
270 calories

Never before
have so few calories tasted so good.

Taste, after all, is the pleasurable part of eating.
So, Stouffer's® makes sure that every Lean Cuisine® entree tastes so good,
you'll enjoy every bite.
Yet each dish is less than 300 calories. Beef dishes,
chicken, fish, seafood, even pastas.
Sound too good to be true?
No, simply too good to miss.

Lean Cuisine: From Stouffer's.
It's not just the calories that count. It's the taste.

Lean Cuisine, 1984

"I
love the way
it looks on
me."

"Stouffer's Lean Cuisine,
Less than 300 calories.
I love the taste, I love what I see,
I love feeling good about being me.
I love the way it looks on me.
And so does he."

Lean Cuisine. From Stouffer's.
You'll love the way it looks on you.

Lean Cuisine, 1983

THE WHOLE FAMILY WAS BIG ON CHEESE.

CHEESEBURGER MACARONI

Hamburger Helper

ADD HAMBURGER

Happily, there's Hamburger Helper
Cheeseburger Macaroni,
loaded with cheese to please the big cheese
appetites in your family. Not to mention
mountains of macaroni and beef.

© General Mills, Inc. 1988

Cheeseburger Macaroni! Just one of 17 great
Hamburger Helper dinners. All so different,
hamburger will never be the same.
Hamburger Helper makes
a great cheesy meal.

Hamburger Helper, 1988   ▸ *Suzi Wan Packaged Chinese Food, 1988*   ▸▸ *Canned Food Information Council, 1985*

Bring home the taste of the Far East

Suzi Wan™ BRAND Dinner Recipes

Surprise your family with Sweet 'n Sour Chicken, Teriyaki Beef, Pepper Beef Oriental or Chicken Imperial. They'll love it, and you'll love how easy it is to take your ordinary chicken or beef, add it to our long grain rice, special spices and unique sauces to come up with something extraordinary in just 10 minutes. Find them in the Packaged Dinner Section.

Suzi Wan™ BRAND Fried Rice Side Dishes

To make any dinner special, serve it with Suzi Wan™ Stir Fry Rice with Chicken Stock, Teriyaki Rice, Sweet 'n Sour Rice or Vegetable Rice Oriental. It's real fried rice that cooks up in just 10 minutes. Find them in the Rice Section.

© Uncle Ben's, Inc. 1987

Make the ordinary extraordinary in just 10 minutes™

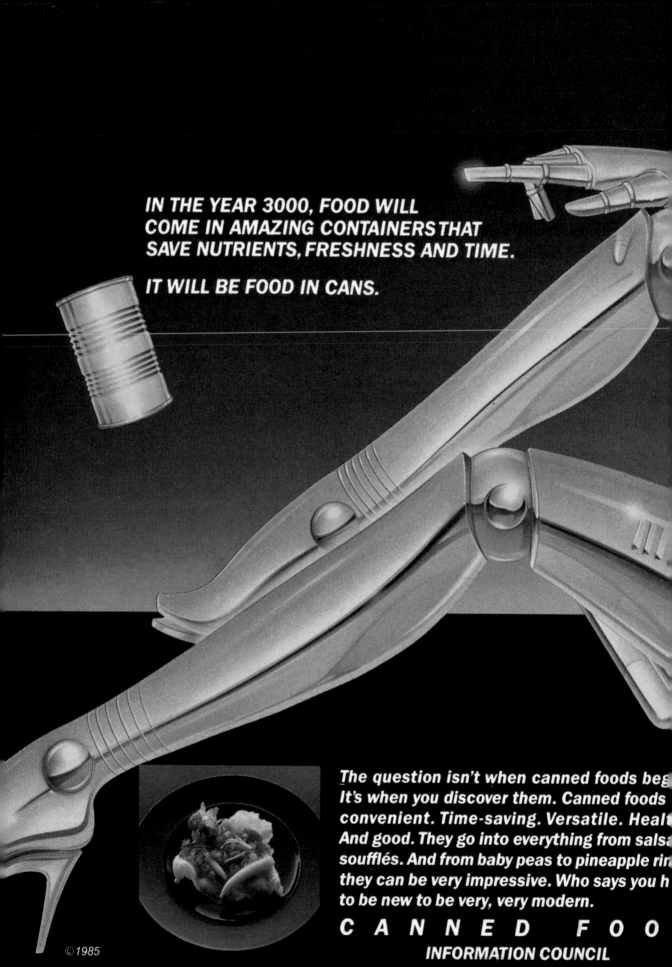

IN THE YEAR 3000, FOOD WILL COME IN AMAZING CONTAINERS THAT SAVE NUTRIENTS, FRESHNESS AND TIME.

IT WILL BE FOOD IN CANS.

The question isn't when canned foods beg
It's when you discover them. Canned foods
convenient. Time-saving. Versatile. Healt
And good. They go into everything from salsa
soufflés. And from baby peas to pineapple rir
they can be very impressive. Who says you h
to be new to be very, very modern.

C A N N E D   F O O
INFORMATION COUNCIL

©1985

PUT THE BITE ON DUNKIN' DONUTS FOR OVER 1,500,000 CASH AND FOOD PRIZES.

Right now, at all participating Dunkin' Donuts shops, we're having an exciting new game called "3 For The Money."™

You don't have to buy anything to play. Just come in and pick up your free game ticket and scratch off the little circles to see what's underneath.

If you collect the words "It's Worth The Trip" you're eligible for Dunkin' Donuts' $25,000 grand prize drawing.

And even if you don't collect the words "It's Worth The Trip", it's still worth the trip.

There are 2 other games.

One gives you the chance to win instant cash prizes up to $1,000. The other instant game gives you the chance to win delicious food prizes. Altogether we're offering over 1,500,000 cash and food prizes.

"3 For The Money" is open to anyone 16 years or older. It's void in Maryland and where prohibited by law and the game ends July 26, 1980.

So hurry. Because while everyone is trying to take a bite out of your dollar, Dunkin' Donuts is giving you the chance to bite back.

(Ohio residents may obtain a free game ticket by sending a stamped, self-addressed envelope, by July 12, 1980, to Ticket Request, Promotional Marketing Corp., 16 Wilton Road, Westport, CT 06880.)

**$25,000 GRAND PRIZE.
3 WAYS TO WIN.
3 GAMES TO PLAY.
PLAY "3 FOR THE MONEY"
AT DUNKIN' DONUTS.**

Dunkin' Donuts, 1980

CHEW YOUR BRAINS OUT WITH BUBBLE YUM AND WIN FREE RECORDS

YUM IT UP FOR A FREE ALBUM OR CASSETTE.
Be one of 15,000 winners. Just look for winning wrappers inside specially marked packages.* Game ends 4/30/89.

PLUS! EVERY BUBBLE YUM.WRAPPER IS WORTH $1.00.
Every outside Bubble Yum wrapper is worth $1.00 off any single record, cassette or CD of your choice, up to a total of $3.00 per album.
Order your first selection today or send for a free catalog. No album limit. Offer ends 12/31/88.

WRAPPERS FOR RECORDS TOP SELECTIONS

BRUCE SPRINGSTEEN
TUNNEL OF LOVE
MADONNA/*TRUE BLUE*
AEROSMITH
PERMANENT VACATION
BILLY IDOL/*VITAL IDOL*
MICHAEL JACKSON/*BAD*
U2/*JOSHUA TREE*
DEF LEPPARD/*HYSTERIA*
JOHN MELLENCAMP
THE LONESOME JUBILEE
WHITESNAKE/*WHITESNAKE*
PINK FLOYD
A MOMENTARY LAPSE OF REASON
GEORGE MICHAEL/*FAITH*
INXS/*KICK*

**NO ALBUM LIMIT!
SEND FOR FREE CATALOG**

$ _____

Name _____ Age _____

Address _____

City _____ State _____ Zip _____

Phone # (_____)

☆ **I'VE CHEWED MY BRAINS OUT. I WANT...** (Single albums only please, no double albums.)

_____   _____
(Artist)   (Title)

$9.98 LP or Tape; $15.98 CD (List price)

List price.	Deduct $1 for each outside wrapper enclosed, up to $3.	Discount price.	Postage & handling per order.	NYC residents add 8¼%; NY State 4¼%.	Total amount enclosed. Make check payable to Express Music.
—	=	+ $1	+	=	

☆ **I'M GOING TO CHEW MY BRAINS OUT ALL YEAR LONG!**
Send me a Bubble Yum Wrappers for Records Catalog. No purchase necessary. No album limit. Enclose a self-addressed stamped envelope and send request to: WFR, Box 919, Wilton, CT 06898.
Send all orders for albums to: Bubble Yum Wrappers For Records, Express Music Catalog, 50 West 17th Street, New York, NY 10011.

*Or send a self-addressed stamped envelope by 4/1/89 (WA & VT residents may omit return stamp) for free wrappers and official rules to: BYGP, Box 901, Wilton, CT 06898. Void where prohibited. **No purchase necessary.**

We are not responsible for lost or misdirected mail. Your discount rights may not be assigned or transferred. Offer good only in USA. Orders postmarked after 12/31/88 will not be processed. Your selections will be on their way to you within 72 hours of receipt of valid request.

Bubble Yum, 1988

A bowl of raspberries.

No, it's not an ice cream. Nor, a sherbet.
What you're looking at is a delightfully different type of dessert.
It's called sorbet.
Light to the taste, creamy in texture (even though unlike sherbet or ice cream, there's no cream in it), you'll find it's only half the calories of rich ice creams.
You'll also find it's deliciously smooth—a blend

of real fruit, pure juice and natural sweeteners.
Which means, it's of course, 100% natural.
And why indeed a bowl of raspberry sorbet can taste just like a bowl of rich, ripe raspberries.
Also in Strawberry, Peach, Mandarin and Pineapple.
Dole® Fruit Sorbet. Look for it next to the other fine frozen desserts in your store.

Dole Fruit Sorbet

Dole Sorbet, 1986

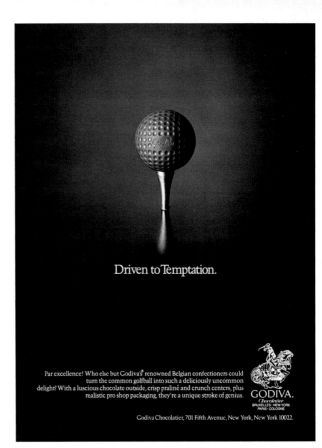

Driven to Temptation.

Par excellence! Who else but Godiva's renowned Belgian confectioners could turn the common golfball into such a deliciously uncommon delight? With a luscious chocolate outside, crisp praliné and crunch centers, plus realistic pro shop packaging, they're a unique stroke of genius.

GODIVA.
Chocolatier
BRUXELLES · NEW YORK
PARIS · COLOGNE

Godiva Chocolatier, 701 Fifth Avenue, New York, New York 10022.

Godiva Chocolatier, 1983

Creamy rich ice cream

in a luscious chocolatey coating.

Delicious,

bite-sized,

and simply irresistible.

BonBons
from ®
Vanilla
Ice Cream Nuggets

The Finger Food Ice Cream.™

Fudgsicle Fudge Pops, 1989 ◄   Bon Bons, 1986

It is now socially acceptable to eat Häagen-Dazs® ice cream with your fingers.

Häagen-Dazs

© 1989 The Häagen-Dazs Company, Inc.

GOURMET / OCTOBER 1989   173

Häagen-Dazs Ice Cream, 1989

Life Savers, 1986

Brach's Halloween Candy, 1985

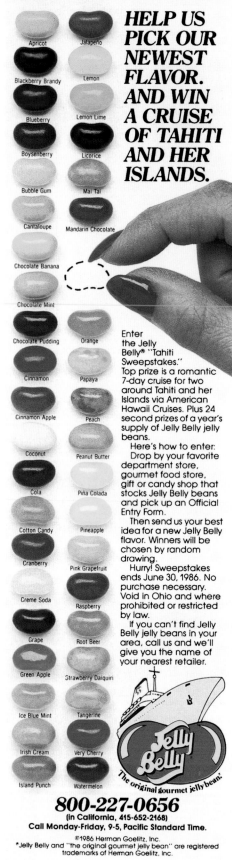

HELP US PICK OUR NEWEST FLAVOR. AND WIN A CRUISE OF TAHITI AND HER ISLANDS.

Enter the Jelly Belly® "Tahiti Sweepstakes." Top prize is a romantic 7-day cruise for two around Tahiti and her Islands via American Hawaii Cruises. Plus 24 second prizes of a year's supply of Jelly Belly jelly beans.

Here's how to enter:

Drop by your favorite department store, gourmet food store, gift or candy shop that stocks Jelly Belly beans and pick up an Official Entry Form.

Then send us your best idea for a new Jelly Belly flavor. Winners will be chosen by random drawing.

Hurry! Sweepstakes ends June 30, 1986. No purchase necessary. Void in Ohio and where prohibited or restricted by law.

If you can't find Jelly Belly jelly beans in your area, call us and we'll give you the name of your nearest retailer.

800-227-0656
(in California, 415-652-2168)
Call Monday-Friday, 9-5, Pacific Standard Time.

©1986 Herman Goelitz, Inc.
®Jelly Belly and "the original gourmet jelly bean" are registered trademarks of Herman Goelitz, Inc.

Jelly Belly Candies, 1986 ▶ *Cheez Whiz, 1983*

Still life with Cheez Whiz®
A Rather Addictive Blend of Natural Cheeses.

Cheese, Glorious Cheese

Brie
over giant strawberries

Blue Cheese
flower ball

Fontina
baked over salmon slices

Port Wine Cold Pack
in avocado

Limburger
burger

Edam
wrapped in prosciutto

With over 750 varieties
of the world's finest cheeses
made right here in the United States,
and hundreds of ways to enjoy
each of them, the possibilities,
to say the least, are glorious.

Taste the greatness of
American-made real cheese.

America's Dairy Farmers
National Dairy Board

Muenster
cut-outs

Port du Salut
stuffed pecans

Camembert
baked in pastry

Gouda dip

Provolone
melted over asparagus

National Dairy Board, 1987

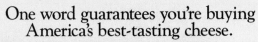

One word guarantees you're buying
America's best-tasting cheese.

Wisconsin.

Once again, cheeses from
America's Dairyland dominated
the U.S. Championship Cheese
Contest. Winning 9 of the 13
Best of Class ribbons, plus the
Grand Championship. Proving,
beyond any doubt, America's
most delicious cheeses are made
in Wisconsin.

So look for the word
"Wisconsin" on the next package
of cheese you buy. Then taste
the taste worth looking for.

**Dairy Farmers
of Wisconsin**
Wisconsin Milk Marketing Board

Lindsay Olives, 1983 ◄ *Dairy Farmers of Wisconsin, 1988*

Make a meal for summer.

Natural
RyKrisp
Whole grain rye snack crackers

Cracker Barrel
SHARP NATURAL CHEDDAR CHEESE
KRAFT

Crisp, rich and juicy!
A summer splendor of great
natural tastes—whole grain rye,
aged golden cheddar, juicy slices of
peach, plum and nectarine. Perfect for
lunch in the park, a late evening
supper or a quick meal anytime.

Cracker Barrel cheddar
RyKrisp Crackers
California Summer Fruits

RyKrisp
KRAFT

California Tree Fruit Agreement

RyKrisp Crackers, 1980

Kraft Singles, 1980

Put a little love in lunch with Skippy.

Serving Skippy® is a loving way to give your kids the good nutrition they need. Because it's the only leading national brand to give them both high protein and less sugar. And kids really go for the taste of Skippy. Now that's a combination any mother can love!

For good nutrition straight from the heart.

LESS SUGAR THAN OTHER LEADING NATIONAL BRANDS

SKIPPY®

CREAMY PEANUT BUTTER

© 1985 Best Foods, CPC International Inc.

Skippy Peanut Butter, 1985

Del Monte Dried Fruit, 1985

HE DOESN'T GET MANY DATES.

If he did, he might trade that chopper in for a ten-speed. After all, dates can give anyone a healthy outlook. They're low in calories and have nearly every nutrient a body needs. So who knows? If he showers, shaves and eats a few dates, he might marry a debutante. Stop running from officers. Start running for office. Maybe win.

California Dates!

California Dates, 1988

Sad is the salad never seasoned with Bertolli.

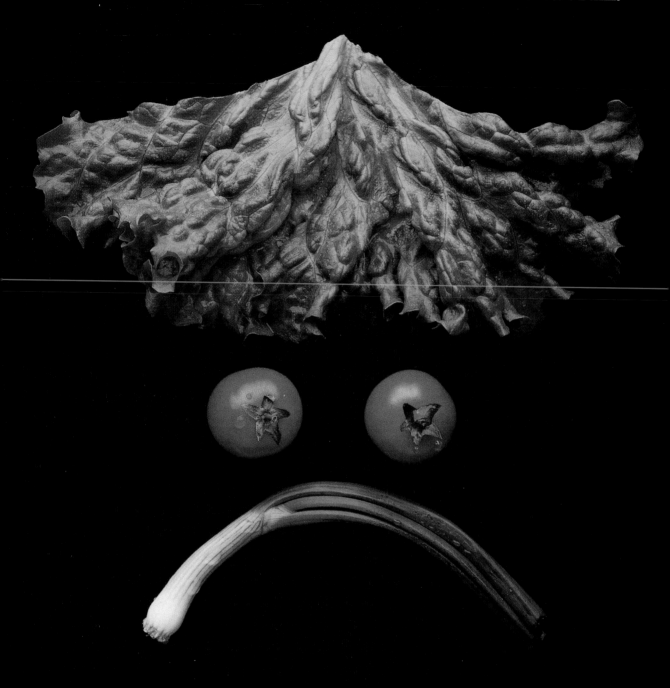

Can you blame it? When just 3 tbsp of Bertolli® Extra Light™ Olive Oil and 1 tbsp Bertolli Fine Wine Vinegar, tossed with oregano and Parmesan, make a salad sensational. In fact, Bertolli Extra Light has such a delicately mild flavor it can enhance the taste of any recipe that uses oil. And Bertolli Olive Oil can actually help lower your cholesterol.*

*Use Bertolli Olive Oil as part of a balanced diet.
© BERTOLLI USA INC. 1988

BERTOLLI
BUON APPETITO

You're sort of small for a spoon, aren't you kiwifruit?

I taste big. Sourpuss. Sweet without sugar.

CALIFORNIA SWEET
KIWIFRUIT

Name one fruit loaded with vitamin C, natural fiber and potassium. Did you say kiwifruit? Did you say "Who cares?" Oh. Then, take one bite. Hello! Nothing tastes like a kiwi. One brave new bite.

That's all it takes to persuade anyone. Friendly persuasion. Just published and free. No-holds-barred new booklet. **Mother never told me about kiwifruit.** Full of recipes, wild

suggestions, health and happiness ideas. Send a business-sized self-addressed, stamped envelope to Kiwifruit, 1540 River Park Drive, #120, Sacramento, CA 95815.

California Kiwi Fruit, 1988

CREATE YOUR OWN CLASSIC. WITH BEST FOODS.

CLASSIC POTATO SALAD
Potato salad tastes as good as it always did with Best Foods® Real Mayonnaise.

1 cup Best Foods Real Mayonnaise
2 tablespoons vinegar
1½ teaspoons salt
1 teaspoon sugar
¼ teaspoon pepper
4 cups cooked, peeled, cubed potatoes (5 to 6 medium)
1 cup sliced celery
½ cup chopped onion
2 hard-cooked eggs, chopped

In large bowl, stir together first 5 ingredients until smooth. Add remaining ingredients; toss to coat well. Cover; chill. Makes 5 cups.

Best Foods Mayonnaise, 1986

Short Order Cook.

If you've got ripe California Avocados and five minutes, you've got lunch or dinner made. Because they're so easy to prepare. What's more, they complement almost any dish. And bring just as many compliments to the cook.

California
AVOCADOS

They're ripe with possibilities.

Bertolli Olive Oil, 1988 ◄ *California Avocados, 1986*

POMPEIAN

POMPEIAN INC.   BALTIMORE MD. 21224

Pompeian Olive Oil, 1984

"Compare your coffee to my Mellow Roast.®" — Roger Miller

COFFEE AND GRAIN BEVERAGE

You'll taste the delicious difference of Mellow Roast.®

"Dang me, that's good!"

Mellow Roast® has the country secret for great coffee taste without bitterness. And all it takes is one sip to show you the difference that country secret can make—a rich aroma and big, full-bodied taste. That's because Mellow Roast takes rich coffee and adds roasted grain to smooth away the bitterness. Compare Mellow Roast® Coffee and Grain Beverage to your coffee. Then you'll say, "Dang me, that's good."

GENERAL FOODS

Mellow Roast...great coffee taste without bitterness.

Mellow Roast Coffee Beverage, 1980

▶ *Maxwell House Instant Coffee, 1986*

Earth's First Soft Drink.

Perrier. Not manufactured, but created by the earth when it was new.

Perrier. Earth's First Soft Drink.

Not manufactured
but created by the earth
when it was new.

SEND FOR COLOR CATALOG $2.00 (REFUNDABLE WITH FIRST MAIL-ORDER PURCHASE) AND LIST OF AUTHORISED STOCKISTS. CRABTREE & EVELYN LTD, BOX GO/13, WOODSTOCK HILL, CT 06281, 124 NEWBOLD COURT, LONDON, ONTARIO N6E 1Z7, CANADA.

Gatorade Sports Drink, 1980 ◄ *Crabtree & Evelyn Tea, 1982*

BODY LANGUAGE LESSON #2

Make your walk talk.

You can come on bold. You can come on bouncy. But your body has to be healthy and strong to get the message across.

GRACE UNDER PRESSURE

Healthy bone joints are like shock absorbers—they actually compress for an instant with every step you take. The nutrients you get from milk each day help build your bones and joints so they can take the pressure, and you can pull off those beautiful, smooth moves.

STAYING LIMBER

Milk has protein, vitamins and minerals like calcium that strengthen your bones and help you stay supple and loose. And enough calcium and exercise will help your bones stay younger as you get older.

Two glasses of milk a day give you over half the calcium you need but only an eighth of your calories.* So listen to your Body Language. To stay loose, drink up.

THE WADDLE OR THE STRUT?

The stronger your bones, the more you can strut your stuff. If your bones were weak and brittle, you'd lose the flow of motion that makes you graceful. So listen to your Body Language. Drink milk. And start a moving conversation that'll do a body proud.

*Based upon Recommended Dietary Allowance for women, 13 to 23

Milk. It does a body good.

NATIONAL DAIRY BOARD
1984 © C.M.A.B.

National Dairy Board, 1985

THERE'S A REAL DIFFERENCE TO THE GREAT TASTE OF MINUTE MAID.® AND THIS IS WHERE IT STARTS.

Lemons. Lots of fresh, juicy, real lemons. That's where the great taste of Minute Maid Lemonade starts.
Unlike some drinks that are just lemonade flavored, Minute Maid Lemonade is made from the juice of real lemons. It's always natural.

And we make sure that every drop has that delicious Minute Maid taste.
So as the days get hotter and you get thirstier, remember that Minute Maid Lemonade makes a real difference. A difference you can taste.
MAKE SURE. MAKE IT MINUTE MAID.

"Minute Maid" is a registered trademark of The Coca-Cola Company. © 1983. The Coca-Cola Company.

Minute Maid Lemonade, 1983

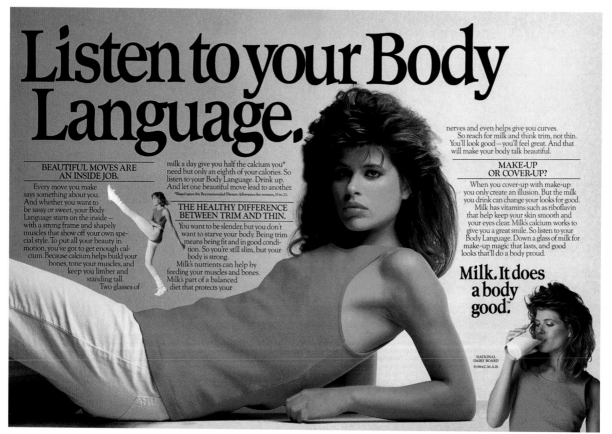

Listen to your Body Language.

BEAUTIFUL MOVES ARE AN INSIDE JOB.

Every move you make says something about you. And whether you want to be sassy or sweet, your Body Language starts on the inside—with a strong frame and shapely muscles that show off your own special style. To put all your beauty in motion, you've got to get enough calcium. Because calcium helps build your bones, tone your muscles, and keep you limber and standing tall. Two glasses of milk a day give you half the calcium you* need but only an eighth of your calories. So listen to your Body Language. Drink up. And let one beautiful move lead to another.

*Based upon the Recommended Dietary Allowance for women, 13 to 23.

THE HEALTHY DIFFERENCE BETWEEN TRIM AND THIN.

You want to be slender, but you don't want to starve your body. Being trim means being fit and in good condition. So you're still slim, but your body is strong.

Milk's nutrients can help by feeding your muscles and bones. Milk's part of a balanced diet that protects your nerves and even helps give you curves.

So reach for milk and think trim, not thin. You'll look good—you'll feel great. And that will make your body talk beautiful.

MAKE-UP OR COVER-UP?

When you cover-up with make-up you only create an illusion. But the milk you drink can change your looks for good.

Milk has vitamins such as riboflavin that help keep your skin smooth and your eyes clear. Milk's calcium works to give you a great smile. So listen to your Body Language. Down a glass of milk for make-up magic that lasts, and good looks that'll do a body proud.

Milk. It does a body good.™

NATIONAL DAIRY BOARD
©1984 C.M.A.B.

National Dairy Board, 1985

Diet 7Up, 1981

Diet 7Up, 1982

Five Alive Fruit Beverage, 1984

Capri Sun Fruit Drink, 1983

After the show, we always show up at McDonald's

Summer appetites really get big after the sun goes down. And when your stomach starts talking, McDonald's has the answer. Big Mac® or Filet-O-Fish® Sandwiches. Shakes. Sundaes and McDonald's world famous fries are some of the delicious menu choices McDonald's offers you. With fast, friendly service and prices that fit any family budget. McDonald's "sure is good to have around."™

McDonald's®

You deserve a break today

Body by Tab.

TRADE-MARK ®

Jayne Kennedy

McDonald's, 1982 ◄   Tab, 1983

And the winner is...

Back to the Fifties

At a time when the Surgeon General was warning American consumers to avoid the pitfalls of excessive caloric intake and cholesterol-laden food, along comes this tribute to fifties' excess. The Uncle Ben's® test kitchens went into overdrive, coming up with this unique spin on an otherwise healthy food product. Doomed to obsolescence? An understatement. A pizza crust made from rice? Blasphemy. Add to that globs of cheese and chunks of Oscar Mayer® wieners and you have a recipe for a heart attack. (Someone call the doctor.)

Futtern wie bei Muttern

Zur selben Zeit, als die amerikanischen Gesundheitsbehörden die Verbraucher vor dem Verzehr von zu vielen Kalorien und ungesunden, cholesterinhaltigen Lebensmitteln warnte, wurde dieses Tribut an die Fressfeste der Fünfziger aufgetischt. In der Uncle Ben's®-Testküche hat man offensichtlich keine Mühen gescheut, diese einzigartige Verwurstung des ansonsten gesunden Produkts Reis auszutüfteln. Veraltet? Weit untertrieben. Auf den Pizzateig aus Reis werden zähe Käsefäden und deftige Oscar-Mayer®-Würstchen gehäuft und schon hat man das Rezept für den nächsten Herzinfarkt. (Doktor, zu Hilfe!)

Retour aux années 50

Au moment où le Directeur du service de santé publique mettait en garde les Américains contre une consommation excessive de nourritures trop riches, paraissait cet hommage aux excès des années 50. Les cuisines laboratoires de Uncle Ben's® ont tourné à plein régime pour inventer une nouvelle préparation pour un aliment par ailleurs parfaitement équilibré. Condamné à l'oubli ? C'est un euphémisme. Une pâte à pizza à base de riz ? Un sacrilège. Ajoutez une bonne quantité de fromage et des morceaux de saucisses Oscar Mayer® et vous avez la recette pour une crise cardiaque. (Appelez le SAMU).

¡Que vivan los años cincuenta!

En una época en la que la Dirección General de Salud Pública advertía a los consumidores estadounidenses que convenía evitar los riesgos de los alimentos hipercalóricos y con colesterol, Uncle Ben's® se desmarcó con este tributo a los excesos de los años cincuenta. La empresa puso la directa y dio un giro a este producto alimenticio por lo demás sano. ¿Condenado a la obsolescencia? Un eufemismo. ¿Masa de pizza a base de arroz? ¡Menuda blasfemia! Añádale pegotes de queso y trozos de salchichas Oscar Mayer® y obtendrá un excelente receta para un ataque de corazón. (¡Que alguien avise a un médico...!)

50年代に還って

公衆衛生局長官が過度のカロリー摂取とコレステロールまみれの食べ物に対する誘惑をしりぞけるようアメリカの消費者に警告したのと同じ頃、この50年代の過食への賛辞が現れた。アンクル・ベンの試作品調理部門は別のヘルシーな食品の開発に猛然と取り掛かった。では生産中止宣告？控え目過ぎ。お米で作ったピザの台は？冒涜。あれにチーズを少しと、大量のオスカー・マイヤーのウィンナーを加えたら、あなたはもう心臓麻痺のレシピを手にしている。(誰か医者呼んで！)

Big smile, low price. Pizzeria Rice!

You'll get savings worth smiling about with budget-minded Pizzeria Rice. Save 3 ways with the coupons on the facing page from Uncle Ben's, McCormick or Schilling, and Del Monte. Then save again, with more coupons on specially marked boxes of Uncle Ben's Converted Brand Rice and packages of Oscar Mayer Wieners or Beef Franks.

PIZZERIA RICE

1 cup UNCLE BEN'S® CONVERTED® Brand Rice
⅓ cup grated Parmesan cheese
1 can (16 oz.) DEL MONTE® Stewed tomatoes, including liquid
2 tablespoons cornstarch
1 teaspoon McCORMICK or SCHILLING SEASON•ALL® Seasoned Salt

1 package (1 lb.) OSCAR MAYER® Wieners or Beef Franks, cut into ½" pieces
¼ cup chopped green pepper
1 teaspoon McCORMICK or SCHILLING Oregano Leaves
½ cup shredded mozzarella cheese, or to taste

Cook rice following package directions, omitting butter. Add Parmesan cheese; mix well. Grease and flour a 12" pizza pan or two 9" pie pans. Firmly press hot rice mixture on bottom and ½" up sides of pan to form crust. Bake at 450°F. 12 minutes.* Meanwhile, combine tomatoes, cornstarch and Season•All in saucepan. Cook, stirring, over medium-high heat until thickened. Remove crust from oven. Spread tomato mixture over crust. Add hot dogs and green pepper. Sprinkle oregano and shredded cheese over top. Bake 10 minutes longer. Makes 6 servings.

*Recipe may be prepared to this point and held overnight.

©Uncle Ben's® Inc., 1980

Uncle Ben's Rice, 1980

BOS
5-6270
BOS
270 (4-80) MADE IN U.S.A.
DTW
72-4394
DTW
PAS.270 (4-80) MADE IN U.S.A.
MSY
07-5013
MSY
S.270 (4-80) MADE IN U.S.A.
KANSAS CITY

Pan Am.
First In Space.

The first thing you notice as you enter the First Class Cabin of a Pan Am 747 or L-1011 Clipper® is the extraordinary feeling of space.

First In Comfort.

And as you settle into your Space Seat, your Pan Am Sleeperette® Seat, this sense of spaciousness becomes even more impressive. There's space in front of you, around you, above you. But above all, space to give you something so very rare in air travel today, a sense of privacy.

First In Food And Wines.

And because of the comfort so much space offers, Pan Am's Five Star Dining is gracious dining. Offering a wide selection of international entrées from the trolleys. Served on fine china. On snowy linen. And you'll whet your appetite with some of the world's most respected wines, especially selected from the wines of the world by Pan Am's international wine consultant.

First In Service.

Pan Am enjoys a 56 year tradition of fine service, impeccable service. Truly First Class from the time you're welcomed aboard till your coat is returned. It seems, in fact, as though we invented luxury in the air. But then, after all, we did.

For reservations and information call your Travel Agent or Pan Am.

Pan Am. You Can't Beat The Experience.®

Pan Am Airlines, 1985

SPEND A WEEK
IN THERAPY.

RELAX. FLY EASTERN AND USE THE AMERICAN EXPRESS® CARD.

If you find today's world traumatic, perhaps you have a subconscious desire to run away.

What you need is a vacation in Florida, Mexico, the Caribbean or the Bahamas.

Where your alarm clock is the morning surf, the loudest horns blow from gentle cruise ships and there's only one responsibility.

And that's to yourself. So spend a week in therapy. You'll feel better.

Eastern can take you to 37 therapeutic vacation places.

And with the American Express Card, you can charge Eastern's affordable vacation, dine at terrific restaurants and shop at exciting stores. The Card is welcome almost everywhere.

When you take an Eastern vacation and use the American Express Card, life seems easy.

For details about an Eastern vacation, call Eastern or an Accredited Travel Agent.

The American Express® Card. Don't leave home without it.®

EASTERN
WE EARN OUR WINGS EVERY DAY®

Eastern Airlines, 1985

Power lunch.

There are lots of ways to get ahead in the business world.

You can aim a little higher than the competition, work a lot harder.

Even call on more of the top 100 business centers than anyone else.

Or, better yet, just have lunch with the right people.

Amtrak Railway, 1983 ◄ United Airlines, 1985

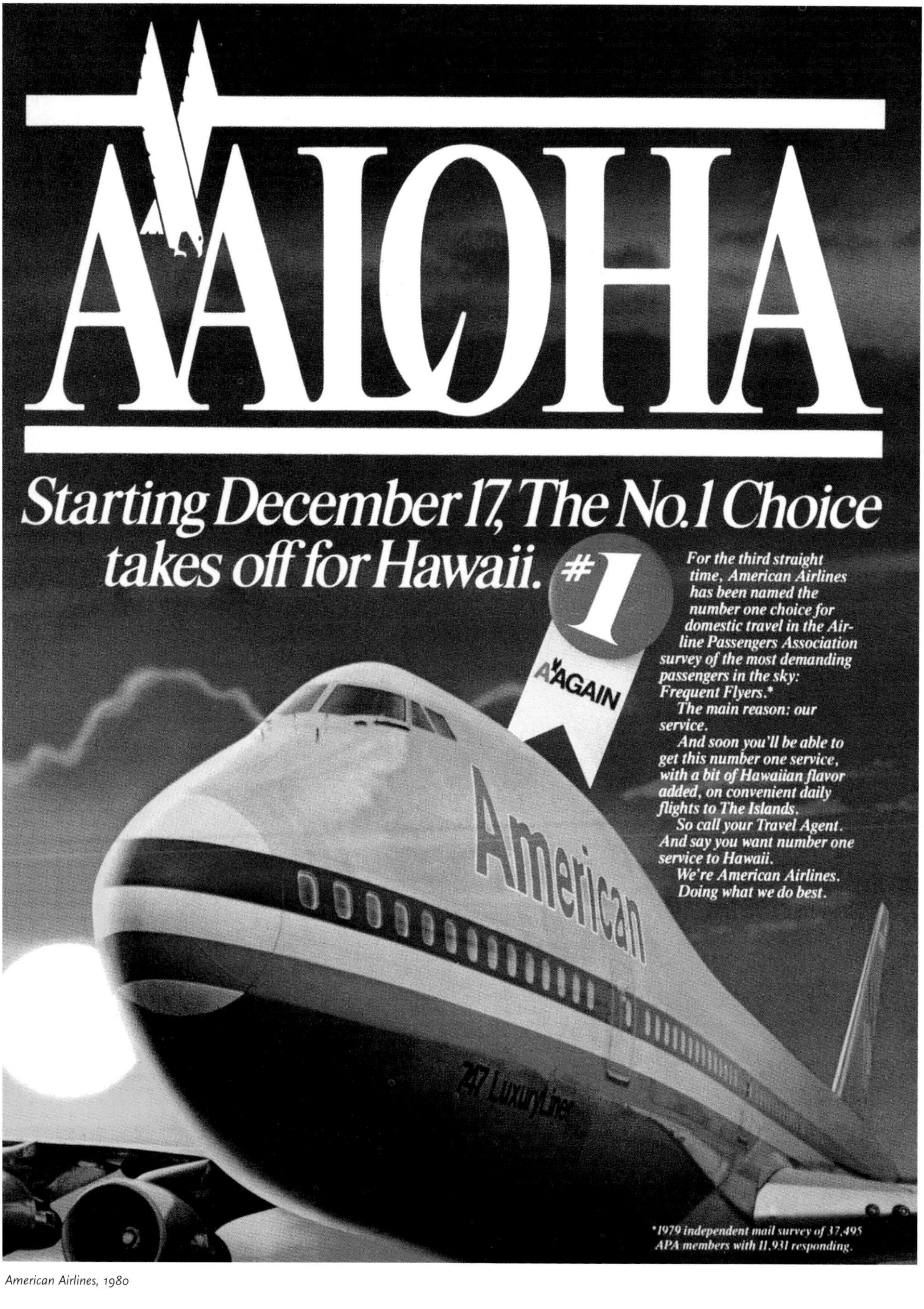

AALOHA

Starting December 17, The No.1 Choice takes off for Hawaii.

#1 AA AGAIN

For the third straight time, American Airlines has been named the number one choice for domestic travel in the Airline Passengers Association survey of the most demanding passengers in the sky: Frequent Flyers.*

The main reason: our service.

And soon you'll be able to get this number one service, with a bit of Hawaiian flavor added, on convenient daily flights to The Islands.

So call your Travel Agent. And say you want number one service to Hawaii.

We're American Airlines. Doing what we do best.

*1979 independent mail survey of 37,495 APA members with 11,931 responding.

American Airlines, 1980

After you dive into Cartagena's ancient walled city where the pirates hid, peer into a magical deep sea world. Play on a native island. It all happens in Colombia's Caribbean. From **$379.**

Per person price based on double occupancy & includes roundtrip Avianca GIT jetfare from New York ($319 from Miami), Class A hotel, baggage handling, transfers, U.S. departure tax, city tour. Airfare subject to change.

Paradise is a sun-soaked, moonlit escape called Santa Marta. White sands, blue water, balmy nights. Romantic Colombia. From **$553.**

Per person price based on double occupancy & includes roundtrip Avianca GIT jetfare from New York ($439 from Miami), jetfare to Santa Marta; three days in Cartagena, Class A hotel; four days in Santa Marta, top hotel, all transfers, U.S. departure tax, city tours. Airfare subject to change. American Express calls this tour "Spanish Legend." Prices slightly higher after December 31, 1980.

First airline of the Americas, second oldest in the world.

Avianca Vacation Center / 4299 N.W. 36th St. / Miami Springs, Fla., 33166
I want to dive into Colombia. It sounds warm and wet and perfectly wonderful. I'm packing. Send me more information, but I'll talk to my travel agent anyway. ☐ Cartagena ☐ Spanish Legend

Name _____ G/SEPT.

Address _____

City _____ State _____ Zip _____

Travel Agent _____
         (Name & address)

Avianca
We fly to all of South America

Avianca Airlines, 1980

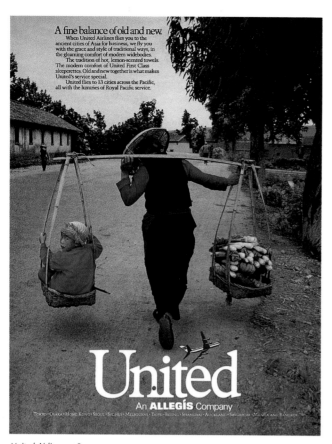

United Airlines, 1987

United Airlines, 1989

USAir Airlines, 1984

TWA Airlines, 1982

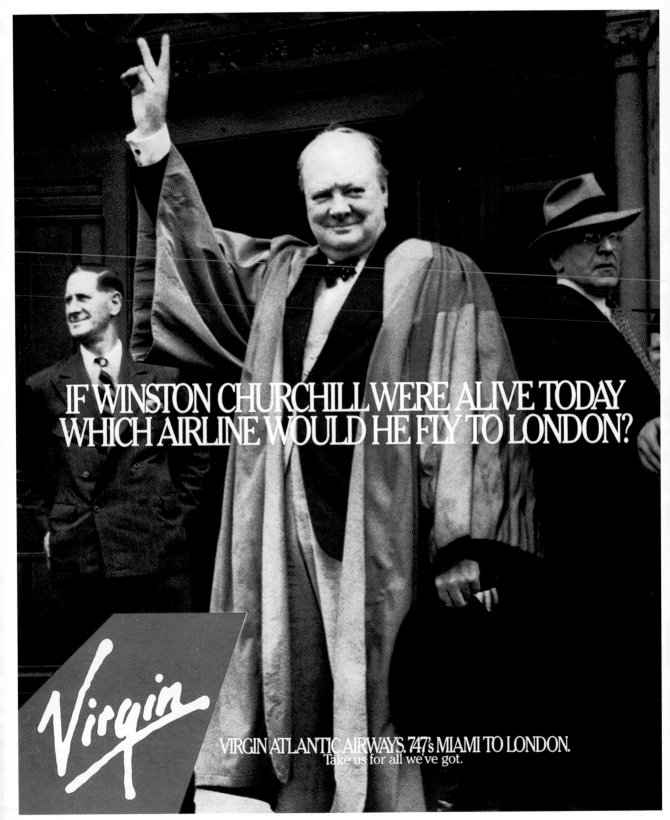

IF WINSTON CHURCHILL WERE ALIVE TODAY
WHICH AIRLINE WOULD HE FLY TO LONDON?

VIRGIN ATLANTIC AIRWAYS. 747's MIAMI TO LONDON.
Take us for all we've got.

Virgin Atlantic Airways, 1986

In a world of airlines, one airline has always been something special.

At first glance, all airlines may appear to be the same. But when you look closer, one airline offers you a special way to fly.

It's an airline so large it carries over 30 million people a year; yet so personalized, you can reserve your seat a year in advance.

It's an airline so committed to saving you time, you can get all your boarding passes for all your flights before you ever get to the airport.

It's an airline that's led the way by being innovative, not imitative. American Airlines. In a world of airlines, it's the one special airline that can make your trip something special.

American Airlines
Something special in the air.

American Airlines, 1984

Sometimes the best cure for cabin fever is another cabin.

You know about cabin fever. It's that cooped up feeling you've had all winter. Well, we have a cure. A 14 million acre, unspoiled, uncrowded cure called Colorado's national forests. Where you can sit for hours and let those nine to five pressures fade like a beaver's wake on a quiet pond. Our 52 page Colorado Adventure Guide can help point you in the right direction. So call 1-800-255-5550 or send this coupon for your copy today. Then call your travel agent or Frontier, Colorado's airline.

⊖ FRONTIER AIRLINES
Colorado Tourism Board "I Guess Held Rather Be in Colorado" © 1971 Cherry Lane Music Publishing Co., Inc.

Guess I'd rather be in Colorado.

P.O. Box 38700 Dept. BHGM Denver, Colorado 80238
___ Please send me a free copy of the Colorado Adventure Guide in 4-6 weeks.
___ Please rush my copy. I have enclosed $1.00 for UPS delivery.

Name _____
Address _____
City _____ State ___ Zip ___

Colorado Tourism Board, 1985

TWA's 747 BUSINESS LOUNGER ⌐ TO EUROPE vs. THE SEAT ⌐. YOUR FEET ARE

TWA Airlines, 1985

More of the Pacific from the airline that brings you more of the U.S.

From the spectacular fjords of New Zealand to the hallowed ground of Japan's Mount Fuji.

From the Great Barrier Reef to the Great Wall. From a serene and ancient temple in Thailand to the heart of Hong Kong, the city that never sleeps.

United brings you thirteen incredible cities across the Pacific, with more nonstops from more U.S. cities than any other U.S. airline.

With the style and comfort of United's Royal Pacific Service every step of the way.

Call your Travel Agent or United for reservations or information on all-inclusive tours.

You're not just flying, you're flying the friendly skies.

Tokyo	Taipei	Singapore
Osaka	Hong Kong	Sydney
Seoul	Manila	Melbourne
Beijing	Bangkok	Auckland
Shanghai		

United

United Airlines, 1986

A fresh breeze across the Pacific.

The airline that serves more top business centers in the United States now serves more top business centers across the wide Pacific with more nonstops than any other airline.

Convenient service to thirteen cities in all, with all the advantages that come with one airline service.

One airline to handle ticketing, seat assignments, boarding passes, and baggage for your whole trip.

And, of course, United's incomparable Mileage Plus, offering a whole world of exciting travel awards.

You'll enjoy United's famous Royal Pacific Service, the best of the friendly skies in First Class, Business Class, and Economy.

Best of all, you'll be flying with a friend. United Airlines. Now the friendly skies covers the wide Pacific.

Call United or your Travel Agent. *You're not just flying, you're flying the friendly skies.*

United

United Airlines, 1986

NOT ↘. YOU'LL BE AMAZED WHAT IT DOES TO THE REST OF YOU.   LEADING THE WAY. TWA.

Japan Air Lines, 1981

Air France Airlines, 1985

United Airlines, 1986

United Airlines, 1980

▶ *Hawaiian Air, 1986*

e bring you Hawaii. And more.

ur Premier Pacific Service leaves for paradise from Los Angeles,
n Francisco, Seattle and Las Vegas.
    Aboard our spacious widebody L-1011 jets with personal Premier
cific Service along the way. Everything from tempting hot entrees to
iles that welcome you to Hawaii as no one else can.

om the Mainland to the Neighbor Islands, no charge for direct
nnection.
    Hawaiian Air is the only airline, serving West Coast cities and all Hawaii,
ng you a direct connection to the Hawaii Neighbor Island of your choice
m Honolulu at no extra cost. And you can expect to earn more Gold Plus
nts per mile in the sky with our frequent flyer program.
    Hawaii's largest and most experienced airline invites you to come share
Island hospitality in the air. Call us toll free in Hawaii at 1-800-367-5320,
our travel agent. ©1985 Hawaiian Airlines, Inc.

HAWAIIAN AIR.
Hawaii's first choice. Hawaii's first airline.

A Five Star Grand-Luxe Hotel

Those Who Appreciate The Differ

Beverly Wilshire

"There may be one place that pampers you more than the Beverly Hills Hotel. But do you really want to live with your mother again?"

The Beverly Hills Hotel
and Bungalows

RIDE INTO THE SUNSET

THE AMERICAN EXPRESS® CARD TAKES YOU THERE

After a hard day's shooting up the countryside or serenading the locals, do what entertainment people have been doing ever since happy endings. Riding into the Sunset. Securely tucked in the heart of Hollywood, the Sunset Marquis Hotel is an elegant respite removed from the busy-ness and the busy-bodies. Here, your needs are met 24 hours a day, from state-of-the-art equipment to state-of-the-smart appointments. From transcontinental

SUNSET MARQUIS
hotel and villas

communications to our tension-taming health spa. Then when you're ready to roll, our complimentary limousine service will have you at any major studio in the surrounding area in minutes. With an American Express® Card Assured Reservation, your suite or villa will be waiting for you, however late you arrive. For reservations, call 1 (800) 858-9758 and let us do the rest. Because when the American Express Card takes you into the Sunset, all you have to do is enjoy the ride.

Membership has its privileges.®

Sunset Marquis Hotel and Villas, 1988

Days Inn is a better place to stay. For less.

Stay with us on your next trip and you'll see why.

At Days Inn motels, you'll get clean, quiet accommodations with two double beds, color TV, direct dial phone, plus, a well lighted and appointed bathroom with separate dressing area. You'll also enjoy great food and friendly, quick service in our restaurants.

Best of all, when you stay at most Days Inn motels your kids 12 and under eat free ...breakfast, lunch and dinner. That's value! With convenient locations all across America, you're sure to find a Days Inn motel close to where you're going. Try us. Just once. And compare. You'll see why we're a better place to stay...for less.

Try us. And compare. Call 1-800-325-2525

© 1984 Days Inns of America, Inc.

DAYS INN

Days Inn, 1984

Ramada Inn, 1987

ECONOMICAL LODGING, ACROSS AMERICA, FOR TODAY AND TOMORROW.

Days Inn pioneered economical, clean and comfortable lodging across America.

Today, while we are exploring new ideas for tomorrow, Days Inn is committed to giving you consistent value and comfort.

DAYS INN

• Host to more Walt Disney World guests than any other lodging chain.
• Stay with us and your "Kids Eat Free."®

FOR RESERVATIONS CALL FREE **1-800-325-2525** OR YOUR TRAVEL AGENT.
*Participating properties across America ©1982, Days Inns of America, Inc.

Days Inn, 1982

There is no such thing as just a room

at a L'Ermitage Hotel. At the Mondrian,

as in all our hotels, we only have suites.

Anything less would cramp your style.

L'ERMITAGE HOTELS
A Collection of Originals

1-800-424-4443

WEST HOLLYWOOD · BEVERLY HILLS
L'Ermitage · Bel Age · Mondrian · Valadon · Le Parc · Le Dufy · Le Rêve

L'Ermitage Hotels, 1989

**Marriott Resorts.
Vacations From Your
Point Of View.**

You've just arrived. And already you're wishing
you'd never have to leave. As the sun melts the worries
away, the soft waves lull you. And a moment later, you
forget you've ever been anywhere else.

Marriott vacations are made up of moments like
these. With dedicated, pampering service and every
activity you can envision.

For your free vacation guide to our 20 extraordinary
Marriott Resorts, call 1-800-PARADISE, or your travel
professional. Marriott vacations. They're everything
everyday life isn't.

Marriott
R E S O R T S

Marriott Resorts, 1989

UNIQUELY HYATT.

The works of man and nature mingle
with incomparable grandeur at the
Hyatt Regency Grand Cypress at
Orlando. Nothing so close to paradise
has ever been so close to home.

Sun, sport and setting magically
come together, with a challenging
Scottish style golf course designed by
Jack Nicklaus. Restaurants where the
food and ambience are elegant, yet
refreshingly unpretentious. Sprawling
grounds with a magnificent outdoor
pool and artifacts from around the world.

There's a lake for sailing and
facilities for tennis, racquetball, hand-
ball, jogging and hiking. And EPCOT
Center is only a few minutes away.
For reservations call 800 228 9000
or 305 239 1234 or contact your
travel planner.

Don't you WISH
YOU WERE
HERE

HYATT REGENCY ⊕ GRAND CYPRESS
AT ORLANDO

Hyatt Regency Hotels, 1986

L·I·F·E
ON·THE·BEACH

Life on the beach is ever
so much better than life *at* the
beach. The all-suite, all-luxury
Alexander hotel is *on* Miami
Beach. Recently, we have been
transformed into one of the
most tastefully exciting hotels in
America. And when you dine,
you'll dine at Dominique's,
which is four-stars and for-

gourmets. Or at Le Café for dining that's just as delicious, but
more casual. When you add all
our amenities, our service, our
pool and our ocean, you'll know
this. When you spend some
small part of your life with us:
you can do nothing. Gloriously.

*For our free brochure or reservations,
call 800 327-6121 or your travel planner.*

THE
ALEXANDER
ALL-SUITE LUXURY HOTEL
Elegance with a splash.

5225 Collins Avenue,
Miami Beach, Florida 33140

The Alexander Hotel, 1988

Palm Beach Polo and Country Club, 1981

Grand Cypress Resort, 1987

Desert Princess Resort, 1988

Palm Springs Convention and Visitors Bureau, 1985

Las Vegas Convention and Visitors Authority, 1982

Las Vegas Convention and Visitors Authority, 1981

COME FACE TO FACE WITH SPACE.

Climb inside a real space capsule. Encounter simulated zero-gravity. Fire rocket engines and lasers. And even pilot a spacecraft by computer. At The Space and Rocket Center in Huntsville, Alabama, over 60 hands-on exhibits put the space program at your fingertips.

You'll also experience our spectacular Spacedome theater. Here, engulfed by a wraparound screen and 48-speaker sound system, you'll thrill to our new film, "The Dream is Alive".

Next door at Marshall Space Flight Center, you'll witness the development of NASA's Space Station and see where our astronauts prepare for missions.

During your visit, you can catch your breath at the Huntsville Marriott, located on the grounds.

Without a doubt, it's the best place to really get in touch with the space program. So, take a day or two and come face to face with 30 years of American adventure. At The Space and Rocket Center.

Get the right stuff for planning a visit, plus information on the incredible U.S. Space Camp. Call toll-free for a copy of our free brochure.

THE SPACE AND ROCKET CENTER.
Huntsville, Alabama
800/633-7280 or 205/837-3400

NASA Space and Rocket Center, 1986

"PALATIAL"

CAESARS PALACE AND AMERICAN EXPRESS.®
YOU'VE GOT OUR WORD.℠

It's a treasure of endless delights. Historic fact. Romantic legend. And the myths of the gods. It's another world. A palatial world. The world of Caesars Palace in Las Vegas.

THE PALACE OF REGAL PLEASURES.

Inside Caesars, you'll experience an impeccable commitment to service. As well as exquisite food and drink from restaurants of boundless quality and selection. You'll enjoy the giants of entertainment. Invigorating health spas. A magnificent marble-inlaid pool. Indulge in your favorite games. Encounter championship gladiators in action. Explore the world's largest electronic Race and Sports Book. And visit the fascinating theatre of the future, Omnimax.

THE CARD OF ROYAL WELCOMES.

There's no better way to relive the grandeur of ancient Rome than with the American Express® Card. Even a Roman emperor couldn't receive better service. And with an American Express® Travel Service Representative in the lobby, Cardmembers can make travel arrangements, cash personal checks or receive emergency card replacement.

If you don't have the American Express Card, call 1-800-THE-CARD. Or pick up an application in Caesars' lobby. You can also make reservations at Caesars Palace by calling 1-800-634-6661.

One word best describes the Roman Empire called Caesars Palace. Palatial. And one card lets you enjoy it all. The American Express Card. You've got our word.

Caesar's Palace Hotel and Casino, 1986

Red Chips. White Chips. Blue Chips.

The quiet clicks of red and white chips add up to a roar of blue-chip business at American casino hotels—over $7 billion in 1985 revenues. And more and more of that business is Bally business.

Bally's Atlantic City is an established leader—and the city's most consistently profitable casino hotel. And the former MGM Grand Hotels are now Bally's Las Vegas and Bally's Reno casino hotels. Which makes Bally a major player in those major markets.

But casino hotels are just one part of Bally's strength in the leisure business category. Which should come as no surprise—because Bally *created* the leisure business category. Besides casino hotels, Bally is the leader in four other major areas of the category—public lottery games, gaming equipment, health and fitness centers, and amusement games and arcades. And no one can match the presence of Bally's Six Flags in regional theme parks.

Leisure is America's most exciting growth industry—$25 billion in revenues last year, with a growth rate almost seven times the GNP. And with sales of over $1.6 billion, Bally is a growing and diversified leader in this growing industry.

Because wherever America spends its leisure time, Bally leads the way.

For more information, write William H. Peltier, V.P. Corporate Communications, 8700 W. Bryn Mawr, Chicago, IL 60631. Or call 1-312-399-1300.

Bally
THE LEISURE LEADER.

Bally's Casino Hotels, 1987

San Diego's best just keeps getting better.

Sea World is a living, changing place—
alive with new animals to meet and new ways to have fun
every time you visit. Shamu™ and his trainers constantly give
you the world's newest, most thrilling animal show.
You'll flip over our new dolphin show and this summer
"Up With People," direct from their Super Bowl appearance,
will lift your spirits with their new show. Bring your family
back to Sea World. It's a whole different world every day.

You've gotta see what's new at

Sea World™

Mission Bay, San Diego

Sea World, 1982

SEE WHAT MOVIES ARE MADE OF.

What makes the Universal Studios Tour the most unique experience in Southern California? It's the only place where you can actually see movies like the stars do—from behind the scenes!

Your day begins with a tram ride through our huge 420-acre movie backlot. You'll see 640 outdoor sets, buildings and facades, representing some of the most famous movie sets and locations ever created. Your journey includes an unforgettable encounter with some of Hollywood's greatest special effects, like the "Jaws"® attack, the parting of the Red Sea, a collapsing bridge and a chilling alpine avalanche. And just when you think you've seen it all, there's more action around the corner.

We'll take you to a sound stage where you'll learn the secrets of how movie makers create space battles and other spectacular feats.

In our fabulous Entertainment Center, you'll experience five live shows each depicting a different dimension of film making. You can discover your hidden talents when you star in our SCREEN TEST COMEDY THEATRE, witness the action-packed STUNT SHOW, be dazzled by real movie

ANIMAL ACTORS, experience the awesome CONAN—A SWORD & SORCERY SPECTACULAR, and learn how WOODY WOODPECKER comes alive on the screen.

It's a full day of movie magic, live shows, shopping and dining. So, come be a part of the stuff dreams are made of at Universal Studios Tour.

UNIVERSAL STUDIOS TOUR
AN MCA COMPANY
Celebrating Our 20th Year

Admission price covers Tram Tour, all shows and attractions. Hollywood Fwy. at Lankershim. Open daily. Tours run continuously. For information, call (818) 508-9600, groups (818) 508-3771. © 1984 Universal Studios, Inc.

Universal Studios Tour, 1984

MEET THE BIGGEST STARS IN HOLLYWOOD.

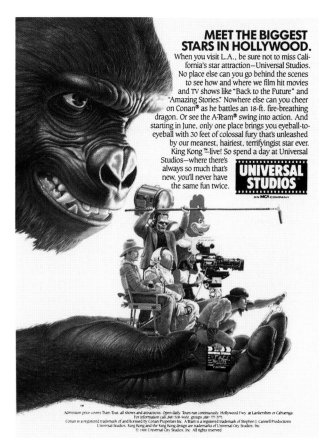

When you visit L.A., be sure not to miss California's star attraction—Universal Studios. No place else can you go behind the scenes to see how and where we film hit movies and TV shows like "Back to the Future" and "Amazing Stories." Nowhere else can you cheer on Conan® as he battles an 18-ft. fire-breathing dragon. Or see the A-Team® swing into action. And starting in June, only one place brings you eyeball-to-eyeball with 30 feet of colossal fury that's unleashed by our meanest, hairiest, terrifyingist star ever. King Kong™ live! So spend a day at Universal Studios—where there's always so much that's new, you'll never have the same fun twice.

UNIVERSAL STUDIOS
AN MCA COMPANY

Admission price covers Tram Tour, all shows and attractions. Open daily. Tours run continuously. Hollywood Fwy. at Lankershim or Cahuenga. For information call (818) 508-9600, groups (818) 777-3771.
Conan is a registered trademark of and licensed by Conan Properties Inc. A-Team is a registered trademark of Stephen J. Cannell Productions. Universal Studios, King Kong and the King Kong design are trademarks of Universal City Studios, Inc. © 1986 Universal City Studios, Inc. All rights reserved.

Universal Studios Tour, 1986

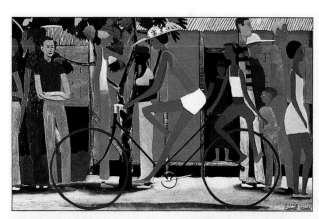

Discover a world the world hasn't discovered.

TRINIDAD & TOBAGO

Fly BWIA International
For reservations, call 1-800-327-7401
In New York, call 212-581-3200

Trinidad & Tobago Tourist Board, 1982

The past is ever present in the Caymans.

Not surprising that artists find inspiration in village scenes little changed in a century. Or that the design of many of the new holiday apartment complexes recapture the charm of early Cayman architecture.

Or that the most beautiful beaches in the West Indies are open and unspoiled and the ecology of the wondrous undersea world of the Caymans is protected.

Or that the Caymans are the only major British Crown Colony remaining in the Caribbean, with all the English traditions of civility and gracious hospitality.

An hour's flight from Miami on Cayman Airways. A little longer from Houston. But a world apart.

Good travel agents will tell you about the Caymans. Or contact Cayman Islands Department of Tourism, 250 Catalonia Ave., Coral Gables, FL 33134. Phone (305) 444-6551.

CAYMAN ISLANDS

Cayman Islands Department of Tourism, 1982

Tourism British Columbia, 1983

Florida Division of Tourism, 1981

Alaska Division of Tourism, 1985

Santa Fe Poster, 1986

Nebraska Department of Economic Development, 1985

Michigan Travel Bureau, 1985

Colorado Tourism Board, 1985

Washington State Tourism Development, 1985

MAGICALLY MAUI.

"Maui no ka oi," said Hawaii's warrior kings of this magical island. "Maui is the best."

The Hyatt Regency Maui on Kaanapali Beach captures the magic of Maui with an unforgettable blend of natural beauty and modern elegance.

You can lounge at the opulent outdoor pool with lush green mountains at your back. Play championship golf with endless vistas of the Pacific before you. Or follow the waterfalls and lagoons that wander through the grounds, with exotic birds and fish darting into view.

Your first visit to the Hyatt Regency Maui is unforgettable. Your second, inevitable. A fabulous touch of Hyatt on magical Maui. Don't you

WISH YOU WERE HERE

HYATT REGENCY ⬡ MAUI

For reservations, call your travel planner or 800 228 9000.

Hyatt Regency Hotels, 1986

Arizona...where Nature plays a grand, guileless trick on winter. Relax in gracious surroundings... from value-oriented lodgings to luxurious resorts. Dine against the backdrop of the world's most wondrous natural contrasts. Let our beautiful fairways test you. Feel your heart warm, your skin bronze. In Arizona, we never turn a cold shoulder. Come join us.

ARIZONA *Evergrand*

For information write: Arizona Office of Tourism, 1480 East Bethany Home Road, Phoenix, Arizona 85014

Arizona Office of Tourism, 1985

Club Med, 1980

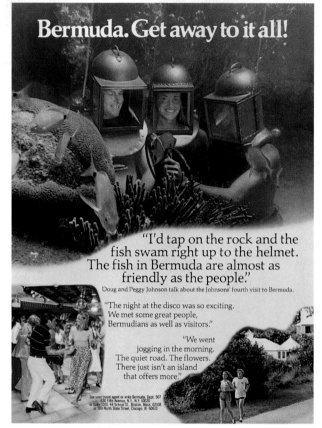

Bermuda, 1980

Puerto Rico Tourism Company, 1984

The Bahamas, 1981 ▶ *United States Virgin Islands Department of Tourism, 1981*

The summer of 82°

82°F. That's the average mean temperature in the summer in the American paradise. With trade winds blowing almost without exception from an easterly direction. (Now that doesn't sound mean at all!) See your travel agent.

United States Virgin Islands

St. Croix · St. John · St. Thomas

On the island of Lombok,
they've perfected the art of fly-fishing.

The locals know the big fish swim in the depths, out beyond the island's coral reef.

So they have developed a unique way of casting out their lines.

They build a simple kite from a dried leaf and two sticks. Then they attach their baited hooks and fly them up, and far out to sea.

From the calm waters of the lagoon, they watch the soaring kite. When it takes a sudden dip, they know it's time to reel in their dinner.

Lombok is a peaceful, tropical island in the warm Indian Ocean, just 15 minutes from Bali.

And thankfully, the fishing kite is one of the few technological advances you'll find here.

Except, of course, for your luxurious hotel.

For information about our flights, call (800) 3-GARUDA. For tour information call Garuda Orient Holidays (800) 247-8380.

Garuda Indonesia
Proud to welcome you aboard.

Garuda Orient Holidays, 1989

Freeport/Lucaya.
You may not want to do it all, but it's nice to know it's there.

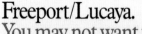

Underwater beauty.
A fling with Lady
Luck. Exotic gifts.
Championship golf. Gourmet meals.
Soft powdery beaches. Sailing into
the sunset. It's all there.

Freeport Abaco
Bimini
FLORIDA Eleuthera For reservations at Freeport/Lucaya and West End, see your travel agent. Or call toll
Nassau free Bahamas Reservation Service 800-327-0787. In Dade County, 443-3821.
Andros
Exuma **It's Better In The Bahamas.**

Bahamas Reservation Service, 1986

A CLUB MED VACATION BEGINS WHERE CIVILIZATION ENDS.

Imagine, for a moment, nothing. No clocks. No ringing phones. No traffic jams. No radios. No newspapers. No crowds.

Now imagine this. An island village where aqua seas brush dazzling white shores. Where lush green palms line wandering pathways. Where crystal blue skies change magically to golden sunsets.

Where you can indulge in everything from wind-surfing, snorkeling and tennis, to afternoon classes in water aerobics or painting, to secluded moments on miles of sun-drenched beach.

Activities vary by village. © 1988 Club Med Sales, Inc., 40 West 57th Street, New York, NY 10019.

Imagine not just three meals, but three gourmet banquets every single day. With freshly baked breads and pastries and free-flowing wine.

Where evenings are always filled with entertainment, dancing and a special atmosphere that turns new faces into old friends in moments.

If all this captures your imagination, drop by and see your travel agent or call 1-800-CLUB MED. It just may be the beginning of the end of civilization as you know it.

CLUB MED
The antidote for civilization.

Club Med, 1988

Get lots of rest and plenty of liquids. Tahiti.

Tahiti Tourist Board, 1986

Garuda Orient Holidays, 1989

BERMUDA IS YOU.

Reflections on a pastel dream.

It is everything you hoped it would be. It is the warmth of a

ISN'T IT?

smile, the coolness of pink sand. It's the clatter of hoofs down St. Anne's Road and the flutter of hearts in the moonlight. No place on earth feels anything like Bermuda.

Call your travel agent or:

1-800-BERMUDA

Name   Address   City   State   Zip

4101

Greet the Irish morning
from your room in an Irish castle.

Ashford Castle, Co. Mayo

When you come to Ireland you don't just look at our castles, you stay in them. And when you stay at Ashford Castle in western Ireland your visit is an unexpected blend of history and modern luxury. Pamper yourself with a traditional Irish breakfast before an early morning round of golf. Or take a sunset cruise on Lough Corrib, the much-fabled lake that this thirteenth-century castle was built to guard. And after you've worked up an appetite exploring the surrounding countryside, you'll find some of the best seafood in Ireland here in County Mayo.

Getting to Ireland is a pleasure on Aer Lingus. For great fares, widebody 747s, and our special Irish hospitality see your travel agent or call Aer Lingus.

IRELAND
The unexpected pleasures.

Bermuda Department of Tourism, 1987 ◄   *Irish Tourist Board, 1987*

ON ALITALIA, BUSINESS COMES FIRST.

On international flights you'll find Alitalia's new Business Class right up front, where other airlines usually place first class. Why? Because our Business Class now offers all the comforts of first class at a cost only slightly higher than economy fare. For more room, Alitalia has reduced the number of seats. That's two seats per row, not three across. And our new reclinable seats invite total relaxation. For your enjoyment, there are free feature films and stereo music for good listening. Our menu offers a wide selection of authentic Italian cuisine, along with your choice of cocktails or excellent Italian wines. Our distinctively Italian ambience is enhanced by superior service and the kind of personal attention that is so rare, yet so Alitalia. Our Business Class is such a pleasure, you just might forget all about business.

Business Class B747

Alitalia

Alitalia Airlines, 1982

France
It's so worth it.

Alsace invites you to lose yourself to the romance of another place in time, as you stroll through tiny cobblestoned villages untouched in all their medieval splendor. It's no wonder that the sculptor Bertholdi got his first inspiration in Colmar to create the Statue of Liberty.

Treat yourself to a lazy country picnic with a glass of local Riesling along the ancient Route des Vins. And be sure to experience a leisurely cruise on the charming canals of Strasbourg, followed by a steaming plate of choucroute and heady local beer in a bustling brasserie.

Rent a car with Jet Vacations (only $109 per week with unlimited mileage*) and stay in a charming hotel for as little as $17 per person including breakfast.** Alsace awaits your visit and Jet Vacations makes it so easy to take this journey back in time.

*Two week advance reservation required.
**Per night, double occupancy with continental breakfast, service and taxes included.

AIR FRANCE

Please send me more information.

Name ___
Address ___
City State ___
Zip ___

French Government Tourist Office
Write: Dept GM2, F.G.T.O.
P.O. Box 2858
Lake Ronkonkoma, N.Y. 11779

Air France Airlines, 1986

We've Cut The Cost Of A Brazilian Vacation Dramatically.

Now you can spend a week in Rio for as little as $693-$929, including airfare and hotel accommodation.* So the cost of a vacation in Rio is now a very good reason to go, and no longer a reason not to.

The individuality and style of Brazil, its language, culture and cuisine make it quite unlike any other South American country. And so do the 11,000 beautiful miles of beaches.

Looking across Rio at Sugar Loaf.

Aren't You Ready For The World Famous Copacabana And Ipanema Beaches?

These spectacular beaches are the spiritual home of the people of Rio.

At dawn the runners begin to appear, to exercise along the sand. Then comes the sunbathing, and the swimming. The soccer.

And the volleyball games. The sellers of cold drinks and ices. And everywhere the miniature Brazilian bikinis.

Aren't You Ready For A City That Gets Hotter At Night?

Anyone who has been to Rio and experienced the people and the nightlife will tell you it's true. If you have an icy reserve, prepare to watch it melt.

Aren't You Ready For Pan Am's Rio?

When you fly down to Brazil, Pan Am, the Brazilian Tourism Authority and your local Travel Agent will make sure you know all there is to know. So you'll be ready.

☐ Yes, I'm Ready For Rio.

PAN AM ● BRAZILIAN TOURISM AUTHORITY EMBRATUR

Please send me information about Pan Am's new low cost vacations to Rio, and about Brazil.

Name ___
Address ___
City ___ State ___ Zip ___

Brazilian Tourism Authority
60 East 42nd Street, Suite 1336
New York, NY 10165

GO10P

*All prices are per person based on double occupancy and include airfare from Miami. Varying effective dates and reservation, length of stay and advance purchase requirements apply. Departures Mon.-Thurs. Prices subject to change without notice.

Aren't You Ready For Rio?

Pan Am Airlines, 1983

Aruba Tourism Authority, 1989

México Tourism Office, 1986

Mexican Government Tourist Office, 1980

Club Pearl Cruises, 1984

SPAIN

Where more Europeans vacation than anywhere else in the world.

This is your year to visit Spain. Where prices are among the least expensive in all of Europe.

Just ask your travel agent and you'll understand why more Europeans vacation in Spain than anywhere else in the world.

Spain is the total travel experience. See the fiery flamenco dancing in Madrid and Sacramonte gypsy caves in Granada.

Visit the legendary castles in Segovia and Belmonte. Explore the Roman ruins in Merida and Tarragona. Tour the royal palaces in Madrid. La Granja, El Escorial and Aranjuez. And Spain offers more. Much more. Exciting bull fighting in Pamplona and Madrid.

Beautiful fiestas and festivals. The sun-drenched Costa del Sol. Idyllic Majorca, Ibiza and the Canary Islands. Spain offers everything for a memorable European vacation. Including the right price. Come to Spain this year.

For more information, contact the nearest Spanish National Tourist Office: 665 Fifth Avenue, New York, New York 10022 / 845 No. Michigan Avenue, Chicago, Ill. 60611 / 3160 Lyon St., San Francisco, Calif. 94123 / Casa del Hidalgo, St. Augustine, Fla. 32084.

SPAIN
A lot more vacation for a lot less money.

Spanish National Tourist Office, 1980

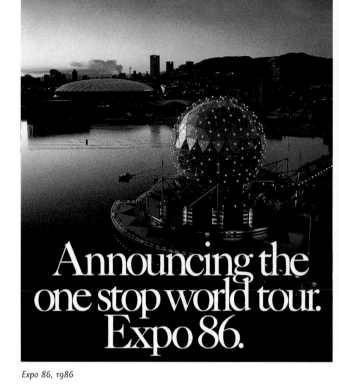

Announcing the one stop world tour. Expo 86.

Imagine. Over forty countries and nary a border in sight. From May 2nd to October 13th, 1986 Vancouver becomes the world. The U.S.S.R. China. England. The U.S. Frankly we couldn't think of a better place on earth for this to happen. Come. Touch the future or travel back to Ancient Egypt. Explore the British Columbia you've always wanted to see. Naturally the people here are SuperHosts. Call ResWest at (604) 662-3300 for your hotel bookings. Don't miss it for the world.

Hon. Claude Richmond, Minister Tourism/Expo 86

Super, Natural British Columbia CANADA

Expo 86, 1986

THE PEOPLE OF PORTUGAL

Come brush shoulders with a people who invite you to share the richness of their country, the beauty of their islands, and the treasures of their culture. The faces on this page are only a sample of the friendly people you'll meet in this welcoming land of discoveries.

Portugal Where Europe meets the Atlantic

For an information kit write: Portuguese National Tourist Office, P.O. Box 9016, Dept. 3G9, East Setauket, N.Y. 11733-9016.

Portuguese National Tourist Office, 1989

For once, view the works of the Spanish masters without flipping pages.

Goya. El Greco. Velázquez. Miró. Picasso.

From the pages of art books, their paintings have fascinated and inspired you.

Yet the printed page does not really allow you to see them. For what makes each a masterpiece is what it demands of the viewer: a personal relationship in which the work reveals itself layer by layer. Until finally, standing before it, you come to experience the full emotional and spiritual power the artist intended you to feel.

At the Prado in Madrid—and in many other museums throughout Spain—you will find hundreds upon hundreds of the world's greatest works of art. And you will recognize many from reproductions you have seen.

But as you fix your gaze on them you will recognize something else.

That you are looking at them for the first time.

The Prado. An extraordinary destination along your journey of discovery.

Spain
Everything Under The Sun.

The Duchess of Alba
by Francisco de Goya.
Courtesy of
The Hispanic Society
of America, New York.

Spain, 1989

Only In Australia Can You Catch The Perfect Wave Everyday.

Some of the world's best surfing can be found along the Australian coast. The perfect wave, however, is miles from any ocean.

Western Australia's Wave Rock swells to 45 feet and has been forming its curl for 2.7 billion years. Like so much else about the Land of Wonder, it remains mysterious and eternal.

Where The Real Waves Are.

The oceanic beauty of Western Australia offers sharp contrast to the undersea riches found on the Great Barrier Reef.

Nurtured over geologic spans of time, the 1200-mile long Reef is home to 400 species of coral, 1500 species of fish and an infinite number of emotions that only mysterious beauty such as Australia's can evoke.

All That Water Can Make You Thirsty.

Snorkel or skin dive the Reef, explore a few of its 500 islands—like Lizard or Heron—and you can work up a demanding thirst. Usually for something dry.

In that case, we recommend a day in the Barossa Valley. It produces more award-winning vintages than any other region in Australia.

A little over an hour's drive north of Adelaide, the Barossa is a short, narrow valley with some 40 wineries. It's there you'll taste the unmistakable German influence, both in the excellent food and the quality of the wine.

Farm Yourself Out.

To taste all the complexity of Australia, though, you should experience a farm stay.

Found all over Australia, from just outside cities to deep inside the Outback, host farms are a great way to get acquainted with our land.

You'll get country cooking at its best. And though you're not required to, you might even lend a hand at some chores, an eternal necessity on any farm.

Come And Say G'day.

The need for information also seems eternal. So get our free Aussie Holiday Book. Call 1-800-445-3000 and ask for Dept. G005.

Which should leave you with one last thing to catch. The next flight Down Under.

Australia
The Wonder Down Under.

Australia, 1988

Add a little spice to your life

If variety is the spice of life, then dining in Thailand is living life to the full.

Nowhere in the world will you find such exquisite blends of exotic ingredients in such infinite variety. Shrimps, green papaya, red and green chillies, lemon juice, peanuts, palm sugar, garlic, tomatoes, fish sauce - and they're just the ingredients to 'Som Tam' - a simple Thai salad!

Good food is second nature to Thais. And a gourmet tour around Thailand is a unique way to sample the cuisine and understand the culture from which it originates. It's also a great way to pick up Thai handicrafts which make beautiful souvenirs.

Wherever you go you'll find luxury hotels with standards of service other countries can only aspire to.

Call your travel agent today or fill in the coupon and enjoy a gastronomic adventure in the land of smiles.

EXOTIC **Thailand**
GOLDEN PLACES, SMILING FACES

For more information on exotic Thailand fill in this coupon and mail to : Tourism Authority of Thailand, (East Coast) 5 World Trade Center Suite No. 2449, New York, N.Y. 10048, U.S.A. (West Coast) 3440 Wilshire Blvd., Suite 1101, Los Angeles, CA 90010 U.S.A.

Name _____ Address _____ Postcode _____

AG 10/89
GOURMET / OCTOBER 1989
265

Tourism Authority of Thailand, 1989

599

Grand touring Alaska's Inland Passage with your own loyal staff.

Edging up to Glacier Bay in your own glittering yacht.

Commanding a place at your own dining table or gaming table.

Royalty?

Yes. Royal Viking

EURAILPASS PRICES ARE FALLING THIS FALL

Now's a great time to buy a 15-day Eurailpass because we've just lowered the price. With a Eurail Saverpass, 2 or more people travelling together can enjoy unlimited first-class train travel through 17 European countries for only $230* per person. Send for our free brochure and start planning your trip today.

EURAILPASS
A FIRST CLASS VIEW OF EUROPE
Please rush me a free Eurailpass color brochure.

Name
Address
City_____State____Zip____
Mail today to: Eurailpass, P.O. Box 10383, Stamford, CT 06904

*Available 10/1/89–12/31/89
$240 per person 1/1/90–3/31/90

Eurailpass, 1989

Eurailpass admits there may still be a less expensive way to see Europe.

Eurailpass gives you lots of ways to save money on European travel. With our Eurail Saverpass, for example, you get unlimited first-class rail travel in any or all of 16 European countries for only $199 per person* That's less than $14 per day.

Of course, there is a way to travel around Europe that costs even less. If you like to pedal.

*Applies to 15-day pass, when three or more travel together. Other inexpensive rates are available for one or two people.

EURAILPASS
Please rush me a free Eurailpass color brochure.

Name
Address
City_____State____Zip____
Mail today to Eurailpass, Box Q, Staten Island, New York, 10305.

Eurailpass, 1986

"GOOD MORNING. YOUR EGGS ARE FRYING, YOUR BACON IS CRISP, AND YOU'VE JUST TRAVELED 400 MILES."

While you were sweet dreaming on your pillow, Amtrak was whisking you 400 miles closer to your destination, and you didn't even bat an eye.

Now Amtrak's full service kitchen is preparing breakfast to your order, and it will be served with a smile and a passing view. Where else but on one of the most advanced passenger train systems in the world...Amtrak.

In the last 10 years, Amtrak has replaced 75% of its trains with all new equipment, and has refurbished the other 25%. We boast one of the best on-time performance records of any carrier in the transportation industry. Our computerized reservations system is second to none, and now there are over 10,000 travel agents at your service.

So come and feel the magic, as 19 million riders a year do. Call your travel agent or call Amtrak at 1-800-USA-RAIL. You'll find traveling so easy, you can do it with your eyes closed.

ALL ABOARD AMTRAK

Royal Viking Cruises, 1984 ◄ *Amtrak Railways, 1985*

And the winner is...

Yo Ho Ho and a Bottle of Sun Screen

What's this? A cruise to the Caribbean or an invitation to a clothing-optional beach? Tell me, Cap'n Mike, just how loose did you want your shipmates to be? No doubt a healthy dose of rum helped unleash the libidos of many a passenger hoping to unravel her problems on a high seas adventure. Forget about those floating geriatric hotels and wheelchair-clogged island excursions that dominated the cruise industry in the eighties. This is one love boat that put unabashed sex to the fore. Sign me up.

Ho Ho Ho und ne Buddel voll Sonnenmilch

Was ist das denn? Eine Kreuzfahrt in die Karibik oder die Einladung an einen FKK-Strand? Sagen Sie schon, Käpt'n Mike, wie unbekleidet hätten Sie's denn gern auf Ihrem Schiff? Ein ordentlicher Schluck Rum hat sich sicherlich positiv auf die Libido all der Kreuzfahrer ausgewirkt, die ihre Probleme bei einem Abenteuer auf hoher See zu vergessen hofften. Wie weggewischt sind die Erinnerung an die schwimmenden Altersheime und von Rollstühlen blockierten Landausflüge, die in den achtziger Jahren die Regel waren. Auf diesem „Love Boat" sagt endlich mal jemand, worum es wirklich geht: um Sex! Wo kann man buchen?

Ohé du bateau !

Qu'est-ce que c'est ? Une croisière aux Caraïbes ou une invitation pour aller sur une plage où le port du maillot est facultatif ? Dites, Capt'ain Mike, vous les aimiez dégourdies, vos coéquipières ? Aucun doute qu'une bonne dose de rhum a aidé plus d'une passagère à libérer sa libido, espérant ainsi oublier ses problèmes dans des aventures en haute mer. Adieu les hôtels flottants du troisième âge et les excursions dans les îles au milieu des fauteuils roulants, si typiques des croisières des années 80. C'est pour une croisière romantique où le sexe sans complexes a la priorité. Je vais m'inscrire.

Vacaciones en el mar

¿Qué es esto? ¿Un anuncio de un crucero por el Caribe o una invitación a una playa nudista? Explíqueme, capitán Mike, cómo de sueltos quería que anduviesen sus camaradas de a bordo. Sin duda, una dosis saludable de ron debió de ayudar a desatar las libidos de muchos pasajeros con ganas de resolver los problemas de esta joven durante una desatada aventura en alta mar. Al diablo con esos hoteles geriátricos flotantes y excursiones a islas en sillas de ruedas que dominaban el sector de los cruceros en los ochenta. Este barco del amor vendía sexo sin tapujos. Apúnteme.

"ヤッホー"と日焼け止め

これは何だ？カリブ海へのクルーズ、それともヌーディストビーチへの誘い？ マイク船長、教えてくれ、君の船のお客さん達をどのくらい解放的にしたいの？ かなりの量のラム酒が、冒険の波にさらわれて「問題」を解決したいと望むたくさんの女性客の性衝動を開放したことは間違いない。80年代のクルーズ業界のメインであった、そこいらにある年寄りくさいホテルや車椅子だらけの島への旅行なんて忘れなさい。これは恥ずかしがる必要もなくセックスをおおっぴらにできる愛の船ですよ。さあサインして。

the bonds of city life and unravel your problems on a Windjammer cruise. Surrender to the majestic ocean and enchanting ports of call. Let the currents guide you to peace of spirit, mind and body. Master the Windjammer knot and untie yourself from everyday hassles. Experience the real you.

Your share of the six day Windjammer adventure can be as little as $400.

For reservations only call toll free 1-800-327-2600.

Loosen up

Cap'n Mike, please send me a free Adventure Booklet in full color.

Windjammer 'Barefoot' Cruises LTD
P.O. Box 120, Miami Beach, Fla. 33119
Phone 305/373-2090

Windjammer Barefoot Cruises, 1983

603

Index

All-American Ads   Ed. Jim Heimann

20s

ALL-AMERICAN ADS OF THE 20s
Steven Heller, Ed. Jim Heimann / Flexi-cover,
format: 19.6 x 25.5 cm (7.7 x 10 in.), 640 pp.
ONLY € 29.99 / $ 39.99
£ 19.99 / ¥ 5.900

The Roaring Twenties

Advertising for the Jazz Age

Prohibition made liquor illegal and all the more fun to drink. Speakeasies, luxury cars, women's liberation, bathtub gin and a booming economy kept the country's mood on the up-and-up. Women sheared off their locks and taped their chests, donning flapper dresses and dancing the Charleston until their legs gave out. Gangsters flourished in big cities and gangster movies flourished in Hollywood. It was the roaring twenties in America: a singular time in history, a lull between two world wars, and the last gasp before the nation's descent into the Great Depression. Forging the way into the future like a modern ocean liner in a sea of antiquity, advertising in the twenties sought to bring avant-garde into the mainstream—which it did with great success.

The author:
Steven Heller is the art director of *The New York Times Book Review* and co-chair of MFA Design at the School of Visual Arts. He has edited or authored over eighty books on design and popular culture including *Merz to Emigre and Beyond: Avant-Garde Magazine Design of the 20th Century* and *Design Literacy Revised*.

The editor:
Jim Heimann is a resident of Los Angeles, a graphic designer, writer, historian, and instructor at the Art Center College of Design in Pasadena, California. He is the auth of numerous books on architecture, popular culture, and Hollywood history.

ALSO AVAILABLE

ALL-AMERICAN ADS OF THE 30s
Steven Heller, Ed. Jim Heimann /
Flexi-cover, 768 pp.

ALL-AMERICAN ADS OF THE 40s
W.R. Wilkerson III, Ed. Jim Heimann /
Flexi-cover, 768 pp.

ALL-AMERICAN ADS OF THE 50s
Ed. Jim Heimann / Flexi-cover, 928 pp.

ALL-AMERICAN ADS OF THE 60s
Steven Heller, Ed. Jim Heimann /
Flexi-cover, 960 pp.

ALL-AMERICAN ADS OF THE 70s
Steven Heller, Ed. Jim Heimann /
Flexi-cover, 704 pp.

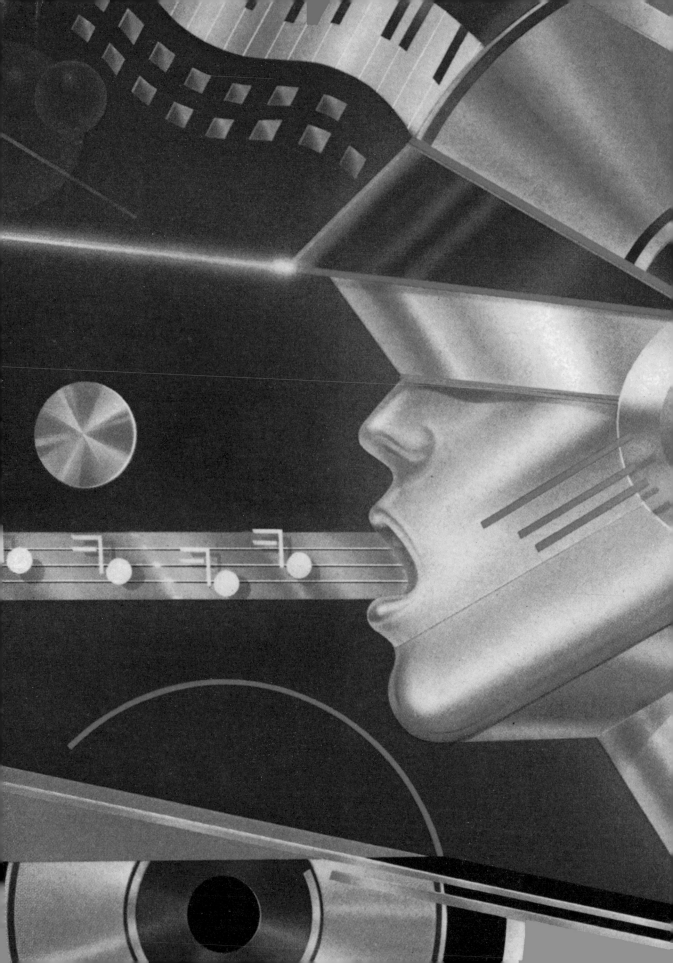